Africa beyond
Liberal Democracy

African Philosophy
Critical Perspectives and Global Dialogue

Series Editors
Uchenna B. Okeja, Rhodes University; and Bruce B. Janz,
University of Central Florida

Editorial Board
Anthony Appiah, Valentine Mudimbe, Gail Presbey, Achille Mbembe,
Robert Bernasconi, Samuel Imbo, Tsenay Serequeberhan, Thaddeus Metz, Katrin Flikschuh, Niels Weidtmann, Christine Wanjiru Gichure,
Kai Kresse, Joseph Agbakoba, Souleymane Bachir Diagne,
Dismas. A. Masolo, Pedro Tabensky

The African Philosophy: Critical Perspectives and Global Dialogue book series aims to promote emerging critical perspectives in different branches of African philosophy. It serves as an avenue for philosophers within and between many African cultures to present new arguments, ask new questions and begin new dialogues within both specialised communities and with the general public. By merging the critical and global dimensions of thoughts pertaining to important topics in African philosophy, this series beams the lights and rigour of philosophical analysis on topical as well as classical questions reflective of the African and African diaspora search for meaning in existence. Focussed on the best of African philosophy, the series will introduce new concepts and new approaches in philosophy both to intellectual communities across Africa, as well as the rest of the world.

Recent Titles in the Series

Africa beyond Liberal Democracy: In Search of Context-Relevant Models of Democracy for the Twenty-First Century, edited by Reginald M. J. Oduor

Menkiti's Moral Man, by Oritsegbubemi Anthony Oyowe

Partiality and Impartiality in African Philosophy, by M. Molefe

Menkiti on Community and Becoming a Person, edited by Edwin Etieyibo and Polycarp Ikuenobe

African Philosophical and Literary Possibilities: Re-reading the Canon, edited by Aretha Phiri

Derrida and Africa: Jacques Derrida as a Figure for African Thought, edited by Grant Farred

Afro-Communitarian Democracy, by Bernard Matolino

A Discourse on African Philosophy: A New Perspective on Ubuntu and Transitional Justice in South Africa, by Christian B. N. Gade

Disentangling Consciencism: Essays on Kwame Nkrumah's Philosophy, edited by Martin Odei Ajei

The Rule of Law and Governance in Indigenous Yoruba Society: A Study in African Philosophy of Law, by John Ayotunde Isola Bewaji

Africa beyond Liberal Democracy

In Search of Context-Relevant Models of Democracy for the Twenty-First Century

Reginald M. J. Oduor

ROWMAN & LITTLEFIELD
Lanham • Boulder • New York • London

Published by Rowman & Littlefield
An imprint of The Rowman & Littlefield Publishing Group, Inc.
4501 Forbes Boulevard, Suite 200, Lanham, Maryland 20706
www.rowman.com

86-90 Paul Street, London EC2A 4NE

Copyright © 2022 by The Rowman & Littlefield Publishing Group, Inc.

All rights reserved. No part of this book may be reproduced in any form or by any electronic or mechanical means, including information storage and retrieval systems, without written permission from the publisher, except by a reviewer who may quote passages in a review.

British Library Cataloguing in Publication Information Available

Library of Congress Cataloging-in-Publication Data

Names: Oduor, Reginald M. J., editor, author.
Title: Africa beyond liberal democracy : in search of context-relevant models of democracy for the twenty-first century / Reginald M. J. Oduor.
Description: Lanham, Maryland : Rowman & Littlefield, [2022] | Series: African Philosophy: Critical Perspectives and Global Dialogue | Includes bibliographical references and index. | Summary: "The contributors to this volume ask whether democracy is universal or culturally bound, how the adoption of Western liberal models of democracy has hindered democratisation in Africa, and how indigenous African political thought can be utilised to design models of democracy suitable for twenty-first-century African countries"—Provided by publisher.
Identifiers: LCCN 2022011965 (print) | LCCN 2022011966 (ebook) | ISBN 9781666913811 (Cloth) | ISBN 9781666913835 (pbk) | ISBN 9781666913828 (ePub)
Subjects: LCSH: Democracy—Africa. | Postcolonialism—Africa. | Africa—Politics and government—1960-
Classification: LCC JQ1879.A15 A3195 2022 (print) | LCC JQ1879.A15 (ebook) | DDC 320.46—dc23/eng/20220309
LC record available at https://lccn.loc.gov/2022011965
LC ebook record available at https://lccn.loc.gov/2022011966

To all who tirelessly work
for the true liberation of the peoples of Africa

Contents

Preface	ix
List of Figures	xi
Acknowledgements	xiii
Introduction	1

PART 1: RATIONALE FOR THE "AFRICA BEYOND LIBERAL DEMOCRACY" PROJECT

1. African Political Ideology and Practice in the Era of Globalisation: Can a Return to African Humanistic Socialism Combat Afro-Libertarianism? 13
   Sirkku K. Hellsten

2. Promoting Indigenous Values to Facilitate the Emergence of Suitable Forms of Democracy 27
   Thomas Menamparampil

3. Colonialism and the Challenge of Western-Style Democracy in Africa 41
   Dennis Masaka

4. The Snares of Liberal Democracy: Lessons from Electioneering in the Democratic Republic of Congo 55
   David Ngendo-Tshimba

PART 2: CRITIQUE OF THE "AFRICA BEYOND LIBERAL DEMOCRACY" PROJECT

5. Democracy as Falsehood: Seek but Do Not Expect to Find 81
   Donna Pido

6. Gender-Sensitive Followership in Africa: The Case of Uganda 97
   Robinah S. Nakabo

PART 3: PROPOSALS FOR CONTEXT-RELEVANT AFRICAN MODELS OF DEMOCRACY

7. Co-operative Collegial Democracy: An African Context-Relevant Governance Model 117
   Emefiena Ezeani

8. The Traditional Roots of Democratic Verbal Discipline: Insights from the Akan 137
   Emmanuel Ifeanyi Ani

9. An Appeal for a Communitarian Model of Democracy 153
   Munamato Chemhuru

10. Elements of an Indigenous African Model of Democracy 165
    Joseph Situma, Kisemei Mutisya, and Christine Buluma

11. Democracy and the Right of the Minority in Africa 179
    Moses Oludare Aderibigbe

12. Critical Reflections on the Quest for a Monolithic Democratic Alternative to Liberal Democracy for Africa 191
    Tayo Raymond Ezekiel Eegunlusi

13. Groundswell: An Unavoidable Democracy, with Special Reference to the Acholi of Uganda 213
    J. P. Odoch Pido

14. In Defence of Ethnically-Based Federations in Post-Colonial African States, with Special Reference to Kenya 235
    Reginald M. J. Oduor

Epilogue 275
Reginald M. J. Oduor

Index 281

About the Contributors 287

Preface

The chapters in this volume represent a wide variety of perspectives for two main reasons. *First*, they have been written by scholars based in South Africa, Zimbabwe, Uganda, Nigeria, Ghana, Finland, India, and Kenya. *Second*, the authors come from a variety of disciplines, namely, political philosophy, political science, design, anthropology, and mass communication.

The authors seek to answer one or more of the following questions:

1. Is democracy universally applicable, or does it require adaptation to cultural realities?
2. To what extent has the adoption of Western liberal models of democracy hindered democratisation in post-colonial African states?
3. How can indigenous African political thought be utilised in the endeavour to design models of democracy that are suited to the socio-cultural realities of post-colonial African states?

It is my earnest hope that the chapters in this volume will contribute to the discourse on post-colonial reconstruction—a task which continues to be hampered by neo-colonial domination at the economic and political levels, and by a hegemonic Western mode of knowing at the academic level.

Reginald M. J. Oduor
December 15, 2021

List of Figures

Figure 7.1	Co-operative Pyramidal Democratic Structure Source: Adapted from Ezeani (2013, 152)	127
Table 7.1	A Sample of CCD's List of members of Federal College with voting results. Federal Republic of Nigeria—Presidential Election. List of Zonal Representatives: The Federal College	131
Table 7.2	A Sample of CCD Election Form. Federal Republic of Nigeria—Presidential Election Form for Members of the Federal College	132

Acknowledgements

I am deeply indebted to Dr. Hu Yeping and the Council for Research in Values and Philosophy (RVp), as well as to my two colleagues at the University of Nairobi, Drs. Oriare Nyarwath and Wamae Muriuki, for all their logistical assistance in the early days of this book project.

I am grateful to Dr. Donna Pido of the Technical University of Kenya, herself a contributor to this volume, for looking through three of the other chapters with the eye of a speaker of English as a first language.

My friend James Gichuhi, Managing Director of Itac Consulting Ltd. and himself a person with total visual disability like myself, consistently and generously assisted me with his vast knowledge of adaptive information and communication technology whenever I had a technical challenge in the course of editing this volume, for which I am truly grateful.

My heartfelt gratitude to Lexington's Senior Acquisitions Editor Jana Hodges-Kluck, her two assistants Matthew Lumbard and Deanna Biondi, as well as to Lexington's Production Editor Michael Hals, for their outstanding support in the preparation of this manuscript.

Last, but certainly not least, I thank my dear wife, Lilian, and our two amazing boys, Kue and Kinda, for their patience over the many months that I worked on this volume, taking away precious time from them.

Reginald M. J. Oduor
December 2021

Introduction
Reginald M. J. Oduor

In the early years after political independence, a considerable number of African political leaders, among them Julius Nyerere, Kwame Nkrumah and Sekou Toure, questioned the adequacy of liberal democracy for post-colonial African states. However, partly due to the debilitating authoritarianism in the one-party states that many of them established in place of the independence liberal democratic constitutions, many theorists believed that the only remedy was the restoration of multi-party systems. The triumph of the liberal West at the end of the Cold War emboldened advocates of party pluralism in Africa, and their campaigns were augmented by financial and diplomatic support from the Western powers. Nevertheless, almost three decades after the optimism occasioned by the return to multi-party rule from the early 1990s, both civilian regimes and military juntas are shattering the dream of genuine democracy in the continent, just as they did soon after political independence.

Yet while massive scholarly and political energies have been spent on the repeatedly unsuccessful bids to entrench Western liberal democracy in the continent, much less effort has been invested in the endeavour to develop homegrown African models of democracy that strike resonance with the worldviews and current experiences of the continent's diverse peoples. Besides, while there is currently much talk about the need to use indigenous African knowledge to address various challenges facing African societies, it is usually limited to endeavours such as preserving agricultural produce, motivating the poor to engage in birth control, or indigenous African legal systems are viewed as junior partners of the dominant Western-style legal systems on the continent.

Thus, regrettably, in the contemporary African context, "democratisation" has come to be incorrectly construed to be synonymous with the entrenching of liberal democracy. Nevertheless, if culture is understood to be the totality of a society's inventions and innovations aimed at enabling it to sustain its existence in a specific environment, then a political system is part and parcel of the culture in which it develops. Consequently, it is a truism to state that a political system that is appropriate in the cultural context in which it arose may be blatantly out of place in another. Thus the failure of liberal democracy in Africa at the dawn of independence in the late 1950s and early 1960s, and again soon after the promulgation of the so-called second-generation constitutions in various African polities from the mid-1990s, should prompt political theorists to ask how suitable it is in the African context. More important, the repeated failure of liberal democracy in Africa should motivate African and Africanist scholars to explore ways in which the rich and diverse indigenous political heritage of the continent could be utilised to develop models of democracy that strike resonance with the communalistic worldviews of the continent's peoples.

It is noteworthy that a number of theorists and politicians working in non-Western contexts have already questioned the purported universal applicability of liberal democracy. Indeed, the title of the present volume is inspired by Daniel A. Bell's *Beyond Liberal Democracy: Political Thinking for an East Asian Context* (2006)—a bold challenge to the 'copy-and-paste' approach to liberal democracy in non-Western cultures, with an introduction appropriately titled "One Size Doesn't Fit All". Almost a century earlier, Mohandas Karmachand ("Mahatma") Gandhi, in *Hind Swaraj; or Indian Rule* (1909), contended that liberal democracy was inadequate for the Indian context. In addition, Thomas Pantham's "Thinking with Mahatma Gandhi: Beyond Liberal Democracy" (1983) provides an illuminating discussion of the socio-political context of Gandhi's dissatisfaction with liberal democracy. Furthermore, several Latin American countries have been experimenting with their own indigenous models of democracy in place of liberal democracy (Whitehead 2010), and such experiments presume alternative theoretical and ideological frameworks.

Moreover, with the failure of the second attempt to establish liberal democracy in African states from the 1990s, Tukumbi Lumumba-Kasongo's edited volume, *Liberal Democracy and Its Critics in Africa* (Lumumba-Kasongo ed. 2005) explores various critical questions in the context of particular elections and particular countries in Africa including Ghana, Nigeria, Kenya, the Congo, Cameroon and the Central African Republic. It also shines the spotlight on problems arising from the transplantation of liberal democratic institutions, and asks whether democratic processes as currently practised in Africa are having a positive impact on the lives of the citizens of various African polities.

Besides, a growing number of African and Africanist post-colonial theorists are calling for the development of alternative models of democracy for the continent that draw from indigenous African cultures. Among such authors are Wamba-dia-Wamba (1994), Wiredu (1996), Mojola (1996), Mafeje (2002), Chweya (2002), Bradley (2005), Claxton (2008) and Sium (2014). It is worth emphasizing that many of these thinkers take cognizance of the impossibility of reverting to pre-colonial political formations and modes of governance. What many of them emphasise is the need to creatively combine traditional African thought and practice with innovative approaches to democracy from other parts of the world, all in the light of current realities. This is why Paulin J. Hountondji speaks of 'endogeneity' rather than 'indigeneity' (Hountondji ed. 1997).

However, Achille Mbembe, the renowned critic of post-colonial theory, questions the concept of "indigeneity," holding that Africa cannot correctly be viewed in terms of a fixed racial category, and proposes that pan-Africanism and Afrocentrism be replaced with Afropolitanism, which views Africa as intensely entangled with the rest of the world (Mbembe 2001; Mbembe in Balakrishna 2016). As Syrotinski (2012, 413) explains, Mbembe's criticism of post-colonial theory is threefold: "firstly, its tendency to privilege the single moment of colonization within the long history of formerly colonized societies; secondly, the conflation of resistance (anti-colonial or otherwise) with the very different problematic of subalternity; and finally, the overemphasis on the language of 'difference' and 'alterity', and the consequently closed and constraining nature of this discourse."

Nevertheless, I opine that there are ready replies to Mbembe's three objections outlined in the previous paragraph, and therefore ample justification for the continuation of post-colonial theory from the point of view of the right to cultural group identities. *First*, as Frantz Fanon (1963) graphically illustrated, the pernicious effects of colonialism were at several levels, not least the psychic and economic ones. Similarly, Walter Rodney (1973) pointed out that colonialism, and slave trade before it, dealt an almost fatal blow to the long-term economic well-being of African peoples. Consequently, a catastrophe so far-reaching still deserves close scholarly attention almost six decades after its formal demise. *Second*, the problem of subalternity is actually the direct result of Western imperialism and can therefore not be addressed in isolation. *Third*, despite the fact of immigration into Africa from various other parts of the world, there is substantial evidence that cultures that can be traced to Africa and identified with Africa on considerably strict criteria are still dominant in the continent, and thus warrant speaking of indigeneity within the African context, on condition, of course, that the influence of immigrant cultures is taken into consideration. Indeed, indigeneity, as conceptualised in this volume, is not about the first occupants of various locales in Africa, but rather about perspectives that have developed within the African continent, even with input from immigrant cultures. This is what Paulin J. Hountondji refers to as "endogeneity" (Hountondji ed. 1997).

Francis Fukuyama famously celebrated the triumph of the liberal democratic West at the end of the Cold War in his declaration that the event marked "the end of history" conceived as a clash of ideologies (Fukuyama 1992). Nevertheless, as Fayemi (2009, 108) memorably observed, "Fukuyama's liberal democracy cannot be the end of human history, simply because we are not at the end of human intelligence. Diverse nations have every right to construct new conceptions of democracy, which respond to their religious, economic, and social needs." This brings to mind Frantz Fanon's exhortation to newly independent African countries to delink from the ways of their erstwhile colonisers:

> If we want to turn Africa into a new Europe . . . , then let us leave the destiny of our countries to Europeans. They will know how to do it better than the most gifted among us.
>
> But if we want humanity to advance a step further, if we want to bring it up to a different level than that which Europe has shown it, then we must invent and we must make discoveries. (Fanon 1963, 315)

The volume is divided into three sections. The four chapters in Section 1 offer rationales for the "Africa beyond Liberal Democracy" project.

According to Sirkku K. Hellsten, the Western attempt to offer two contrary trends of liberalism (*political liberalism* and *economic liberalism*) in one package as the model for ideal development has failed to entrench liberal democracy in Africa, but has instead succeeded in killing the humanistic side of African indigenous political ideologies that inspired the struggle for political independence. As a result, observes Hellsten, many African states have now adopted the instrumental values and profit-maximization of economic liberalism, but set aside the human rights and democracy agenda based on the originally humanistic values of *political liberalism* and liberal democracy.

Similarly, Thomas Menamparampil argues for the need to promote indigenous values so that forms of democracy suited to specific peoples may emerge. He contends that pretension to cultural superiority on the side of one group over others is unrealistic, and that we need to give *equal respect to the many streams of cultures* and civilizations that contribute to the ultimate destiny of the human race.

On his part, Dennis Masaka's central claim is that by virtue of its hegemonic relations with Africa, the West has no moral high ground from which to lecture Africa on the necessity of adopting the West's liberal paradigm of democracy. He further contends that the legacy of undemocratic rule that the Western colonisers left behind in Africa influenced the sprouting of 'post-independent' undemocratic African governments. He therefore asserts that African countries have a right to draw a democratic ethos from their own indigenous systems of governance, as well as from non-indigenous sources which they, without coercion, consider to be important in enriching their own model of democracy.

David Ngendo-Tshimba sketches the contours of the pitfalls of post-war Democratic Republic of Congo's electioneering in the 2006, 2011 and 2019 general elections. His over-arching argument is that the insistence on the organisation of elections for purposes of legitimising power in post-conflict polities may simply not be very meaningful in the first place, or, even worse, may lead to a renewal of violence only capable of worsening an already bad situation. In the circumstances, the aim should be meaningful citizen participation rather than a liberal democratic ritual termed as "free and fair elections".

Section 2 contains two chapters by contributors who, from a feminist vantagepoint, are patently critical of the quest for alternative models of democracy for African polities. The inclusion of critiques of the "Africa beyond Liberal Democracy" project guards against a dogmatic approach to the focus of the book by encouraging debate on it. As John Stuart Mill famously observed, "However unwillingly a person who has a strong opinion may admit the possibility that his opinion may be false, he ought to be moved by the consideration that, however true it may be, if it is not fully, frequently, and fearlessly discussed, it will be held as a dead dogma, not a living truth" (Mill 1956, 73).

Donna Pido points out that the disruptive forces of colonialism, Western arrogance and waning Western hegemony have contributed to contemporary East African efforts to stabilise culture and governance in democratic ways through rhetoric and popular discourse. Her argument, ultimately colored by feminist theory, culminates in a cynical but optimistic cross-cultural critique of 'democracy' and efforts to operationalise it.

Robinah S. Nakabo argues that the quality of leadership is a function of the quality of followership. Thus as the quality of followership in much of Sub-Saharan Africa changes due to factors such as formal education, urbanization and globalization, the quality of leadership and democratic governance are bound to change. Consequently, avers Nakabo, whereas the volume theme seeks a break with liberal democracy, there is an urgent need for qualitatively changed followership. She asserts that implicit in her reflections are the hypotheses that: (1) the disgraced liberal democracy would work in our favor if only we had a closer look at the phenomenon of followership, and (2) the changing quality of followership might lead to more African democratic models sprouting from below rather than those suggested in academic fora that adopt a top-down approach.

The eight chapters in Section 3 make substantive proposals for alternative models of democracy that, in their authors' view, stand a much better chance of taking firm root in contemporary African states than does liberal democracy.

Emefiena Ezeani contends that in spite of all the perceived benefits of political parties in fostering a democratic culture, in Nigeria, as well as in many other African and non-African states, the party system functions differently from how it does in its Western cradle lands and undermines democracy in a number of ways. He argues against the current *competitive* model of democracy and presents and defends an alternative governance model—*Cooperative Collegial Democracy*—for African societies free from the bureaucratic, costly and controversial general elections.

Emmanuel Ifeanyi Ani observes that the multi-party system of democracy in Africa has seen the emergence of verbal aggression in the contest for power. This, according to him, threatens the very foundations of peace, especially since empirical studies have revealed that physical aggression is frequently preceded by verbal aggression. He points out that African polities will still need verbal discipline regardless of whatever future evolution their democracies undergo. He avers that certain traditional cultures of Africa (such as that of the Akan of Ghana) place a high premium on linguistic discipline and have built a network of norms that discourage verbal aggression. He suggests ways in which public policy could do for contemporary societies what culture has done for certain traditional societies.

On his part, Munamato Chemhuru notes that since coups d'état, civilian dictatorships and disputed elections have remained the hallmark of many post-colonial African states for well over five decades now, it is doubtful if Western liberal democracy ought to be a model for the African state. Consequently, without suggesting that traditional African societies did not have their own problems, he proposes a revisiting of communitarian traditional systems of governance as a plausible basis for democracy in Africa.

For Joseph Situma, Kisemei Mutisya and Christine Buluma, in view of the diversity of African ethnicities and the intensity of ethnic identities, the challenge is to harness and propagate indigenous values and virtues that engender strong national sentiments. Consequently, they reflect on some indigenous African norms and values, and argue that a number of them are viable elements for an indigenous model of democracy for the twenty-first century.

According to Moses Oludare Aderibigbe, the principle of the supreme right of the majority which elections uphold in liberal democratic thought and practice amounts to the majority imposing its will on the minority. Besides, asserts Aderibigbe, given the tendency of many Africans to vote according to their ethnic or religious identities, democracy will have to mean more than voting at elections. To this end, he argues that the universal values of democracy ought to be contextualised by taking into consideration the African reality and adopting some indigenous African values to domesticate democracy and make it sustainable. He holds that values such as the autonomy of the individual, coupled with the importance of consensus and tolerance, have the potential of protecting the rights of the minority in the society by involving kinship groupings such as extended families and lineages in decision-making processes.

Tayo Raymond Ezekiel Eegunlusi questions the possibility of a universal alternative African model of democracy. While conceding that liberal democracy has failed Africans, he argues that writers often take at least three things for granted in their search for its substitute. First, since people define democratic practices in relation to particular cultures, suggesting an over-arching democratic model for Africa is unrealistic. Second, considering African peoples' diverse identities and experiences, preference for any democratic model from any region may be perceived as culture-imposition by other African states and regions. Third, liberal democracy's failures mainly emanate from people's moral failure. Thus while Western colonialism is correctly adjudged to be responsible for the failure of liberal democracy in Africa, similar moral failures characterising the governance systems of pre-colonial African societies have also contributed to the failure.

J. P. Odoch Pido highlights the difference between 'trickle down' and 'groundswell' approaches to design. He observes that the trickle-down model can be considered to be democratic when an innovation receives widespread acceptance by members of a group. Groundswell, intensely democratic, is what the masses actually do and how their behavior affects the decisions and actions of those in power. He notes that neither of these apparently opposing trends can be stopped or controlled without considerable, often very undemocratic, effort. As part of the search for truly African models of Democracy, Pido reflects on numerous examples in which either 'trickle down' or 'groundswell' have occurred globally and in East Africa.

Reginald M. J. Oduor offers a rationale for ethnically based federations in ethnically plural post-colonial African states, with specific reference to Kenya. He notes that despite globalisation, ethnocentricism continues to be a salient feature of socio-political reality in many parts of the world, a large number of post-colonial African states included. He further points out that group identity is an essential component of the individual's sense of self-respect. From this he infers that liberal democracy's repudiation of the collective right of members of an ethnic group to pursue their political aspirations in the context of their cultural group is not simply defective but is actually an act of violence. He therefore avers that ethnic loyalties ought not to be vilified or wished away but ought rather to be carefully factored into the socio-political engineering of multi-ethnic African polities.

In sum, this book is a contribution to the discourse on post-colonial reconstruction—an indispensable and ongoing endeavour because destruction always takes a much shorter time than rebuilding; and five hundred years of Western imperialism, first as the slave trade, then as colonialism, and now as neo-colonialism, have destroyed and continue to destroy Africa's peoples socially, politically, economically, spiritually, psychologically and in many other ways. This is why those who insist that we have no business blaming colonialism for our woes more than fifty years after independence are in gross error. To those who may wonder why, in the light of current geo-politics, scholars would deliberate on a topic such as the one signified by the title of this book, I reply that visionaries are by definition people who see beyond their circumstances and their time. The lives of many people in Africa today have already been grossly degraded by the instabilities occasioned by dysfunctional liberal democracy. Consequently, it behooves them to bequeath to the next generation possible road maps to a better future, and this volume is a contribution to this discursive endeavour. As the saying goes, societies are made great by those of their elders who plant trees whose shades they know they shall never sit under.

REFERENCES

Balakrishnan, Sarah. 2016. "Pan-African Legacies, Afropolitan Futures: a conversation with Achille Mbembe". *Transition*, No. 120, pp. 28–37. https://www.jstor.org/stable/10.2979/transition.120.1.04.

Bell, D. A. 2006. *Beyond Liberal Democracy: Political Thinking for an East Asian Context*. Princeton: Princeton University Press.

Bradley, Matthew Todd. 2005. "'The Other': Precursory African Conceptions of Democracy". *International Studies Review*, Vol. 7 No. 3, pp. 407–31. https://www.jstor.org/stable/3699757.

Chweya, Ludeki. 2002. "Western Modernity, African Indigene, and Political Order: Interrogating the Liberal Democratic Orthodoxy". In Chweya, Ludeki ed. *Electoral Politics in Kenya*. Nairobi: Claripress, pp. 1–27.

Claxton, Mervyn. 2008. "African Culture: A Source of Solutions for Africa's Problems?" *Présence Africaine*, New Series, Vol. 2 No. 175/177, pp. 589–615. https://www.jstor.org/stable/43617550.

Fanon, Frantz. 1963. *The Wretched of the Earth*. Constance Farrington, trans. New York: Grove Weidenfeld.

Fayemi, Ademola Kazeem. 2009. "Towards an African Theory of Democracy". *Thought and Practice: A Journal of the Philosophical Association of Kenya*, Premier Issue, New Series, Vol.1 No.1, pp. 101–26. https://www.ajol.info/index.php/tp/article/view/46309.

Fukuyama, Francis. 1992. *The End of History and the Last Man*. London: Penguin Books.

Gandhi, M. K. 1909. *Hind Swaraj; or Indian Rule*. Gujarat: Indian Opinion.

Hountondji, Paulin J. ed. 1997. *Endogenous Knowledge: Research Trails*. Dakar: CODESRIA.

Lumumba-Kasongo, Tukumbi ed. 2005. *Liberal Democracy and its Critics in Africa: Political Dysfunction and the Struggle for Social Progress*. Dakar: CODESRIA Books

Mafeje, A. 2002. "Democratic Governance and New Democracy in Africa: Agenda for the Future". Paper prepared for presentation at the "African Forum for Envisioning Africa" in Nairobi, Kenya, 26–29 April 2002. www.worldsummit2002.org/texts/ArchieMafeje2.pdf.

Mbembe, A. 2001. *On the Post-colony*. Berkeley: University of California Press.

Mill, John Stuart. 1956 (1859). *On Liberty*. Shields, Currin V. ed. Upper Saddle River, NJ: Prentice Hall.

Mojola, A. O. 1996. "Democracy in Pre-colonial Africa and the Search for Appropriate Models in Contemporary African Society". Oloka-Onyango, Joseph, Kivutha Kibwana and Chris Maina Peter eds. *Law and the Struggle for Democracy in East Africa*. Nairobi: Claripress, pp. 329–40.

Pantham, T. 1983. "Thinking with Mahatma Gandhi: Beyond Liberal Democracy". *Political Theory*, Vol.11 No.2, May 1983, pp. 165–88.

Rodney, W. 1973. *How Europe Underdeveloped Africa*. Dar-Es-Salaam: Tanzanian Publishing House.

Sium, Aman. 2014. "Dreaming Beyond the State: Centering Indigenous Governance as a Framework for African Development". *Counterpoints*, Vol. 443: Emerging Perspectives on 'African Development': Speaking Differently, pp. 63–82. https://www.jstor.org/stable/42982048.

Syrotinski, M. 2012. "'Genealogical Misfortunes': Achille Mbembe's (Re-) Writing of Postcolonial Africa". *Paragraph*, Vol. 35 No. 3, pp. 407–20. https://www.jstor.org/stable/43263849.

Ta' I Wo`, Olu Fe'mi. 2004. "Post-Independence African Political Philosophy". Wiredu, Kwasi ed. *A Companion to African Philosophy*. Malden, MA: Blackwell Publishing Ltd., pp. 243–59.

Wamba-dia-Wamba, E. 1994. "Africa in Search of a New Mode of Politics". Himmelstrand, U., K. Kinyanjui, and E. Mburugu eds. *African Perspectives on Development: Controversies, Dilemmas and Openings*. London: James Currey, pp. 249–61.

Whitehead, L. 2010. "Alternative Models of Democracy in Latin America". *Brown Journal of World Affairs*, Vol. 17 No. 1, pp. 75–87. https://www.jstor.org/stable/24590758.

Wiredu, K. 1996. *Cultural Universals and Particulars: An African Perspective*. Bloomington: Indiana University Press.

Part 1

RATIONALE FOR THE "AFRICA BEYOND LIBERAL DEMOCRACY" PROJECT

Chapter One

African Political Ideology and Practice in the Era of Globalisation

Can a Return to African Humanistic Socialism Combat Afro-Libertarianism?

Sirkku K. Hellsten

In this chapter, I examine the current state of African political ideology in the context of globalisation. I ask why liberal democracy has not succeeded to become the preferred governance model in contemporary Africa. I then argue that it is high time African political philosophers, political scientists and political decision-makers stepped up the search for a consistent ideological basis for Africa's development broadly construed. I further argue that this can only be achieved if greater emphasis is laid on developing alternative political theories that take Africa's context and history seriously and challenge the applicability of current hegemonic development ideals championed by Western powers and financiers. In this regard, I suggest that an excellent starting point is the re-assessment of the merits and shortcomings of the African liberation ideology and African humanistic socialism, both of which combatted exploitation by Western imperialistic capitalism and global neo-liberalism during the struggle for de-colonisation and the early years of independence.

LIBERAL DEMOCRACY: THE IDEAL FOR AFRICA'S DEVELOPMENT?

Since the end of World War II, the ideal for international development has been presented within the political value framework of liberal democracy, with a market-based economic system. Western powers created this development ideal to challenge socialism during the Cold War (Escobar 1985). Besides, following the collapse of the Soviet Union in 1991 and the subsequent disintegration of the Eastern (socialist) Bloc, liberalism (in its various formulations) remained the only 'respectable' choice, and eventually achieved global dominance (Rist 2002; Hellsten 2013). Thereafter, Western states provided development aid to African polities on condition that the recipients demonstrated commitment to governance systems and institutions that would eventually lead to working liberal democracies.

Philosophically, liberal democracy is based on various formulations of the social contract theory, from the pre-Enlightenment ideas of Thomas Hobbes and John Locke, to those of the Enlightenment such as Adam Smith, Jean-Jacques Rousseau and Immanuel Kant, who were looking for a theoretical justification for the modern nation-state.[1] This state was based on the consolidation of public power, that is, on the will of citizens who chose their leaders and made their laws as autonomous moral and political agents. Economic development occasioned by the Industrial Revolution led to the increased popularity of capitalism, which was also believed to increase the individual's awareness of his or her autonomy, giving rise to an increasing need for the exchange of information. In recent years, social contract theory has been developed further still, being reformulated to fit the current political and economic context, and to legitimise and reinforce the purported universality of liberal values and ideals in the era of globalisation.

Furthermore, the Structural Adjustment Programmes, imposed on many African states by the Bretton Woods institutions (chiefly the World Bank and the International Monetary Fund) from the 1990s, were based on the assumption that countries that adopted free market economic policies would also commit themselves to liberal democracy. Only recently have such institutions recognised that economic growth alone does not guarantee democratic governance, and now emphasise that a market economy and privatisation should be based on the principles of 'good governance' in order to lead to 'inclusive growth', that is, economic development which benefits the citizenry more equally.

Besides, in the various United Nations human rights initiatives such as the Millennium Development Goals (2000–2015) and the current Sustainable Development Goals (2015–2030), the targets are based on the idea of universalising liberal democratic values. Moreover, many Western development agencies are prone to the wishful thinking that with the worldwide establishment of institutions such as those typically found in Western polities, most countries would also commit themselves to humanistic liberal values such as inclusion, participation, equal rights and opportunities, as well as tolerance of difference. Indeed, those agencies set these values as the "underlying principles" for much of their development co-operation with African states.

After World War II, an expanding market economy and a growing middle class were seen as the best way to get Western European countries back on their feet, and the same thinking has subsequently been applied to post-colonial Africa, despite its markedly different socio-political context. In Europe, democratic development within the nation-state has had a significantly long history spanning more than two centuries. On the other hand, Africa's newly independent, culturally heterogeneous states set out from a much weaker point, being vulnerable to conflicts that easily lead to social and political fragmentation—a fact which was recognised by liberation ideologists such as Julius Nyerere and Kwame Nkrumah, who emphasised the need to reinforce national unity and solidarity. From their point of view, liberal democracy with a market-based economy in the weak, post-colonial polities would create too many interest groups, resulting in competition and conflict (Nyerere 1967; Collier 2009; Hellsten 2013; UNDP 2013; World Bank 2013).

Nevertheless, by Western powers insisting that democratisation in Africa go hand in hand with a free market economy, and by co-ordinating their aid accordingly, they conflate two very different liberal traditions—economic liberalism and political liberalism. Not surprisingly, given that these two liberal traditions have very different value frameworks, this merger has not always proceeded harmoniously. While economic liberalism is based on pragmatic and instrumental materialist values and the ideal of self-interested profit-maximising agents, political liberalism has its roots in Enlightenment humanism, which viewed individuals as moral and political agents working together to realise mutual interests. In today's political reality, economic liberalism has taken the upper hand in this uneasy 'liberal union'. Thus, while many countries across the world have adapted to the instrumental interests of economic liberalism, few are committed to the ideals of political liberalism based on the notion of equal human worth that imply the imperative to pursue social justice manifested in equal rights, equal opportunities, and equal participation, among others. In other words, the 'liberal development project' has failed to enhance pluralistic political liberalism.

What is more, while capitalist neo-liberalism is currently dominating economic policies, on the governance side political liberalism is still vigorously competing with authoritarian regimes. Besides, the post–World War II development ideal championed by the U.S.-led Western hegemony has been challenged by various actors and factors. Economically, the BRICS (Brasilia, Russia, India, China, and South Africa), as well as many countries in Asia and Africa, are playing a growing role in global economics and politics. China, in particular, has taken up an important position in the world's economy, with an expanding middle class and rising consumerism promising continued economic growth. Furthermore, China offers an alternative model of governance to that of Western liberal democracy, with its state capitalism presenting an authoritarian form of governance that can compete robustly in a global business environment.

Yet China is not alone in opting for an authoritarian and centralised governance model. Indeed, anti-liberal political ideologies have been on the rise, particularly in Asia and Africa, and even the United States and Western Europe have seen developments that challenge the victory trajectory of liberal democracy, with the expansion of populist politics, conservative republicanism, religious fundamentalism, nationalist protectionism, new forms of fascism and other forms of extremism, and the increased threat of terrorism in the birthplace of liberal democracy (Diamond et al. 2016). As such, the analysis of Samuel Huntington (1991) of the progressive 'waves of democracy' no longer seems to apply, with the ongoing 'fourth wave' of global political change appearing to shift towards more authoritarian governance systems worldwide. Thus, even though Western type democratic institutions have been widely adopted across the globe, they now appear to be increasingly used to legitimise conservative and/or illiberal systems representing various forms of authoritarian libertarianism/neo-liberalism (Diamond et al. 2016).

Elsewhere, majoritarian democracy is challenging pluralistic liberal democracy. Majoritarian democracy does not necessarily respect the rights of minorities, voices of the marginalised, equality of opportunity, and other pluralistic, liberal values—particularly when 'the invisible hand of the market' is given a major role in politics. In Africa, for example, majoritarian democracy can be seen in the politics of 'numbers', where politicians form (usually ethnically based) alliances to guarantee votes that will keep them in power. These alliances ignore the interests of those who are not part of them, and gain support by focusing on division rather than on trying to find ways to promote unity within nations. They use democratic institutions to capture and retain power, but within a traditional patriarchal value system that is based on sub-national rather than national loyalties, and is currently mixed with neo-liberal self-interest, that is, the obsession with amassing private property.

In addition, over the past decade or so, illiberal powers have gained influence within the global trade arena in many other parts of the world. Leading authoritarian countries such as China, Iran, Russia, and Saudi Arabia have developed new tools and strategies to contain the spread of liberal democracy, and to challenge the international political order based on liberal values while remaining economically competitive. Meanwhile, the so-called advanced democracies of the West have experienced internal challenges and have failed to respond to the threat posed by the authoritarians (Diamond et al. 2016). It is worth noting that the European Union currently views defending liberal democracy as part of the European value system, instead of calling for universal values. Thus, the Enlightenment ideals are now localised and openly culturally embedded in European history and political practice and are thus no longer disguised as manifestations of 'universal reason'.

AFRO-LIBERTARIANISM AND AUTHORITARIAN NEO-LIBERALISM

In this section, I examine the state of politics and political ideologies in Africa today, before concentrating on the current state of political theory in the continent. In the contemporary African context, it is particularly important to view theory in relation to political practice in order to clearly distinguish between facts and values, traditions and ideals, practice and ideology. Indeed, as Immanuel Kant famously noted, experience without theory is blind, but theory without experience is mere intellectual play (Kant 1998).

African political practice has widely adopted a form of governance that I have labelled 'afro-libertarianism' (Hellsten 2009). It is important to emphasise here that 'afro-libertarianism' is not a carefully designed ideology, consciously constructed political theory, or deliberately chosen policy direction. Rather, it is a predatory political practice that is taking over African politics. It does not offer normative guidelines on the role of the state or government in deciding economic or social policies (state interference/maximum or minimum state). Instead, it is built upon a reactionary and inconsistent policy agenda that is dependent upon external pressures, donor conditions, business offers from any partners, and the personal interests of the leaders rather than those of the people. As a result, this political practice is neither moving towards the ideals of liberal democracy, nor in the direction of the core values of African collectivist humanism upon which the push for African liberation from Western European colonialism was based.

In afro-libertarian political practice, the pre-colonial communalist African value systems that called for loyalty to the group (most often the ethnic group), social duties, and respect for traditional hierarchies have now been integrated within various imported governance models. First came colonial authoritarianism, then, after de-colonisation, most of Africa shifted, albeit nominally, to the contrasting model of liberal democracy—now embraced by the West and competing with socialist authoritarianism and centralisation. The combination of this range of governance systems and institutions in Africa has gradually led to a rapacious political order, in which ideals and methodologies have been integrated in a manner that has produced a series of mixed values and practices. For example, the imported democratic practice of holding regular elections is now often used to legitimise the power of autocrats.[2] In other words, what is done in the name of 'democracy' is often inconsistent with 'democratic values', and contrary to the interests of the people. More specifically, without a commitment to equal participation, 'democratic' elections can be, and have been, manipulated to validate unjust power and resource distribution, with the courts (that are under the not-so-subtle control of incumbents) used to make rulings that uphold the status quo, and the media (that have no genuine autonomy) used to guide public opinion in favour of the affluent and influential.

In the precarious situation described in the previous two paragraphs, public trust in democratic processes and institutions diminishes. Citizens are left without any genuine policies to choose from, or any real options based on consistent ideological positions on the role of the state in economic development and in the citizens' lives generally. Indeed, instead of choosing between sets of alternative political value frameworks, the people end up choosing between charismatic leaders, or voting on the basis of ethnic loyalties and other traditionally communalist and patriarchal considerations (Mazrui 2001, 97–99; Taiwo 2006; Hellsten 2009), and ultimately lose confidence in democracy as a system that can bring about positive change. This is often referred to as the 'failure of democracy in Africa', and yet it is rather a failure on the part of those in power to promote democratic values.

The distinction between values and practices becomes even more blurred if we fail to consider both political philosophy and political science when analysing the different aspects of political developments in Africa. For example, it is essential to consider why African socialist and communalist humanisms did not work in their historical and social contexts: was the problem rooted in their value frameworks, their implementation, external factors, or a combination of all three? As Ali Mazrui (2001, 97–98) aptly noted, under post-colonial—and neo-colonial—conditions, African political theory has responded more to socio-cultural ideologies than to socio-economic ones. These socio-cultural ideologies focus on issues such as identity, ancestry, and sacredness, leaving socio-economic ideologies (that focus on class, economic interests and economic transformation) trailing behind, particularly after the decline of African socialism.

African political philosophy mainly attempts to revive communal governance structures by emphasising indigenous African solidarity values, while African political science often measures political development by orthodox Western standards of 'democratic practice'.[3] In everyday politics, however, the lack of a consistent ideology of development is reflected in ad hoc economic and social policies. In general, political decisions in Africa are reactive to global, regional, and national affairs, rather than driven by long-term, value-based planning. Furthermore, policy formulation is often unrealistic, with inadequate political will to honour election pledges. Without a coherent value-based ideology that offers a blueprint for political responsibility, the people are left without any criteria by which to assess the performance of those who they elect to high public offices.

In today's context of global capitalism, it is important to consider why African liberation ideologists preferred a socialist model based on the African communalist context, given their approach based on experience rather than blind, idealistic theories of change. Having seen firsthand how neo-liberal economic policies exploited African peoples and made the ravages of imperial capitalism manifest in its promotion of exploitation and inequality in the name of 'economic rationality', they saw African socialism as offering an alternative development ideology for de-colonisation and beyond. They saw its collectivist values as more applicable to the post-colonial context than African communalistic traditions, and its call for social responsibility as suitable for building national pride and unity.

Yet while the goal of African socialism was the common good of the people (Kaunda 1966; Nyerere 1967, 1968, 1973; Nkrumah 1970; Shivji 1976; Amin 2014), today many theorists view the failure of African socialism from a solely economic point of view, and from the history of the winner—that is, capitalism with its attendant market economy—and declare that socialism suffered a crushing defeat. In reality, however, due to internal and external pressures, experiments with African socialist democracy never had an opportunity to run their course. Since Western countries themselves have problems formulating consistent policies that balance the two very different kinds of liberalism (political and economic), it is no wonder that much younger post-colonial African states have had difficulties with democratisation within the context of globalisation.

THE FAILURE OF THE LIBERAL AGENDA IN AFRICA AND BEYOND

In current Afro-libertarian political practice, there is a trend towards a rise in authoritarian neo-liberalism, and a drift away from liberal democracy. This direction is fulfilling the predictions of the liberation ideologists that called for humanistic values as the basis for African development and warned of the dangers of a capitalist free market economy. Many of the current African leaders remain cautious about liberal democracy, while wholeheartedly adopting individualistic market-driven economic policies, and, although many leaders may still make rhetorical calls for communalistic solidarity, they merely expect this solidarity from the citizenry without the leaders committing themselves to the common good of the nation.

Thus, when, in line with classical economic liberalism, the ideal of individualistic self-interest manifesting as profit-making is taken as a model for rational citizenship, the value base is different from that of liberal democracy, which views citizens as autonomous moral and political agents. The value base changes even more when profit-maximisation is set in the context of traditional communalistic solidarity with social duties and networks, because communalistic calls for solidarity create biased, sub-national loyalties, as the leaders, and sections of the population, try to protect and advance their own interests rather than promoting the common good. While economic liberalism calls for market rationality, communalism, in the African context, sets this within the networks of traditional patrimonial relations.[4] Political liberalism, grounded in the ideal of an all-inclusive social contract as the basis of democratic decision-making, does not work in a context within which sub-national loyalties prevent impartiality and the autonomy of individual citizens. Yet in the contemporary African context, the leaders and the wider ruling elite create political cleavage by appealing to solidarity towards one's social collective—with this often being one's clan, ethnic, or religious community.

In contemporary African politics, the confusion arising from the ad hoc mixing of various value systems is leading to a move away from the ideals of liberal democracy. A key problem lies in the inconsistent 'development model' set by the West. After World War II, the two kinds of individualistic liberalism (economic and political) were brought together to combat the challenge of socialism and its centralised mode of governance. The Structural Adjustment Programmes (SAPs), and other economic privatisation programmes championed by the Bretton Woods institutions in line with global capitalism, have firmly rooted economic liberalism in Africa. However, the ideal of political liberalism, which emphasises the role of citizens as autonomous and self-governing moral and political agents with equal rights, is less widely and less eagerly adopted (Senghor 1964; Rawls 1971; Nyerere 1973; Shivji 1976; Escobar 1985; Rist 2002; Hellsten 2009, 2013, 2016). The main problem with the Western development agenda in Africa is the incompatibility of the values of these two very different kinds of liberalism. Economic liberalism, which now drives global capitalism, is based on instrumental and materialistic values, and, as such, tends to lead to increasing greed and competition over resources, just as African liberation ideologists Julius Nyerere, Kwame Nkrumah, Kenneth Kaunda, and many others anticipated (See Kaunda 1966; Nkrumah 1970; Nyerere 1967, 1973).

The foregoing observations should enable us to better appreciate why African liberation ideologists preferred the socialist model which was compatible with the African communalist context. Their goal was greater sovereignty through self-reliance for the newly independent African states, with a view to promoting the common good of the people.

Following the abandoning of African socialism, the value basis of African political practice has integrated Western individualist economic and political liberalism in a manner that best suits those in power. Ironically, this African formulation of authoritarian neo-liberalism uses imported and imposed democratic institutions and structures to legitimise patrimonial, often illiberal governance systems. More specifically, autocrats subvert democracies by undermining the institutions that sustain them—legislatures, representative local governments, the judiciary, the media, and other non-state institutions such as civil rights groups—and by whipping up sub-national loyalties, often in the form of politicised ethnicity. The result, in each case, is a polity which institutionally looks like a liberal democracy, but in which the value base is nowhere near that of political liberalism which views citizens as autonomous moral and political agents.

PRACTICAL EXAMPLES

In terms of empirical case studies within Africa, Tanzania offers a useful example of the authoritarian trend in the globalised neo-liberal political economy. The country is grappling with corruption in its diverse manifestations—illicit money transfers, drug trafficking, poaching, among other practices that have lined the pockets of those who are in positions to manipulate rules and regulations if they receive attractive 'compensation'. There is suspicion about 'secret' deals made by public officials regarding the utilisation of the country's vast natural resources. The lack of transparency and commitment to the common good continues to increase fragmentation in Tanzanian society, with the unequal distribution of the country's resources creating tensions among various ethnic groups and social classes.

Besides, the perpetual debate over a new draft Tanzanian constitution illustrates the way in which the question of the distribution of the country's resources is becoming increasingly central and preventing different parties from reaching consensus. The 2015 general election results were the closest since the country's independence in 1961, indicating a significant dwindling of confidence in Chama Cha Mapinduzi (CCM)—the party which has ruled the country since independence.[5] On its part, CCM has become something of an ideological chameleon: despite its constitution defining it as a socialist party, it has in policy and practice changed its political direction from Nyerere's *Ujamaa* humanistic socialism towards a more market-oriented approach, and currently quite openly supports a form of state capitalism.

The present Tanzanian constitution gives the president considerable power, and CCM, as the ruling party, has overall control of state resources and public offices, as well as economic policies and business opportunities in the country. Thus, CCM can use both state-owned enterprises and the private influence of its individual high-ranking members to determine key economic decisions. Consequently, there is often a conflict between the interests of the state and those of individuals occupying state offices. However, during the first year of President John Pombe Magufuli's leadership, there appeared to be some serious efforts to cut public waste, stop tax evasion, and check the influence of political elites on business deals. Magufuli took a firm grip on state affairs, and created a more cautious political atmosphere, where people were worried about losing their positions and connections. Nevertheless, he also proved to be intolerant of criticism, limiting some civil and political freedoms, including the freedom of expression and the independence of the media. It was not quite clear how much control the president had in party affairs, as traditionally the CCM as a political collective has been above, and in control of, any individual it supports at any given time—a similar situation to that of South Africa's African National Congress (ANC) (See Hellsten 2016).

In Mozambique, meanwhile, we see a similar structure, where party power is placed over individual influence in the running of state and business. As with Tanzania's CCM, there has been only one ruling party in Mozambique, Front for the Liberation of Mozambique (FRELIMO), since the country's independence in 1975. All attempts to share power with the Mozambican National Resistance (RENAMO)—the former rebel movement that became an opposition political party after the civil war (1977–1992)—have failed. Frelimo, very much like CCM, is ideologically flexible, and has a firm control on the economy, and on domestic and international business deals in the country. Thus, as in Tanzania, the economy currently has a capitalist orientation, with previously held FRELIMO socialist principles having been long forgotten and replaced by the interests of the ruling elite. A large part of business in the country is controlled by the ruling party and the president, although President Filipe Nyusi, who took office in January 2015, has fewer overarching powers than his predecessor Armando Guebuza.

Overall, both Tanzania and Mozambique present examples of control by autocratic political parties that had previously led the countries' national liberation movements, affording them historical credit and grassroot following that continue to guarantee them support in elections.

Zambia has travelled a path similar to that of Tanzania and Mozambique, although power in the country changed hands from a socialist party to a neo-liberal one, as Kenneth Kaunda's United National Independence Party (UNIP), which had ruled the country since its independence in 1964, lost power to Frederick Chiluba's Movement for Multiparty Democracy (MMD) in 1991 during the first multi-party elections in twenty-three years. Yet the same problems manifested in Zambia, as the winner took it all, fomenting tension among various political factions.

Elsewhere in Africa, other forms of authoritarian neo-liberalism can be found. In Uganda, for instance, the National Resistance Movement (NRM), which took power in 1986 on a liberation platform after decades of instability, is still in power, with Yoweri Museveni, its original leader, unwilling to step down or share power. Yet again, there are countries such as Kenya, that have been consistently market-oriented, and appear to have adapted to democratic handovers of power. However, the ethnic alliances formed to ensure power for particular ethnic leaders are undermining pluralistic liberal democracy in such countries, turning elections into competitions over numbers based on ethnic loyalties—following the divide-and-rule strategy (Cheeseman 2014).

The foregoing examples illustrate how Afro-libertarianism and authoritarian neo-liberalism have found expression in diverse governance models in Africa. In some African states, political parties in power do not allow room for multi-party political competition, despite the citizens' calls for opportunities to choose among genuine ideological alternatives. In others, authoritarian governance appears in the form of charismatic, strong and/or ruthless leaders. While poverty levels remain high in these countries, the rich and powerful continue to acquire vast amounts of wealth through corrupt local and global business deals at the expense of their impoverished subjects. Clearly, in many of these countries, political and economic elites are intertwined.

CONCLUSION

In this chapter, I have sought to show that in many contemporary African polities, there is an incoherent mix of three value systems: traditional African communalist values of solidarity and egalitarianism, that in practice appear as sub-national loyalties and patrimonial power relations, have been awkwardly integrated with two imposed and divergent Western individualist value systems, namely, economic and political liberalism. Consequently, defining actual guiding social values and political principles is becoming increasingly difficult. As such, many African political parties now seldom draw up any clear, consistent, normative ideological frameworks to guide the development of the countries in which they operate. Instead, in their political campaigns, they make vague references to "democracy", "development", "reform", "change", "wealth creation", "national unity", and "national sovereignty". In reality, political practice is based on short-term personal profits for those who capture state power, and not on long-term planning for the common good. When political parties do not offer clear ideological directions, the people quickly begin to look for normative guidelines from elsewhere. This has led to the emergence of various kinds of extremism such as religious fundamentalism, politicised ethnicity, fascism, and extreme egoism, as well as destabilising political movements that espouse various authoritarian modes of leadership, thereby creating a vicious cycle of marginalisation, discontent, and conflict.

Thus, in order to find directions for African development broadly construed, there is an urgent need to take a fresh look at both the philosophy and context of liberation ideologies espoused by leaders such as Julius Nyerere, Kwame Nkrumah, and Kenneth Kaunda. Deploying that African humanistic socialism in the current global neo-liberal context could provide African politics with new options to combat exploitation and to come up with alternative governance structures. Whether such structures would adapt to the values of liberal democracy or to those of African humanism is not as crucial as the attempt to find a path to a more human-centred ideal for development after decades of economic instrumentalism. Thus, the reason for re-emphasising the role of African humanistic socialism in this context is its original point of departure—its focus on alternative, human-centred development that is much broader than mere economic growth or rising standards of living. African humanistic socialism was particularly critical of imperialism and cutthroat global capitalism for their exploitation and for creating a false consciousness among African peoples.

I have further argued that the historical fact that humanistic African socialism as political practice was abandoned does not render its goals, its human-centred values and its core criticism of Western economic liberalism meaningless—quite the opposite, in fact. It is noteworthy that many of the leading liberation ideologists pointed out that adopting individualist capitalistic practices without commitment to any profound humanistic values would lead to vicious competition and social fragmentation. They emphasised that this was particularly problematic in recently de-colonised and often still fragile African states whose borders were artificially set by the colonial powers, resulting in ethnically heterogeneous populations, and their warnings have proved to be well-founded, with the consequences manifest all around us. Indeed, many African states have been ravaged by internal and cross-border conflicts arising from fierce competition for power and resources, often based on ethnic loyalties.

It is therefore high time we re-examined what African humanistic socialism can offer in the fluid and precarious current context of world politics. African and Africanist political theorists ought to take the lead in reconstructing consistent ideological frameworks that could guide African development and politics in the era of globalisation and give African states an original and powerful role in global politics, instead of them playing endless 'catch-up' with Western states that have, quite unjustifiably, set up their own historical development, political systems, and value frameworks as the ideals for global development.

NOTES

1. Political philosophers such as John Rawls and Robert Nozick have had great influence by emphasizing various aspects of liberalism in democratic societies, Rawls focusing on political liberalism, and Nozick on economic neo-liberalism. Further attempts to re-justify liberal democracy as the global development ideal have been presented by a number of cosmopolitan theorists, including Martha Nussbaum and David Held (See Hobbes 1962; Rawls 1972; Nozick 1974; Locke 1980; Rousseau 1987; Montesquieu 1989; Held 1995; Nussbaum 2015).
2. Currently, elections are regularly used to legitimise the position of leaders in power by rigging polls, bribing election officials, buying votes or voting cards, intimidation, etc (see Collier 2009; Hellsten 2009).
3. African development is usually measured using the human development index, governance index, corruption perception index, human rights realisation index, economic growth and business environment indices, among others. When measured against Western countries who develop these indices and present themselves as the ideal, Africa will always be seen to be trailing behind them.
4. Here patrimonialism refers to an authority relationship in which the (male) leader controls an administrative staff selected from his kinship network dominated by male ancestry, and based on personal loyalty to him.
5. Chama Cha Mapinduzi (CCM), which is Kiswahili for "Revolutionary Party", was formed in 1977 through the merger of the Tanganyika African National Union (TANU) and the Afro-Shirazi Party (ASP) which were the sole operating parties in mainland Tanzania, and the semi-autonomous islands of Zanzibar and Pemba respectively. Since the restoration of a multi-party system in Tanzania, CCM has won the previous six general elections (in 1995, 2000, 2005, 2010, 2015, and 2020) both in the mainland, as well as in Zanzibar and Pemba. In 2005, CCM presidential candidate Jakaya Kikwete won by a landslide, receiving more than 80 percent of the popular vote, while the 2015 elections were much closer between the CCM candidate John Magufuli and the (somewhat) united opposition and CHADEMA's candidate Edward Lowassa.

REFERENCES

Amin, Samir. 2014. *The Implosion of Capitalism*. London: Pluto Press.
Collier, Paul. 2009. *Wars, Guns, and Votes: Democracy in Dangerous Places*. New York: Harper Collins Publishers.
Cheeseman, Nic. 2014. "Does the African Middle Class Defend Democracy?" *WIDER Working Paper 2014/096*. UNU/WIDER, Helsinki. https://www.wider.unu.edu/publication/does-african-middle-class-defend-democracy.
Diamond, Larry, Marc Plattner and Christopher Walker. 2016. *Authoritarianism Goes Global: The Challenge to Democracy*. Baltimore: The John Hopkins University Press.

Escobar, Arturo. 1985. *Encountering Development: The Making and Unmaking of the Third World*. Princeton: Princeton University Press.

Hellsten, Sirkku. 2009. "Afro-Libertarianism and the Social Contract Framework in Post-Colonial Africa: The Case of Post-2007 Elections Kenya". *Thought and Practice: A Journal of the Philosophical Association of Kenya*, New Series, Vol. 1 No. 1, pp. 127–46. https://www.ajol.info/index.php/tp/article/view/46311/0.

———. 2013. "African Humanism in Re-conceptualisation of Global Development: Bringing Ethics back to Governance?" *Zanzibar Yearbook of Law*, Vol. 3, pp. 3–24. https://travelsdocbox.com/84966865-Africa/Zanzibar-yearbook-of-law.html.

———. 2016. "Deconstructing the Myth of African Middle Class". Melber, Henning ed. *The Rise of Africa's Middle Class In Africa*. London: ZED books.

Huntington, Samuel. 1991. *The Third Wave: Democratisation in the Late Twentieth Century*. Norman: University of Oklahoma Press.

Kant, Immanuel. 1998. *Critique of Pure Reason*. Guyer, P. and A. Wood eds. Cambridge: Cambridge University Press.

Kaunda, Kenneth. 1966. *A Humanist in Africa*. London: Longmans Green.

Mazrui, Ali. 2001. "Ideology and African Political Culture". Kiros, Teodros Ed. *Explorations in African Political Thought: Identity, Community, Ethics*. New York: Routledge.

Nkrumah, Kwame. 1970. *Consciencism: Philosophy and Ideology for Decolonisation and Development with Particular Reference to the African Revolution*. London: Panaf Books.

Nyerere, Julius. 1967. *Freedom and Unity*. Oxford: Oxford University Press.

———. 1968. *Ujamaa: Essays on Socialism*. Oxford: Oxford University Press.

———. 1973. *Freedom and Development*. Oxford: Oxford University Press.

Rawls, John. 1972. *A Theory of Justice*. Oxford: Oxford University Press.

Rist, Gilbert. 2002. *The History of Development: From Western Origins to Global Faith*. London: Zed Books.

Senghor, Leopold. 1964. *Négritude et humanisme*. Paris: Seuil.

Shivji, Issa. 1976. *Class Struggles in Tanzania*. London: Heinemann.

Taiwo, Olufemi. 2004. "Post-Independence African Political Philosophy". Wiredu, Kwasi Ed. *A Companion to African Philosophy*. Oxford: Blackwell.

UNDP. 2013. "Human Development Report 2013—The Rise of the South: Human Progress in a Diverse World". http://hdr.undp.org/en/media/HDR_2013_EN_complete.pdf

World Bank. 2013. "Africa's Pulse 2013". http://www.worldbank.org/content/dam/Worldbank/document/Africa/Report/Africas-Pulse-brochure_Vol7.pdf.

Chapter Two

Promoting Indigenous Values to Facilitate the Emergence of Suitable Forms of Democracy

Thomas Menamparampil

It is increasingly being recognised that democracy is the most suitable form of government for human growth and social betterment. However, the democratic structures being proposed are those that developed in the West over centuries. While recognising their merit on their own right, it is prudent to take note of certain limitations to absolutising them. *First*, the Western models of democracy differ greatly among themselves. *Second*, on the admission of Western political observers themselves, there are many flaws in the workings of various democratic systems as they function in the West itself today. *Third*, those countries in East Europe, Latin America and other parts of the world that hastily adopted the Western models of democracy are finding it difficult to get them working. Consequently, it would be expedient for each polity to undertake deep reflection, with a view to determining what democratic structures would best serve its needs.

Exploring their history, members of a society will notice how gradually their society emerged from isolation through the leadership of a creative minority which interpreted the society's identity and indigenous values, and how their society thereby attained its present stage of development. This intelligent minority helped the society especially in those periods of its history when it had to face severe challenges. As long as the creative minority remained an inspiring force guiding the people through persuasive ways, the society lived by some form of democratic values in keeping with its ancient traditions and continued to make progress.

Historically, this ideal situation did not always last. Force was deployed either by a ruling elite within a society or by a greater power without. The use of force leads to violence, both within and without a society. Traditional democratic values weaken and even vanish in a society subjected to violence over a considerable period of time. A return to democracy is possible only by reviving a society's ancient values that will eliminate the use of force as a determining element in human relationships.

No society can return to its distant past in its original form, but it can make its cherished values come back to life and exert an influence on its present way of functioning, for example on its economy and the quality of human relationships. Only a form of democracy based on the ancient value system of a particular society will have a future within it. Even when a society borrows elements from other traditions, it must make them fit in with its indigenous values. The thinking element in every society, whom I call Philosopher-Friends, plays a dynamic role in leading the society to success in this mighty endeavour.

Consequently, in this chapter, I argue that each society ought to study its own ancient traditions, identify values in those traditions that served human and social interests best, promote them, and use them to lay solid foundations for its political organisation. Towards this end, I set out with reflections on some of the challenges of democratisation, after which I argue that building synergy is the only path to greatness. I then examine the pivotal place of humane ideals in a genuine democracy. That is followed by reflections on the self-defeating nature of violence in the struggle for democratisation. Finally, I examine the role of intellectuals as the persuasive creative minority, before making some concluding remarks.

CHALLENGES OF DEMOCRATISATION

It is important to make the road to our togetherness smooth according to the best traditions in our various cultures. There is no shortcut to success—we need to think, plan, work hard, be fair to people, that is, be ready to pay the price for that which we wish to obtain: "If we ask what the right thing to do is, there are clear, fundamental answers. End poverty. Eliminate disease and squalor. Educate children. Teach women to read. In short clean up the mess" (Martin 2006, 25).

When newly independent countries seek to introduce modern structures of democracy, they are likely to meet with some difficulties, particularly if such institutions were not part of their older heritage. For example, when Australia gave independence to the Solomon Islands in the 1970s, the Westminster style of government was triumphantly introduced there. However, the entire system was so new to the cultural world of the local communities that it was difficult to get it to function meaningfully. The liberal democratic system which had developed in the Western world through the political efforts of generations—a way of self-government especially suited to the Anglo-Saxon worldview—was being thrust upon the Pacific islanders, whose life together was expressed in a totally different manner. It was not easy to rouse a sense of national feeling among groups that were ethnically very different among themselves, and whose collective existence was always expressed in cohesion within individual ethnic groups than in a togetherness of a vast variety of ethnic groups. Political parties made little sense to them, as their social relationships were largely confined to their own kinsfolk, clans and related ethnic groups. Their leaders used to be chosen for their ability to grant personal favours rather than for the quality of their ideology or the appeal of their political programs. The chaos that followed was understandable (see Dinnen and Firth 2011).

Newly independent countries that profess to be democratic keep struggling to stabilise. In any case, even in the West, forms of democracy differ greatly, say, the British from the French; similarly, American and Italian, Spanish and Greek. They differ not only in form, but also in the sturdiness of their democratic traditions. Besides, among professing democratic countries, the number of dysfunctional democracies is great. After the fall of the Berlin Wall, the countries of Eastern Europe struggled hard with democratisation, but success still eludes them. In Latin America, democracy gained considerable ground after the 1970s, but of late there is significant faltering there.

Furthermore, countries such as Russia, Venezuela and Iran, while professing democracy, reportedly manipulate elections, silence independent press, control opposition activities, and thus weaken the checks and balances typical of modern democracy. Some of the successor states to the Soviet Union in Asia have developed an uncertain position in this regard, neither authoritarian nor meaningfully democratic, thus remaining in a grey zone (Fukuyama 2011, 4).

Other countries are democratic, but their governments are not able to deliver the basic services expected of them. Thus, in Ukraine the ruler ousted in the Orange Revolution had to be re-called and re-elected when his democratic opponent was found to be incompetent; and in Venezuela, minority ethnic groups feel excluded from the life of the polity. Indeed, the failure of governance plagues many so-called democratic countries, perpetuating gross inequalities.

Thus, the inability of many countries to deal with their social and economic problems enfeebles their legitimacy as democracies (Fukuyama 2011, 5). Fukuyama alleges that Indian democracy is weakened by criminal politicians, fractious groups, extreme inequality, corruption and chaos. On the other hand, China gets its plans executed with amazing efficiency, but its government remains undemocratic.

When we look carefully, we notice that the ailments of professed democracies are many: authoritarianism (Russia), corruption (India), failed-states status (many countries that got their political independence from Western powers from the mid twentieth century), and entrenched interest groups (U.S.A.): no one is perfect (Fukuyama 2011, 10). It is, then, no use finding fault with only Afghanistan, Iraq, Syria, or other non-Western countries: all need to be understood, encouraged and helped.

If the path to democracy has been hard for those countries that have been long on it, it will mean the same for others. Nation-building is laborious and costly, and much effort has to be put into bringing sturdy institutions into existence. Many things must go ahead to prepare the way—expanded access to education, intelligent use of information technology, and the spread of ideas, especially on the benefits of democratic values and their relationship with a modern economy. Most important, the indigenous values and traditional attitudes of each community ought to be promoted in public life, so that a form of democracy suited to a particular country may emerge in it.

SYNERGY: THE ONLY PATH TO GREATNESS

As Martin (2006, 386) observed, "A principle of a great civilisation ought to be that it focuses intensely on how to develop the capability latent in everybody. The more that is done, the more we all benefit from one another." Democracy is about developing people. As societies emerge from their relative isolation and interact with other societies and civilisations, the synergy thus created makes amazing things happen. A society grows to greatness in proportion to the skill it develops in keeping the components of its culture—economic, political, ethical and aesthetic—in harmony with one another (Toynbee II 1969, 140).

One of Toynbee's central arguments is that great societies rise on hard terrain, not on easy ground: earnest and sincere effort is the only way to greatness. Thus, the Sumerian civilisation came up on the jungle-swamps of the Tigris-Euphrates (Toynbee I 1969, 95). Likewise, the civilisation of China rose on the marshy banks of the Yellow River (Hwang Ho) amidst jungles and high water (Toynbee I 1969, 97). Similarly, the Hellenic civilisation was born on the rocky and hard soil of Greece, such that, for example, the austere land of Attica favoured the emergence of a creative and enterprising people. When Attica's pasturelands dried up and plough-fields grew barren, the Athenians explored the subsoil, developed silver mines, introduced currency, and made pottery and ships (Toynbee I 1969, 113–14).

The measure of effort a society puts in for its very survival provides it with the stamina needed for further achievements. Toynbee argues that it was the exertion that the early Romans put into transforming their barren soil that gave them the energy to build up their vast empire extending from Egypt to present-day Britain (Toynbee I 1969, 108). Similarly, it was the hard soil of Tyre and Sidon that raised the Phoenicians to greatness, and it was from them that we received the alphabet. In the same way, it was on the rocky hills of Judea that the Hebrews gained their religious insights, which gave birth to two great religious traditions, Jewish and Christian, which continue to inspire the world to this day (Toynbee I 1969, 117–18). In like manner, Eastern Germany produced the resolute Prussians, who unified Germany and built up the German Empire; and the barren soil of Scotland brought up a well-educated people with a strong sense of economy and outstanding stamina (Toynbee I 1969, 120).

The more successful countries today would jeopardise their own survival if they decided to settle down to a comfortable way of life; for, as William James noted, "a permanently successful peace-economy cannot be a simple pleasure-economy. We must make new energies" (cited in Barzun 2001, 673). The most precious value for a rising society, therefore, is a culture of hard work according to its own individual tradition and determination to press its way forward with courage.

It is not the harshness of the environment alone that stirs a society to achievement: challenge can be of diverse nature, including pressure or competition from neighbouring societies. In the history of civilisations, it was societies under intense pressure that achieved greatness. Nevertheless, they achieved it only if they found a way to offer an adequate response to the challenge. Toynbee adduces numerous examples to illustrate this point. He shows how the South of Egypt was prominent when political pressure was from the South, and how Northern Egypt rose to prominence when the pressure was from the North (Toynbee I 1969, 139); how the Byzantine challenge provoked the Turks to expand Westward into the European mainland (Toynbee I 1969, 140); how the Orthodox tradition in Russia expanded eastward, reaching as far as the Pacific under pressure from those regions (Toynbee I 1969, 141).

The most interesting part of Toynbee's argument is that it was the Persian pressure that awakened the sleeping Greek states, and ultimately led to the rise of Alexander; that it was the Carthaginian aggressiveness that stirred the Roman energies to throw back the invading forces and sent them conquering Gaul, Spain and North Africa, with the energies so generated; that the Westward expansion of Islam was a belated response to the thrust of Greece and Rome into Asia, and that it was this long Islamic pressure on the West that provoked the European society to gather strength not only to drive the alien forces out of the Iberian peninsula, but also "carried the Spaniards and Portuguese overseas to all the continents of the world" (Toynbee I 1969, 193). The Spanish and Portuguese imperial experiences inspired France, the Netherlands and England to venture on an empire-building drive all around the world (Toynbee II 1969, 238).

Taking Toynbee's argument further, we may see in the rise of many states in Asia and Africa a belated response to the colonial pressure. Recent trends suggest that the economies of these countries are awakening in a big way. The future belongs to those who choose the right options, whether the change they choose "is moving in productive or destructive directions, and whether it is creating balanced growth across income classes, ethnic groups, and regions, or precarious imbalances" (Sharma 2012, 12). The wisdom of the ancients must help a society to make the correct choice in the face of a crucial challenge.

DEMOCRACY IS ABOUT PURSUING HUMANE IDEALS

Regrettably, in our time, "mass education, cheap consumer goods, the popular press and mass entertainment are combined with deeply felt rootlessness, confusion and anomie" (Mishra 2012, 302). Furthermore, today we judge a society's stature by its technological advance and GDP. Toynbee observes that it was precisely when the Athenian economy expanded, with plantation-farming for export, that the Athenians introduced slavery into the colonies of Agrigentum and Sicily. However, this was not a step forward for the Athenian civilisation (Toynbee I 1969, 232). We do not deny that technological skills and economic assets are of enormous importance; but of even more importance are the less visible assets such as relationships that hold a society together, the values that it lives by, the ideals it places before its members, and the spiritual dreams that it assiduously pursues.

In many ancient cultures, the wise person used to be held in high esteem; but today the one who wins admiration is the boaster, the amoral economic performer, and the partisan bully who can push his or her community's interests ahead. However, in our eagerness to promote our immediate interests, we cannot afford to forget the human person and his or her dignity, communities and their long-term good, as well as humanity and its civilisational heritages and value systems. There is an abundance of moral rhetoric in the statements of leading political and commercial personages of our day, but too little seriousness. Thus Hobsbawm (2013, 2) wrote: "None of the mission statements I have come across says anything worth saying, unless you are a fan of badly written platitudes" (Hobsbawm 2013, 2).

Five decades ago, Toynbee warned that schools of economy forget that even an economic world order cannot be built on economic foundations alone (Toynbee I 1969, 337). Universal values of fairness and healthy human relationships ought not to be sacrificed to the self-interest of a few who control affairs. While it is true that the market is productive and raises living standards, it tends to concentrate wealth in the hands of a few, pass on environmental costs to society, and abuse workers and consumers. Consequently, "Markets must be tamed and tempered" (Stiglitz 2012, p.xiii). Big corporations and bankers ought not to be allowed to have recourse to fraudulent and unethical ways (Stiglitz 2012, p.xxiii), or to take advantage of the weaker sections of society. The government ought to play a regulating role, when, for example, producers seek to make profit by making their products more addictive or are indifferent to the damage they inflict on the environment (Stiglitz 2012, p.xviii), or when consumer interests are ignored.

The ethical consciousness in society has to be kept alive, and the market too must be given a 'moral character.' Yet the movers of the economy today seem to have lost their 'moral compass' (Stiglitz 2012, p.xvii). The consequence is the constant restlessness we notice in society. Anger is intensifying. When genuine grievance gets mixed up with anger engineered by people with political interests, matters become more complicated. There is an ascendancy of criminality in politics (Das 2012, 200–3). In many places we are in such situations; and our options are becoming limited.

In any case, if a political structure only reinforces the unfair system rather than correct it, difficult days lie ahead. The anxiety is that the rewards of the new economy are not always going to the most deserving: "Much of this vast rise in private wealth has gone to a small segment of the ultra-rich . . ." (Hobsbawm 2013, 50). The 1 percent that profits most are not great thinkers or innovators (Stiglitz 2012, 27); instead, they are self-rewarding executives. They are people who know how to manage the government machinery for their own interests: they know how to skirt the law, shape it in their favour, and take advantage of the poor (Stiglitz 2012, 37); they know how to win monopolies, and get control over natural resources (Stiglitz 2012, 49), sell to the government above market prices (Stiglitz 2012, 40), get taxes and wages lowered (Stiglitz 2012, 63), silence unions (Stiglitz 2012, 64), fire workers (Stiglitz 2012, 67), marginalise minority groups (Stiglitz 2012, 68), and push austerity programs to the areas of medical care and education to the disadvantage of the poor (Stiglitz 2012, 230–31). For them even unemployment serves a useful purpose, since it creates a climate that favours the lowering of wages (Stiglitz 2012, 263). What is more, corporations are competing against countries—not simply against other corporations (Charan 2013, 7).

Yet the tragedy is that the economically privileged minorities in economically disadvantaged countries aspire for nothing higher than the conveniences and gadgets of their Western consumer counterparts (Mishra 2012, 308). What is more, some cities in such countries are growing as monsters, serving a vigorous economy but not the interests of communities nor the sustainability of the natural environment. Many societies are fast becoming more and more impersonal with scope for human growth narrowing every day.

It is sobering to realise that growing inequality in the economy can spell doom for the economy itself, because it impairs efficiency by weakening the motivation of the workers and undermines growth by distorting market mechanisms or introducing asymmetries and unfairness in competition (Stiglitz 2012, 6). In other words, the market becomes inefficient if it ignores the human dimension (Stiglitz 2012, xi–xii). If you create wealth, society is enriched; but if you take it from others through malpractices such as inflated prices and adulterated goods, society is impoverished (Stiglitz 2012, 32). Unequal societies create continuous political instability. On the other hand, in more egalitarian societies people work hard and seek to preserve social cohesion (Stiglitz 2012, 77). It is in such societies that high levels of social responsibility are achieved and rules for environment protection respected (Stiglitz 2012, 100). There, people see the need to invest in infrastructure, education, health and research (Stiglitz 2012, 93).

Consequently, human values must be given their proper place in the economy for the success of the economy. This implies that Freedom for enterprise and venture must be combined with responsibility for the common good (Toynbee I 1969, 339).

Toynbee lamented that the mass education of his day did not include the uplifting of interests and motivation (Toynbee I 1969, 339); instead, it led to the 'vulgarisation' of tastes in society. He went on to observe that ardent consumers in his day hardly realised how much they were being 'used' by profit-makers, being treated to the trivialising entertainment provided by commercial entrepreneurs and being taken advantage of by the propaganda of interested parties such as political ideologues and media barons (Toynbee I 1969, 340). With the emergence of the so-called new media, this lament should now be augmented several times over.

In times of trouble, we need to carefully observe the stirrings among the exploited masses because their insights are always dynamic. It is they who make a decisive choice between a violent approach and a peaceful one. On one hand, ongoing exploitation can result in a pervasive sense of helplessness, stir up collective anger, culminating in a revolution: that is what happened in troubled times in places such as France, Russia, and China. On the other hand, such troubles can lead to the stirrings of the inner person in search of deeper meaning and fulfilment, as well as in a quest for intelligent social change.

It is at the breakup of an old order that a new one comes into existence. Toynbee sees Abraham emerging during the disintegration of the Sumerian civilisation, and Moses during the decadence of the 'New Empire' in Egypt (Toynbee I 1969, 442), each time from among the most oppressed people. Judaism takes birth among the Jews who were most hard-pressed and helpless during their Babylonian exile, wailing "by the rivers of Babylon" (Psalm 137:1). We are probably beginning to experience similar pains.

Before the disruption occasioned by the novel coronavirus around the world from early 2020, certain new trends were emerging, described by Charan (2013, 5) as follows: "Wealth is moving from North to South, and so are jobs. Companies in the south, big and small, have a fierce entrepreneurial drive. Many are revelling in double-digit revenue growth, bringing jobs and prosperity to their home countries." Francis Fukuyama believes that later modernisers are actually advantaged relative to more established industrial powers, just as earlier liberal trade theories had predicted (Fukuyama 1992, 101). However, poverty is still widespread in many parts of the world, now aggravated by the COVID-19 pandemic which threatens to wipe out the impressive gains of the past few decades.

THE SELF-DEFEATING NATURE OF VIOLENCE

It is tempting to resort to force in a bid to agitate for democratisation in Africa. In *The Prince*, Niccolò Machiavelli proposed force as the sole means of shaping human destinies (Machiavelli 1998). However, history shows that force is counterproductive—it is always confronted by force in response. Referring to European history, Fernando Braudel (1993, 416) observed: "The basic rule was always the same. When a State seemed to be too powerful ... its neighbours would jointly tilt the scales in the opposite direction so as to make it more moderate and better behaved."

During the dynamic period of a society, the ideals and values of the creative minority within it win enthusiastic acceptance. As long as the various elements of a culture or civilisation are in harmony, it continues to grow (Toynbee I 1969, 327). However, at a later period of history, some form of imbalance creeps into that society, inequality grows among its members, and the leadership and the upper classes become exploitative in the political and economic fields. Unfairness deepens. The creative minority atrophies into a closed clique of vested interests: it degenerates into a dominant and exploitative minority which seeks to maintain itself in power by the use of force.

The consequences of Assyrian militarism ultimately caught up with the Assyrian Empire, even though the Assyrians dominated southwest Asia for two and a half centuries. Their mighty power disappeared altogether, and even the name 'Assyrian' was forgotten where it had held absolute sway. Xenophon was not even aware of such a name (Toynbee I 1969, 390).

In like manner, the impressive democratic institutions of ancient Greece ceased to function because its energies were lost in internal struggles, and ultimately it had to submit to Macedonian imperialism. Thus, Hellenism withered from within as the free cities were torn asunder by mutual hatred and by class wars: "They found no place for the greatest minds of the age" who had to take shelter with tyrants (Dawson 2002, 62). Those who emerge victorious in an awe-inspiring war are tempted to rejoice at their success. However, victory imposes its own type of punishment on the winners: "Victory, like revolution, can devour its own children, particularly those who expect more from it than what it actually delivers. The idealists who realise too late that violence never achieve their goals are among history's most common losers in victory" (Schivelbusch 2004, 98). Macedonians who went conquering countries right up to India turned against each other in a suicidal conflict soon after their victories (Toynbee I 1969, 395).

Similarly, the democratic traditions of the Roman senate gave way to the Augustan empire. The polarisation between classes, communities, and interests in the ancient Roman society led to such tensions and instances of violence, so that its weakened democratic society had no choice but to surrender to an absolute ruler. Thus, the Roman Empire was born over the dead bones of Roman democratic traditions (Toynbee I 1969, 344). The Republic was overwhelmed, and the ambition for money and power devastated the 'republican virtues' that were the greatest pride of Roman citizenship (Friedman 2012, 31). What Friedman calls "republican virtues" I call "indigenous democratic values." Something similar happened yet again in France after the cries of "Equality, Fraternity, and liberty" had grown fainter, and Napoleon emerged from the ranks to take up absolute power: the noble values of the revolution were clean forgotten.

Things were no different for the imperialist European states that, after reducing the rest of the world to colonies, turned against each other during the two so-called world wars. It was a suicide attempt on the part of Europe. Furthermore, today, many neighbouring states in the former Western colonies in Africa, Asia, Central America and South America are busy at the same game, learning little if anything from the experiences of Europe in the first half of the twentieth century.

Thus, once a society gets divided into a dominant minority and an exploited majority, force begins to play a greater role in its functioning. As a result, the ideals and goals that were greatly esteemed and enthusiastically pursued come to be imposed. The leaders cease to be admired or respected, and ordinary people sink to the level of the oppressed. Finally, a stage comes when such a society is forced to yield either to internal revolution or to external aggression. The greater the suppressing energies of the exploiting minority, the more violent the revolution (Toynbee I 1969, 326–27). Ultimately the old system collapses, and a new creative minority takes over and drives things in a new direction. In France, Russia, China, and Vietnam there were bloody revolutions. This is the destiny of any society which reaches a peak of achievement but creates several forms of imbalances within itself or in its neighbourhood.

Furthermore, as the art of war develops, the greatest loss of all is the weakening of culture, especially on the winning side. The democratic values present in the ancient indigenous cultures of warring societies are greatly weakened or even lost altogether. In 1871, Nietzsche said that great victories pose great dangers, and that the triumph of the German empire would lead to the demise of German culture (cited in Schivelbusch 2004, 4).

Barzun (2001, 700) correctly noted that during wartime, the hostile feelings that anyone may have against his or her fellows, employers or state authorities find release in being turned against an anonymous foe. It is also sobering to bear in mind that the winners of a war are tempted to think that once the enemy (another class, caste, ethnic group, economic, or political interest group, or country) is humbled, their own future is safe. They forget that they have just wounded a tiger, and that they do not know when it will bounce back. The humiliation of Athens by the Persians in 480–479 B.C.E. made Athens build up a fleet that led it to the victory of Salamis and to the glory of the Periclean times. Xerxes, the successor of Darius, took aggression to European Greece, provoking a Hellenic counterattack under Alexander (Toynbee I 1969, 610).

In the context of an arms race between neighbouring states in economically disadvantaged regions, the foregoing reflections gain even greater importance. In the immediate context, technology related to war may seem to make progress, but it is humanity that takes the blow when one community inflicts cruelties on another. No one wins a war today except arms-producing corporations—they alone have the last laugh. Thus, the concepts of "equality, fraternity, and liberty," that are found in every cultural tradition, ought to be brought back to lie and cease to be mere slogans.

THE ROLE OF INTELLECTUALS AS THE PERSUASIVE CREATIVE MINORITY

Fernandez-Armesto (2001, 560) noted that "Increasing inter-connectedness seems to lead to increasing interdependence, which in turn demand [*sic*] new, ever wider, ultimately worldwide 'frameworks' for action, transcending old nations, blocs and civilisations." This is the challenge before creative thinkers in our times—becoming not anti-other, but pro-everyone. Only then will a sure future become possible.

Progress comes when a group of people in a society causes some kind of shaking in it. Toynbee called such people creative personalities: they re-shape others after their own thinking (Toynbee I 1969, 251). Allow me to refer to such intellectuals who stir their societies to beneficial activity—a minority of enlightened individuals committed to common good—as "Philosopher-Friends." New and creative ideas often come into the minds of several persons at the same time quite independently: that is the law of nature. Ordinary people have remained much the same all through history. They depend on a "creative minority" who think, reflect, and transform themselves and dare to introduce unforeseen changes into their society (Toynbee I 1969, 253–54). This is the task we assign to intellectuals who understand the old values and traditions and make them relevant to present-day problems. New ideas rooted in the old, not imposed but introduced by creative individuals through their inspiring style and persuasive ways, are true pointers to the future (Toynbee I 1969, 255).

There may be differences of perceptions among countries about free enterprise or regulated economy, but there will not be much difference in convictions about the need for a global ethic that promotes an equitable world order, that is, a spiritual vision of the human and cosmic realities. We want to remain human, and to build our lives on genuine human values. We draw closer to attaining this goal when there is a true encounter of cultures: "The great civilisations of the past have often been focused on their own cultures. In the future, they will increasingly study the greatness of other civilisations" (Martin 2006, 388).

Keeping true to Toynbee's vocabulary, the "internal proletariat" of the globalised world today are seeking a new Inspiration, a Fresh Enlightenment, a relevant spiritual insight, a Peaceful Revolution. It is always a creative minority that formulates it in their behalf and makes it intelligible. That ought to be the mission of intellectuals today.

CONCLUSION

In every society, the creative and persuasive minority, that is, the intellectuals, must show the way. They must return to the masses and help them to understand themselves, enabling them to visualise a new future. This mighty task cannot be done by the intellectuals of one society in isolation because human destinies are interlinked. We are not at the parting of ways, but at the converging point of civilisational urges. Many societies joining hands can open up some hitherto unknown avenue for an unprecedented spiritual advance in order to prevent fratricidal wars among aggressively nationalistic states (Toynbee II 1969, 322), or among classes, castes, ideologies or ethnic groups. This can only be achieved through societies that cherish democratic values within their own territories and in the world at large; and those values have a future only if they are rooted in the indigenous cultural traditions of diverse societies.

REFERENCES

Barzun, Jacques. 2001. *From Dawn to Decadence: 1500 to the Present—500 Years of Western Cultural Life*. New York: Harper Perennial.
Braudel, Fernando. 1993. *A History of Civilisations*. London: Penguin Books.
Charan, Ram. 2013. *Global Tilt*. London: Random House Books.
Das, Gurucharan. 2012. *India Grows at Night*. London: Penguin.
Dawson, Christopher. 2002. *Dynamics of World History*. Wilmington, Delaware: ISI Books.
Dinnen, Sinclair and Stewart Firth. 2011. *Politics and State Building in Solomon Islands*. Canberra: ANU E Press.
Fernandez-Armesto, Felipe. 2001. *Civilisations*. London: Pan Books.
Friedman, George. 2012. *The Next Decade*. New York: Random House.
Fukuyama, Francis. 1992. *The End of History and the Last Man*. London: Penguin Books.
Hobsbawm, Eric. 2013. *Fractured Times: Culture and Society in the 20th Century*. Delhi: Little Brown.
Machiavelli, Niccolò. 1998. *The Prince*. Bondanella, Peter ed.; Bondanella, Peter and Mark Musa trans.s. Oxford: Oxford University Press.
Martin, James. 2006. *The Meaning of the 21st Century*. London: Eden Project Books.
Mishra, Pankaj. 2012. *From the Ruins of the Empire*. London: Penguin.
Schivelbusch, Wolfgang. 2004. *The Culture of Defeat*. London: Granta books.
Sharma, Ruchir. 2012. *Breakout Nations*. London: Penguin.
Stiglitz, Joseph. 2012. *The Price of Inequality*. London: Penguin.
Toynbee, Arnold. 1969. *A Study of History*. D. C. Somervell's Abridgement, Vol I and II. New York: Dell Publishing Co.

Chapter Three

Colonialism and the Challenge of Western-Style Democracy in Africa

Dennis Masaka

The West considers liberal democracy as a requirement for African governments if they are to promote virtues such as individual freedoms, multi-party politics and good governance (Sklar 1983, 12; Jotia 2012, 622). Nevertheless, in this chapter, I advance the view that Western-style liberal democracy has not been well received in some "post-colonial"[1] African countries partly because of the West's hegemonic relations with such countries from colonial times to the present. Indeed, colonial rule in Africa negated the very fundamentals of liberal democracy. As Fatton (1990, 457) observed, "it was only in the last decade of colonialism, when independence[2] became a certainty, that the imperialist powers gradually began to institute democratic reforms in what had hitherto been structures of exploitation, despotism, and degradation." However, this transition to democratic rule was nominal because the economic, cultural and bureaucratic domains remained fundamentally untransformed (Fatton 1990, 457). Thus, it is not surprising that some African countries are suspicious of the West's call to adopt liberal democracy. If anything, some of them seem to favour continuing with the authoritarian system of governance that they inherited from the Western imperialists.

I set out, in the next section, by contending that by promoting a highly authoritarian system of governance, colonialism had a negative impact on democratic politics in contemporary Africa. I further argue that the struggles for liberation across Africa were testimony to the undemocratic rule that the colonial authorities imposed on the continent. That is followed by a section in which I argue that the call by the "former"[3] Western colonisers to African countries to adopt Western liberal democratic principles of governance is at odds with their own authoritarian rule during the colonial era that left them with a compromised moral standing on matters concerning democracy. In the penultimate section, I suggest that African countries have a right to chart their own destinies. Here, I have in mind the creation of democracies that are grounded on indigenous African systems of governance, with special emphasis on consensus-based decision-making, albeit supplemented by worthwhile aspects of non-indigenous forms of democracy that are freely chosen rather than imposed. In my view, this is necessary so that the system of governance which African countries adopt effectively speaks to their existential situations.

COLONIAL RULE IN AFRICA

The partitioning of Africa during the "Scramble for Africa" by Western powers during the Berlin Conference in 1884–1885 was principally capitalist driven (Uzoigwe 1985, 19). As the phrase "Scramble for Africa" implies, it was actually a stampede by some Western powers to appropriate as much land as possible with their own economic benefit in mind. In other words, the partition was primarily motivated by economic reasons rather than by other considerations such as the alleged "civilising mission" for the sake of the colonised. Although the colonial authorities imposed some elements of their civilisation such as education and religion on the indigenous peoples of Africa, they manipulated these elements to create conditions that were conducive to exploiting the indigenous peoples' economic resources without much resistance from them.

While I do not pretend to portray the colonial experiences of African countries as the same, I think that there are certain fundamental elements of colonial rule that were common throughout the continent. As Keller (2007, 46) observes, "The modality of colonial rule varied from one colonial power to the next, but the end result was always domination, exploitation, and organised repression." This makes it possible to talk of the nature of colonial rule in Africa. Colonial governments in Africa were created to serve the interests of Western owners of capital. As such, repressive measures were established to prevent dissent from the colonised masses (Moyo 1992, 307). The voices of the colonised people were muzzled in the face of the denigration of their humanity (Flikschuh 2014, 4) and the plunder of their resources for the exclusive benefit of the owners of capital. Commenting on the immorality of colonialism, Nyamnjoh (2012, 132) states that "it repressed where it should have fostered, tamed instead of inspired and enervated rather than strengthened." Even the creative abilities that allowed indigenous peoples to exploit their resources for their own benefit were systematically doubted. They were largely excluded from having a say in the governance of their own countries (Taiwo 1993, 896).

At this point, it is necessary to outline some attributes of colonial rule in Africa, with a view to establishing whether or not such rule can be classified as democratic.

One key aspect of colonial rule in Africa was its exclusive control of the colonised territories (Taiwo 1993, 897). Through the use of military might, the indigenous peoples of Africa were effectively subdued. Indigenous leaders were forcibly removed from their positions as the colonial authorities asserted their hegemony. Key structures of governance became the exclusive preserve of the colonisers. Besides the use of military might, the colonial authorities employed quasi-peaceful means to gain some level of acceptance of their rule among the indigenous peoples. For example, the indigenous structures of power such as those of chiefs were systematically manipulated to support the status quo. In some cases, in order to ensure support for the colonial project, existing chiefs were replaced with individuals who were not in the hereditary lines of chieftainship, and who would therefore return the favour by facilitating the foreign domination of their communities. The overall objective was to exclude the indigenous peoples from the control of their own countries; and any attempts at resisting this manipulation were met with further repression.

Besides, to enable the exploitation of the resources of the colonised territories, the colonial authorities had to ensure that the indigenous peoples were rendered wholly dependent on them for their sustenance. This was partly attained by dispossessing them of their sources of wealth, such as their fertile lands and livestock. Land is an important resource for human beings: it defines their sense of belonging, entitlement and wealth. Colonial authorities expropriated the indigenous peoples' rich ancestral lands and resettled them in uninhabitable lands (Austin 1975, 28). This made it impossible for them to fend for themselves. As a result, they had no choice but to become unwilling labourers who aided the predominantly extractive development paradigms of colonial authorities (Rodney 1985, 337).

In addition, colonial authorities ensured that indigenous peoples received the barest education to keep them perpetually subservient (Rodney 1985, 339–40). As Austin (1975, 35) argued in reference to the situation in the then Rhodesia, "the corollary of deliberately fostered African inferiority is the perpetuation of white superiority. There is a vicious circle [*sic*] in which white oppression of the African produces a depressed condition among Africans, which in turn is used to justify the majority's continued oppression." The segregation policies ensured that the supposed racial superiority of the colonisers over the indigenous peoples was created and maintained. In this light, the services and privileges enjoyed by the colonial settlers were meant to foster their assumed superiority while the indigenous peoples suffered oppression and sub-standard services. In the light of the organised repression, domination and exploitation that characterised colonial rule in Africa (Keller 2007, 46; Nyamnjoh 2012, 132), it was manifestly authoritarian rather than democratic.

Furthermore, although the indigenous peoples had their own civilisations that reflected their own existential situations (Gelfand 1981, 62), the paternalistic approach which the colonial authorities employed to control them meant that the alien authorities reduced them to inferior beings that required such foreign authorities to "uplift" them to a "civilised" existence (Taiwo 1993, 896; Bassil 2005, 32). Thus based on the assumed inferiority of the indigenous peoples (Bassil 2005, 28), the colonial authorities excluded them from participating in the governance of their own countries (Fatton 1990, 458). In some cases, a few indigenous people were co-opted into the structures of government. Nevertheless, they did not have the power to influence the colonial governments' decisions.

Moreover, to ensure that the interests of the colonial settlers were best served, the colonisers prevented the indigenous peoples from competing with the European settlers in the economy generally, and in the ownership of land in particular (Rodney 1985, 345). Some of the measures that the colonisers put in place to control the indigenous peoples included restrictions on movement within the colonies, punitive taxes and poor working conditions (Stoneman 1981, 130).

Consequently, the indigenous peoples showed an aversion to the colonial system from its inception. They were dissatisfied with the fact that colonial authorities denied them their basic rights, grossly restricted their freedom to control their natural resources, and, most crucially, repudiated their humanity (Taiwo 1993, 898). Even though there were attempts by the alien authorities to portray their rule in a positive light, resistance to it was evident across the continent (Boahen 1985, 3; Ranger 1985, 47; Mukandala 2001, 5). Oppression, by any stretch of the imagination, is not in accord with the so-called democratic principles.

However, even at present, some regard colonialism as a positive development in Africa, especially in respect to the promotion of democratic rule. For instance, Bernhard, Reenock and Nordstrom (2004, 227) claim that "the end of European overseas colonialism brought hopes that areas that had been subject to it would be able to assimilate the positive aspects of modernity, like democracy and development. This hope did not bear out."

The struggles for liberation across Africa gave rise to "independence". I use the term "independence" in reference to African countries with reservations in this chapter because genuine independence is yet to be attained (Oduor 2012, 238). Indeed, African countries have external signs of "independence," but in reality, the colonisers still have significant influence on their internal affairs. Thus, for the indigenous peoples of Africa, authentic liberation has remained illusory (Mungwini 2016, 523). Nevertheless, this "independence" at least points to the Africans' quest for sovereignty. Since this "independence" is an outcome of struggles against oppressive colonial governments, the expectations were that "independent" African states would avoid the authoritarian style of governance of colonial regimes.

POST-INDEPENDENCE AND THE CALL FOR LIBERAL DEMOCRACY

The struggles for liberation led to the forced departure of colonial authorities from positions of direct control of African countries. However, it is curious that after the end of overt colonial rule, there has been a call by the "former" colonisers, especially to their "former" colonies, to embrace Western-style liberal democracy. They make this call in the light of the observation that many "post-colonial" African governments have exhibited authoritarian tendencies. However, it is problematic for the West to pretend that the emergence of authoritarian rule in Africa is a "post-colonial" problem. In fact, it is now widely believed that the "independence" that Africans attained simply meant the replacement of colonial state operatives with indigenous ones without any fundamental change in the old repressive system of governance. As Mazrui (2002 [1975], 71) noted, "In most African countries, independence meant the transfer of power from the West to the westernised. The new politicians were those with a good command of the imperial language and a substantial imitation of the Western life-style." To be sure, some changes have been implemented in order to affirm the dignity of the indigenous peoples by extending to them services that were principally the preserve of the colonisers. Nevertheless, the fundamental character of colonial rule, whose distinctive feature is lack of accountability to the governed, has been largely retained in many African countries.

In the light of the foregoing observations, it becomes difficult for the West's message of democracy to be heard and accepted by some African governments. Here, I have in mind those "post-colonial" African governments that are still headed by leaders of former liberation war movements who have firsthand experience of the injustices of colonial rule. Such leaders may feel that the West does not have a moral high ground from which to prescribe a system of governance to "independent" African states (Healey and Robinson 1994, 11). Thus, the call for the implementation of liberal democracy in place of the present authoritarian rule in some African countries has been resisted by some African regimes (Fatton 1990, 457).

Although African governments may have their own reasons for retaining systems of governance that are not in accord with the aspirations of the citizens, I am of the view that prescribing alien systems of governance to African countries is not viable either, being likely to be regarded as continued interference in the internal affairs of "independent" and "sovereign" African states. Indeed, African countries have a right to appeal to their own indigenous systems of democracy that resonate with their varying existential situations. If they are to borrow certain traits of democracy from other geopolitical centres, they ought to do so without coercion. This is necessary if the "independence" which African countries have attained is to become genuine. As Wamba-dia-Wamba (1992, 32) argued, African countries must move away from basing their internal affairs on paradigms that are constructed elsewhere if they are to attain the emancipation that they yearn for. Self-determination in respect to nurturing their own governance systems that might not necessarily be in accord with the ones that the West prescribes to them might be a panacea to the failed experiments with imposed alien paradigms of democracy (Sklar 1983, 18). I pursue this position below.

IN DEFENCE OF AN INDIGENOUS AFRICAN CONSENSUAL MODEL OF DEMOCRACY

The call for indigenous forms of democracy in African countries is premised on the fact that even after the attainment of "independence," the "former" colonial authorities are still keen on influencing events in Africa. More specifically, each "former" Western colonial power still retains a significant hegemonic relationship with its "former" colony or colonies in Africa. In other words, the "former" colonial authorities are still influencing the governance of their "former" colonies (Tar 2010, 83). Whenever there is a problem in the "former" colonies, the respective colonial masters are quick to offer prescriptions or threats of punishment to them.

The continued hegemonic relations between the West and African governments point to the fact that colonialism has not completely ended. In particular, all indications are that the West still thinks that its paradigm of democracy is ideal for African countries despite the fact that it is unsuitable to their existential situations. Ghanaian thinker, Kwame Nkrumah (1965, p. x) argued that colonialism has survived decolonisation, and now exists in a new form, which is neo-colonialism. For Nkrumah, what makes the two appear to be different is that colonialism is overt, while neo-colonialism is covert. Yet both colonialism and neo-colonialism are instruments of domination. Nkrumah (1965, p. xi) considers neo-colonialism as the worst form of imperialism, and "for those who practice it, it means power without responsibility and for those who suffer from it, it means exploitation without redress." It is, as it were, dominance by remote control. As Nkrumah (1965, p.x) noted, "A state in the grip of neo-colonialism is not master of its own destiny." In line with Nkrumah's view, Diaspora philosopher Walter D. Mignolo (2005, 112) asserts that "independence changed the *actors* but not the *script*."

Consequently, African countries ought to seek liberation from foreign domination by developing paradigms of democratic governance based on indigenous African modes of democracy that flourished in pre-colonial times, that resonate with the present existential circumstances of these countries, and that have survived attempts at destroying them by foreign powers. As Ramose (1992, 64) correctly observed, the peoples of Africa must construct their own epistemological paradigms as a way of expressing their authenticity and true liberation. In matters of governance, this translates to the imperative for African countries to ground their politics on indigenous forms of democracy. This liberation is necessary if the peoples of Africa are to defeat what Ramose (1992, 67) referred to as "the condition of sameness" that the West imposed on them.

In defining "the condition of sameness," Ramose (1992, 66) stated that the hegemonic peoples of the West have a certain understanding of what it means to be a human being, and what it means to exist in relationship with others which they have imposed on diverse cultures. In other words, the West assumes that its understanding of inter-human relations has a trans-cultural applicability. Nevertheless, this understanding has proved to be fundamentally different from the indigenous African conceptions of "the human being and the universe" (Ramose 1992, 66). Since the Western paradigm of democracy is an imposition on Africa and has resisted dialogue with indigenous forms of democracy, it cannot deliver the authentic liberation that the peoples of Africa seek.

Nevertheless, I do not seek to romanticise what was part of pre-colonial African democracies. Indeed, those indigenous systems of democracy probably had some elements that may no longer speak to the present circumstances of African countries. Yet the same is true of paradigms of democracy from other geo-political centres. Nevertheless, it is expedient for African countries to be guided by systems of democracy that are indigenous to them. The point here is that besides Western liberal democracy, other worthwhile paradigms of democracy exist. This concurs with the position held by Oduor (2017) that "liberal democracy is *not* synonymous with democracy." In other words, democracy is not reducible to liberal democracy.

Besides, the utilisation of indigenous African modes of democracy would serve as a corrective to the problems that African countries have faced as a result of the adoption of Western-style liberal democracy. Wamba-dia-Wamba (1992), Ramose (1992), Wiredu (1996), and Gyekye (2013) defend the necessity of using indigenous paradigms of democracy as the basis for constructing a system of governance for African countries. This is partly out of the realisation that Western-style liberal democracy is not suited to the circumstances of Africa's indigenous peoples, as it has not facilitated the solving of the problems of the "post-colonial" state in Africa. For example, multi-party politics is central to Western liberal democracy. However, it cannot assure the civil liberties that it purports to uphold because it is preoccupied with capturing state power rather than with fundamentally changing the operations of the state to make it accountable to the people (Wamba-dia-Wamba 1992, 31).

Furthermore, in a multi-party system, competition for power is emphasised at the expense of enabling the participation of ordinary people in governance. As Wamba-dia-Wamba (1992, 31) noted, "The multi-party parliamentary mode of politics is characterised by its State-centeredness, oppressiveness and tendency to freeze creativity and imagination." Those in the opposition claim to have workable solutions to the problems facing their respective countries. However, they are required to take over the reins of power first before they can put their ideas into practice. They may also not be willing to avail those solutions to the sitting governments because they cannot "arm the enemy". Thus, their claims to have solutions to their countries' problems is often a mere pretext to ascend to power.

Consequently, multi-party politics turns out to be a means of manipulating people's emotions in order to attain the selfish goals of the members of the contesting political parties. Political parties become new oppressors of the voters by promising certain benefits on condition that they are voted into power. As Ramose (1992, 75) observed, "the oddity of adversarial politics is emphasised even more by the fact that quite often this kind of politics degenerates into opposition for the sake of opposition." In fact, in some cases, it has actually given rise to deceptive appearances of a multi-party system, as the ruling parties devise strategies to defeat the multi-party system (Wiredu 1996, 188; 1997, 309). For example, they may form some fake opposition parties to give the outside world the impression of a multi-party system at work.

In reference to the Western-style liberal democracy currently in use in Africa, Wiredu asserts:

> Current forms of democracy are generally systems based on the majority principle. The party that wins the majority of seats or the greatest proportion of the votes, if the system in force is one of proportional representation, is invested with governmental power. Parties under this scheme of politics are organisations of people of similar tendencies and aspirations with the sole aim of gaining power for the implementation of their policies. (Wiredu 1996, 186–87)

One important objection that Wiredu (1996, 187–89) raises against the multi-party system is that it tends to exclude the losers from decision-making. In my view, the bitterness of losing and the reality of being excluded from decision-making make it difficult for contestants to accept defeat. As a result, warlike campaigns for elections under the multi-party system in Africa are common. Contestants often resort to the use of any means, fair and foul, to win elections in order to ascend to or retain power. This is often a source of tensions and even violent conflicts, leading to political instability.

Consequently, Wiredu (1996, 189; 1997, 310) thinks that a no-party consensual democracy, where governments are formed through negotiation among citizens, can be a corrective to the problems that the multi-party system has caused in African countries. I concur with Wiredu and others in proposing democracy by consensus which has been part of the traditions of Africa's indigenous peoples from pre-colonial times, and which can adequately respond to Africa's current governance challenges if aligned to her present circumstances. This is despite Eze's reservations with such an approach, especially in respect to whether or not consensus can be realistically attained (Eze 1997b, 320–21). By consensual democracy, Wiredu (1996, 182) means a system whereby decisions on law and policy are negotiated and agreed upon by the people's representatives, who are themselves chosen by way of negotiation rather than through a majoritarian system. The call for consensus arises from the recognition that people hold diverse opinions (Wamba-dia-Wamba 1992, 34; Ramose 1992, 76; Wiredu 1996, 183).

Consensus decision-making regarding choosing representatives who would then form government, as well as the manner in which government conducts its business, would be effective because it would take the input of the governed seriously. Nevertheless, it might not be possible for everyone to be in agreement regarding an issue being negotiated. As Wiredu (1996, 183) observed, "consensus usually presupposes an original position of diversity. Because issues do not always polarise opinion on lines of strict contradictoriness, dialogue can function, by means, for example, of the smoothing of edges, to produce compromises that are agreeable to all or, at least, not obnoxious to any."

What can be discerned from Wiredu's view above is that in a consensual system, there is extensive discussion among the people concerned before an agreed course of action is arrived at. In such a system, debate is independent and robust, and the input of every member is considered (Wamba-dia-Wamba 1992, 34; Gyekye 2013, 244). There is evidence of democracy in the way in which the representatives of the people are chosen and decisions of government arrived at. It is therefore untrue that the absence of a multi-party system in the political cultures of indigenous Africans makes them defective

(Ramose 1992, 76). In fact, the imposed multi-party democracy undermines the virtues of consensual democracy such as equality and solidarity. It is for this reason that I consider consensual democracy to be better suited for African countries than the imposed Western-style multi-party democracy.

Is it possible to totally ignore alien paradigms of democracy as African countries seek to return to their indigenous forms of democracy? Ramose (1992, 65) correctly observed that as African countries search for an emancipatory epistemological paradigm, it is impossible for them to ignore the political culture of the West because it has become part of Africa's governance culture. I think that African countries may incorporate some elements from other geo-political centres into their paradigm of democracy if they consider them to be enriching to their own circumstances, as long as they do so freely and not because of pressure from the West as is presently the case with liberal democracy. Nevertheless, indigenous African political culture ought to remain the foundation for constructing a paradigm of democracy for African countries.

CONCLUSION

In the foregoing discussion, I have contended that the rejection of Western-style liberal democracy by many Africans is partly out of the realisation that it does not speak to their existential situations, and is therefore unlikely to lead to the authentic emancipation that they seek. Nevertheless, I have also advanced the view that the rejection of Western-style liberal democracy in Africa is not a denial of the imperative for democratic rule. Indeed, it is erroneous to assume that there is only one paradigm of democracy, that is, Western-style liberal democracy, which ought to be embraced by all cultures. Yet this is not to say that African countries have nothing to learn about democracy from other geo-political centres. Nevertheless, they ought to adopt elements from alien models of democracy out of choice rather than from coercion, and as long as they ensure that indigenous African political culture is the foundation of their systems of governance.

NOTES

1. In reference to African countries, I prefer to enclose the term "post-colonial" in quotation marks because I subscribe to the thinking that, at present, African countries have not realistically gone past the colonial era (Eze 1997a, 14). There is a sense in which the colonial order has not been totally defeated and replaced with what I would

regard as authentic independence. In this light, I use the term "post-colonial" in the present chapter with caution.

2. The "independence" that African countries have attained may be described as cosmetic, because it has not delivered genuine liberation of the indigenous peoples of Africa from Western domination. Consequently, I use the term "independence" in reference to African countries with caution.

3. I use the term "former" in reference to the Western colonizers of Africa with caution because it is highly doubtful that they have ceased to influence events in Africa.

REFERENCES

Austin, Reginald. 1975. *Racism and Apartheid in Southern Africa: Rhodesia*. Paris: The UNESCO Press.

Bassil, N. Noah. 2005. "The Legacy of Colonial Racism in Africa". *Australian Quarterly*, Vol. 77 No. 4, pp. 27–32.

Bernhard, Michael, Christopher Reenock and Timothy Nordstrom. 2004. "The Legacy of Western Overseas Colonialism on Democratic Survival". *International Studies Quarterly*, Vol. 48, pp. 225–50.

Boahen, A. Adu. 1985. "Africa and the colonial challenge". Boahen, A. Adu ed. *General History of Africa, VII: Africa under Colonial Domination 1880–1935*. Paris: United Nations Educational, Scientific and Cultural Organisation, pp. 1–18.

Eze, Emmanuel Chukwudi. 1997a. "Introduction: Philosophy and the (Post)colonial". Eze, Emmanuel Chukwudi ed. 1997a. *Postcolonial African Philosophy: A Critical Reader*. Cambridge: Blackwell Publishers Ltd., pp. 1–21.

———. 1997b. "Democracy or Consensus? A Response to Wiredu". Eze, Emmanuel Chukwudi ed. 1997b. *Postcolonial African Philosophy: A Critical Reader*. Cambridge: Blackwell Publishers Ltd., pp. 313–23.

Fatton, Jr., Robert. 1990. "Liberal Democracy in Africa". *Political Science Quarterly*, Vol. 105 No. 3, Autumn 1990, pp. 455–73.

Flikschuh, Katrin. 2014. "The Idea of Philosophical Fieldwork: Global Justice, Moral Ignorance, and Intellectual Attitudes". *The Journal of Political Philosophy*, Vol. 22 No. 1, 2014, pp. 1–26. https://doi:10.1111/jopp.12006.

Gelfand, Michael. 1981. *Ukama: Reflections on Shona and Western Cultures in Zimbabwe*. Gwelo: Mambo Press.

Gyekye, Kwame. 2013. *Philosophy, Culture and Vision: African Perspectives: Selected Essays*. Accra: Sub-Saharan Publishers.

Healey, John and Mark Robinson. 1994. *Democracy, Governance and Economic Policy: Sub-Saharan Africa in Comparative Perspective*. London: Overseas Development Institute.

Jotia, Agreement Lathi. 2012. "Liberal Democracy: An African Perspective". *Academic Research International*, Vol. 2 No. 3, pp. 621–28. https://www.savap.org.pk.

Keller, Edmond John. 2007. "Africa in Transition: Facing the Challenges of Globalisation". *Harvard International Review*, Vol. 29 No. 2, pp. 46–51.

Mazrui, Ali Al'Amin. 2002 (1975). "Africa and Cultural Dependency: The Case of the African University". Laremont, Ricardo Rene and Fouad Kalouche eds. *Africa and Other Civilisations: The Collected Essays of Ali A. Mazrui*, Vol. 2. Trenton, NJ: Africa World Press, pp. 57–93.

Mignolo, Walter D. 2005. "Prophets Facing Sidewise: The Geopolitics of Knowledge and the Colonial Difference". *Social Epistemology*, Vol. 19 No. 1, pp. 111–27. https://doi:10.1080/02691720500084325.

Moyo, Jonathan Nathaniel. 1992. "State Politics and Social Domination in Zimbabwe". *The Journal of Modern African Studies*, Vol. 30 No. 2, June 1992, pp. 305–30.

Mukandala, Rwekaza. 2001. "The State of African Democracy: Status, Prospects, Challenges". *African Journal of Political Science*, Vol. 6 No. 2, pp. 1–10.

Mungwini, Pascah. 2016. "The Question of Re-centring Africa: Thoughts and Issues from the Global South". *South African Journal of Philosophy*, Vol. 35 No. 4, 2016, pp. 523–36. http://dx.doi.org/10.1080/02580136.2016.1245554.

Nkrumah, Kwame. 1965. *Neo-Colonialism: The Last Stage of Imperialism*. New York: International Publishers.

Nyamnjoh, Francis B. 2012. "'Potted Plants in Greenhouses': A Critical Reflection on the Resilience of Colonial Education in Africa". *Journal of Asian and African Studies*, Vol. 47 No. 2, pp. 129–154. https://doi:10.1177/0021909611417240.

Oduor, Reginald M. J. 2012. "Odera Oruka's Account of the Foundation of Human Rights: A Critique". *Thought and Practice: A Journal of the Philosophical Association of Kenya (PAK)*, New Series, Vol. 4 No. 2, December 2012, pp. 219–40. http://ajol.info/index.php/tp/index.

———. 2017. "Democracy Free from Western Hegemony: Opening Remarks". Address at the International Conference on Beyond Liberal Democracy: The Quest for Indigenous African Models of Democracy for the Twenty-First Century, Nairobi, Kenya, organised by the Department of Philosophy and Religious Studies, University of Nairobi, Kenya, and the Council for Research in Values and Philosophy (RVP), Washington, D.C., U.S.A., 22–23 May, 2017.

Ramose, Mogobe Bernard. 1992. "African Democratic Tradition: Oneness, Consensus and Openness—A Reply to Wamba-dia-Wamba". *Quest: Philosophical Discussions—An International African Journal of Philosophy*, Vol. VI No. 2, December 1992, pp. 63–83.

Ranger, Terence Osborne. 1985. "African initiatives and resistance in the face of partition and conquest". Boahen, A. Adu ed. *General History of Africa, VII: Africa under Colonial Domination 1880–1935*. Paris: United Nations Educational, Scientific and Cultural Organisation, pp. 45–62.

Rodney, Walter. 1985. "The Colonial Economy". Boahen, A. Adu ed. *General History of Africa, VII: Africa under Colonial Domination 1880–1935*. Paris: United Nations Educational, Scientific and Cultural Organisation, pp. 332–50.

Sklar, Richard L. 1983. "Democracy in Africa". *African Studies Review*, Vol. 26 No. 3/4, pp. 11–24.

Stoneman, Colin. 1981. "Agriculture". Stoneman, Colin ed. *Zimbabwe's Inheritance*. London: The College Press (Pvt) Ltd., pp. 127–50.

Taiwo, Olufemi. 1993. "Colonialism and its Aftermath: The Crisis of Knowledge Production". *Callaloo*, Vol. 16 No. 4, Autumn 1993, pp. 891–908.

Tar, Usman A. 2010. "The challenges of democracy and democratisation in Africa and Middle East". *Information, Society and Justice*, Vol. 3 No. 2, pp. 81–94. www.londonmet.ac.uk/isj

Uzoigwe, G.N. 1985. "European partition and conquest of Africa: an overview". Boahen, A. Adu ed. *General History of Africa, VII: Africa under Colonial Domination 1880–1935*. Paris: United Nations Educational, Scientific and Cultural Organisation, pp. 19-44.

Wamba-dia-Wamba, Ernest. 1992. "Beyond Elite politics of Democracy in Africa". *Quest: Philosophical Discussions—An International African Journal of Philosophy*, Vol. VI No. 1, June 1992, pp. 29–42.

Wiredu, Kwasi. 1996. *Cultural Universals and Particulars: An African Perspective*. Bloomington: Indiana University Press.

———. 1997. "Democracy and Consensus in African Traditional Politics: A Plea for a Non-party Polity". Eze, Emmanuel Chukwudi ed. *Postcolonial African Philosophy: A Critical Reader*. Cambridge: Blackwell Publishers Ltd., pp. 303–12.

Chapter Four

The Snares of Liberal Democracy

Lessons from Electioneering in the Democratic Republic of Congo

David Ngendo-Tshimba

In the aftermath of the Cold War—which was paradoxically hot (in the literal sense) and lethal on the African continent—a vast majority of African states still struggle to overcome the challenges characteristic of a post-war context, as they strive for political and socio-economic paradigms that would rid them of institutional fragility. The Democratic Republic of Congo (DRC) is no exception to this trend. Drawing from contemporary events and scholarly literature on scenarios of electoral engineering in post–Cold War Africa, I seek in this chapter to illuminate the political, social, and economic predicaments associated with the conducting of elections after violent conflict as a means to rebuilding broken political structures and so restoring a democratic political order in a state. Whereas, ideally, a theory and practice of civics in which sovereignty is lodged in the assembly of all citizens who choose to participate in the decision-making processes to shape their own destiny is quite appealing, I argue that premature increases in political participation in a post-violence context, including prioritisation of elections as is the case in the DRC, have a high likelihood of destabilising fragile political systems.

In this critique of Western liberal democracy, I first examine the pitfalls of post-war DRC's electioneering in the 2006, 2011 and 2018 general elections. On the basis of these three sequential yet profoundly dissimilar electoral experiences (although prior to each of which armed conflict had weighed heavily on both state and non-state agencies), I argue that resorting to the ballot rather than the bullet is no guarantee that in the aftermath of a countrywide devastating armed conflict, sustainable political order will be established. To illustrate this, even after having twice emerged as winner of presidential elections (although his victories were contested), President Joseph Kabila's regime was unable to consolidate its war-torn political, economic, social and security apparatuses, the intense engagement of the international community notwithstanding. It is against this backdrop that I argue that the insistence on the organisation of elections for purposes of legitimisation of power may simply be a hollow ritual, and, more so, one that does provide an otherwise despotic regime with a façade of legitimacy—or, worse still, may lead to a renewal of violence only capable of worsening an already bad situation.

Finally, I posit that whereas, according to the tenets of liberal democracy, credible elections constitute the hallmark of a democratic political order, the context within which this ideal is pursued must be appropriate. This is due to the fact that in a previously war-ravaged state faced with serious political and socio-economic challenges, as was the case in the DRC after two episodes of armed conflict, elections—good intentions notwithstanding—may not constitute the necessary steps along the road to a viable democratic political order. Instead, making the post-war society governable (by synchronising different as well as differing social forces for sound civic participation) constitutes a proper sequencing essential to the eventual political institutionalisation, which is, in turn, a crucial step towards a truly democratic order after politically inspired mass violence.

LIBERAL DEMOCRACY-CUM-'ELECTOCRACY'

According to Wamba-dia-Wamba (1994), two dominant historical modes of politics have been specified: the parliamentarian mode of politics—which includes liberal democracy—and the Stalinian or Third International mode of politics. To Wamba-dia-Wamba, however, neither the parliamentarian mode nor the Stalinian mode (which is not the same thing as the Soviet Union under Stalin, that is, Stalinism) "support[s] a process of human and social emancipation today" (Wamba-dia-Wamba 1994, 249).

By the mid-1990s, the momentum for political reforms had effectively become an unstoppable Africa-wide movement. To borrow the recent words of American political theorist Francis Fukuyama, with the collapse of the Soviet Union in 1991, "the Marxist left largely collapsed, and social democrats were left to make their peace with capitalism" (Fukuyama 2019, 113). With the triumph of capitalism came the re-launch of the liberal democratic experiment in many African countries, with the single-party and military dictatorships that had been erected in the mid-1960s to the mid-1970s giving way—one after the other—to popular domestic pressures not only for liberalisation, but even for outright democratisation of the political space. This post–Cold War wave of democratisation ushered in the restoration of multi-party politics, the organisation of elections, the licensing of private electronic and print media, and the removal of the worst restrictions on the organisation of public political meetings.

Thus, there seemed to be growing agreement as to how political power ought to be transferred—the holding of periodic and democratic elections ('electocracy') being the sine qua non of political stability and of society's peaceful development. Indeed, if the winds of democracy are blowing over Africa, one reason for them, according to Sylla and Goldhammer (1982), may be that democracy provides a rational solution to the problem of succession. Sylla and Goldhammer (1982, 12) further maintain that in a sense, liberalisation of the political process forces a country to establish a rational system for transferring power.

In post–Cold War sub-Saharan Africa in particular, there has been a rapidly growing reliance on electoral processes as the principal way to legitimise governance at national, regional and local levels. Coming from the context of a bipolar world where the crisis and the collapse of one side (communism) seemed to have validated the victory and superiority of the other (capitalism), Ernest Wamba-dia-Wamba (1994) pointedly noted that the political death of bureaucratic socialism propelled the parliamentarian mode of politics (characteristic of liberal democracy) to a hegemonic position. Celebrants of capitalism in the West, Wamba-dia-Wamba underscored, seized the occasion to intensify the propaganda for a free-market economy and multi-party democracy. Hence, this Western-induced parliamentarian mode of politics has been perceived as an inescapable means for stimulating the development of democratic governance through the choosing of representatives, the forming of governments, and as a means of conferring legitimacy upon a new political order.

As the most visible feature of liberal democracy, universal suffrage in independent Africa has been treated as democracy's defining characteristic. Often, the main answer of the international community to the problem of inertia or systemic dependency in the aftermath of severe conflict is the rapid organisation of elections, which, it is hoped, will produce a legitimate government with a mandate to shape a new and better society. This post-conflict democracy solution, however, contains major problems. Citing the work of Robert Bates, *When Things Fell Apart* (2008), Straus and Taylor (2012) reiterated that the early optimism about Africa's democratic transition has met with new scepticism to the extent that political liberalisation (by way of a dispensation of liberal democracy) came to shorten the time horizons of African leaders during the past two decades, increasing the likelihood that such heads of state would cause the atrophy rather than the development of institutions for the common good. Furthermore, Uvin (2002) argued that, against a backdrop of extreme poverty due to dilapidated socio-economic infrastructures, disorganisation of the then political scene, and the legacies of violence that continue to suffocate the delivery of public goods, elections might simply not be ultimately very meaningful.

The debate on electoral systems in post–Cold War Africa has often presupposed that the key institutional players in this process—most notably political parties—do represent the aspirations of the electorate, and that the general elections merely come into play to arbitrate over which of the contesting parties is deemed by the voting majority as best at addressing their concerns. Yet, in a post-war setting where violence-ridden states are apt to have stronger patronage networks in comparison to others, the demands of loyalty supersede efficiency, inclusivity and the rule of law; hence, electoral violence is likely because power is sought by any means necessary (Bekoe 2012). More often than not, therefore, the predominant route to state power in most parts of Africa today has been the orchestration of political violence, of which electoral violence is the most common.

Assessing Africa's new governance models, Olukoshi (2007) notes that where citizen pressure became an exercise in futility under political regimes that were supposed to have derived their mandate from the populace through elections, the essence of governance had not really changed in spite of the framework of electoral pluralism that had been introduced. Furthermore, the cost of getting the elected government to pay attention to domestic concerns has actually been high, involving the organisation of domestic protests, the deployment of brutal state apparatuses, the routine abuse of power in order to undermine domestic political opposition, and the rigging of elections to foil the popular will and block the extension of the frontiers of democracy (Olukoshi 2007). To add to such gloomy stories of suffocated democratic dispensations, Oloka-Onyango (2007) noted that by the time he was writing, only six of Africa's independence leaders were replaced in free and fair elections: the rest were either overthrown, forced to resign, died in office, or were stopped by an assassin's bullet. That a sheer lack of genuine political pluralism has been conspicuous in post–Cold War Africa is an indisputable fact, the façade of multi-party democracy notwithstanding.

It is no exaggeration to posit that the tide of democratisation that swept over Africa in the aftermath of the Cold War brought to the fore a category of elites whom Gros has labelled "opportunistic democratisers" (Gros 1998 cited in Berhanu 2007, 102–3). As Berhanu (2007) noted, constitutional reforms and the conduct of periodic pluralistic elections alone are actually not sufficient for effecting transformation with a positive bearing on the socio-economic and political life of the citizenry and the good of the entire society (including non-citizens) at large. Hence, replacing authoritarian regimes with apparently democratic ones, rather than making new arrangements in the realm of political governance that can practically benefit society in socio-economic terms, may turn out to be futile. Despite the fact that elections remain a prerequisite for broader democratic practices, electoral exercises and democratic political order are certainly not synonymous.

THE CASE OF 'ELECTOCRACY' IN THE DRC

It was widely believed that the promulgation of the 2005 DRC constitution would usher in the Third Republic, starting with the elections of 'new' leaders with political legitimacy, and so complete the democratic transition which had begun in the early 1990s, but which was interrupted by the two wars. Whereas the West, led by the United States, applauded the new DRC constitution as, in the words of Thomas Turner (2007), establishing "a balance of power between the branches of government, ensuring protection and development of minorities, and providing for a limit of two presidential terms", critics judged it to be "vague both as regards the form of state (unitary or federal) and the form of governing regime (presidential and parliamentary)" (Turner 2007, 183–84). It was against this backdrop, and within the contours of this newly promulgated constitution, that the 2006 DRC general elections were held.

THE 2006 DRC ELECTION EXPERIENCE

The holding of the 2006 general elections (both presidential and legislative) followed a decade of one of the deadliest internationalised conflicts that made the DRC the theatre of what was called Africa's Great War or African World War (Reyntjens 2009, 1; Prunier 2009, 1). It was a democratic experiment the country was to undertake only the second time, the first being the election of Patrice Lumumba to lead the maiden government of the independent republic as Prime Minister in the May 1960 elections. Turner (2007) noted that many Congolese voted for peace, but their votes led, paradoxically, to a second-round choice between the two leading warlords: Joseph Kabila and Jean-Pierre Bemba. Furthermore, the elections were supposed "to put an end to 'partition and pillage' but territorial reunification was far from complete when the elections were held, and pillage continued" (Turner 2007, 166).

As Prunier (2009) observed, these elections followed the promulgation of the new constitution, which had been submitted to a popular referendum at the end of 2005 and approved by 84.3 percent of the voters, signifying a resounding triumph for the two-year-long transition process. Almost as soon as the electoral process began to acquire greater credibility, the conduct of elections was called into question. Because the civilian population concurred with the argument of Apollinaire Malu Malu (who then headed the Independent Electoral Commission) about the politicians' delaying tactics, anti-postponement riots spread very quickly across the major cities of the country. Beyond the vagaries of individual politicians, the main national problem the Congolese state faced during the entire transition period was—and still remains long after the constitutional referendum—security. By some estimates, the bigger problem was how to reintegrate structures of often anomic destruction into "new structures of controlled violence"—at least in accordance with the classical definition of the state as an entity having the monopoly of legitimate violence over a certain territory (Prunier 2009, 306).

By 2006, election fever had started to grip the country. The looming future was filled with both hopes and fears—the elections having turned into a "Holy Grail" (Prunier 2009, 309). At the time of elections, the *Mission d'Organisation des Nations Unies au Congo* (MONUC), that is, the United Nations Peacekeeping Mission in the Congo—already deployed in the country half a decade earlier—together with the *Comité International d'Accompagnement de la Transition* (CIAT), that is, International Committee in Support of the Transition, which included the five permanent members of the UN Security Council in addition to Belgium and Canada, as well as four Southern African Development Co-operation (SADC) member-states (Angola, Mozambique, South Africa, and Zambia), struggled against high odds to ensure that the crucial elections epitomised the standardised norms of a free, fair, transparent and non-violent electoral process acceptable to the so-called international community. In April 2005, the European Union had contributed USD 21 million towards setting up an auxiliary military force of two thousand men under a Franco-German coordinated command (Turner 2007; Mbavu 2011).

While the DRC could not have completed the transition from open warfare to the elections of 2006 without substantial support from the so-called international community, this strong support paradoxically became a political problem: A number of opposing candidates, and people associated with the major non-candidate, Etienne Tshisekedi, claimed that the international community was imposing its choice, namely, Kabila (Turner 2007, 165). Already in the first round of those elections, a post-war DRC deeply divided between east [Swahili-speaking] and west [Lingala-speaking] (Turner 2007, 166) was brought to the fore. Had Horowitz (2001) not persuasively argued that the common tendency of different ethnic groups to support opposing political parties provides a situation conducive to the mingling of ethnic and partisan violence?

Upon collecting the declaration forms of candidacy and the electoral deposit fee (USD 50,000 per candidate), the Independent Electoral Commission published a list of thirty-three presidential candidates (Turner 2007, 164).

A dozen 'new political parties' sprang up; these were, according to Prunier (2009, 309), parties "in name only" since they were mostly ethnic or regional gatherings around the name of one or two well-known local politicians. On August 20, which was the voting day of the first round, given the stiff competition during the campaign period, none of the contenders won an absolute majority in the first round: Joseph Kabila (then Transitional President) had 44.81 percent of the votes compared to Jean-Pierre Bemba's 20.03 percent. According to the then promulgated constitution of the Third Republic, for a presidential contender to be declared winner, he or she must have got an absolute majority, that is, 50 percent plus one vote. Subsequently, in the second round of the presidential race, the densely populated Swahili-speaking eastern and southern regions ensured victory for Joseph Kabila who had consolidated his electorate base through a robust political alliance known as the *Alliance pour la Majorité Présidentielle* (AMP), that is, Alliance for the Presidential Majority, against the Lingala-speaking northwestern and western regions which gave solid support to Jean-Pierre Bemba. Kabila was declared winner after the second round of voting which took place on October 29, with 58 percent of the votes to Bemba's 42 percent. The turnout had been 65.4 percent of the registered voters (Prunier 2009, 310). By and large, these elections were reported to be free and fair.

The massive clamour that had accompanied the charmed conduct of the 2006 general elections was soon followed by severe military activism, which terrorised the grass roots both in the rural areas of the eastern provinces and the urban centres of the western provinces. Undoubtedly, this widened the schism between the impatient populace and an incapable elected government on the one hand, and the poorly esteemed United Nations peacekeeping forces (blue helmets), on the other.

In the year following the general elections, the frustrated government called for the withdrawal of these blue helmets, notwithstanding a seriously fragile state security infrastructure, especially in the east of the country "where a multitude of militias had virtually made it ungovernable" (Mbavu 2011, 250). Thus, the argument of Tordoff and Ralph (2005) that the holding of multi-party elections is not by itself enough to secure the establishment of a democratic political order was validated.

THE 2011 DRC ELECTION EXPERIENCE

The 2011 presidential and legislative elections were conducted in a much more tense socio-political atmosphere than the elections of 2006. Willame (2011, 2) reports that more than 18,000 candidates registered to run for positions of members of parliament, as opposed to 10,000 in the previous elections. Equally shocking, of the 450 political parties on whose tickets these candidates ran, 417 were recognised by the Ministry of Internal Affairs in August 2011, in contrast to the 203 recognised in 2006. Peculiarly, independent candidates outnumbered candidates claiming adherence to either the ruling party coalition or to opposition parties. Even the incumbent, President Joseph Kabila, presented himself as an independent candidate.

Nonetheless, there were only eleven presidential candidates compared to the thirty-three in 2006. One of the reasons for this cutback could have been the fact that the electoral deposit fee, which is non-refundable, for presidential candidature had doubled from USD 50,000 to USD 100,000 (Willame 2011, 3). Of the eleven candidates, four had previously not had much impact on the national political scene, three had stood in the 2006 presidential race, while two were freshly contending for the presidency although they commanded some degree of influence on the national political scene. Not surprisingly, the incumbent, Joseph Kabila, could only worry much about the latter two, namely, Vital Kamerhe—previously chief campaigner for Kabila in the 2006 race and subsequently President (Speaker) of the National Assembly (lower chamber of Parliament)—and Etienne Tshisekedi, an old emblematic figure of the opposition since the Mobutu era, and who polarised the presidential race in much the same way as Jean-Pierre Bemba did in 2006.

In the end, the 2011 presidential race almost turned into a two-man contest—Joseph Kabila versus Etienne Tshisekedi. The former certainly enjoyed the privileges of incumbency and took advantage of the state's four estates (the executive, the legislature, the judiciary, and the media) as well as the security apparatus over the former. While Kabila's manoeuvres during the campaign resonated with part of the citizenry that had recently shifted to the privileged side of society, Tshisekedi took up a grassroots approach and directed his political discourse towards the poor—those under-privileged by hegemonic structures of the state, and whom his populist rhetoric enticed. According to Willame (2011, 4), the DRC's godfathers, including the United States, the United Nations Security Council, Belgium, China, the World Bank, and the International Monetary Fund (IMF), among others, did not seem to empathise with the many frustrations articulated by Tshisekedi during his campaign.

In the midst of the rapidly growing tension, both from within the country and from the diaspora, the renamed electoral management body, *Commission Electorale Nationale Indépendente* (CENI), that is, "Independent National Electoral Commission", released preliminary results of the polls on 9 December 2011. The final detailed results declared Joseph Kabila winner of the presidential vote with 49 percent against 32 percent for his main challenger, Etienne Tshisekedi

(Stearns 2011, 2; Willame 2011, 3). This was taken to be a constitutional win, as both the Senate (upper chamber of Parliament) and the National Assembly (lower chamber) had already passed in January 2011 an amendment to the 2005 constitution including (i) a one-round plural majority win; and (ii) the president's prerogative to dissolve provincial assemblies, rescind governors, and call for referenda. Analysts of the DRC's political system had pointed out that the amendments of the constitution should have been much more thoughtful by taking into consideration the spirit of the law, not simply its letter. Essentially, the amendments made the presidency much more powerful while causing reluctance on part of the Legislature to press for an effective decentralisation project as required by the constitution (Stearns 2011, 9).

Marred by significant irregularities and malpractices that breached national and international standards, the 2011 elections could not have made any significant contribution towards a radical transformation of the country. Indeed, the 2011 polls overshadowed the hard-won precedent of the 2006 elections, leading many to pessimistically question the DRC's capacity to address its governance shortcomings and consolidate the structures of a democratic political order.

THE 2018 DRC ELECTION EXPERIENCE

2016 presaged a crisis of legitimacy of power on the political tapestry of the DRC. Joseph Kabila, at the country's helm since 2001, exhausted his constitutionally sanctioned hold on power on 19 December 2016 following his re-election for a five-year term in 2011. For the Congolese National Independent Electoral Commission (CENI) as well as for the ruling party and its political coalition, the Alliance for Presidential Majority (AMP), the holding of the next presidential and legislative elections squarely hinged on reviewing and updating the 2011 voter register—an exercise which called for a new population census envisaged for August 2017. For the political opposition and most of the Congolese civil society organisations, as well as for the so-called international community (the self-proclaimed "mature democracies" of the geo-political West), the holding of the elections within the framework of the St. Sylvester Accords of 31 December 2016 was crucial. Mediated by the Congolese Catholic Church, these Accords underscored that elections should be held in 2017 and that the constitutional provision on presidential term limits should not be changed.

At the heart of the talks at St. Sylvester was the vexing question of how to organise a democratic transition of power with a fairly unwilling incumbent (International Crisis Group, December 2017). The untimely death of Etienne

Tshisekedi—a key signatory to the St. Sylvester Accords—in the first quarter of 2017 further set the country on an unprecedented motion of constitutional and political crisis, to which the ruling party and its increasingly unpopular political coalition kept responding with 'context-conditioned elections'—a euphemism for the postponing of impending polls ad infinitum.

The regime of Joseph Kabila, way past its second and final term in office, finally agreed to the holding of the December 2018 presidential and legislative elections. The stakes in these elections were substantially higher than they were in the previous two polls, aggravated by the fact that for the very first time in its post-independence history, the country was eagerly looking forward to having a former president alive! The Kabila regime emphasised that the elections would be a substantially Congolese affair. In this regard, the government spokesperson and minister of communication, Lambert Mende, stated in August 2018 that the elections would be *of* the Congolese, *by* the Congolese and *for* the Congolese (Reid 2018).

However, to the end-of-tenure Kabila regime, elections "of the Congolese" ironically meant the tactfully deliberate purging of some eligible Congolese citizens from the ballot. The bids of three highly influential presidential aspirants (Moise Katumbi Chapwe, Jean-Pierre Bemba Gombo, and Antipas Mbusa Nyamwisi) were therefore not received by the Corneille Nangaa-chaired Independent National Electoral Commission (CENI). Furthermore, elections "by the Congolese" pointed, at least rhetorically, to the entire funding of the CENI and the events prior, during, and after the voting, solely by Congolese public funds, that is, with no external aid. Lastly, elections "for the Congolese" came to signify that the mandate of announcing the election results was exclusively that of the CENI, and that in the event of any electoral dispute of the CENI-announced results, only the country's Constitutional Court—which the outgoing regime had recently restructured and whose personnel it had reshuffled not long ago—would have the final say over any such dispute.

Furthermore, many a lesson was drawn from the previous two electoral experiences. To be sure, in his exclusive interview with *Foreign Affairs* managing editor, Stuart Reid, two weeks to the planned 23 December 2018 polls (finally conducted on 30 December 2018), outgoing President Joseph Kabila revealed the following: "in 2011, we were very adamant that elections had to take place, but had we listened to advice from one or two or three people we probably would have pushed those elections for another six months in order for them *to have been perfect*. But we're bringing *the lessons we learned to these elections of 2018*" (quoted in Reid 2018; italics added).

What, for the Kabila regime in the run up to the 2018 polls, did "perfect elections" mean? A related question is: what were the lessons learned from the previous election experiences? The answers to these questions can be summed up in two observations. *First*, the 2006 experience made it clear to the ruling party that the constitutional rule of absolute majority win (50 percent and one vote) was not only a costly affair, but also, and more important, an obstacle to easy election rigging, particularly in the event of a re-run. *Second*, the 2011 experience endorsed the view on the side of the ruling party that even in the event of the removal of the absolute majority rule, a presidential race conspicuously akin to a face-off between one candidate of the ruling party and the other of the opposition would prove to be an even greater obstacle to a win by the ruling party candidate. As a way out, maintaining a third candidate in the race, stemming from within the opposition, would be key in the bid to keep the floodgates of rigging open in a presidential race with the absence of an absolute majority win rule. Thus, the regime conceived the 2018 presidential elections as a mere civic ritual to facilitate a superficial change of guard without a real change of the actual holders of power.

Less conspicuously, but more perniciously, was the striking resemblance between the independence May 1960 elections organised by the Belgian colonisers and those of December 2018. Preoccupied with turning the momentum of decolonisation into a classic case of transition to neo-colonialism, outgoing Belgian colonial administrators initially conceived of a process of power transfer to "a virtually hand-picked group of people who had undergone a necessary period of apprenticeship and who could therefore be trusted not to endanger the long-term interests of the departing colonialists in the country" (Nzongola-Ntalaja 1987, 104). One is left to wonder whether the outgoing Kabila regime turned to the colonial books for strategies to apply the lessons learnt from the two previous polls.

Strikingly akin to the Belgian colonial scheme, the end-of-tenure Kabila regime reinvented, at the eleventh hour, a new political dynamic of the ruling coalition into what became known as the *Front Commun pour le Congo* (FCC), that is, "Common Front for the Congo". From the FCC—being the emerging political arrangement meant to guarantee the continuation of the expired Kabila tenure on new terms that would circumvent the two-term rule—President Kabila, as the patron of the FCC, selected one Emmanuel Ramazani Shadary as the ordained FCC flag bearer. Shadary, to say the least, was one archetypal supporter of the Kabila regime, who, to parody the words of Nzongola-Ntalaja, "had undergone a necessary period of apprenticeship and who could therefore be trusted not to endanger the long-term interests" of the scheming outgoing regime.

In view of the machinations of the Kabila regime to stay in power in disguise, all major opposition parties quickly coalesced into an alliance known as *Lamuka*—a rhetorically moving word, in both Kiswahili and Lingala (the two most dominant national languages in the country), meaning "wake up".

Out of a growing sense of necessity, the *Lamuka* opposition alliance resolved to front a single candidate for the presidential race. Thus, on 11 November 2018, the Geneva accords were signed, endorsing one Martin Fayulu Madidi as the sole opposition candidate to face off with the one from the ruling coalition. Signatories to the Geneva Accords included Jean-Pierre Bemba on behalf of his *Mouvement de Libération du Congo* (Movement for the Liberation of the Congo) and allies, Vital Kamerhe on behalf of his *Union pour la Nation Congolaise* (Union for the Congolese Nation) and allies, Moise Katumbi on behalf of his *Ensemble pour le Changement* (Together for Change), Félix Tshisekedi on behalf of his *Union pour la Démocratie et le Progrès Social* (Union for Democracy and Social Progress) and allies, Adolphe Muzito on behalf of his *Nouvel Elan* (New Momentum), and Martin Fayulu on behalf of his *Dynamique de l'Opposition* (Dynamic of the Opposition).

So resolute, it appeared, were the ambitions of the *Lamuka* opposition coalition that the first of its seven objectives was "to realise a democratic change of power by free, transparent, inclusive, peaceful and credible elections", while the last was equally succinct: "to assure the victory of the opposition on the 23 December 2018 elections". The writing on the wall could not have been any clearer for the outgoing Kabila regime and the newly established FCC.

There is a second aspect of the striking resemblance between the May 1960 elections and the December 2018 polls: the Belgian colonisers were overwhelmed by the radicalisation of the anti-colonial struggle through unexpectedly decisive mass participation, and, particularly by the substantive mobilisation in the rural areas through which the radical nationalist parties won 71 of 137 seats in the lower house of Parliament. Consequently, it became apparent to the colonisers that their initial strategy might not work. The major stumbling block to the Belgian strategy of neo-colonialism, as Nzongola-Ntalaja (1987) notes, consisted of Patrice Lumumba and his coalition of radical nationalist leaders. In the scheme of departing Belgian colonial masters and their allies, removing this obstacle meant "do[ing] everything possible to prop up the moderate side of the major political cleavage within the nationalist movement" (Nzongola-Ntalaja 1987, 105). Similarly, fifty-eight years later, to the FCC, the singly sanctioned candidature of the united political opposition in the person of Martin Fayulu, lucidly pointed to the fact that the outgoing regime's initial scheme might not yield the desired results.

In addition to the unanimity of the major opposition parties inside and outside the country regarding the candidature of Martin Fayulu, his bid seems to have enjoyed the favour of the higher echelons of the Roman Catholic Church in the country, particularly through the labour of the increasingly influential *Comité Laïc Chrétien* (Christian Lay Committee)—a reincarnation of the famous civil organising of the historic 16 February 1992 March that forced the Mobutu regime to reopen the National Sovereign Conference—under the leadership of Isidore Ndaywel, one of Congo's leading intellectuals of great international repute. The tacit endorsement of Fayulu's candidacy by the Roman Catholic Church leadership in the country and their followers—a significant percentage of the general electorate—was expressed in the phrase, "*Que les médiocres dégagent!* (Let the unfit vacate)", words uttered almost a year to the polls by a no less influential figure in the country's public life, Laurent Cardinal Mosengwo Pasinya.

As was the case with the colonial script for the May 1960 elections, Fayulu along with his new crew of allies radically opposed to the FCC became a serious obstacle to the Kabila regime's continuation strategy, and as such, to again parody Nzongola-Ntalaja (1987, 105), the regime was determined to prop up the moderate side of the major political cleavage within the Lamuka opposition coalition. Thus, less than forty-eight hours after the signing of the Geneva Accords, Félix Tshisekedi (with his UDPS) and Vital Kamerhe (with his UNC) announced their respective withdrawals from the Lamuka coalition, and together they soon formed their own side coalition, Coalition pour le Changement (CACH), that is, Coalition for Change. In this way, the formidable challenge of Lamuka against FCC was significantly eroded.

With the numerical advantage of Lamuka demolished thanks to the emergence of CACH, the floodgates of electoral rigging (in line with the "lessons" learnt from the 2011 polls) were now open. Asked, in the interview with *Foreign Affairs* managing editor Stuart Reid earlier cited, if the outgoing regime would accept the outcome of the vote in the event that FCC flag bearer Shadary did not win, President Kabila revealingly retorted: "We have organised these elections in order to accept the results of the elections. When those results are announced by the electoral commission *and confirmed* by the constitutional court, they will be accepted by everybody" (Reid 2018; italics added).

Meanwhile, the country's Constitutional Court had experienced a significant change in its professional corps following the dismembering of the Supreme Court into three separate jurisdictional organs, namely, the Court de Cassation (High Appellate Court), the Conseil d'Etat (State Council) and the Cour Constitutionnelle (Constitutional Court) itself. Of the nine justices on its bench, three were directly appointed by President Kabila, three others by Parliament, in which the outgoing ruling coalition had an overwhelming majority so that President Kabila's will was again effected, and the remaining three were appointed by the Conseil Supérieur de Magistrats (High Council for Magistrates), almost all of whom had been appointed by President Kabila himself.

The resignation of Justice Jean-Louis Esambo—a professor of constitutional law and a senior judge—in the immediate aftermath of CENI's release of the 2018 electoral calendar spoke volumes about the expected performance of that court in line with the whims of the executive. Hence, that the electoral body, CENI, declared, in its final analysis, Félix Tshisekedi as the victor in the presidential race, had very little to do with what transpired from the casting of the ballots to the tallying of the results. Besides, the Constitutional Court, before which the filing of an electoral dispute had been rendered inevitable, was eagerly pre-set in the mood to "confirm" the verdict of the CENI.

CONSPIRING AGAINST DEMOCRATISATION IN THE DRC?

The liberal world order, Fukuyama painstakingly notes, has historically not benefited everyone, including in "developed [liberal] democracies" (Fukuyama 2019, 4). In fact, of the current global leader of liberal democracies—the United States—Fukuyama revealingly posits that the current dysfunction and decay of its political system "is related to the extreme and ever-growing polarisation of American politics, which has made routine governing an exercise in brinkmanship and threatens to politicise all of the country's institutions" (Fukuyama 2019, 117). If dysfunction and decay can still characterise the liberal democratic experiment in its Western cradle at this time, more decadence arising from the embrace of liberal democracy in the non-West is much less shocking.

At least three encumbrances have rendered periodic elections ineffective in contributing to the building of a viable democratic polity in the DRC:

1. A political elite deeply involved in cancerous corrupt dealings that rob its citizenry of the basic services that a state is obligated to offer;
2. A quasi-absence of state institutions (especially security and judicial apparatuses) to protect the inalienable freedoms of the citizenry;
3. The practice of the so-called international community of unquestioningly providing massive support for periodic general elections in the midst of rampant abject poverty and human insecurity devouring the citizenry due to state indifference. After all, for more than 30 years, Mobutu Sese Seko had monopolised political space in the country, so that the renewed multi-party competition in the 1990s had led to the emergence of two vast, ill-defined political tendencies—"the presidential tendency and the 'sacred union' of the opposition" (Turner 2007, 170).

Against this backdrop, Van Reybrouck (2014) argues that it was an illusion to hope that proper elections would immediately lead to a proper democracy in the DRC. Indeed, the West has been experimenting with forms of democratic administration for the last two and a half millennia, "but it has been less than a century since it has started putting its faith in universal suffrage through free elections" (Van Reybrouck 2014, 512). With these periodic experiences of 'electocracy', the result seems to be the same: elections in the post-war context of the DRC are but a political mechanism to deal with structural issues pertaining to the country's governance through the use of unbalanced procedures administered in a skewed and unprincipled manner. Hence Van Reybrouck (2014, 312) posits that the holding of general elections "should not be the kick-off to a process of national democratisation", but the crowning glory of that process—or at least one of its final steps.

However, even within the exceptional wish that fundamental values of political legitimacy and accountability be attained through the holding of democratic elections, a crucially important yet taken-for-granted question still lingers: Should the holding of democratic elections actually be at the pinnacle of a post-war political agenda? Put differently, what exigencies are being responded to by quickly holding elections in a post-war scenario? Equally important is the concern about substantial grassroots civic education prior to, during, and even after the holding of such elections. Will the continued conduct of such periodic general elections bring about a truly democratic political order in the body politic of an ill-governed citizenry still grappling with socio-economic woes in the face of state absenteeism? The three instances of both presidential and legislative elections (2006, 2011 and 2018) have exposed not only the extent to which Congolese state institutions are feeble, but also the utter lack of political will (nationally and internationally) to restructure and reaffirm these state institutions already submerged by both 'agentification' (proliferation of non-state agencies in the delivery of public goods) and 'donorisation' (excessive flow of foreign financial aid to the government).

That a post-war country resorts to ballots rather than bullets to choose its leaders is no guarantee for peace and stability thereafter. Instead, political institutionalisation, in terms of procedures of political action encompassing all social forces across the governed territory, is "the foundation of political stability and thus the precondition of political liberty" (Huntington 1996, 461). Holding free elections, an exercise that falls within the purview of political liberty, should logically never precede the realisation of political institutionalisation—the bedrock of any political order, democratic or otherwise. This less-trodden path (political institutionalisation and political consciousness-raising) is more crucial than the quick fixes of electoral engineering in the quest for a democratic political order, more so in the aftermath of mass political violence.

In quintessence, the various predicaments of social existence in most African countries emerging from bloody conflicts—including abject poverty, systemic corruption, and political violence arising from the militarisation of society, as well as almost non-existent legitimate and accountable state structures—are not simply incidental problems which the conduct of elections can easily fix. Rather, these structural pitfalls are sustained by a kind of political imagination deeply entrenched in a seemingly pre-ordained mode of politics for social and economic governance. Of the English Parliament—considered to be the Mother of Parliaments—Mohandas K. Gandhi, in his seminal book originally published in 1909, *Hind Swaraj*, presented a poignant critique of this parliamentary mode of politics as follows:

> The Parliament is without a real master. Under the Prime Minister, its movement is not steady, but it is buffeted about like a prostitute. The Prime Minister is more concerned about his power than about the welfare of the Parliament. His energy is concentrated upon securing the success of his party. His care is not always that the Parliament shall do right. Prime Ministers are known to have made the Parliament do things merely for party advantage. All this is worth thinking over. (Gandhi 1921, 212)

It is therefore no exaggeration to suggest that unless another sort of political modus operandi is envisioned and deployed, and then institutionalised by way of organisation of dialectic procedures of state and society, post-war democratic political order will remain elusive. Such a modus operandi would insist on setting the right priorities—establishing and applying political arrangements in accordance with the consensus of members of the political community.

In the aftermath of political violence, the daunting task of re-wiring the politics, that is, applying the 'glue' that ensures that all social forces are balanced out, is what is required to restore order. In this endeavour of putting in place a dependable political order, the holding of general elections cannot be conceived of as primary. The pursuit of democracy through universal suffrage in a multi-party electoral system (for which the term 'electocracy' sounds appropriate) simply tends to reduce politics to a matter of numbers. Yet, politics, and more especially in the aftermath of political violence of *longue durée* as in the case of the DRC, is too serious a matter to be reduced to the counting of votes. In fact, as Gyimah-Boadi (2007) cogently argued, many a political party in post–Cold War Africa is largely conceived and organised as a vehicle for capturing the state: it is hardly conceived and developed as an institution for representation, conflict resolution, political opposition for the promotion of accountability, or institutionalisation of democratic behaviour and attitudes in the first place. Little wonder, then, that "there tends to be very little party activity between elections" (Gyimah-Boadi 2007, 25). At any rate, the organisation of elections under a multi-party system would not suffice to induce the emergence of political consciousness capable of a socially emancipatory politics and thus a truly democratic political order.

The most challenging yet far more rewarding task relating to the question of establishing a democratic political order, therefore, is to specify the requisite steps (of which the holding of general elections is one, but certainly neither the first nor the only one), and determine the process for the operationalisation of a quintessentially democratic dispensation. Good intentions, or pressures both from within and without a post-violence country such as the DRC, ought not to shy away from this arduous task. In this respect, the pursuit of electoral engineering in the DRC sponsored by the so-called international community ought to have been reconciled with the pragmatic necessities of a previously war-ravaged state and society.

Having taken his readers through the story of the origin of Western democracy as practised by classical Athenians, Claude Ake had to reiterate that ancient Athens was just as precise about what the rule of the people means as it was about who the people are:

> It [ancient Athens] stuck uncompromisingly to direct rule by the people and shunned notions of consultation, consent and representation. . . . All citizens formed the sovereign Assembly whose quorum was put at 6,000. Meeting over 40 times a year, it debated and took decisions on all important issues of public policy including war and peace, foreign relations, public order, law making, finance and taxation. The Assembly was regarded as *the incarnation of Athenian political identity and collective will*. To underline this, it preferred to take decisions by consensus rather than votes. The business of the Assembly was prepared by a council of 500 which had a steering committee of 50 headed by a President who held office for only one day. The executive function of the polis was carried out by magistrates who were invariably a committee of 10 usually elected for a non-renewable term of one year. (Ake 2000, 8; italics and words in brackets added)

As Ake (2000) notes, humanity today cannot complain of not knowing what the meaning of democracy was to those who are said to have invented it, and to the only people who are recorded to have tried to practise it without trivialising it. From his scrutiny of the political development (theory and practice) in most of post–Cold War Africa, Tukumbi Lumumba-Kasongo (2005) observes that the system of governance that has been adopted in most parts of Africa since the early 1990s is that fragment of liberal democracy commonly referred to as multi-party politics. Anchoring his critique of liberal democracy on a paradox between what is expected of liberal democracy and its implications for social and economic progress in Africa,

Lumumba-Kasongo (2005) posits that while post–Cold War Africa is adopting liberal democracy as the most promising formula for unleashing individual energy and generating political participation, post–Cold War social and economic conditions in the continent are worsening at the same time. This paradox seems to suggest a crucial invitation to post–Cold War Africa to search for another kind of democracy in theory and in practice.

CONCLUSION

A close reading of the political history of most of post-independence Africa, and the DRC in particular, suggests that very little progress has been made in terms of strengthening the institutional capacity to build viable governance structures for conflict management. Sadly, it is as though the DRC is either bereft of any significant lessons from its own experiences recorded in its socio-political annals (oral and written), or impervious to learning lessons (whether classical or much more recent) from the available literature of its very own experiences or those of its neighbours (in both historical and contemporary contexts). It is no exaggeration to assert that on a balance sheet of political governance, owing to this failure to learn lessons from history, the DRC (and the continent at large) still registers more liabilities than assets; and this is reflected in the disillusionment with the way in which the performance of liberal democracy, with its emphasis on periodic general elections, is now akin to an attempt at squaring circles. In his reflections on the ideal type of political community, Jean-Jacques Rousseau once pondered:

> If Sparta and Rome have perished, what state can hope to last for ever? If we want the constitution that we have established to endure, let us not seek, therefore, to make it eternal . . . The political body, like the human, begins to die as soon as it is born, and carries within it the causes of its own destruction. But the one and the other can be more or less robustly constituted, so as to be preserved for a longer or shorter time (Rousseau 1994, 172).

Is it not time, indeed if not long-overdue, that the Congolese body politic, as well as its bona fide well-wishers, took a cue from Rousseau's insights above? In book 3 of his *Politics*, Aristotle describes three forms of government and the three corruptions of them—tyranny as a deviation from monarchy, oligarchy from aristocracy, and democracy from polity (*politeia*). Aristotle posits that tyranny is rule by one person for the benefit of the monarch, oligarchy for the rich, and democracy for the poor. Hence, none of these forms of government ("constitutions"), according to Aristotle, is for the common good. However, when the multitude governs for the common good, it is called by the name that is common to all constitutions, that is *politeia*. Remarkably, as the past three experiments with elections in the DRC have shown, resorting to the ballot rather than the bullet is no guarantee that the restoration of firm political order, let alone a *politeia*, will be achieved. A deep-seated conviction runs through the contemporary Congolese political class regarding the solution to the country's political conundrum. Across the political divide, there seems to be sheer agreement about a recourse to the holding of general elections à la liberal democracy script. What is more, both political party members and civil society activists are in agreement regarding the purported vast potentials of liberal democracy as defined by the vanguard states of the so-called international community led by the United States. Yet, as Huntington (1968) insightfully observed, when an American is asked to design a government, he or she comes up with a written constitution, bill of rights, separation of powers, checks and balances, federalism, regular elections, competitive parties—all excellent devices for limiting government. The Lockean American, Huntington further points out, is so fundamentally anti-government that he or she identifies government with restrictions on government: his or her general formula is that governments ought to be based on free and fair elections. Perhaps a question worth our considered reflection is whether this formula is truly relevant to the DRC's peculiar history and contemporary political circumstances.

At least the three consecutive experiments with elections in the DRC discussed in this chapter (the second and third more so than the first) lucidly demonstrate that the practice of universal suffrage for the presidency and the legislature was a wrong prioritisation of items on the political "to-do" list of a politically fragile country. Following the suffocation of a truly democratic choice in the immediate aftermath of its independence (with the blessing and sustained interest of the self-proclaimed democratic West), an entrenched autocratic political culture under the thirty-two-year-long Mobutu regime, and decade-long devastating armed conflicts after the fall of Mobutu, coupled with glaring state absenteeism in the dispensation of public goods, the holding of general elections in the DRC in observance of a yet ahistorical, acontextual and deeply apolitical liberal democracy script was, and still is, akin to applying a bandage to a fractured limb for which serious surgical intervention is required.

Indeed, Western political experts, as Van Reybrouck succinctly puts it, often suffer from "electoral fundamentalism" in the same way macroeconomists from the IMF and the World Bank not so long ago suffered collectively from market fundamentalism: They believe that meeting the formal requirements of a system is enough to let a thousand flowers bloom in even the most barren desert. For a country that, since its foundational moment in contemporary times, has almost always been on the brink of utter collapse and which is still predominantly characterised by incessant pockets of political strife and civil disorder, the organisation of general elections per se in the quest for a democratic political order ironically suffocates all opportunities for a 'democracy-from-below'. At the very best, therefore, the insistence on liberal democracy as chiefly manifested in periodic electioneering has been an obstacle to the establishment of a firm democratic political order in the DRC.

The characteristic winner-takes-all kind of elections (as have been witnessed in the previous three Congolese polls) can only contribute to worsening an already bad post-war situation. The pursuit of liberal democracy (reduced to 'electocracy') becomes a matter of life and death, a zero-sum game, whereby the elected government focuses on the systematic annihilation of the defeated elite together with the constituencies (real or perceived) that support them. In the final analysis, the script of liberal democracy is ironically performed against the grain of a truly democratic order: the hunger for free and fair elections only ends up producing a power-hungry political elite characteristically hostile to the notion of democracy as once practised by the ancient Athenians. This, in a sense, becomes the greatest paradox of liberal democracy.

Thus, in the context of the DRC, observing the liberal democracy script to the letter only appears to be *ahistorical*, *acontextual*, and deeply *apolitical*. It is worth bearing in mind that since its very first instance in 1957, elections in the DRC have been, in the main, a typically elitist petite bourgeoisie affair at best, and a facade at worst. The 1957 and 1959 elections that were limited to urban settings exemplify the former characteristic, while the 1970 and 1977 polls characterised by withdrawn ballot papers for opposition candidates is strong testimony to the latter.

Besides, what seems to have ensued from 2006 onwards is a vile combination of exclusive petite bourgeoisie affairs and sham exercises in the holding of elections. To be sure, neither the continuation of old officeholders nor the ushering in of new ones through 'electocracy' can herald a fundamental change to a truly democratic order in today's DRC. Consequently, more than ever before, the onus squarely rests on the Congolese to exercise their political imagination beyond the template of binary thinking characteristic of the liberal democratic project. Such political imagination should inaugurate the Congolese effort—arduous as it may be—to transform the current challenge into an opportunity to govern themselves, free from terms imposed upon them by the liberal democracy script. After all, there is no better concretisation of a *politeia* than for a people to govern themselves rather than to be governed by a hijacking political elite, whether or not it results from a ritualised 'free and fair' election.

To be sure, there seems to be no better window of opportunity for a real pursuit of 'democracy-from-below' in the DRC than there is today, as the current growing dissatisfaction (both inside and outside the country) with the December 2018 polls unfolds. Preoccupation with a dichotomous reasoning (new officeholders versus old ones) only blurs appreciation for the true potential of this auspicious opportunity to draw a better governance compact. MacIver succinctly sums up this imperative:

> Even after a government is established it remains more the guarantor rather than the maker of the law. The structure of order in any society is a rather elaborate affair. It is the result of long-time adjustments between man and man and between man and the environment. (MacIver 1965, 47)

REFERENCES

Ake, Claude. 2000. *The Feasibility of Democracy in Africa*. Dakar: CODESRIA Books.

Aristotle. 1998. *Politics*. Reeve, C.D.C. trans. Indianapolis: Hackett Publishing Co.

Bekoe, Dorina A. 2012. "Introduction: The Scope, Nature, and Pattern of Electoral Violence in Sub-Saharan Africa". Bekoe, Dorina A. ed. *Voting in Fear: Electoral Violence in Sub-Saharan Africa*. Washington, DC: USIP Press, pp. 1–14.

Berhanu, Kassahun. 2007. "Constitutional Engineering and Elections as Sources of Legitimacy in Post–Cold War Africa". J. Oloka-Onyango and N.K. Muwanga eds. *Africa's New Governance Models: Debating Form and Substance*. Kampala: Fountain Publishers, pp. 101–21.

Bøås, Morten. 2012. "Liberia: Elections—No Quick Fix for Peacebuilding". *New Routes*, Vol. 17 No. 1, pp. 15–17.

Fukuyama, Francis. 2019. *Identity: The Demand for Dignity and the Politics of Resentment*. New York: Picador.

Gandhi, Mohandas K. 1921. *Hind Swaraj; or Indian Rule*. Gujarat: Indian Opinion.

Gyimah-Boadi, Emmanuel. 2007. "Political Parties, Elections and Patronage: Random Thoughts on Neo-patrimonialism and African Democratisation". Basedau, Matthias, G. Erdmann and A. Mehler eds. *Votes, Money and Violence: Political Parties and Elections in Sub-Saharan Africa*. Scottsville: University of KwaZulu-Natal Press, pp. 65–81.

Horowitz, Donald L. 2001. *The Deadly Ethnic Riot*. Berkeley: University of California Press.

Huntington, Samuel P. 1968. *Political Order in Changing Societies*. New Haven: Yale University Press.

International Crisis Group. 2017. "Time for Concerted Action in DR Congo". *Africa Report*, No. 257, 4 December 2017. https://www.crisisgroup.org/africa/central-africa/democratic-republic-congo/257-time-concerted-action-dr-congo.

Lumumba-Kasongo, Tukumbi. 2005. "The Problematics of Liberal Democracy and Democratic Process: Lessons for Deconstructing and Building African Democracies". Lumumba-Kasongo, Tukumbi ed. *Liberal Democracy and its Critics in Africa: Political Dysfunction and the Struggle for Social Progress*. Dakar: CODESRIA Books, pp. 1–25.

MacIver, Robert M. 1965. *The Web of Government*, Revised Edition. New York: The Free Press.

Mbavu, Vincent M. 2011. *Revitaliser un Congo en panne: un bilan 50 ans après l'indépendence*. Geneva: Globalethics.net.

Nzongola-Ntalaja, Georges. 1987. *Revolution and Counter-Revolution in Africa: Essays in Contemporary Politics*. London: Zed Books.

Oloka-Onyango, Joseph. 2007. "Not Yet Democracy, Not Yet Peace! Assessing Rhetoric and Reality in Contemporary Africa". Oloka-Onyango, Joseph and N. K. Muwanga eds. *Africa's New Governance Models: Debating Form and Substance*. Kampala: Fountain Publishers, pp. 230–50.

Olukoshi, Adebayo. 2007. "Assessing Africa's New Governance Models". Oloka-Onyango, Joseph and N.K. Muwanga eds. *Africa's New Governance Models: Debating Form and Substance*. Kampala: Fountain Publishers, pp. 1–25.

Prunier, Gérard. 2009. *From Genocide to Continental War: The 'Congolese' Conflict and the Crisis of Contemporary Africa*. London: Hurst & Co.

Reid, Stuart. 2018. "Big Man in Congo: A Conversation with Joseph Kabila". *Foreign Affairs*, 14 December 2018. https://www.foreignaffairs.com/interviews/2018-12-14/big-man-congo.

Reyntjens, Filip. 2009. *The Great African War: Congo and Regional Geopolitics, 1996-2006*. Cambridge: Cambridge University Press.

Rousseau, Jean-Jacques. 1994 [1762]. *The Social Contract*. Betts, C. trans. Oxford: Oxford University Press.

Stearns, Jason K. 2011. "As criticism of election proliferates, time runs out for opposition". http://congosiasa.blogspot.com/search?updated-max=2011-12-13T04:18:00-08:00&max-results=7.

Straus, Scott, and Charlie Taylor. 2012. "Democratisation and electoral violence in sub-Saharan Africa, 1990-2008". Bekoe, Dorina A. ed. *Voting in Fear: Electoral Violence in Sub-Saharan Africa*. Washington, DC: USIP Press, pp. 15–38.

Sylla, Lanciné and Arthur Goldhammer. 1982. "Succession of the Charismatic Leader: The Gordian Knot of African Politics". *Daedalus*, Vol. 111 No. 2, pp. 11–28. http://www.jstor.org/stable/20024783.

Tordoff, William, and Ralph Young. 2005. "Electoral Politics in Africa: The Experience of Zambia and Zimbabwe". Tordoff, William and Ralph Young eds. *Government and Opposition*. London: Blackwell Publishing.

Turner, Thomas. 2007. *The Congo Wars: Conflict, Myth and Reality*. London: Zed Books.

Uvin, Peter. 2002. "The Development/Peacebuilding Nexus: A Typology and History of Changing Paradigms". *Journal of Peacebuilding and Development*, Vol. 1 No. 1, pp. 5–24. https://www.tandfonline.com/doi/abs/10.1080/15423166.2002.9792033266676.

Van Reybrouck, David. 2014. *Congo: The Epic History of a People*. Garrett, S. trans. London: Fourth Estate.
Wamba-dia-Wamba, Ernest. 1994. "Africa in Search of a New Mode of Politics". Himmelstrand, Ulf, Kabiru Kinyanjui and Edward Mburugu eds. *African Perspectives on Development: Controversies, Dilemmas and Openings*. London: James Currey, pp. 249–61.
Willame, Jean-Claude. 2011. "Ébullitions électorales au Congo: de Charybde en Scylla" http://www.revuenouvelle.be/Ebullitions-electorales-au-Congo-de-Charybde-en.

Part 2

CRITIQUE OF THE "AFRICA BEYOND LIBERAL DEMOCRACY" PROJECT

Chapter Five

Democracy as Falsehood

Seek but Do Not Expect to Find

Donna Pido

Philosophers have wonderful, well-thought-out ideas about democracy that stimulate thought and discourse while guiding our civilisations. Anthropologists have slightly different points of view expressed in the changing historical trends on the ground and in anthropological theory. The disruptive forces of colonialism, cultural arrogance on all sides and waning Western hegemony have contributed to contemporary East African efforts to stabilise culture and governance in democratic ways through rhetoric and popular discourse. However, the very pursuit of "African" or "contemporary" or "21st century" or any other democratic models includes an element of falsehood for reasons related to human biology and history. In this pursuit, cultural factors have interfered with our ability to recognise, analyse and utilise indigenous models. In particular, in spite of all the rhetoric to the contrary, patriarchy has effectively disabled purely democratic praxis.

My goal in this chapter is to take a critical but optimistic look at the ultimate falsehood of pure democracy, and other so called "democratic models". My thesis is that no matter what we humans do or say or plan, we are limited in our momentary understanding because of language, epistemological boundaries, biological programming, and the minute details of our own cultures and histories. My argument, ultimately coloured by feminist commitment, culminates in a cross-cultural critique of "democracy" and efforts to operationalise the concept in reality.

I begin with an introduction to the concept of democracy from an anthropological perspective, and then describe issues that are relevant to the concept of 'liberal democracy' that arise within the four traditional sub-fields within anthropology as a discipline, namely, linguistics, archaeology/paleoanthropology, biological anthropology and cultural/social anthropology. There follows a summary and conclusion which includes a consideration of post-modernist theory within the field of anthropology.

AN INTERDISCIPLINARY ARGUMENT BY A NON-PHILOSOPHER

The two fields which I straddle are based almost entirely on empirical evidence sometimes fitted into abstract theoretical frameworks. As an anthropologist/designer of concrete hands-on products based on empirical evidence, and of systems based on observation, I have spent an adult lifetime making novel connections, a core methodology of both anthropologists and designers. As a participant observer, I have some empirical knowledge of how democracy appears to work and not to work. Designers know that their work involves taking apparently disparate elements and bringing them together in a cohesive and insightful way. This chapter is, in part, about debunking the propagandistic use of the concept of "rule of the people". To do this, we must go back to the very roots of the notion that political formations can be effectively governed by the people, the mob, the community, the elite or any other category of humans.

Using a combination of the Design Paradigm—that of gathering evidence widely for creative problem solving—and walking through the four divisions of anthropological inquiry, namely, linguistics, archaeology, biological and cultural anthropology, I can keep to safe ground in the cross-disciplinary context. While I have taken post-modern theory into account, if there is a theoretical framework or foundation of this work, it is feminism. It is this overarching paradigm that stops us females in our tracks whenever we are tempted to accept patriarchal forms, interpretations, propaganda and mythologies without question. The anecdotal character of many of my examples and citations may lead some readers to imagine that they do not represent a great many similar experiences of some fifty years of participant observation in Kenya. Indeed, accumulated anecdotes constitute 'data' in ethnographic description and analysis of cultures.

LANGUAGE

"Rule of the people" sounds good, but the ancients who coined the term never once imagined that the "people" could include women, children, the landless or the enslaved. Over the millennia, philosophers and other academics have refined this definition and made it complex in many ways (Christiano 2006).

We can identify words of equivalent meaning to the Greek terminology and belief system and other European concepts of democracy in other European languages. Thus far, I have not found terminology attached to the concept of "democracy" in many languages outside the Indo-European orbit. The hallowed dictionary put together by the Former Inter-territorial Language Committee of East Africa in the 1930s defines "democracy" with a description of what it is, not with a single term in Kiswahili (Johnson 1939, 141). The Kiswahili *demokrasia* is clearly a direct loanword from English.

If we are to distinguish "democracy" from other forms of governance, it is important to note that there are democratic mechanisms that are formalised and institutionalised in non-Western systems. This brings us to definitions that, historically, have been applied to forms of government that often purport to be democratic but are not. This should come as no surprise to the global community today. We can list a host of descriptive terms that tell us who is actually in control. Among these are Oligarchy (rule by a small group), Plutocracy (rule by the rich), Phallocracy (control by males), Gerontocracy (rule by old men), Kleptocracy (domination by thieves), "Lootocracy" (a Kenyan colloquial variation of Kleptocracy), Aristocracy (rule by the social or hereditary elite), Meritocracy (control by the professionally worthy), and Theocracy (rule by a religious institution). There are some that are hypothetical, such as Demonocracy (rule by devils, although political oppositions often believe that the parties in power are devils), or aspirational such as Juvenocracy (rule by the young) and Ochlocracy (rule by the mob). There are also those that are commonly de-emphasised, such as Albocracy (rule by white people). Then there are two that we rarely hear of, and which seldom appear in print, cyber space or speech. One is Gynocracy or Gynecocracy (rule by females), and the other is Negrocracy (rule by black people)—a term which does appear on the internet, but with various localised definitions. Terms such as "majority rule" and "rainbow nation" often mask Negrocracy because of other communities' fear and possible flight. Each of these words identifies a segment of the "demos" that is actually in control, thus telling us that "pure demo-cracy" is not necessarily a real thing.

We can then consider re-combinations of some of these terms that further qualify the concept of Democracy. Among these are Parliamentary Democracy, Representative Government, Constitutional Monarchy, and Presidential Democracy. Finally, there is a particularly memorable term used in Cuba in the 1970s to describe that country's political structure: they called it "Dictatorship of the Proletariat" in spite of the de facto Autocratic Dictatorship that was in place at that time (Andres Perez[1], personal communication).

Reading between the lines of all these modified terms for democracy, we can see that there is some clarity in people's understanding of their own systems, and that there is some acknowledgement that pure democracy may not exist. Teaching schoolchildren that they will actually have a say in how their countries and institutions are run when they grow up is an initial propagandistic use of the recombination of terminology and concepts. This happens everywhere and in all times. The continuation of the propagandistic promotion of the concept of democracy has led us all into various historical political disasters such as the one unfolding in the United States in the second half of the second decade of this century. Rhetoric, bravado and falsification have marshalled the notion of American greatness and exceptionalism in manipulating structures that were designed to be democratic by placing a demagogic, aspiring autocrat at the head of the state. This sort of thing can happen anywhere.

ARCHAEOLOGY

If we can include ancient history in archaeology, we know that the concept of rule by the people has origins several centuries before Cleisthenes, who is credited with having been its father in 508 B.C.E. (Davies 1993). At that time the demos did not include women, children, foreigners, the landless, or slaves. At about the same time, the Romans founded a republic, but it lasted only a few years. We can observe the early Greco-Roman religions which featured personal gods, family gods, community gods, task or interest specific gods, and a high god with his family. In these we can see a system that allows considerable freedom in interpretation and application at all levels. This model of dispersed and personalised authority, based on the family, worked well in the relatively containable Greek and Italian peninsulas.

For the last six hundred years or so, Europeans have been aware of the religions of West African peoples, the Yoruba and Dahomean people in particular, that are based on the same paradigm. As the Roman Empire became too extended to govern effectively, the Emperor adopted Christianity as the state religion in part because it was modelled on absolute, centralised authority. Ironically, the spread of the Yoruba and other West and Central Africans throughout the Western Hemisphere as slaves encompassed much more territory and enabled perpetuation of the original model disguised as the centralised, authoritarian paradigm.

As will be seen below, concrete evidence of East African Democracy seldom, if ever, appears in the archaeological record, so we cannot say whether or not it was there. We can, however, take some insights from paleoarchaeology and human paleontology. We must consider, as a major factor in our present existence, the overwhelming importance of predator risk (Jack Harris, personal communication). We cannot discount the segregation/protection of females and the sexual division of labour as connected to group protection from predators. For example, if a menstruating woman were to participate in a hunting expedition, the risk to all the hunters would be increased because predators can smell her more easily than they can detect a non-menstruating woman or a man.

Many of our strategies in creating shelter and in our social organisation are related to reduction, avoidance or elimination of predator risk. The earliest structures put in place by very early humans were crescent shaped, low rows of stones put in place possibly as a wind break, but definitely to give a position from which to take a stand. Women, who could reproduce, and children would have been protected behind these rock barriers. Male protectors could be replaced, but female producers could not (Howell 1966).

Living in the proverbial cave conferred the advantage of reduced predator risk on the inhabitants, especially if there were guards outside whose scent was less likely to attract predators. In places where predator risk is still very real, people know that the smell of smoke on one's body and clothing after leaving a human house is a deterrent to predators of species that have tended to learn to stay away from prey that smells like people. In modern days, wild animals have learned from their predecessors that the smell of smoke from a domestic fire signals more danger to themselves than is worth risking. Wise travellers to deep rural areas in Kenya make sure to spend some time in a house with a wood fire before walking around in the "bush".

The concrete archaeological record, long and widespread as it is, gives us few clues to how societies have been governed other than the existence and remains of palaces for the rulers, slums for the demos, and places of public assembly. Settlement patterns, even those in existence today, can tell us more about economic and class differentiation than about who is actually in power. However, striking differences in the allocation of space and the quality of housing can make some strong suggestions as to the distribution of power and influence. Lamentably, the physical structures seldom reveal the minute details of governance.

An example is the Roman Forum that housed the Senate (from the Latin root that gives us "senile", meaning old and worn out). That building, which still stands, housed the group of Senators who ran the government. The structure does not tell us that the Senators were appointed from the aristocracy. Neither does it tell us that they enjoyed a close relationship with the general populace who surrounded the senate in the extensive markets and public buildings of the Forum. In the standing built environment, we can identify houses of parliament in many countries, but their effective use in democratic processes is not always clear. Huge temples and other places of worship point primarily to mass congregation for worship, but do not necessarily tell us what else, other than prayer, went on or goes on within their walls. Only in a few places of worship is it clear that males and females were segregated, or that females were not allowed in at all. We have no way of knowing what other categories of people were excluded entirely.

Since the invention of writing and the use of drawn, painted and sculpted imagery, we have plenty of evidence to the effect that the societies of the last ten thousand years or so (since the development of settled agriculture) have been centralised, patriarchal and authoritarian, even though pantheons have been gender inclusive. In many of the states and empires of history, the king is somehow connected with God either as an intermediary, a descendent, or as deity itself. This pattern has characterised many political entities from Japan all the way around through Europe, Asia and Africa to Mexico and Peru. When the centralised authority is a female, she is often symbolically represented as a male, as in the case of the Egyptian Queen Hatshepsut, who is represented wearing a false beard.

BIOLOGY

Biologically, all of us humans have, as our nearest relatives, two other primate species—the chimpanzee with whom we share 98 percent of our DNA, and the gorilla with whom we share 97 percent. Most of the developments from lower to higher primates, including bipedalism, upright posture and dexterity (use of hands and fingers), have taken place in East Africa, notably Northern Kenya and Ethiopia, over the last 2 million years (Johanson 1981; Leakey 1994). Some of the sources of valuable insights are the ever-growing body of wildlife cinematography focused on primate behaviour and the fast growing literature, both scientific and popular, on human body language and small group social organisation (Morris 1977; Pease 2004). The basic model among the higher primates is that groups form around a senior, dominant male who controls and directs the females and children, while the older juvenile males and young adult males leave the troop, at least temporarily (Jolly 1972, 91–121; Davidson 1996).

These mammals form families, extended families, troops, and we humans do all three. It is the process of troop formation and its outcomes that informs my understanding of democracy. Between 1988 and 2013, I served at various times as administrator and academic advisor for student exchange programmes in Kenya. The groups that I worked with were composed of students from the United States who had an interest in Africa, and especially Kenya. They were drawn from different universities and colleges that fed into several one or two semester programs organized by specific institutions in Kenya. The result was that students with similar interests were thrust together for the first time, either at the airport as they were departing for Kenya, or on their first day in the country. About eighty percent of these students were female, while about five percent were either "non-white" or non-American. The thrusting together of new faces, along with composition of extreme gender and minority imbalance, probably generated the democratic or undemocratic responses that we administrators saw.

What we were able to observe was a troop-like formation with lines of dominance, submission, exclusion, and social ranking firmly in place within the first hours of the students' coming together. The basic structure consisted of an Alpha male, a sub-dominant male, as well as submissive males and females who followed the Alpha male. Variations on this theme and impacts on our administration of the program were as interesting as watching the basic structure play itself out.

Our most difficult administrative experience was with an all-female group, because they would be constantly bickering and bothering the administrators. The next most challenging administrative experience was with a group where the aspiring sub-dominant male could neither share with, nor take power from, the Alpha. In one rare group there were two equal dominant males who smoothly and amicably shared decision-making and control. In another group there was a sub-dominant male whose failed attempts to take control of the group appeared to be the source of frustrations in the group. There was often a dominant female who aligned with the Alpha male in keeping the sub-troops of females in line. Another group had a single male who ran the show well but excluded a dominant female from matters concerning the group; it was apparent that he could not tolerate her. She left the programme halfway through the semester. We were not sure why she left. What we know of troop dynamics is that members may temporarily or permanently expel a member, but in this case those expelled had to remain attached because of the institutional structure of their programmes. Finally, one group fragmented into small clusters because of the overbearing behavior of one female who managed to wrest control and become the Alpha. Several of the fragments actually explained to the administrators that they left the larger group to get away from her and her small loyal group which included both the females and a very submissive male.

The point is that in spite of what we claim to do, we humans tend to centralize ourselves around a dominant male with many variations on the basic structure. One of the institutions that the groups came from was run by Quakers using Quaker principles of equality and consensus. Although all the student groups had ostensibly democratic components in their programmes, it was particularly interesting to observe those in the Quaker groups—they acted within their equality and consensus framework, while often struggling in the dominance/submission continuum among both males and females. At a point of challenge of the Alpha in a Quaker group, we were able to observe the "cheerleader" phenomenon when the females broke into small groups and physically arranged themselves behind the contesting males in the struggle, much to our surprise and to the validation of Allison Jolly (1972, 188).

CULTURAL/SOCIAL ANTHROPOLOGY

The observational and written analysis of human and other primate behaviour, including our material remains and our languages, can be taken into account as we examine, in not very great detail, the tiny tip of the social and cultural iceberg. Dealing with the social and cultural aspects of "democracy" would take a whole library and several lifetimes of study and writing by many scholars. Let me focus on democratic forms in my native land of the United States, and in Kenya as instances of how the concept of democracy works and does not work.

The Anglophone peoples take great pride in the moment in history when the evil King John was forced to sign the Magna Carta in 1215, a document which decreed his sharing of power and authority with the nobles. They seldom mention that power was shared only with a relatively small aristocracy and a few churchmen to the continuing neglect of the demos.

So dedicated were the Anglophones and many other Europeans to their mitigated and socially hierarchical form of parliamentary democracy that they imposed it on all the peoples they colonised, even on those who already had kingdoms in place. Where they encountered small kingdoms as in West, Central, and Southern Africa, they incorporated these into larger colonial entities, later to become nation-states. This has caused unending grief for the peoples who had only weak or no kingships, but who were swept with the same broom into contrived modern nation-states, Uganda being a striking example.

The Americans, in framing their constitution, wisely took the lead of the Iroquois people, by adopting a federal system—a model that was unknown in Europe in the 1700s. This gave our states, most of which are bigger in territory than most of the nation-states of Europe, a degree of autonomy within, with a firm connection to the whole federation, which they called the United States of America. Having worked with the British unitary system for many years, Kenyans, in their 2010 constitution, adopted some aspects of the

American structure through devolution of power and bestowing a degree of autonomy on the counties newly converted from the old districts.

Why is all this important to Kenyans? The answer is simply because in many East African societies, there were and still are democratic structures that, in common with the non-African democracies, ignore or exclude large swaths of the population while functioning in structurally, popularly and vocally democratic ways. The biggest excluded swath is females—those who may have de jure access to power but have little or no de facto voice or input in any decision making, and who are constrained by traditions that deny them the right to spiritual, economic or social independence.

If, setting aside the deficit status of females, we can consider democracy and centralisation as diametric opposites, we can observe a constant tension between the dispersal of power and authority against their concentration in the hands of a single person or delineated group.

In order to demonstrate the existence and nature of structural democratic forms in East Africa, I focus on the Maasai, presently of Narok and Kajiado Counties and a large part of Northern Tanzania (Jacobs 1965; Galaty 1977; Klumpp 1987; Pido 1989).

Several centuries ago, the people who would become the Maasai constituted themselves orally and structurally to prevent centralisation of authority and control, while protecting their territorial, cultural, social, economic, environmental, and individual integrity. They did this by consensus in the division of territory into Enaiposha, the cool wet highlands and Ol Kaputiei, the hot dry lowlands. Then they divided the vast expanses of grazing land into territories designated for their major political units called Sections in English, Iloshon in Maa. Ol Kaputiei and Enaiposha formed coalitions of Iloshon, meaning "plateaus or grazing territories" designated by the colours white and black. While these political entities (Iloshon) operate independently of one another, they are joined within the two coalitions, Enaiposha and Ol Kaputiei, just as the Iroquois Five Nations were (Beauchamp 1905), and the fifty states of the United States are now. Political and geographical separation required mechanisms for flexible unification and dispersal. Five exogamous clans were formed and required to send members to each of the eleven Iloshon, thus dispersing kinsmen everywhere in Maasailand. Any Maasai, travelling to any other part of Maasailand, can identify clansmen and count on their support. Clans could not isolate themselves and accumulate power within any Olosho because they were required to be exogamous. Thus, there is constant mixing of people who belong to their father's clan, but who also know who their mother's clansmen are (Klumpp 1987, 55).

As a further measure to ensure non-centralisation and non-concentration of power, the early Maasai, who certainly had an age grade system in place beforehand, now established corporate, time-bounded age sets. Unlike the Samburu and many other communities who initiate a steady stream of boys into warrior-hood, the Maasai set time limits that delimited, fixed and named sets of young men who remained as corporate entities for the rest of their lives. This ensured that even if a traveller could not locate a clansman to help him, he would definitely find men of his own age who shared his membership in one, clearly defined age set. Authority and power to make decisions for the whole unit—Clan, Section, or Coalition—was vested in the sitting set of Senior Elders and was reinforced by their supervision of the ceremonial cycle through which subsequent generations were recruited and groomed for corporate leadership (Klumpp 1987, 59).

This system worked very well in protecting the integrity, ecosystems, and people of Maasai territory right up until the day some ignorant intruders from a constitutional monarchy walked in looking for a king, queen, or other head of a centralised state. They were unable to deal with diffused authority, so they categorised the Maasai as "savages", although they were undeniably "noble" as well. Then, culture-bound, ethnocentric, and in need of a recognizable hierarchy, they appointed "chiefs", and the rest is well known history.

Originally, democratic behaviour among the Maasai was self-designed, self-imposed, purpose driven, and structural both vertical in the passage of individuals through life and horizontal in space. It was democracy dominated by the senior males balanced and decentralised through spatially lateral distribution of their authority. This system was reinforced by consensus of old and young, and by economic sanctions (deprivation of cattle) as well as supernatural sanctions against those who did not comply. It also excluded females de jure as well as de facto.

In sharp contrast to the structural democracy of a single East African community, we can also consider the more vocal, frenetic, and openly active and participatory democracy of the United States Building on a long history of print media involvement in politics and an education system designed to increase sophisticated judgment by the electorate but which is actually used to lull them into submission, the additional electronic media have enabled Americans for over a century to make a lot of noise in selecting their leaders. In school we were taught that the electoral college was put in place to protect the rural states with small populations from dominance by the urbanised ones with high populations. In the wake of the 2016 election, even the most gullible of Americans now knows that the electoral college was devised to preserve the dominance of white racial minorities in states with large, recently emancipated black populations.

DISCUSSION

Are we now in a position to do as the Maasai did and build in structures that will ensure more equitable distribution of power, authority and participation? Maasai religion protects the integrity of the grassland savannah ecosystem in all its variations. The best efforts to introduce horizontal features to Kenyan democracy through devolution to the counties are still being tested. Can citizens of various self-professing democratic countries put in place protections for future generations that will prevent the misappropriation of power by demagogues or groups of bullies? For example, how can we in Kenya prevent the development of an entrenched aristocracy as happened so long ago in Europe? Will we need supernatural sanction to do that?

The mere existence of supernatural sanction is worthy of investigation. People follow injurious rules out of fear for the fate of their souls after they die, or out of fear of ancestral punishment on their succeeding generations. When supernatural authority is dispersed there is some leeway to negotiate eternal damnation, but when it is unitary and uncompromising, people have few choices. How can any of this work in the search for true democracy in Africa? For example, we know that according to a belief widespread among Nilotes, Bantus and others, women and children risk all manner of supernatural devastation if they dare to eat chickens or eggs, those tasty small packages of protein that men eat just to prevent them from going to waste.

When we have to face up to the intensely anti-female systems of East Africa, we are forced to look at the anti-female dysfunction of non-African systems as well. We can link this anti-female dysfunction to primate troop structure and to my observation of mixed-gender and single-gender groups of American students. We must also remind ourselves that in only two primate species do males universally and constantly harass females for no apparent reason other than genetics. One is chimpanzees, the other is us humans (see Nat Geo n.d.).

It is noteworthy that in all nations and all times, rules are set that effectively exclude females from political participation with the flimsiest of excuses. The Egyptian parliament put a law into place several years back in which women are allowed to participate in "public life" only after they have taken care of their families. No parallel law exists for men. I spent some time with a neighbour in Lemek, Narok District, who had been raped by two men on her way home from a ceremony. When she took the matter to her local gerontocrats, they judged that she had been drunk so it was in order, and that she had not said *no* correctly, so, in reality, it was not a rape. The elders were bending the customary system to benefit the woman's attackers. If women cannot be treated fairly by the gerontocrats in the wake of personal injury, how can we expect them to be included in political processes?

Note that many of the people who decided not to vote for Hillary Clinton in 2016 were liberal female members of the Democratic Party. To understand this phenomenon, we can go back to troop dynamics and the propensity of female humans to single out one of their number for vicious persecution to the detriment of all (Jolly 1972). This phenomenon is widely reported in the various national presses, including Kenya, and was widely discussed in the mass media in the wake of the American presidential election of 2016. It is a well-documented and widely experienced phenomenon of polygynous families.

On 1 May 2017, Al Jazeera TV news featured a story about a Ugandan lady named Fatuma who was running for office. She was violently stripped naked in public by a mixed male and female group of police. How many male candidates have any of us ever seen or heard of who were stripped naked just for standing for public office?

Women who excel or hold high positions are often accused of sexual misconduct. Many of us will recall Idi Amin's dismissal of his Minister for Foreign Affairs, Elizabeth Bagaya, because he claimed that she had had sex with a French diplomat in a public toilet in one of the airports near Paris. In Kenya, in keeping with a widespread and time-tested tradition, female political candidates have been treated to physical and sexual violence and have been accused of sexual misconduct—an accusation that is seldom, if ever, voiced for male candidates.

Highly motivated and constructively active Kenyan women are routinely labelled "*malaya*", meaning "prostitute" in Kiswahili.

One measure of female competence in public life is the accusation, whispered furtively by people "in the know", that so and so is in the habit of having sex in public toilets. We know the woman must be excellent in her work when she is not only accused of sex in public toilets but also sex "with strangers" in public toilets. Not so ironically, women who take leadership roles, whether in the family, community or the nation are often accused of diluting male sexuality. The term for this kind of woman in New York Yiddish is "*ballebusta*", which means "breaker of testicles". In sharp contrast to such pejorative descriptions, in English and a number of other languages, the term for a man who excels in leadership is "hero".

Exclusion of females is not always consciously done. Kenya's first feature-length dramatic film, *Kolormask*, was released in December 1985, just a few days before the death of S. M. Otieno triggered nationwide introspection on the role and status of women. Written, produced and directed by Kenyan Sao Gamba, the movie was a polemic for male supremacy, yet Gamba himself was certain that it was about the good and bad in people regardless of their race or culture. He saw his film as a demonstration and defence of African culture (Sao Gamba: personal communication).

The Constitution of Kenya 2010 requires that neither gender occupies more than two-thirds of appointive and elective positions at the national and county levels. In partial compliance with this provision, the government has appointed a number of competent females to high public offices. However, due to a parliament with an overwhelming male majority, the constitutional provision is yet to be operationalised through an enabling piece of subsidiary legislation. The deleterious effect of the male-dominated parliament was also graphically illustrated when, in 2014, the legislators tried to pass the Marriage Act with a provision enabling Kenyan men to marry as many wives as they wanted without so much as informing any of them of the others' existence. Nevertheless, the provision was later revised to allow polygyny only for Islamic and African customary marriages (Republic of Kenya 2014).

Without dwelling on any more of the details of anti-feminism and all its insidious variations in "democracies", it is this very limitation and exclusion that gives the ultimate lie to any and all claims of democracy by anyone. At least the churches try to argue that the Adam and Eve story is not an indictment of women, and to convince their congregants that God gave women special status and special powers that were too good or big to be included in decision making or in the leadership of their communities.

Without the full inclusion of women, there can be nothing that we dare to call "democracy". All the propaganda and persuasive rhetoric that our male counterparts can muster could work only when women had no alternatives because of male control of the means of production. Those days are over. Even the threat of supernatural sanction in the form of God and/or the ancestors will not work anymore.

Having said this, those of us who are old enough or observant enough will know about the rapid erosion of women's traditional rights with the bestowal of title deeds on men, and especially the destruction of women's secret societies that enabled symmetry of power with men if not full equality with them. They are still known in West Africa (Jedrej 1990; Phillips 1995) but are very rarely mentioned or acknowledged in Kenya. In the first few decades of the national women's organisation Maendeleo ya Wanawake (MYWO), many Kenyan communities still had something similar. Observers who could not figure out why MYWO thrived in some parts of the country while it withered in others were failing to recognise its function as an overlay on pre-existing structures that had functioned to uphold the integrity and rights of women in their ethnic communities in deep history. The colonial failure to recognise these low-key but very powerful organisations was based on their absence in European cultures. It was only because of the extreme tenacity of West African women's societies that I ever thought of looking for them in East Africa, or of extrapolating their existence from observational data and many verbal mentions collected over a long time and quietly verified by senior women.

CONCLUSION

Carrot-and-stick propaganda, conceptual social marketing of appealing ideas, ascription of culpability to females or people with darker skins are all arbitrary and are used to lead the masses to believe that they have some control. Though the masses may be participating, it would be difficult to find a nation-state where the proletariat really does dictate. If we consider democracy and centralisation as diametric opposites, we can observe a constant tension between the dispersal of power and authority against concentration in the hands of a single person or delineated group. There is also a constant tension between inclusion and exclusion. Further, there is a constant stream of propagandistic rhetoric at all levels that is intended to lead people to believe that the place they occupy is the right one, and that whatever they are doing is contributory in a way that supports their own best interests.

I am picking on all concepts of democracy, not just the African ones. African models of democracy are no more or less democratic than others. Several writers advocate that 'cultural realities' be taken into account when developing alternatives to liberal democracy for twenty-first-century Africa. To a female reader, this smacks of male efforts to oppress women with a smile on everybody's faces, which was what Gamba did in *Kolormask* without realising it. Of course, it is entirely possible that 'cultural realities' means that the entry of many women into democratic participation at all levels from the household to the top is stimulating more inclusive thought and contemplation in our male counterparts.

The bottom line is that we are biologically programmed to be autocratic, phallocratic, and hierarchical. All our efforts at creating and maintaining democratic, gender-neutral, and non-hierarchical organisations are struggles against biology. Sometimes we win and sometimes we lose, but we can never abandon our struggle to become the kind of humans we like to think we are.

NOTE

1. Andres Perez was my Cuban classmate at Columbia University in the mid 1970s who was deeply dedicated to the Chinese-Cuban communist model.

REFERENCES

Beauchamp, William Martin. 1905. *A History of the New York Iroquois*. Albany: New York State Education Department.
Christiano, Tom. 2006. "Democracy". Zalta, Edward N. ed. *Stanford Encyclopedia of Philosophy*. https://plato.stanford.edu/entries/democracy/.
Davidson, Bruce. 1996. *Mountain Gorilla: A Shattered Kingdom*. a documentary film. London: ITN Source.
Davies, J. K. 1993. *Democracy and Classical Greece*. Cambridge, MA: Harvard University Press.
Galaty, John. 1977. "In the Pastoral Image: The Symbolic Dynamics of Maasai Identity". Ph.D. Thesis, Mc Gill University, Montreal.
Howell, F. Clark. 1966. *Early Man*. New York: Time-Life Books.
Jacobs, Alan. 1965. "The Traditional Political System of the Pastoral Maasai". Ph.D. Thesis, Nuffield College, Oxford.
Jedrej, M.C. 1990. "Structural Aspects of a West African Secret Society". *Ethnologische Zeitschrift*, Vol. 1, pp. 133–42.
Jolly, Allison. 1972. *The Evolution of Primate Behavior*. New York: Macmillan Company.
Johanson, Donald, and Maitland Edey. 1981. *Lucy: The Beginnings of Humankind*. St Albans: Granada.
Johnson, Fredrick. 1939. *A Standard Swahili-English, English-Swahili Dictionary*. N.P.: The Former Inter-territorial Language Committee of East Africa.
Klumpp, Donna. 1987. "Maasai Art and Society: Age and Sex, Time and Space, Cash and Cattle". Unpublished Ph.D. Thesis at Columbia University, New York.
Leakey, Richard E. 1994. *The Origin of Humankind*. Science Masters Series. New York: Basic Books.
Morris, Desmond. 1977. *Man Watching*. New York: Harry Abrams.
Nat Geo Wild. n.d. "Wild Congo". https://www.youtube.com/watch?v=B363LoZneiE.
Pease, Allan, and Barbara Pease. 2004. *The Definitive Book of Body Language*. London: Orion Books Ltd.
Phillips, Ruth. B. 1995. *Representing Woman: Sande Masquerades of the Mende of Sierra Leone*. Los Angeles: UCLA Fowler Museum of Cultural History.
Pido, Donna. 1989. "Ethnic Identity and Color Code: The Maasai Center and Periphery". Paper presented to the Eighth Triennial Symposium on African Art, Washington D.C., 15–17 June.
Republic of Kenya. 2014. "The Marriage Act". Nairobi: Government Printer.

Chapter Six

Gender-Sensitive Followership in Africa

The Case of Uganda

Robinah S. Nakabo

Leadership rather than followership predominates in discussions about democracy. It is easy to point fingers at those holding leadership positions as the cause of all failures in the workings of democracy, but this ignores the other side of the coin—followership. In Africa, especially, followers place their leaders above all other human beings, and most times above the law—something that springs from socialisation. This undermines liberal democratic principles such as accountability, participation, and the rule of law. As such, we might assume that liberal democracy is not suitable for Africa, and that it is therefore reasonable to look back in search of what is truly African democracy. However, how does African democracy look like after all the interferences and intercultural exchanges? Both followership and leadership are bound to be affected by the changes in education, technological advancements, and the current massive volume of information, all of which catalyse intercultural exchanges.

I argue in this chapter that the neglecting of followership in many patriarchal African societies is the missing link in efforts to address the challenges of democratisation in the continent. I have divided the chapter into two main sections. In the first of the two, which follows this introductory one, I reflect on the meaning of followership, the classification of followership, and the crucial role of followership in enhancing democratisation in Africa. In the second, I examine the socialisation of followership in Africa, with special reference to Uganda. I conclude that Uganda in particular, and African states at large, do not need to jetison liberal democracy in the twenty-first century, but rather to raise exemplary, gender-sensitive followership.

FOLLOWERSHIP: MEANING, CLASSIFICATION, ROLES, AND PREPARATION FOR LIBERAL DEMOCRACY

Literature on followership and leadership mainly proceeds from the recognition that followership has been neglected (see for examples Bjugstand 2006; Kelley 1988; 2008). Some authors urge that discussions on leadership be handled side by side with those on followership, as separating them results in incomplete accounts of both. For instance, Yung and Tsai (2013) refer to followership as a mirror image of leadership. Grit (2011) avers that resources are wasted if focus is placed on creating "perfect" leadership but sustaining "flawed" followership.

In his review of Kellerman's *Followership: How Followers Are Creating Change, and Changing Leaders* (2008), Harle (2009) highlights the symbiotic relationship between followership and leadership. Social psychologists inform us that even when groups desire to be without leaders, followership and leadership simply emerge (Vugt 2006). This is enough reason to jointly reflect on them—they have a mutual purpose, and together move institutions forward (Chaleff 1995; Jerry II 2013). In the foreword to *The Art of Followership* (Riggio, Chaleff and Lipman-Blumen eds. 2008), MacGregor Burns notes that the bifurcation of followership and leadership was never necessary. In his psychoanalytic discussion of the difference between followers and leaders, Cluley (2008) argues that the difference between these two terms is illusory. Thus it is prudent to jointly consider followership and leadership with clear roles (Kelley 2008), abilities and responses (Maroosis 2008) in order to adapt to new times (Chaleff 1995; Howell 2008; Rost 2008; Stech 2008).

THE MEANING OF FOLLOWERSHIP

Followership has generally had negative connotations. As a result, several organisations focus on leadership traits, and put substantial effort into developing and strengthening leaders (Kellerman 2008). Followership and leadership do not run parallel to each other; rather, they are interlinked, often switching roles (Howell & Mendez 2008; Stech 2008). The word "Follower", from the Old High German word *Follaziohan*, etymologically means "to assist, succour, or minister to" (Eui-Jung 2012, 9). In an attempt to clarify the meaning of "followership", Rost (2008) distinguishes it from followers. He notes that, like most words with the suffix "ship", it denotes an ongoing process: "Followership is what followers do when they follow" (Rost 2008, 54). However, Rost (2008) points out that to look at followership in this fashion is to uphold the industrial view of followership and leadership. He therefore contends: "Followership is an outmoded concept that is dysfunctional and even destructive in a post-industrial world. Followership, as a concept, is out of touch with the world we live in" (Rost 2008, 56). Due to the fact that many of his respondents negatively perceived "followership", Rost resolved to use "collaboration" instead.

Rost's view that followership is a dysfunctional and outmoded concept, one that is disruptive in a post-industrial era, poses a challenge in the African context. In contrast to Rost's context, most African countries are in the process of industrialisation. This being so, is it justifiable for them to join in banishing followership as a concept? At what cost is Africa continuing to embrace the industrial view of followership and leadership? How is this affecting the quality of leadership? Are African peoples willing to embrace the idea of questioning the industrial view of followership and leadership? What would it mean for African leaders to accept that followers are collaborators? Are the various African cultures compatible with this view? There is need for research to answer these questions exhaustively. Whatever the case, there is need to examine the African understanding of followership, and how it might be affecting the growth of the kind of democratic leadership that many Africans yearn for. The fact is that leadership without followership results in disappointment.

For Barbara Kellerman (2008), followers are as important as leaders, if not more important. Nevertheless, Kellerman (2008) also views followership as a response by subordinates to the leader's directives. This is inconsistent with the importance she assigns to followership; for if followership is as important as leadership, or even possibly more important, there cannot be a subservient relationship between leaders and followers. I agree with Kellerman on the crucial place of followership because the nature of followers has a direct impact on leadership, because if followers choose to remain aloof or to isolate themselves, there cannot be leadership. Followers must be physically and psychologically present for a meaningful relationship of followership and leadership to flourish. Yet with or without leadership, common interests can motivate individuals to act collectively. Thus Kellerman's view that followership is a response to a leader's directives is very limiting. I also do not agree with Kellerman that the quality of followership depends on the quality of leadership. The more correct position, in my view, is that the dialectical relationship between the two shapes them both.

Followership sets the pace for leadership because every new leader, having been first moulded within a particular context as a follower, tries out his or her leadership style with keen interest on how those occupying the position of followers respond. Thus the leader is like a person testing the depth of a pool of water by dipping in his or her leg as far as the water allows. He or she can only rest his or her foot if the pool provides supportive ground. The person might appear to be superior to the inanimate water, but the water has the power to kill him or her if he or she carelessly goes into it. The water here represents the nature of followership—whoever assumes leadership needs to have learnt the art of followership first—its context, and how to listen to its communication. Death here might not be physical but rather psychological, moral or social.

The point of the analogy of the pool of water in the previous paragraph is that although, by habit of mind, many people tend to conceive of followership as inferior to leadership, it has implicit power unmatched by any unskilled leadership type—it has its own unstated rules (which may be contextual) that cannot be ignored. As such, successful leadership is that which has learnt well how to interpret communication from followership. In contrast to the view that leaders succeed when they teach their followers both how to lead and to follow, I subscribe to the view that "leadership is the property and consequence of a community rather than the property and consequence of an individual leader" (Grit 2011, 7). The community here represents the followers who produce and sustain leadership.

According to Maroosis (2008, 21), "followership is acting properly and well in a given situation". Of course "properly", "well", and "situation" can be defined relatively, and this is likely to give rise to ambiguity, but through these terms Maroosis emphasises that followership ought not to be characterised by passivity. Maroosis, like Chaleff (1995 and 2008), also notes that just like leadership, followership ought to possess certain abilities that catalyse both effective followership and leadership. For instance, Chaleff writes that both followers and leaders need to be courageous, because it might be attractive to be a leader, but to trust someone enough to follow him or her requires courage, and hence it is more honorable to follow than to lead. In other words, for autonomous individuals to allow another to make decisions on their behalf requires substantial inner strength, as it involves subjecting their wills to his or hers. Due to the humility involved, it is more honourable to follow than to lead.

Furthermore, Attridge asserts that "good followership is more vital to a democracy than excessive leadership" (Attridge 1949, 12; cited in Yung 2013, 48). The actions that ensue from the courage of both followers and leaders prepare them for the mutual learning exchange between them (Hollander 1992, cited in Yung 2013, 48). Maroosis (2008, 18) refers to the desirable qualities that equip both followers and leaders to correctly do what different situations demand as "response-abilities". They aid followers and leaders to do "first things first", which in this context are "the moral things" (Maroosis

2008, 21). Maroosis contends that followers and leaders must do the right things (things that are efficient and effective) and say the right words (Maroosis 2008).

Blame can no longer be placed on leadership alone: followers have a moral duty to create a conducive environment for a healthy followership-leadership relationship. In his closing remarks at the conference in which this chapter was first presented, the host chair of the conference, Dr. Reginald Oduor, directed the delegates' attention to Étienne de la Boétie's view that tyranny would come to an end if those who submit to it stopped doing so (Oduor 2017). Dr. Oduor's remarks were in the context of the total liberation of Africa from Western imperialism, highlighting the fact that Western imperialism appropriates whatever it uses to exploit Africa from Africa itself. Nevertheless, his observation is relevant to the point of this chapter, namely, that if, in a liberal democracy, leaders are not delivering what is expected of them, followers are accomplices in the failure.

CLASSIFICATION OF FOLLOWERSHIP

Followership theorists have proposed different ways of classifying followers on the basis of their behavior and thinking patterns. Kelley (2008) points out that followers' personalities, culture, upbringing, education, peer pressure, and sometimes context, all contribute to moulding, though not determining, individual followership styles. Kelley (2008) classifies followers thus:

1. Sheep, who are passive, dependent, and uncritical thinkers;
2. Yes people, always at the leader's side, ready to do anything—conformists, dependent and uncritical;
3. Alienated (Isolated), who feel discriminated against, but can think independently and critically;
4. Pragmatists, who first culculate the benefits of performing an action before making a decision for or against it;
5. Star followers, who think independently, are active and engaged, question and criticise leadership. Some call these Exemplary followers (Kellerman 2008) or courageous followers (Chaleff 1995; 2008).

Kellerman (2008) classifies followers into isolates (similar to "alienated"), bystanders (simply observe with no action), participants (engaging), activists (can work hard for or against leaders), and diehards (fanatics who can willingly lay down their lives for their leaders).

However, there is need to critically examine various classifications of followership with cultural and gender differences in mind. For instance, should we consider the same classifications in African contexts? What about women and men in African societies? Can they also be categorised in the same way if we take into consideration the kind of socialisation in different cultural settings?

If we are to understand why liberal democracy is problematic in Africa (and I do agree that it is), we need to shift our focus from leadership traits to followership traits in African contexts, in the hope of raising pertinent questions touching on a persistent problem. The roles that followership plays range from partners, collaborators, informants, the moulding of good leadership, and when necessary, rising to the challenge of leadership. According to Chaleff (1995, 1), "leaders rarely use their power wisely or effectively over long periods unless they are supported by followers who have the stature to help them do so". This help comes through communication, specifically feedback to leadership. In the introduction to *The Art of Followership: How Great Followers Create Great Leaders and Organisations*, Benis emphatically writes: "if I had to reduce the responsibilities of a good follower to a single rule, it would be to speak truth to power" (Benis in Riggio, Chaleff and Lipman-Blumen eds. 2008, p. xxv). By far this seems to be the critical role of followership. However, unless the environment is conducive to followership playing this role, all we can expect is "sheep" and "yes-people" who allow dictatorship to thrive instead of keeping it in check in order for liberal democracy to thrive. Chaleff (2008, 67–87) therefore advocates for courageous followership to counter leadership that resembles Saddam Hussein's style, which he (Chaleff) uses to illustrate his point.

FOLLOWERSHIP FOR LIBERAL DEMOCRATIC LEADERSHIP

One would wonder why there is a shift from focusing on leadership to followership in achieving liberal democracy. Kelley (2008) notes that focusing on leadership worked well for the industrial era, where it was simply required of followership that it manifests obedience in carrying out assigned tasks. After his earlier work, *In Praise of Followership* (1988), Kelley (1992) reiterated the importance of followership, drawing attention to the danger of inordinate focus on leadership. Kellerman (2008) designed a followership course in her leadership training program on the basis that leadership needs followership, and yet followership can do without leadership.

The fact that followers can do without leaders is illustrated in *The Courageous Follower: Standing up to and for Our Leaders* (Chaleff 1995), and is dramatised in a film titled *Minions* (Coffin and Balda 2015) which shows some small creatures desperate to have a hero—a being different from them to be their leader. The irony is that in their attempt to identify such a being, they organise themselves successfully on their own, but insist on finding someone who is unlike them, thereby confirming that effective followership gives rise to effective leadership. The minions master the art of following— they so desire to follow that leadership emerges spontaneously from amongst themselves. The minions exemplify the fact that rather than followership revolving aroung leadership, both followership and leadership revolve around a single purpose. Indeed, the Minions end up killing the leaders themselves (unknowingly, of course), indicating the power that followership has over leadership.

Other authors remind us of the culturally plural nature of contemporary societies which renders old leadership models irrelevant. For instance, Chaleff (1995, 2) observes that we need to transcend "authoritarian models that strip followers of accountability". Whereas leaders are vital to the day-to-day running of organisations, to imagine that the rest must follow without asking questions is problematic. This is due to the fact that it is pretentious for followers to be blind to the wrongs that the leaders commit and to blow their leaders' successes out of proportion. With advancements in the flow of information, a healthy exchange between followers and leaders is imperative.

What does neglecting followership mean for Africa? Various commentators on African politics complain that liberal democracy is not working (Amukugo 2013), or that it is not meant for Africans (Tar 2010). Indeed, the conference for which I originally wrote this chapter was convened to search for indigenous African models of democracy because, allegedly, liberal democracy is alien to Africans. However, my view is that the challenge is that Africa has not awoken to the fact that leadership might not be the problem, but rather followership—that Leadership is what followership has moulded it to be. Cluley (2008) concluded that it is the psychology within groups (followers) that pushes the leaders to appear individualistic through the group's idealisation and identification processes. Apparently, these two processes are important in keeping followers together, as they idealise the leader and identify with him or her. However, African leaders have opportunistically misused this phenomenon to dehumanise their followers.

Nevertheless, the failure of liberal democracy in Africa ought not to be blamed exclusively on the leadership, because the followership is an accomplice in the abuse. Why, for example, should we blame Mobutu Sese Seko, who ruled the Congo for over thirty years? (Leon 2010, 2). Why should we condemn the incumbent President Yoweri Museveni of Uganda, who has also ruled for more than thirty years, and yet during the 1990s he was hailed for denouncing African presidents for staying in power for too long? If such leaders have followership around them, what are they (the followers) doing? Are they simply "sheep" or "yes-people"—without independent and critical minds? Why does Africa fail to raise a strong, independent and critical followership to keep African leadership in check, thereby nurturing liberal democracy? In the next section, I attempt to provide possible answers to these questions, although there is need for further research into this phenomenon.

SOCIALISATION OF FOLLOWERSHIP IN AFRICA: THE CASE OF UGANDA

In order to understand why followership is neglected in Africa, we need to take a close look at the family, formal education, culture, and politics. It is in the family that most informal training of the young takes place. In addition, most African societies are built on a partriarchal ideology, which means that boys grow up in families where they enjoy higher status than girls. As boys are socialised to be leaders with independent and critical frames of mind that equip them to make important decisions, girls are socialised to be followers, dependent and to say "yes" to directives. It is not accidental, therefore, that such simple matters as disciplined driving become complex, creating unnecessary traffic jams in African cities. Whereas there might be other causes for the jams, such as an increasing number of people owning cars without a corresponding expansion of the roads, one major cause of the jams is that many male drivers come from their homes with the attitude that they are more important than other road users, resulting in a clash of egos and the consequent clogged roads.

It is also in families that feminisation of followership is introduced and concretised. Girls and women are socialised to believe that they are simply passive followers—they are rewarded when they do not speak back to their husbands, or when they do not show their husbands that they know better in many, if not all, situations. Many cannot dare say anything when they find their husbands in error, or even make decisions concerning their sexuality and health because society has given this role to men. Thus, although hierarchy in the family has some advantage in that it maintains peace, that peace is myopic if it is devoid of moments of truth-telling. This feminisation of followership in Africa causes leadership to be equally faulty. If a wife cannot participate actively in keeping the husband's power in check, the results are ills such as unwanted pregnancies, sexually transmitted diseases, family economic crises, orphaned children, street children, child abuse, and domestic violence. Research by Morton et al. (2012) on effects of family leadership styles and adolescent dietery behavior indicates that leadership at this level ought to be approached with great care, as it has a significant impact on the children's decision making abilities when they attain adulthood. It is therefore in the family that the grooming of blind followership takes place. The focus on leadership at the expense of followership hinders the growth of democratic family relations and is carried forward into other levels of society.

If the majority of families in Uganda raise more than half of its citizenry as "sheep" or "yes" followers, and the rest as potential leaders, there is definitely a problem with followership and therefore leadership, thereby hindering liberal democracy from taking root in the country. This is because power hungry, egocentric males compete for the few available leadership positions. With women as mothers, wives or sisters simply looking on, the situation is not helped at all. This is not to say that there are no women who have transcended this blind followership attitude, but the patriarchal nature of African societies does not encourage the active engagement of women in society. The roles stereotypically assigned to girls as they are growing up cannot cultivate independence and critical thinking, both of which are ingredients of courageous, star or exemplary followership. The few women who are raised to be leaders appropriate that male egocentric model instead of coming up with a distinct style for women that tones down men's egocentricism in order to keep each other in check. Thus, socialisation at the family level ought to be transformed to align it to current demands.

However, the situation is slowly changing: we are seeing many families beginning to raise their girls as leaders. Nevertheless, whereas it is advantageous to have female leadership, socialising all children to be leaders is problematic. All children ought to be raised first as followers. Being a follower is not admired much because it is associated with negative stereotypical feminine characteristics that are not valued in a patriarchal setting. Stech (2008) highlights a number of synonyms of the word "follow", including "to depend", "be inferior", "subordinate", "conforming", and "compliant", all of which denote undesirable traits for those who see themselves as born leaders. However, a family ought to provide for both boys and girls to be star followers. The current feminist debate should also shift focus from empowering the girlchild, which favors one gender, to empowering exemplary followership for democracy in families. This might sound utopian, but it can be tried out through action research and evaluation (Patton 2002), and the journey has already begun, although outside Africa, as I earlier indicated in works by Chaleff (1995), Kelley (2008), and Kellerman (2008), among others.

The fact is that we are all followers. As Kellerman (2008) notes, everyone starts out as a follower, even though we might not recognise this. Williams and Miller (2002, cited in Bjugstand 2006, 304) found out that many executives are actually followers, although they do not admit it due to the stigma attached to followership. Even leaders are following some purpose which they have to make clear to the followers, so that they can together help each other to pursue it (see, for examples, Chaleff 1995; Stech 2008; Maroosis 2008). Warren Benis correctly observed that "the moment when each of us realises he or she is mostly a follower, not a leader, is a genuine developmental milestone" (Benis 2008, pp. xxiii–xxiv).

Besides, since leadership takes only a handful from the entire population, is it not better to first develop exemplary followership, after which leadership can emerge out of it? The challenge in Africa is that many who make their way into leadership have been mini leaders from childhood, and have no idea what followership is all about. Having been dehumanised from childhood, they grow up with a negative attitude which influences various aspects of their lives, with detrimental effects. Perhaps children raised as followers stand a better chance of transitioning into good leadership roles, and also switching roles back to followership whenever situations demand, with minimal conflicts.

The situation in formal education in Uganda also sheds some light onto followership styles in Africa. The current education system in Uganda does not encourage independent and critical thinking in the learner. The teacher is seen as a pitcher from which learners must be "open" to receive. This is not the kind of education which was advocated for by thinkers such as Socrates (Plato 2002), Rousseau (1889), or Freire (2005). The challenges faced by teachers, such as limited funding, poor working conditions, and large numbers in Universal Primary Education (UPE) and Universal Secondary Education (USE), make it difficult for teachers to engage in teaching styles that lead learners to independent and critical thinking (Wabule 2017). In addition, the quality of the teachers themselves leaves a lot to be desired (Mandy 2005). The fact that teaching as a profession is not attracting quality personnel due to poor pay could be the main reason why Uganda's education system is grossly inadequate. It is therefore not difficult to see why the country's education system is churning out passive or "yes" people as followers. Thus even though universal primary and secondary education are in place in Uganda, the result is not exemplary followership that can meaningfully interact with the prevailing leadership.

At the cultural level, there is overwhelming conformism and idolisation of superiors to the point of dogmatic following of those in positions of authority, or those who "appear" to be powerful. This is not to say that superiors ought not to be respected, but rather that the kind of respect that is widespread does not nurture exemplary followership. This kind of respect easily turns into fear, where individuals cannot ask "why" or challenge their leaders, even when they clearly see them making fatal decisions. Many cultures in Uganda mould children into fearful adults not empowered to constructively criticise elders and other people in authority. However, fear itself is an opportunity for an individual to develop courage to take positive action (Chaleff 2008, 21).

I use Sigmund Freud's psychoanalytic idea of the reality principle through the eyes of Cluley (2008) to explain this cultural situation in Uganda. According to Cluley, before human beings can separate between internal and external narcissistic desires, desires are easily satisfied internally without consciousness of external forces that contribute to satisfying them. This changes the moment one realises that one's desires can sometimes be satisfied only through external factors. This realisation is what Freud called the "reality principle" (Cluley 2008, 206). Primary narcissistic tendencies are then repressed in order for the individual to conform to the external environment. Through punishments and rewards, one learns to redesign one's desires to fit within acceptable desire standards in society. If Freud's reality principle and how it operates is true, many cultures in Uganda, especially at the family level, are responsible for producing and nurturing fearful, passive, and conformist followership. It is a culture of acquiescence similar to what Chaleff (2008, 68) says of Saddam Hussein's followers. Chaleff narrates the contents of the documentary footage of Saddam Hussein assuming power in Iraq in 1979 (Chaleff 2008, 68), and how he tearfully gave a speech about the betrayal by some of his officers. One by one their names were read out, and each escorted out to be shot. The men who remained seated were too timid to do anything, only sighing with relief whenever the names read out were not their own.

In sharp contrast to many African cultures, the Chinese have a culture that springs from the philosophy of Confucious, and this has contributed significantly to their current level of development. Whereas in most African cultures individuals are brought up in a manner that does not lead to exemplary followership, the Chinese are brought up in a way that encourages them to educate their minds (Confucius 1963; Dhakhwa 2008). In fact, after Uganda gained political independence, opportunism took over, such that many Ugandans perfected the culture of amassing wealth with little or no effort at all (Hansen & Twaddle 1988). The habit of resorting to witchcraft (Chabal 1999) or religion is widespread among Ugandans—if there is no one to blame for what is challenging and inexplicable, push it to the invisible!

With minimal desire to educate the mind, persistent egoistic leadership, and feminisation of followership, exemplary followership cannot emerge. The reality principle sets in to innitiate individuals into defeatist attitudes that are reflected in followership and leadership styles. Nevertheless, Ugandans in particular, and Africans in general, can transform their cultures to make them competitive at the global level, and liberal democracy is a requirement for this to materialise (Teson 1999). This is because liberal democracy promises fundamental freedoms for all members of society, enabling individuals to actualise their potentials. Nevertheless, because liberal democracy has been misappropriated in most African countries, the challenges associated with it are more pronounced than the benefits that it can produce. Consequently, there is need to carefully study the conditions that enable liberal democracy to thrive elsewhere, and which might be lacking in Africa, before dismissing it altogether.

Drawing from Collins (2012), I find that followership-leadership models at the level of the government of a country mainly get their direction from family structures. Although she was writing from a different context, there is still a correlation between hierarchy in government institutions and families. If the family is the basic unit of society, the recommendation to raise exemplary followers during socialisation of children (Kelley 2008; Kellerman 2008; Chaleff 2008) is reinforced. Instead of following the same old path of trying to unclogg leadership, strategies for moulding exemplary followership ought to be formulated right from the family, hence Collins's title, *It's All in the Family* (Collins 2012). In this regard, Grit and Holt (2011) correctly noted: "complaints about leaders and calls for more or better leadership occurs on such a regular basis that one would be forgiven for assuming that there was a time when good leaders were ubiquitous. Sadly, a trawl through the leadership archives reveals no golden past, but nevertheless a pervasive yearning for such an era" (Grit and Holt 2011, 6).

Socialisation, as it occurs in popular culture through the internet and other channels of communication, gets mixed up with elements from indigenous Ugandan cultures, and get shared by children in schools. Some of these indigenous elements do not tolerate any kind of confrontation from children in their interactions with adults; but because this mixture produces internal contradictions rather than coherence, it is likely to create internal conflicts for those exposed to it. For instance, whereas a film produced in America represents a nurturing of individual initiative and creativity which springs from a considerable level of independence, in Uganda there is still reverence for communal thinking and reluctance to let adults lead an independent life. However, children ought to be socialised to communicate effectively, and to have a considerable level of independence of thought and action, as these are some of the treasured characteristics of exemplary followership. Parents ought to allow this free communication from children to emerge while the children are still surrounded by loved ones in preparation for communicating at other levels.

Language can also be a tool for developing exemplary followership. In this regard, Chaleff (2008, 68–75) suggests encouraging a language that develops followership. For example, he suggests calling a situation of tolerating oppression as cowardice, leadership as stewardship of other people's interests, and followership as partnership with leadership to achieve an objective. John Dewey, in *Democracy and Education* (1916), lays emphasis on language in social learning. The ideals and values of a society are easily expressed through a common language. Members of a society ought to proscribe the act of rewarding those who conceal injustices to protect their leaders. Just as all other habits that develop, for example the use of slang among the youth, a habit of uncritical acquiescence can be constructed or deconstructed through the use of language. Dewey, in *How We Think* (1910), explains how new habits can replace old ones if we only put in the effort to carry them out consistently.

The gender dynamics embedded at all the levels examined in the preceding paragraphs—family, education, culture and politics—are such that wherever women are, there is an apparently natural tendency to think that they take second place. However, now that formal education is becoming accessible to more women along with access to information through the Internet, should we expect leadership to continue being the preserve of men? With more infiltration of contemporary culture through popular music, films and other artistic creations, how feasible is it to engage in discourses that reminisce on political organisations that mostly excluded women? African women are increasingly emerging from kitchens and bedrooms to the discussion table, and they expect to be heard just like their counterparts elsewhere—something that was discouraged in many indigenous African societies. The youth, both female and male, are also demanding greater participation in leadership, and yet indigenous African leadership was, by and large, gerontocratic.

The biblical statement that "a man shall leave his father and his mother, and be joined to his wife" (Genesis 2:24) has philosophical underpinnings that many overlook. According to that saying, men are the ones to cling, and yet this is frequently conveniently overturned or reversed. The "rights" men award themselves while women are busy nurturing everyone else but themselves obscure men's vulnerability. The same is true of political leadership in Africa. As political commentators blame elites for manipulating political institutions for selfish gains, they (the commentators) fail to pay attention to the fact that by neglecting to participate in the processes of governance, followers create the environment for leaders to do so. The rich use the law to manipulate power in order to subjugate others. Rousseau in fact put it correctly when he noted that "The strongest is never strong enough to be always the master, unless he transforms strength into right, and obedience into duty"

(Rousseau 1762, 4). That is why I emphasise that women are partly to blame for their subjugation because of their psychological tendency to "mother" anything and everything as their socialisation trains them to do. In the same vein, followers, both women and men, complain about failed leadership and liberal democracy while abdicating their responsibility to undertake critical and independent thought, leading to their inaction.

Looking back with nostalgic longing for what is authentic to Africa in terms of democracy might be as frustrating as attempting to provide a remedy for leadership while ignoring followership. Deliberations on democracy in Africa should be cognisant of all the changes that have taken place and those bound to occur due to the fast-changing circumstances on the global, regional and local scenes. I am therefore convinced that African politics can be revolutionised and invigorated if focus shifted to developing exemplary followership that is liberated and autonomous. In fact, post-modernism is calling for a new way of interpreting reality and behaving (Lyotard 1984). Women ought to take agency of their lives instead of being overly dependant on men. This includes taking part in decision-making processes that are likely to affect them. It is the idealised leadership models with passive and conformist followerships that are responsible for the historical tragedies from which Africans are still nursing wounds. Gender dynamics will always surface in all political discourses, such that anything that tries to undermine what achievements women have attained is going to be challenged the world over, creating isolated or alienated followers. Consequently, focus ought to be directed towards developing exemplary followership in order for liberal democracy to thrive in Africa. This is not an easy task, but it is worth the effort.

CONCLUSION

Questions arise as to whether or not followership can be subjected to critical reflection side by side with leadership, and whether or not a new culture of exemplary followership can be built away from the existing culture (Riggio, Chaleff and Lipman-Blumen eds. 2008). In an effort to raise the quality of followership in Uganda in particular and in Africa at large, I have highlighted the need to remodel socialisation, and to change education styles to encourage independent and critical thinking. Training for exemplary followership is crucial, especially through informal education. In this regard, socialisation at the family level is critical in shaping the individual's outlook. If what Freud discovered is correct, that all psychology including narcissism is primarily grounded in social interaction (as cited by Cluley 2008, 202), we should be aware of the effects of the social environment on the development of the individual. Rousseau (1889) was therefore correct in proposing moving Emile, his hypothetical learner, from the town to the country to be educated with minimal interruption from interactions with already matured individuals.

All in all, the first step in the effort to develop exemplary followership is to recognise that retrospection ought to be limited to appreciating mistakes in order to eliminate them and to amplify any past successes. Looking back at Africa's indigenous past from a followership-leadership perspective, there were injustices that frustrated not only women and the youth, but also men who preferred to take life easy, if only society had allowed them free choice on how to conduct their lives. It is grossly erroneous to think that all men enjoy taking the lead in various spheres of life. Yet society is quick to pass judgment against whoever behaves contrary to what it expects—not only against women who show interest in leadership, but also against men who do not appreciate leadership positions. Is it really the case that all men are fit to be heads of families, and that no woman can undertake this responsibility? In the contemporary world, followership by both women and men needs to be revamped to counter dissipations of leadership in order for liberal democracy or any other preferred political model to thrive. It is therefore my considered opinion that despite the calls and quest for indigenous African models of democracy to replace liberal democracy in the continent in the twenty-first century, liberal democracy is not the problem in Uganda in particular, or in Africa at large: lack of exemplary, gender-sensitive followership is.

REFERENCES

Amukugo, Elizabeth. 2013. "Liberal Democracy, Education and Social Justice in Africa". *Journal for Studies in Humanities and Social Sciences*, Vol. 2 No. 1, pp. 144–57. www.researchgate.net/publication/282326483_liberal_democracy_education_and_social_justice_in_Africa.

Balda, Kyle, and Pierre Coffin (Film Directors). 2015. *Minions*. https://www.timeout.com/london/film/minions.

Bennis, Warren. 2008. "Introduction". Riggio, Ronald E., Ira Challef and Jean Lipman-Blumen eds. *The Art of Followership: How Great Followers Create Great Leaders and Organisations*. San Francisco: Jossey-Bass, pp. xxiii–xxvii.

Bjugstand, Kent, Elizabeth Thach, Karen Thompson and Alan Morris. 2006. "A Fresh Look at Followership: A Model for Matching Followership and Leadership Styles". *Journal of Behavioral and Applied Management*, Vol. 7 Issue 3, pp. 304–19. https://wenku.baidu.com/view/acc0f4362af90242a895ec.html, https://www.researchgate.net/publication/252457195_A_Fresh_Look_at_Followership_A_Model_for_Matching_Followership_and_Leadership_Styles.

Chabal, Patrick, and Jean-Pascal Daloz. 1999. *Africa Works: Disorders as Political Instrument*. Bloomington: Indiana University Press.

Chaleff, Ira. 1995. *The Courageous Follower*. San Francisco: Berrett-Koehler Publishers.

———. 2008. "Creating New Ways of Following". Riggio, Ronald E., Ira Chaleff and Jean Lipman-Blumen eds. *The Art of Followership: How Great Followers are Creating Great Leaders and Organisations*. San Francisco, CA: Jossey-Bass, pp. 67–87.

Cluley, Robert. 2008. "The Psychoanalytic Relationship between Leaders and Followers". *Leadership*, Vol. 4 issue 2, pp. 201–12. https://doi.org/10.1177/1742715008089638.

Collins, Patricia Hill. 2012. "It's All in the Family: Intersections of Gender, Race, and Nation". Heyes, Cessida J. ed. *Philosophy and Gender: Critical Concepts in Philosophy*. New York: Routledge, pp. 260–78.

Confucius. 1963. *The Source Book in Chinese Phiosophy*. Chan, Wing-Tsit trans. Princeton, NJ: Princeton University Press.

Dewey, John. 1910. *How We Think*. Chicago: D.C. Health and Co. Publishers.

———. 1916. *Democracy and Education*. New York: The Macmillan Company.

Dhakhwa, Sujeeta, and Stacey Enriques. 2008. "The Relevance of Confucian Philosophy to Modern Concepts of Leadership and Followership". *The Osprey Journal of Ideas and Inquiry All Volumes* (2001–2008) *Paper 5*, pp. 1–13. http://digitalcommons.unf.edu/ojii_volumes/5.

Eui-Jung, Suh. 2012. "The Power of Followership: Eight Tips to Make Star Followers". *Weekly Insight*, November 5, pp. 9–12. http://www.seriworld.org/03/wldKetFileDown.html?mn=E&mncd=0302&seriid=&eng=&nextpage=LzAzL3dsZEtldEwuaHRtbD9zb3J0PUMmc2VjdG5vPTMmcF9wYWdlPTU=&gbn=02&key=db20121105001&sectno=3.

Freire, Paulo. 2005. *Pedagogy of the Oppressed*, 30th Anniversary Edition. Ramos, Myra Beryman trans. New York: Continuum.

Grit, Keith, and Clare Holt. 2011. "Followership in the NHS". http://www.kingsfund.org.uk/publications/articles/leadership_papers/nhs_followership.html.

Hansen, Holger Bernt, and Michael Twaddle. 1988. *Uganda Now: Between Decay and Development*. London: Ohio University Press.

Harle, Tim. 2009. "Barbara Kellerman, Followership:How Followers Are Creating Change and Changing Leaders". *Leadership*, Vol. 5 Issue 2, pp. 284–87. http://journals.sagepub.com/doi/pdf/10.1177/1742715009102941.

Hollander, E. P. 1992. "Leadership, Followership, Self and Other". *Leadership Quarterly*, Vol. 3 No. 1, pp. 43–54.

Howell, Jon P. & Maria J. Mendez. 2008. "Three Perspectives on Followership". Riggio, Ronald E., Ira Challef and Jean Lipman-Blumen eds. *The Art of Followership: How Great Followers Create Great Leaders and Organisations*. San Francisco, CA: Jossey-Bass, pp. 25–39.

Jerry, Robert H. II. 2013. "Leadership and Followership". *UF Law Scholarship Repository*, pp. 345–54. http://ssrn.com/abstract=2689243.

Kellerman, Barbara. 2008. *Followership: How Followers Are Creating Change and Changing Leaders*. Boston, MA: Harvard Business Press.

Kelley, R. E. 1988. "In Praise of Followers". *Harvard Business Review*, Vol. 66 No. 6, pp. 142–48.

———. 2008. "Rethinking Followership". Riggio, Ronald E., Ira Challef and Jean Lipman-Blumen eds. *The Art of Followership: How Great Followers Create Great Leaders and Organisations*. San Francisco: Jossey-Bass, pp. 5–15.

Leon, Tony. 2010. *The State of Liberal Democracy in Africa: Resurgence or Retreat?* Washington, D.C.: Center for Global Liberty and Prosperity.

Lyotard, Jean-Francois. 1984. *The Post-Modern Condition: A Report on Knowledge*. Manchester : Manchester University Press.

Mandy, Fagil M. 2009. *Top Secrets of Educating Your Child*. Kampala: MPK Graphics Ltd.

Maroosis, James. 2008. "Leadership: A Partnership in Reciprocal Following". Riggio, Ronald E., Ira Challef and Jean Lipman-Blumen eds. *The Art of Folowership: How Great Followers Create Great Leaders and Organisations*. San Francisco, CA: Jossey-Bass, pp. 17–24.

Morton, Katie L., Lisa S. Perlmutter, Alexandra H. Wilson and Mark Beauchamp. 2012. "Family Leadership Styles and Adolescent Dietary and Physical Activity Behaviors: A Cross-Sectional Study". *International Journal of Behavioral Nutrition and Physical Activity*, Vol. 9 Issue 1, pp. 1–9. https://ijbnpa.biomedcentral.com/articles/10.1186/1479-5868-9-48.

Oduor, Reginald M. J. 2017. "Scholarship in Service of Africa". Closing remarks at the international conference on "Beyond Liberal Democracy: The Quest for Indigenous African Models of Democracy for the Twenty-First Century", organised by the Department of Philosophy and Religious Studies, University of Nairobi and the Council for Research in Values and Philosophy (RVP), Washington, D.C., U.S.A., 22–23 May.

Patton, Micheal Quinn. 2002. *Qualitative Research and Evaluation Methods*. Thousand Oaks, CA: Sage.

Plato. 2002. *Meno*. holbo, J. and B. Waring trans. https://www.staff.ncl.ac.uk/joel.wallenberg/contextsjoelGeoff/meno.pdf.

Riggio, Ronald E., Ira Chaleff and Jean Lipman-Blumen eds. 2009. *The Art of Followership: How Great Followers Create Great Leaders and Organisations*. San Francisco: Jossey-Bass.

Rost, Joseph. 2008. "Followership: An Outmoded Concept". Riggio, Ronald E., Ira Chaleff and Jean Lipman-Blumen eds. *The Art of Followership: How Great Followers Create Great Leaders and Great Organisations*. San Francisco, CA: Jossey-Bass, pp. 53–64.

Rousseau, Jean-Jacques. 2002 [1762]. *The Social Contract, or Principles of Political Right*. Cole, G.D.H. trans. New York: Dover Publications, Inc.

———. 1889. *Emile, or Concerning Education*. Worthington, Eleanor trans. Boston: D.C. Heath & Company.

Stech, Ernest L. 2008. "A New Leadership-Followership Paradigm". Riggio, Ronald E., Ira Chaleff and Jean Lipman-Blumen eds. *The Art of Followership: How Great Followers are Creating Great Leaders and Organisations*. San Francisco, CA: Jossey-Bass, pp. 41–52.

Tar, Usman A. 2010. "Information Society and Justice". *Society and Justice*, Vol. 3 No. 2, pp. 81–94. https://www.scribd.com/document/373606505/Information SocietyAndJustice-v3n2-p81-94-pdf.

Teson, Fernando. 1999. "A Defence of Liberal Democracy for Africa". *Cambridge Review of International Affairs*, Vol. 13 No. 1, pp. 29–40. https://doi.org/10/1080/09557579908400270.

Vugt, Mark Van. 2006. "Evolutionary Origins of Leadership and Followership". *Personality and Social Psychology Review*, Vol. 10 No. 4, pp. 354–71. https://pdfs.semanticscholar.org/0a95/bbec75c7d8a6f414ee97ebee2292a69cd2a3.pdf.

Wabule, Alice. 2017. *Professional Integrity of Teachers in Uganda: Practical Action Strategies*. Gronigen: Globalisation Studies.

Wiebe, Paul D., and Cole P. Dodge. 1987. *Beyond Crisis: Development Issues in Uganda*. Kampala: Makerere Institute of Social Research/ Crossroads Press.

Yung, Chen Tsun, and Chen Kvan Tsai. 2013. "Followership: An Important Partner of Leadership". *Business and Management Horizons*, Vol. 1 No. 2, pp. 47–55. www.macrothink.org/journal/index.php/bmh/article/download/4233/3502.

Part 3

PROPOSALS FOR CONTEXT-RELEVANT AFRICAN MODELS OF DEMOCRACY

Chapter Seven

Co-operative Collegial Democracy
An African Context-Relevant Governance Model
Emefiena Ezeani

Liberal democrats seem to have convinced most of the world that liberal multi-party democracy is the most "civilised" model of governance, as it allegedly entails the best method of both selecting leadership and forming government. In this light, Francis Fukuyama famously claimed that we have reached "the end point of mankind's ideological evolution with the universalisation of Western liberal democracy", which he also argued was "the final form of human government", and so, the best of all democratic models (Fukuyama in Cunningham 2002, 27; see also Fukuyama 1989; 1992). Yet his claims call for a closer re-examination by scholars and statesmen, especially in nation-states where the liberal democratic model has failed. Had Fukuyama contended that democracy, without the prefix *liberal* represents the final phase of humankind's political history, he may not have been far from the truth. Without doubt, democracy is the best form of human government in comparison with *monarchy* or *oligarchy*, and "the most suitable form of government for human growth and betterment" (Menamparampil 2017, 1).[1] What is contentious in Fukuyama's theoretical assumption is "liberal democracy". A question that should disturb the minds of scholars and statesmen is: has *liberal* democracy (a species of the genus *democracy*), which is characterised by institutionalised opposition, party formation, political competition, and struggle for power, proved to be the *best* form of government in *all* societies in which it is practiced?

Although the question above cannot be answered in the affirmative, many people, including African and Western political scientists and political philosophers, have succumbed to the heresy that Western liberal democracy is "the final form of human government". It is this mindset which underscores the Western insistence that democratisation for African states simply means an "unadulterated" adoption of the liberal multi-party model.

The doctrine of the universality of liberal democracy is as much a political fallacy as it is an intellectual superstition. As Menamparampil (2017) has cautioned, while recognising the merit of liberal democracy on its own right, it is prudent to take note of certain limitations to absolutising it because "the western models of democracy differ greatly among themselves", and "there are many flaws in the working of various democratic systems in the West itself". Besides, "those nations in East Europe, Latin America or other parts of the world that adopted in haste the western models are finding it difficult to get them working . . . and the quality of governance has fallen low in some of those nations that claim to be truly democratic" (Menamparampil 2017, 1). Oduor (2017, 3) makes an important observation: "Despite adopting liberal democracy, or even perhaps because of adopting it, the structure of the postcolonial state has, in many cases, proved to be as tyrannical as the colonial one. It therefore needs to undergo radical change for it to move from being a tyrant to a servant".

Contemporary African societies are also plagued by the lethal political dogma that politics is the "seizure, consolidation and use of state power" (Nnoli 1986, 3)—a conception which reduces the notion of politics to the struggle for power. Yet the actual meaning of politics is derived from its Greek root, *polis* ("city" or "state") and *techne* ("skill" or "method"), hence politics (*polis techne*) means the skill or method of governing a state.

A considerable number of African universities have witnessed a generational transmission of all the above-mentioned erroneous and regressive political theories, the praxis of which is grossly responsible for most of the socio-political backwardness and crises in many African states. It is in view of the above political and epistemological aberrations that one would appreciate the significance of the 2017 University of Nairobi Conference on the theme: "Beyond Liberal Democracy: The Quest for Indigenous African Models of Democracy for the 21st Century". This is an indication that some contemporary African scholars are beginning to see that a healthy political and economic situation of African nations cannot be guaranteed by unbridled institutionalisation of the Western liberal political system. Castells (1998, 359) holds that "The most fundamental political liberation is for people to free themselves from uncritical adherence to theoretical or ideological schemes, (and) construct their (own) practice on the basis of their experience, while using whatever information or analysis is available to them, from a variety of sources". All these point to the fact that democracy, as a system of government, is context sensitive. Consequently, this chapter is guided by the strong point inherent in the *context-sensitive theory*, and by advocating *Co-operative Collegial Democracy* (CCD), it seeks to offer solutions to the limitations which are intrinsic to the liberal model of democracy.

Thus, in this chapter, I seek to answer the following questions:

- Is there no better way of recruiting political leaders than the competitive political party system characterised by fraud, colossal monetary waste, inter-religious and inter-ethnic tensions, and violence?
- What are the solutions to the problems posed to African politics, governance, and development by the liberal democratic multi-party model?
- What political structure would ensure the election of people who have uppermost in their minds the general good of the people—leaders who spend most of their time thinking not about the next election, but rather about the development of the society for the benefit of the present and future generations?

The next section highlights the alien character of the Western liberal democratic model in the African context, with emphasis on the negative effects of the party system, political competition, and institutionalised opposition on the consolidation of democracy on the continent. That is followed by a section in which I present the concept and practice of Co-operative Collegial Democracy (CCD) as an alternative democratic model that is practicable in the African context. In the final section, I present a synopsis of some of my major theoretical arguments.

WESTERN LIBERAL PARTY DEMOCRACY: AN ALIEN MODEL IN THE AFRICAN CONTEXT

Western liberal democracy has two faces—the *beautiful* (democratic), and the *ugly* (divisive). The beautiful face encompasses such democratic values as equity, equality, liberty, rule of law/justice, and the popular acclamation that government originates from the people, while the divisive face comprises, among other things, formation of parties, institutionalised opposition, ethnicisation of politics, the struggle for power, political dishonesty, and political aggression or violence.

It seems that only a few Africans are 'privileged' to be aware of the evil face of liberal democracy in the continent. Among them was the late General Murtala Muhammed, the then military head of state of Nigeria, who on 4 October 1975, inaugurated a fifty-member constitution drafting committee, and, concerned about the harmful effects of the party system, asked the members of the committee to see if they could find some other "means by which government could be organised without the involvement of political parties" (quoted in Osaghae 1998, 87). Muhammed realised that traditionally, political parties in Nigeria had existed more like private militia whose activities in the electoral arena were tantamount to 'warfare', with attendant anomic consequences (Momoh and Adejumobi 1999, 114). Like the scholars who organised the "Beyond Liberal Democracy" Conference at the University of Nairobi in May 2017, Muhammed was keenly aware of the harmful effects of liberal democracy in an ethnically plural African state.

For decades, different African states have been governed using the competitive Western liberal political system, with minimal positive impact on the lives of the citizenry if at all, while the privileged, exploitative, and inept political elites enjoy disproportionate power and wealth. Instead of enhancing life, the practice of the Western model of democracy continues to endanger the lives of the people by causing conflicts along ethnic, religious, economic, and political lines. Besides, being a competitive model, opposing groups, euphemistically called 'political parties', struggle against one another to gain control of state power.

In many African states, political competition not only breeds animosity, but also hinders economic progress, as politicians spend most of their time and energy on strategies to capture or retain state power. A good number of African political leaders spend most of the first half of their term in office formulating strategies to amass wealth for themselves and their cronies, and a major part of the second half scheming how to win the next election, with little time to execute their primary duties to the people. For instance, Chimaroke Nnamani, a former Governor of Enugwu State in Nigeria, reveals how his relationship with former President Olusegun Obasanjo was robust, only to turn sour when the issue of a third presidential term crept in as early as the Year 2000 (Nwodo 2009, 1). Hence, within a year during his first term, Obasanjo's major worry was how to achieve his third term ambition in office as President of Nigeria, convinced that his second term was already assured. Obasanjo was a military head of state (1976–1979), and twice a civilian president (1999–2003 and 2003–2007). Thus, most African states end up having high office holders as individuals whose major political ambition is to occupy seats of honour and glory, and to acquire wealth, rather than to render service to their people. Plato, in *The Republic*, calls this type of government "timocracy" (Plato 1987).

One of the major challenges arising out of the imposition of liberal democracy on post-colonial African states is the ignorance of citizens. For example, in the 1997 parliamentary and presidential elections in Kenya, a section of Kenyan voters were said to be illiterate and ignorant, and "had to ask officials for help" (Orr 1997, 9), a situation which is common in most African countries. This reminds one of Plato's observation that it is often the case that ordinary people are manipulated or intimidated by the self-imposed image of the politicians, and that knowledge is essential for making correct choices.

Besides, in a multi-party system, the people have no freedom to select who they want to be their representatives, but are compelled to select from different political party competitors who selected themselves, were selected by their parties, or were sponsored by political godfathers or godmothers, or fronted by business interests. Moreover, party congresses for selection of candidates are often nothing more than bazaars where the highest bidder wins the nomination. Thus, the claim that Western liberal party democracy, with its inherently divisive nature, unites the people and promotes their welfare is evidently untrue.

Another major concern with regard to multi-party democracy relates to state security in African, Asian and Latin American countries with delicate political arrangements. A political party in these countries is an easy gateway to foreign powers to destabilise the state. For example, the West can remove from office a president of an African state who is highly critical of the West by providing financial and logistical support to an opposition party. While the foreign power can go through the military establishment, the existence of political parties provides it with an alternative course of action.

Of greatest concern is the fact that liberal democracy exacerbates conflict in society. The concepts of *struggle* and *competition* have become the defining ideas of contemporary politics. Competition, which is a fundamental element of the party system, conveys the idea of freedom—a value desired by almost everyone in society. Thus, the term *politics* is now commonly understood as the struggle or competition for power. Nevertheless, the element of "struggle for power" is a latecomer in the understanding of politics as an art, skill, or method of governance, only having been added by liberal democratic theorists from the eighteenth century onwards (Held 1999, 81). In pseudo-democracies, recourse to the unfair use of competition is prevalent. Multi-party competition is reminiscent of a 'bone-competition' amongst a horde of dogs, and in both kingdoms the end justifies even the unfair means.

Mwaura (1997) points to a definite connection between ethnic conflict and political, and especially presidential, succession. A fusion of ethnic identity and politics, he opines, is much more pronounced in a multi-party system, especially in places where ethnicisation of politics has become the driving force, and in these places also, the potential for violent inter-ethnic conflict is likely to increase. For example, in Nigeria, to challenge President Mohammadu Buhari or his political party, the All Progressive Congress (APC), is likened to challenging the Muslims and the Hausa-Fulani of Northern Nigeria.

There is overwhelming evidence that competition among political parties in Africa heightens tensions, leading to increased use of violence to achieve political goals. For instance, following the contested 2007/2008 Kenyan elections, more than 1,200 people were reported to have been killed, and 350,000 were displaced (*The Universe*, UK, Sunday April 5, 2009, 12). Almost ten years later, The UK *Independent* newspaper reporters, Tom and Torchia (2017, 1), noted that the August 2017 Kenyan elections took an ominous turn as violent protests erupted in the capital and elsewhere after opposition leader Raila Odinga alleged fraud, and Kenyan police opened fire on people protesting election results. Similarly, in Nigeria, many lives were lost during the 1962, 1965, 2003, 2007, 2011, 2015, and 2019 elections across the country, as well as during the post-election crisis of 2011 in the Northern Region.

Multi-party politics has consistently failed in different African states, including Nigeria, Congo, and Sudan, among others. Why the 'democratic tree' planted in Nigeria and other African countries has not germinated, or, where it has germinated, has not grown to a shrub after 50 years is enough to trigger fundamental philosophical questions and intense academic debates.

Beyond Africa, in a similar incident, more than fifty Pakistanis died during violent protests against the murder of former Prime Minister Benazir Bhutto, an opposition leader for the 2008 Pakistani presidential elections, during a political rally (Fisher 2008). In the United States, the presidential electoral contest between Al Gore and George Bush in the year 2000, and that between Hilary Clinton and Donald Trump in 2016, also put the liberal democratic model to the test. All these incidents of interference, rigging, electoral inconclusiveness, credibility-deficit, violence, and killings across the world in the name of democracy, raise serious questions about the desirability of liberal democracy not only in Africa, but also in other parts of the world.

According to Cunningham (2002, 61), since conflict can be exacerbated by competition, one is left with the option of transforming competitive societies into co-operative ones "in accord with a liberal-democratic socialist alternative". However, it is difficult to see how this would be possible in a society that operates multi-party democracy. Can party members in such a system aspire to leadership positions without competition with one another? How can effective political *cooperation*, which is a significant democratic capital or value, be achieved in multi-party democracies? Can opposition parties easily endorse policies initiated by the incumbent party on the basis of their merits? In posing these questions, I do not wish to advocate for a single-party system either. Nevertheless, a co-operative society would be one whose democracy is not hinged on party politics with its institutionalised opposition.

In more lucid terms, one cannot escape the fact that the party system has become the bane of liberal democracy, especially in African politics. The obsession with wresting power from the incumbent political party has often driven the opposition parties to frustrate the smooth governance and execution of projects by the government of the day. It is often the case that the opposition parties are more preoccupied with denigrating and sabotaging the efforts of the government than with working for the common good. Thus, a failed administration, in the view of these opposition parties, is the best way to acquire power in subsequent elections.

Of particular concern to me in this chapter is the fact that liberal democracy, solidly built on a multi-party system, is alien to the African worldview which has, for many centuries, operated on collegial or co-operative democracy based on principles of equality and equity. This is the root of the popular political dictum among the Igbo, which is, "*Igbo Enwe Eze* (No single person is to be recognised as the King of the entire Igbo nation)". Having witnessed the selfish and exploitative tendencies of a monarch, the Igbo, as a nation, abandoned the centralised monarchical system of government, but at the town level resorted to collegial democracy structured on the principle of *Nze na Ozo*[2] political college.

As Umeh (2017, 252) pointed out, "ancient Igbo Kings were termed *Obi, Oba, Iduu,* or *Iduu na Oba*[3]—these were the traditional King's titles, and the Queens were called *Eze Nwanyi*[4] . . . , before they were replaced by *Nze na Ozo* titled Oligarchy [*sic*] which transformed Igbo society to a kingless society and the earliest democracy in the world". Here, each member of the *Nze na Ozo* is addressed as King in their chosen title names and with no King considered greater than the other. This is also applicable to all the political units that make up an Igbo society—no village is greater than the other no matter its numerical strength. This is encapsulated in the Igbo proverb *Eze aka ibe ya* (No king is greater than the other). Membership to this college (*Nze na Ozo*) is again free to all male members of the Igbo society who fully satisfy the requirements, especially from a moral perspective (exhibiting hard work and integrity). These title holders only stand to lead communal affairs and adjudicate disputes.

Furthermore, among the Igbo, matters pertaining to the well-being of the society are discussed at the *Umunna* (Kinsmen) Council, where every member is given the opportunity to contribute to the well-being of their society. Women too hold a separate Council under the umbrella of *Umuada* (Kinswomen), while the youth are organised under the wing of *Otu Ogbo* (Age grade). These various groups discuss communal affairs and offer their resolutions at the *Nzuko* Session (General Assembly). This General Assembly is again called *Nzuko onye kwuo uche ya* (a session for all to speak out their minds). Thus, the concept of parliament, a word comprising two different words as "*Parler*" (French—to speak) and "*Mens*" (Latin—Mind), which put together translates as "To speak one's mind" suggests that the Igbo might have bequeathed this ancient practice to the Western world which now talks of 'parliamentary system of government'.

The various fora among the Igbo outlined above highlight the point that Africa conceives a nation as a family, and its political structure is modelled after the divisions of a family into father (*Umunna*—Kinsmen), Mother (*Umuada*—Kinswomen), and children (*Otu Ogbo*—Age Grade). With this setting, the idea of divisions into a ruling party and opposition parties, later bequeathed to Africans by the Western colonial administration, was unthinkable to the pre-colonial African.

In indigenous African democracy, every person is inevitably involved in the politics of his or her society, with every political unit enjoying a substantial degree of autonomy. Moreover, equal rights and opportunities, freedom, and justice are granted to all political units as well as to all members of the society. The question of tussling for power, and humiliation from either the party in government or from the opposition parties is absent. This is again so because everyone sees the politics of the community not as an opportunity for self-enrichment, but as a sacred duty—a family affair—in which one is bound to put in one's utmost best for the well-being of his or her society.

This African conceptualisation of a nation as a large family is manifested in the thought of the first President of Tanzania, Julius Kambarage Nyerere, which he referred to by the Kiswahili word *Ujamaa*, which translates as "family-hood" (Nyerere 1966; Schraeder in Gordon and Gordon eds. 1996, 143). No sane family pursues any collective goal or gets a representative by first forming opposing groups or parties; nor are the views of young family members denied serious consideration. On the contrary, the wise (elders) always ensured that the spirit of cooperation was maintained among the family members for the common good. When, therefore, members of the family begin to struggle for power or for a larger portion of the wealth bequeathed to them by their forefathers, the family is doomed.

Is the fact that the above contextual political norm has been neglected not a major reason competitive party democracy is a disaster in Africa? The situation is made worse when members of different ethnic groups in a polity ("family members" in the analogy above) compete for power.

In sum, the liberal democratic party model is quintessentially opposed to indigenous African democracy. It has destroyed the cornerstone of African culture by distorting the African system of social relations, and by encouraging political allegiance along ethnic and religious lines, thereby making it very easy for people without moral integrity and/or requisite governance skills to ascend to positions of leadership. This brings to mind the wisdom in Buddha's three causes of decline and decay of any society, namely, (i) failure to recover that which has been lost, (ii) omission to repair that which has been damaged, and (iii) elevation to leadership of people without morality or learning (Buddha in Blaug & Schwarzmantel eds. 2004, 431). Oduor (2017, 2) makes a pertinent analogy: "Liberal democracy in Africa is like a man in a three piece suit at noon on a hot day in Kisumu".[5] This is one of the reasons why, in his interview with a Nigerian newspaper, *Sun*, Professor Pat Utomi appeals to Nigerians: "Let's crash this democracy . . . We have a fundamental problem. We have to bring this system down completely and rebuild" (cited in Aleshinloye-Agboola 2011, 1). Utomi's stance is predicated on the following argument: "This democratic system is just a gangster arrangement for extracting economic rent from the system. It is not working" (Utomi in Aleshinloye-Agboola 2011, 1).

Yet Africans generally seem to be very optimistic in tenaciously embracing any Western material and ideological product, so that most of them continue to hope that things will be better in future: "after all", the argument goes, "it took Americans and their democracy more than two hundred years to arrive at where they are today". To the African liberal democratic optimists, Peter Ustinov (2004) would say that the point of being an optimist is to be foolish enough to believe that the best is yet to come even when members of a society do not make requisite changes to bring it about.

Furthermore, instead of working towards a context-relevant model of governance, a significant number of African political theorists and commentators hold that emphasis ought not to be placed on the structure of an institution, but rather on the character and performance of its practitioners. From this, they opine that Africans and their politicians ought to be *re-oriented*, *sensitised*, and *educated* to know that the purpose of political office is service, and that it is wrong to vote for someone because of money or ethnic affiliation. However, the problem is not lack of education, but rather absence of political and legal structures capable of altering the people's post-colonial political culture, and preventing, *ab initio*, incompetent and dishonest individuals from acquiring state power. On this hinges the significance of the context-relevant political model which is part of the core of the focus of this work. The political system I shall be proposing, like any other, ought to be tested to determine its suitability or lack thereof.

Uyanne, in one of his November 2019 social media submissions, robustly argued that partisan democracy, being a game of numbers, has been successfully used by some to maintain supremacy over others, and for this, and other reasons, he espouses that "partisan democracy is a rape of real democracy". In view of the fact that party politics has consistently failed Africans, Uyanne (1994, 17) had earlier raised the following question: if one-party structure equals arming a lunatic with an automatic weapon, is the multi-party system not a Tower of Babel where nobody understands the other? Similarly, Barbara Kingsolver, in her novel, *The Poisonwood Bible*, highlights one of the major obstacles to the fruitful implementation of democracy in a pluralistic African state thus:

> "Two *hundred* different languages", he [Anatole] said, "spoken inside the borders of a so-called country invented by Belgians in a parlour. You might as well put a fence around sheep, wolves, and chickens, and tell them to behave like brethren". He turned around, looking suddenly just like a preacher, "Frank, this is not a *nation*, it is the *Tower of Babel* and it *cannot* hold an election." (Kingsolver 1998, 167)

Thus, the persistent unhealthy political situation in African countries calls for an urgent replacement of the liberal democratic system with a political model which adequately addresses the need for a method of recruiting political leaders without the competitiveness characteristic of multi-party politics. In *The Prince*, Niccolò Machiavelli presents what is generally accepted as a realistic picture of human beings as essentially selfish, profoundly aggressive, and intensely acquisitive (see Machiavelli 2011). However, this is not always the case because there are human beings who are, in essence, altruistic, gentle, and generous. Nevertheless, selfishness, aggressiveness, and acquisitiveness are traits that effective political and legal structures ought to tame.

When separated from a context-relevant political structure, the selfishness and acquisitiveness (corruption) as well as aggressiveness (violent political competition) in the people become exponentially pronounced. Consequently, African political scientists and political philosophers must go beyond the regurgitation of the exotic textbook theoretical functions and benefits of the political party system and focus on the post-colonial African milieu instead. For democracy to flourish in an African state, a model of governance that is sensitive to the country's historical circumstances, culture, and strong ethnic cleavages is a desideratum. Such a model has to be the exact antithesis of the Western liberal model which African states have hitherto been practising with little or no success. More specifically, it has to be free from competition, and be characterised by cooperation instead, and to such a model we now turn.

CO-OPERATIVE COLLEGIAL DEMOCRACY: AN ALTERNATIVE TO THE WESTERN COMPETITIVE MODEL

Co-operative Collegial Democracy (CCD) is a system of government that is structured, organised, and regulated in a pyramidal pattern, with a step-by-step method of leadership selection and government formation. Basic units, for example, villages, towns, or wards in a country are the starting points for the formation and organisation of governments as shown in Figure 1 below. In this system, the actual duty of selecting major government functionaries is transferred to colleges of citizens elected or selected by the people at different political levels. The sets of individuals so elected or selected, and who are generally recognised as the people's representatives, constitute Government Bodies ("Colleges") at different political levels. The role of the various sets of representatives (*Colleges*) is two-fold: selection or election of actual political leaders (such as Local Government Chairperson, State Governor, or President) from among themselves, and performing functions similar to those of Local Government councils, State Houses of Assembly, and National Assembly.

Figure 7.1 below is an illustration of where and how selection or election takes place, and how governments at various levels are formed in CCD.

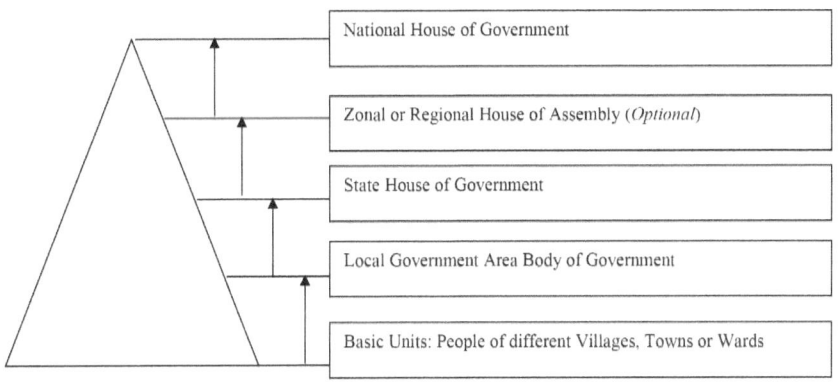

Figure 7.1. Co-operative Pyramidal Democratic Structure. *Source*: Adapted from Ezeani (2013, 152)

Figure 7.1 above shows that in Co-operative Collegial Democracy (CCD), government originates, is organised, and regulated in a pyramidal pattern. Starting the electoral process from basic units forestalls the emergence of politicians not chosen by the people, but who purport to be their representatives or leaders. Such politicians do not feel accountable to the people, as they were not *actually* selected or elected by them, but rather by their respective political parties. With the CCD model, the people elect, at local levels, those whom they know, and who, in turn, are accountable to them (Ezeani 2013, 152 ff.).

The indigenes of different villages would select their representatives to form the Village Assembly; representatives of all the villages would come together to form the Town (or Community) Assembly. Representatives of all Town Assemblies in a Local Government Area would then come together to form the Local Government Assembly. Representatives of all Local Government Assemblies would get together to form a State Assembly, from where would emerge the State Governor, Deputy Governor, and Speaker of the State Assembly, while representatives of all State Assemblies would come together to form the Zonal or Regional Assembly. Representatives of all Regional Assemblies would form the National or Federal Assembly, which would elect or select from amongst themselves the President of the country, as well as some other functionaries such as the Vice-President and Senate President. In other words, all these assemblies would be electoral colleges for various political offices at different levels of government.

The Co-operative Collegial Democracy (CCD) has a selection filtering method known as "Democratic Electoral Filter-ism" (DEF) or as "Pass-through-the-Eye-of-the-Needle-Process", which is one of the most important differences between the liberal democratic multi-party model and CCD. Democratic Electoral Filter-ism (DEF), as a major feature of CCD, is a step-by-step screening process to ensure that major political office holders, such as legislators, governors of states and Head of State (country) are thoroughly evaluated at different electoral levels before they assume high office. It therefore sieves out unqualified political gamblers.

Depending on the political office in question, one who succeeds in the first screening stage at the basic unit has to go through other screening stages (levels)—Town, Local Government Area, State, Regional, and Federal (Ezeani 2013, 150 ff.). Democratic Electoral Filter-ism is also designed to act as a corruption prevention mechanism for people aspiring to capture major political posts using money or through recourse to godfathers. With this measure in place, it would be difficult to bribe one's way through all the screening stages. Besides, since at each political level (Village, Town or Ward, Local Government Area, State, and Federal) every member of the electoral college would select a candidate from each of the comprising political units, it would be very difficult to secure "success" by bribery. Moreover, by enthroning equity and equality, this model would minimise ethnic tensions in the exercise of choice, thereby addressing ethnic minority-majority tensions that have been a major bane in ethnically plural African polities.

In line with indigenous African democratic culture, equity, and equality are part of the hallmark of Co-operative Collegial Democracy (CCD) instead of proportionality and majoritarianism. In addition to the aforementioned positive qualities of CCD, the overall cost of running it is significantly lower than the prohibitive cost of liberal party democracy campaigns and elections. More important, with CCD, the lives and property of the people are protected because politically induced violence is prevented during elections of government functionaries.

Co-operative Collegial Democracy (CCD) is similar to consociationalism as far as both recognise the dangers of winner-takes-all politics, and the institutionalisation of a permanent minority whose political function in society is simply to oppose, and they are both structured to prevent these. Lijphart explains his consociational model thus: "In a consociational democracy, the centrifugal tendencies inherent in a plural society are counteracted by the co-operative attitudes and behaviour of the leaders of the different segments of the population. Elite cooperation is the primary distinguishing feature of consociational democracy" (Lijphart in Hering 1998, 7). However, while Consociationalism works as a coalition or marriage of convenience among a small number of sectional or top party leaders, that is, "government by elite cartels" (Lijphart 1968, 26), CCD does not admit any form of party system, but rather regards the state as a "single party" or "parent" with different political offspring (units) in accord with the philosophy of *Ujamaa* (Kiswahili for "family-hood")—the African concept of the community as a large family (Nyerere 1966; Schraeder in Gordon and Gordon eds. 1996, 143).

Whether Western liberal democracy is practiced in its presidential or parliamentary form, it encourages institutionalised political competition, and is markedly different from Consociational democracy which is an improvement on it. Lijphart's type of consociational democracy, based on contextual political theory (which holds that democracy is of different forms and that it is also sensitive to the socio-political milieu in which it operates), is better than the liberal party model. Indeed, it works well in the Netherlands. However, it is not likely to work effectively in African states because, as Lijphart correctly acknowledges, no two cultures are essentially the same, and democracy is also context-sensitive.

Moreover, despite the merits in the design of Lijphart's consociational democracy, his model, unlike CCD, allows for political parties, which, as we earlier noted, are unsuitable for the ethnically plural post-colonial African states. Besides, Lijphart's consociational model fails to adequately address an important question in democratic practice, namely, the need to guarantee the election of credible and competent candidates: can this political responsibility be effectively exercised by the mass of people who are most unlikely to be aware of the qualities and capabilities of the people they are voting for? This is one area where CCD parts company with Lijphart's Consociationalism. The logic of CCD is that a small group of representatives is much more suited to, and so is vital in, identifying potential talents within their ranks.

Consequently, Co-operative Collegial Democracy (CCD) and Lijphart's consociational democracy can be compared to a tropical apple and a temperate apple respectively: African tropical apples cannot flourish in the Western European climate, and Western European apples will either wither or have stunted growth in African soil. Kingsolver (1998) writes about a missionary family from America to Congo thus: "They carry with them everything they believe they will need from home, but soon find that all of it—from garden seeds to Scripture—is calamitously transformed on African soil" (author's blurb). Some African seeds would also undergo similar transformation on American soil. The problem is neither with the soil nor with the seed, but rather that of incompatibility. That is why liberal party democracy has also been "calamitously transformed on African soil".

I have sought to illustrate that democracy in itself does not mean political competition or struggle for power, neither is it tantamount to political aggression. Rather, it is the process used to vie for power in a liberal democracy (formation of political parties, campaigns and elections) which can be chaotic and susceptible to violence. Compared with the party method of selecting political leaders, Co-operative Collegial Democracy is not violence prone—since competition, which breeds tension and violence, is ruled out. I do not assume that CCD is a perfect democratic paradigm, but rather a political system which, in Millsian parlance, "combines the greatest amount of good with the least of evil" (Mill 1956, 109) when compared with other known models of democracy, and especially when compared with liberal democracy.

Below is a brief illustration of the process of recruiting leadership in CCD. Using Nigeria with six geo-political zones as an example, Table 7.1 below is a list of all the three persons representing each of the six geo-political zones at the Federal level from whom will emerge the President of the State and other Federal Executive Officers.

Using the ballot paper designed as in Table 7.2, each of the zonal representatives selects one person from each of the six geo-political zones. The ones who get the highest score in their respective zones form the federal executive arm of government. In the case of a draw, the final selection is to be determined by lot (*lucky dip*). This seemingly unpopular technique has at least two splendid benefits. *First*, the human and material cost of organising another electoral exercise is saved. *Second*, the lot seems to be the shortest, simplest, and fairest procedure to adopt in the context in question. The six persons who get the highest number of votes in their zones will become members of the Executive College and will choose from amongst themselves the President of the country, the *primus inter pares* ("first among equals"), the First Vice President, the second Vice President, and other office holders, each having a veto as regards any decision taken at the federal level. The remaining twelve members of the Federal College form the legislative arm of government.

Co-operative Collegial Democracy, as a model for leadership recruitment, was first tried out in 2016 and 2017 with Levels 300 and 400 Political Science

Table 7.1. A Sample of CCD's List of members of Federal College with voting results. Federal Republic of Nigeria—Presidential Election. List of Zonal Representatives: The Federal College

S/No	Name	Code No.	Geo-Political Zone	Qualifications	No of Votes	Total
1	Ahmed	NW102	North West	BA (History)	√√√√√	6
2	Sanusi	NW103	North West	PhD (Sociology)	√√√√√√√√	9
3	Yusuf	NW104	North West	(Unavailable)	√√√	3
			TOTAL			18
4	Bello	NE001	North East	MA (Economics)	√√√√	5
5	Dogara	NE002	North East	BSc (Mathematics)	√√√√√√√	8
6	Aisha	NE003	North East	MA (Philosophy)	√√√√	5
			TOTAL			18
7	Yakubu	NC201	North Central	BSc (Mathematics)	√√√	3
8	Ukpai	NC202	North Central	BA (History)	√√√√√√√√√	10
9	Ochefu	NC203	North Central	MA (Pol. Science)	√√√√	5
			TOTAL			18
10	Offor	SE300	South East	PhD (Pol. Science)	√√√√√√	7
11	Ngozi	SE301	South East	MA (Law)	√√√√√	6
12	Mbakwe	SE302	South East	BSc. (C. Engineering)	√√√√	5
			TOTAL			18
13	Onah	SS401	South South	MA (Economics)	√	1
14	Enewali	SS402	South South	MA (Chemistry)	√√√√√√√√√	10
15	Effiong	SS403	South South	PhD (Sociology)	√√√√√√	7
			TOTAL			18
16	Wole	SW500	South West	BA (History)	√√√	4
17	Tunde	SW501	South West	PhD (Accounting)	√√√√√√	7
18	Fumilayo	SW502	South West	PhD (English)	√√√√√√	7
						18

students at the Federal University, Ndufu Alike Ikwo (FUNAI) in Ebonyi State, Nigeria. Most of the participants were of the opinion that it would also be a more orderly and more efficient paradigm for electing Students' Union Presidents and other officers in Universities where political units of a university are made up of Programmes (Courses), Departments, Faculties, and the University as a whole.

Table 7.2. A Sample of CCD Election Form. Federal Republic of Nigeria—Presidential Election Form For Members of the Federal College

	Representative's Name	Code No.	Geo-political Zone
Voter's Name ▶ Choices Made (Names)	Ahmed	NW102	North West
1	Yusuf	NW104	North West
2	Dogara	NE002	North East
3	Ochefu	NC203	North Central
4	Ngozi	SE301	South East
5	Effiong	SS403	South South
6	Fumilayo	SW502	South West

CONCLUSION

I have argued that authentic democracy is essentially about affirming freedom, equality and equity for all, irrespective of minority or majority dichotomies, or any other strengths or weaknesses of various groups in society. This being so, the majoritarian liberal democratic practice of excluding parties that lose elections from power is tantamount to excluding minority groups and their interests from government and governance. Such exclusion is contrary to the primary meaning of democracy, also understood as the opportunity to be adequately represented in decision making. In addition, such exclusion is typically suggestive of hegemony. Nevertheless, with appropriate institutional arrangements in place, there can be stability in ethnically or religiously plural states. The indigenous African political leadership ethos entails the incorporation of majorities and minorities into cohesive polities.

The escalating volatilities stemming from political tensions in ethnically and religiously plural African states are a strong indication of the impracticability in these polities of Western liberal democracy, with its party system and majoritarian principle. As such, Francis Fukuyama's view that Western liberal democracy is "the final form of human government" (Fukuyama 1989; 1992) ignores the fact that the "democratic seed" planted in African countries has not germinated in many of them after more than fifty years, and, where it has germinated, it has not achieved significant growth. This is due to the fact that liberal democracy, characterised by competition through political parties, has not proved to be an effective instrument for institutionalising democracy in ethnically plural African polities. Accepting Fukuyama's hypothesis as a categorical imperative would, therefore, inhibit scholars and statesmen and stateswomen in various non-Western countries, African ones included, from embarking on the task of fashioning context-relevant models of democracy.

Arend Lijphart's consociational democracy (Lijphart 1968), practiced today in some countries, illustrates that liberal democracy is not, after all, the final form of human government.

Consequently, I have made a case for Co-operative Collegial Democracy (CCD) for ethnically plural African states. This is a model of democracy in which "opposing" groups (of any type) select their representatives who join with representatives of other groups to constitute colleges at various political levels. Members of each of the colleges then select or elect from among themselves persons to occupy positions of leadership. CCD makes no provision for different groups to struggle for political power. More specifically, it effectively facilitates conflict resolution in an ethnically plural state, because it is free from the government-versus-opposition approach typical of liberal party democracy. As a result, no segment of society is denied a significant say in governance. CCD is a party-less democratic model. It is founded on the conviction that political cooperation is a structural imperative for an ethnically or religiously plural African state. Unlike liberal forms of democracy, it is *co-operative* rather than competitive. It is also *collegial* because instead of using the masses to elect individuals to political offices as is the practice in liberal democracy, it operates with groups of persons ("colleges") made up of representatives of the people. It is also *democratic* in the true sense of the term because it is the people, starting from the lowest units of society, who elect their representatives from whom government is formed. Failure to adopt such a context-relevant democratic model of governance will continue to hinder the consolidation of democracy in many African states, thereby rendering them dysfunctional polities in perpetuity.

NOTES

1. An updated version appears as a chapter elsewhere in this volume.

2. In each Igbo town, usually made up of several villages, the holders of the highest traditional title are collectively known as Nze na Ọzọ ("*Nze*" = "title-holder", "*na*" = "and", "*Ọzọ*" [pronounced "ozo"] = "group of title holders"; so Nze na Ọzọ literally = "title-holder and group of title-holders", but is dynamically translatable simply as "group of title-holders"). It is from among this group that each village selects its representatives to the King's Palace (the Town's central Government, comprising representatives of all the villages that make up the town), thus becoming members of the King's Cabinet. They are usually regarded as men of high moral integrity who would never compromise justice or truth—virtues they took an oath to uphold during their initiation ceremony. It is important to note that the Igbo, as a nation, do not have one king or queen, but most, if not all, towns have kings. Traditional Igbo towns are made up of villages, and each village, in turn, consists of various *Umu-nna* (clans), where a

clan is a group of families with a common ancestor. Thus, the Igbo, as a nation, have the following organigram: *Igbo nation—Towns—Villages—Clans—Households*, that is, *Family units*.

3. The Igbo have many dialects, which explains why the word 'king' is variously referred to as *Obi, Qba, Iduu, Igwe*, etc. in different Igbo communities.

4. *Eze Nwanyi* literally means a female king, that is, a Queen.

5. Kisumu is a lakeside Kenyan town known for its scorching heat.

REFERENCES

Aleshinloye-Agboola, Mariam. 2011. "Let's Crash this Democracy". *Sun* (Nigeria), Sunday, 13 March, 2011. http://www.sunnewsonline.com/webpages/news/national/2011/mar/13/national-13-03-2011-001.htm.

Blaug, Ricardo, and John Schwarzmantel eds. 2004. *Democracy: A Reader*. Edinburgh: Edinburgh University Press.

Castells, Manuel. 1998. *End of Millennium*. N.P.: Blackwell Publishers.

Cunningham, Frank. 2002. *Theories of Democracy: A Critical Introduction*. New York: Routledge.

Ezeani, Emefiena. 2013. *Cooperative Collegial Democracy for Africa and Multiethnic Societies: Democracy without Tears*. Africa in Development Series, Vol. 13. Oxford: Peter Lang International Academic Publishers.

Fisher, Matthew. 2007. "Elections in Doubt as Pakistan Adjusts to Life without Bhutto". *National Post online*. http://nationalpost.com/news/elections-in-doubt-as-pakistan-adjusts-to-life-without-bhutto/wcm/4d0c2b79-be67-4405-87ea-a6d6f0882d4e.

Fukuyama, Francis. 1989. "The End of History?" Lecture Presented at the University of Chicago's John M. Olin Centre. https://ps321.community.uaf.edu/files/2012/10/Fukuyama-End-of-history-article.pdf

———. 1992. *The End of History and the Last Man*. London: Penguin Books.

Held, David. 1999. *Models of Democracy*, 2nd Edition. Cambridge: Polity Press.

Hering, Martin. 1998. "Consociational Democracy in Canada". http://archiv.ub.uni-marburg.de/sum/84/sum84-6.html.

Kingsolver, Barbara. 1998. *The Poisonwood Bible*. New York: HarperCollins Publishers.

Lijphart, Arend. 1968. *The Politics of Accommodation, Pluralism and Democracy in the Netherlands*. Los Angeles: University of California Press.

Machiavelli, Niccolò. 2011. *The Prince*. London: Penguin Classics.

Menamparampil, Thomas. 2017. "Strengthening Indigenous Values to Facilitate the Emergence of Suitable Forms of Democracy". Paper Delivered at the International Conference on "Beyond Liberal Democracy: The Quest for Indigenous African Models of Democracy for the Twenty-First Century", University of Nairobi, Kenya, organised by the Department of Philosophy and Religious Studies, University of Nairobi, Kenya, and the Council for Research in Values and Philosophy (RVP), Washington, D.C., 22–23 May 2017.

Mill, John S. 1956. *On Liberty*, and *Considerations on Representative Government*. Oxford: Basil Blackwell.

Momoh, Abubakar and Said Adejumobi. 1999. *The Nigerian Military and the Crisis of Democratic Transition: A Study in the Monopoly of Power*. Lagos: Civil Liberties Organisation.

Mwaura, Charles N. 1997. "Political Succession and Related Conflicts in Kenya". A paper prepared for the USAID Conference on "Conflict Resolution in the Greater Horn of Africa", held at the Methodist Guest House, Nairobi, Kenya, 27–28 March, 1997. http://citeseerx.ist.psu.edu/viewdoc/download?doi=10.1.1.540.5512&rep=rep1&type=pdf.

Nnoli, Okwudiba. 1986. *Introduction to Politics*. London: Longman.

Nwodo, Okwesilieze. 2009. "Obasanjo was not Qualified to be PDP Candidate in 1999". *Nigerian Vanguard*, 25 July 2009. http://www.vanguardngr.com/2009/07/25/obasanjo-was-not-qualified-to-be-pdp-candidate-in-1999-okwesilieze-nwodo.

Nyerere, Julius. 1966. "Democracy and the Party Politics". *Freedom and Unity: A Selection of Writings and Speeches, 1952–1965*. Dar es Salaam: Oxford University Press.

Oduor, Reginald M. J. 2017. "Scholarship in Service of Africa: Closing Remarks". Delivered at an International Conference on "Beyond Liberal Democracy: The Quest for Indigenous African Models of Democracy for the Twenty-First Century", Nairobi, Kenya, organised by the Department of Philosophy and Religious Studies, University of Nairobi, Kenya, and the Council for Research in Values and Philosophy (RVP), Washington, D.C., 22–23 May 2017.

Orr, David. 1997. "Violence, Fraud and Floods Mar Kenyan Elections". *The Times* (London), 30 December 1997, pp. 9–10.

Osaghae, Eghosa E. 1998. *Nigeria Since Independence: Crippled Giant*. London: Hurt & Company.

Plato. 1987. *The Republic*, Second Edition. Lee, Desmond trans. London: Penguin Books.

Schraeder, Peter J. 1996. "African International Relations". Gordon, April A. and Donald L. Gordon eds. *Understanding Contemporary Africa*, 2nd Edition. London: Lynne Rienner Publishers Inc.

Umeh, John Anenechukwu. 2017. *The March of Igbo Civilisation*, Vol. I. Saarbrucken: Lambert Academic Publishing.

Ustinov, Peter. 2004. "Can Science Explain Why I'm a Pessimist?" BBC News. www.bbc.co.uk/news/magazine-23229014.

Uyanne, Frank Uzochukwu. 1994. "International Boundaries and Democratisation in Africa". *Democratisation in Africa: Conference Final Report*, Conference organised by ITC & Global Coalition for Africa, Enschede, The Netherlands, March 6–18, 1994, pp. 12–23.

Chapter Eight

The Traditional Roots of Democratic Verbal Discipline

Insights from the Akan

Emmanuel Ifeanyi Ani

Practising the multi-party system of democracy in Africa has seen the emergence of numerous forms of verbal aggression, especially insulting language, in the contest for power. This threatens the very foundations of peace, as indicated in a study involving 6,002 people, in which Jan Stets found that verbal aggression causes physical aggression, and the causality is not just positive but significant (Stets 1990, 508; see also Ani 2015, 150). There is little to learn from Western attempts at verbal discipline, as many Western societies are hardly better off in this regard. It is worth noting that the importance of discipline in the use of language goes beyond the multi-party system: we will still need verbal discipline for whatever future form of democracy we wish to develop. Certain traditional cultures of Africa, such as that of the Akan of Ghana, place a high premium on linguistic discipline and have built a network of norms that discourage verbal aggression. Norms in the Akan culture crystalise into the principle that how we say something is as important as what we say. In this chapter, I extrapolate these principles into the contemporary practice of democracy. I make suggestions about how social policy could do for contemporary society what culture has done for certain traditional societies regarding verbal discipline.

The general rationale is that as long as there is desire for power, there will be desperation on the part of some contestants, and desperation without verbal discipline can lead to verbal aggression. I therefore wish to attend to our contemporary use of language, since this is an important variable in cleaning up our practice of democracy in Africa and is of crucial importance to whatever model of democracy we wish to practice going forward. As such, it is not my purpose in this chapter to discuss the foundational differences between majoritarian and consensual democracy, or among any other forms of democracy. Neither is it the goal of this chapter to propose an alternative to liberal democracy. My aim is to argue for the moderation of the use of language in whatever system of democracy we wish to practice. This is because *argument* remains indispensable to politics. In addition, *bidding* for power is an indispensable part of whatever system of governance we wish to practice; bidding for power goes beyond the multi-party system, and the only alternative to it is monarchy (heredity and no bidding). Nevertheless, bidding for power leads to desperation, which leads to verbal aggression, and we thus need verbal discipline.

In the first section, I describe (with examples) the verbal aggression witnessed in the practice of the multi-party system of democracy in some African countries. In the second, I outline the traditional taboos that the Akan have attached to verbal aggression in its many forms. In the third, I draw out three principles that, in my view, underlie the Akan prohibition of verbal aggression. In the fourth and final section, I reflect on a general application of the said principles to the contemporary practice of democracy in African countries.

VERBAL AGGRESSION AND THE MULTI-PARTY SYSTEM OF DEMOCRACY IN AFRICA

No one would deny that the multi-party system is designed to encourage competition for power by rival groups of people. Mainstream democracy scholars such as Robert Dahl (1971, 3–9), Joseph Schumpeter (1976, 269) and Samuel Huntington (1984, 196) agree that the two pillars of liberal democracy are contestation and participation (see also Ajei 2016, 452). The participation principle is a common denominator that different models of democracy, such as the majoritarian and consensual systems, share. However, the aspect of contest for power is strenuously opposed by some scholars of consensual democracy as a "quintessence of uncooperativeness" (Wiredu 2011, 1061).

The multi-party system institutionalises opposition in such a way that opposition becomes necessary to gain power, and gaining power becomes more urgent than the desire to correct an erring government, giving rise to criticism from the opposition that is often obstructive rather than constructive: it is the political equivalent of asking two gladiators to lock into a tussle in full view of an audience. The difference is that this is supposed to be a contest of ideas about how to better govern the citizens, improve the economy, and provide security, among others. Contestation and participation have informed majoritarian democracy, which has become "the most widely practiced form of democracy in the Western world. It is practiced by the United Kingdom and France, which together colonised over 90 percent of the countries in Africa in which constitutional democracies are currently instituted" (Ajei 2016, 452).

An empirical disquisition of how the multi-party idea has fared in practice in Africa shows mixed results. In this regard, Martin Ajei writes:

> Since the 1990s, some elections in Africa have exhibited a measure of toleration for genuine political pluralism and contest. But since 2000 until October 2015, the outcomes of 26 of the 103 presidential elections held on the continent have been disputed. Eleven of these disputed elections have provoked atrocious violence and the loss of life, property and human security. (Ajei 2016, 453)

If these statistics are correct, the results are mixed because quite a large number of elections have been undisputed. Nevertheless, 26 out of 103 is 25 percent—a quarter of all the elections, which motivates us to keep thinking of how to improve the quality of our elections.

More foundational is the worry that the multi-party system encourages verbal aggression. It is true that the desire for power is universal: we find it in monarchy, dictatorship, aristocracy, oligarchy, and any other system of governance. However, the multi-party system tries to domesticate the desire for power by borrowing the idea of competition from classical liberal economics: the idea is that competition drives prices down while driving quality up. In the case of democracy, it purportedly does this by creating several parties to compete for power. The idea then is that one party's misdeed would become another party's advantage, and the winners would always be the people. Nevertheless, this political arrangement comes with its own problems. Of greatest concern is that it is not always easy to compete *healthily* for power. As earlier noted, practising the multi-party system of democracy in Africa has seen the emergence of numerous forms of verbal aggression in the contest for power. Here I will provide examples from Ghana, where I have worked for several years.

When Kwame Nkrumah's Conventional Peoples Party (CPP) won the Ghana elections in 1954, the opposition, led by Abrefa Busia, adopted a combative stance, proposing alternative systems of government (such as federalism coupled with ethnic-based parties), and this led the CPP supporters to describe them as "arch reactionaries, cocoa-season politicians" (Kukubor 2011, par 7). In response, Busia's newly formed party, the National Liberation Movement (NLM), described the CPP as "those who belong to no family or clan, those who are strangers, not properly trained to appreciate the value of the true and noble Akans" (*Liberator*, 20 December 1955; cited in Kukubor 2011, par 8). The Busia-led opposition had also described a committee composed of some CPP parliamentarians as comprised of "tramps" and "jackals" (*Liberator*, 20 December 1955; cited in Kukubor 2011, par 8).

More recently, two former Ghanaian presidents have engaged in an open exchange of insults. Kukubor writes:

> [John] Agyekum Kufuor referred to Jerry John Rawlings in the Akan language as a "*Sasabonsam*"—a devil, and as "That Thing" which should Not Have Been There as Ghana's president. Jerry John Rawlings also replied by comparing Agyekum Kufuor to Atta Ayi, a notorious armed robber . . . in prison for his criminal activities. Between 1992 and 1996, the late Professor Adu Boahen openly stated that he named his dog after Rawlings because he claimed that his dog was very stubborn just like Rawlings. (Kukubor 2011, par 12)

Regarding an even more recent period in Ghanaian politics, the next report from Kukubor is considerably alarming for the practice of democracy:

> Very recently, the political landscape has been besieged with words such as "*Kookoo ase Kuraseni*" [uncivilised villager], thieves, fruit cake, cocaine barons, Shit-Eating Human-Animal, womaniser, Junkie Parasite, chimpanzee, war monger, wee smoker, stupid fool, Arsonist, homosexual, ill-health ridden president, Professor do Little, and a "confused and blind folded President who is walking in the forest without direction". These insults were mostly traded by the NDC and the NPP. (Kukubor 2011, par 13)[1]

The successor to President John Kufuor, President John Evans Atta-Mills (a professor of law), expressed his concern about the deepening culture of insults, which in his view was subverting national development. He observed that this corrupts the younger generation, and could be a disaster (see Baffoe 2010, par 1). Similarly, Larbi-Odei observed that insults have dominated recent politics in Ghana:

> In the 2012 elections, insulting/offensive comments, unsubstantiated allegations and provocative remarks were the three most frequently used types of indecent expressions against political opponents of a list of 10 of such expressions. There was an average of four (4) indecent expressions recorded on daily basis by the Media Foundation for West Africa (MFWA) between April and December. For the nine-month monitoring period, 2,850 programmes were monitored on the 31 radio stations. A total of 509 indecent expressions were coded on those programmes with as much as 404 indecent expressions by political party affiliates. (Larbi-Odei 2016, pars 11–12)

Similar events are witnessed in Western democracies. Donald Trump, who seems to be the leading user of vulgar language, described the collaboration between two of his rivals (Jeb Bush and Marco Rubio) as "political BS", and told a crowd "you bet your ass" he would revive waterboarding as an interrogation technique (Flegenheimer and Haberman 2015, par 9). He frequently addressed his political opponents as "losers", "jerks", "clowns", and "morons" (Dryer 2017). About four decades earlier, President Richard Nixon was known to be blasphemous and obscene: he often used salacious and scatological words (Rothman 2016, par 5).

It is this rude verbalisation which threatens the very foundations of peace. This is because, as I earlier indicated, empirical studies have revealed that physical aggression is usually preceded by verbal aggression (Stets 1990, 508; see also Ani 2015, 150). Let me quote my own summary of Stet's findings:

> The finding was that there is virtually no one who is physically aggressive without having been verbally aggressive as well, which leads to the conclusion that people are generally physically aggressive only after they have become verbally aggressive. Although the time lag between the two is not certain, it is clear that verbal aggression induces negative feelings that fester until they find expression either in further verbal aggression or in physical aggression. (Ani 2015, 150)

Stets's study focused on verbal and physical aggression within marriage, but his findings have the same implications for social interaction in general, since Fagan et al. (1983) found that those who are aggressive to family members are also aggressive to non-family members (see also Stets 1990, 505). Verbal aggression is not only dangerous for the practice of politics: it also has health implications. Some scholars have linked psychopathy to a history of witnessing physical (and ultimately verbal) aggression (see Weiler and Widom 1996, 253–57; Lang et al. 2002, 93, 96–99; Ani 2015, 151).

The multi-party system encourages verbal aggression, especially by desperate politicians. Nevertheless, given the dangerous potential of verbal aggression to produce physical aggression, exploring ways of dealing with it in our practice of democracy is a worthwhile academic venture. Besides, as I earlier pointed out, the importance of verbal discipline goes beyond the multi-party system, because we would still need verbal discipline in whatever future form of democracy we choose to develop. Let me now turn to a refreshing study of the verbal discipline in the Akan traditional system.

THE AKAN VERBAL CULTURE

Samuel Obeng reports that the Akan of Ghana believe that how we say a thing is as important as what we say (Obeng 1994, 41). This ethnic group believes that conversation should be governed by the "maxim of manners" (Obeng 1994, 38; Ani 2015, 151). Kofi Agyekum also observes that, in the view of the Akan, we acquire language freely, but our usage of it is "constrained and conditioned by the sociological norms, values and conventions of the society" (Agyekum 2010, preface). In *Akan Verbal Taboos*, he detailed the things that the Akan believe we ought never to say. By labelling these things as *taboo*, the Akan raised them to the level of *sacred* negativity, whose most important punishment is a social loss of face. The Akan believe that when we discuss an issue with other people, we must "maintain our face", and to do so, we must also "maintain the face" of those with whom we interact. To try to "remove their face" is interpreted as losing one's own face as well. Agyekum gives an example of this when he reports that if one uses the Akan invective "*woye bonini* (you are barren)", which negatively affects the feelings of the target, "the speaker loses his respect before the public and disgraces himself and possibly his whole family" (Agyekum 2010, 13). He further reports that in Akan society, people show interest in those "who normally present their positive faces in interaction, since this involves the use of appropriate language in a social context bearing in mind the desires of the addressee(s)" (Agyekum 2010, 13). The Akan particularly treated the use of insults as taboo:

> Invectives sometimes take the form of linguistic warfare between participants in a communicative situation. The participants are the combatants and the weapon is the language they use to psychologically affront and hurt the feelings of one another. The abusive expressions throw psychological bombs at the hearts of the opponents and damage their emotions. Invectives tarnish and curb co-operation between people. It is the antagonistic nature of the verbal expressions and their effect that we try to avoid. This is why they are considered as verbal taboos. (Agyekum 2010, 109–10)

Agyekum further writes of the Akan:

> Invectives undermine peace in society. To bring about peace, there is need for linguistic disarmament. The disarmament takes the form of prohibition, inhibition and the restrictions of certain expressions. . . . these prohibitions, inhibitions and restrictions are the proscribed taboo expressions we have labelled *atennidie*, 'invectives.' (Agyekum 2010, 110)

The Akan have various ways of identifying invectives. *First*, they generally identify expressions that aim to denigrate or humiliate the addressee. *Second*, they consider certain expressions to be more offensive when they are spoken in public. The appropriateness or inappropriateness of such expressions also depends on the kind of people present and the overall social context (Agyekum 2010, 110). *Third*, the Akan identify as invectives those expressions that aim to show that the addressee is deviating from the norm. Usually, they consider such expressions to be invectives when the purported deviation from the norm is exaggerated (Agyekum 2010, 110).

Fourth, there are instances where an individual attributes a property of an animal to a human being. An example is where one refers to a person as a dog: although dogs are very good pets, they are also considered to be promiscuous, and they steal, and are also quarrelsome and greedy (Agyekum 2010, 112). Other animals have their negative qualities (that Agyekum extensively documents, but cannot be listed here), and it is equally taboo to refer to a person in terms of those other animals.

Fifth, there are expressions that refer to persons in terms of certain diseases that have been "tabooed because they inflict emotional pain on the addressee" (Agyekum 2010, 118). This includes references to conditions such as barrenness, tuberculosis, and epilepsy, or suggesting dysfunction or improper use of a person's intellect, such as references to foolishness or madness (Agyekum 2010, 118–21). Equally tabooed are derogatory references to a person's characteristics such as ethnic affiliation, sex, age, race, or genealogy (Agyekum 2010, 122–28).

Sixth, the Akan take note of expressions intended to denigrate the addressee's or target's physical structure or personal behaviour. Since our physical and behavioural attributes vary, "any attempt to compare oneself to the addressee in an attempt to reduce him and demean his personality is regarded as an insult" (Agyekum 2010, 128). This includes attacks on a person's "intellect, capability and achievement in the society, his occupation, religion and marital connections" (Agyekum 2010, 128). No matter how bad a person may be, it is forbidden to refer to him or her as a "worthless" human being. It is also offensive to downgrade a male by referring to him as a female or "one who does not go to war" (Agyekum 2010, 130). This is very offensive, especially when a woman directs it at a man, and it derives its gravity from the time when men used to go to war leaving women at home to do domestic work. Referring to a man as a woman has a range of traditional connotations, including "cowardice, impotence, inability to achieve something and an irresponsible fellow" (Agyekum 2010, 131). Agyekum explains that in a game of marbles, if someone is afraid of putting forward his marbles for fear of losing them, there is a temptation to call him a female, and if he responds by also calling his attacker a female, "both of them are immediately barred from the competition" (Agyekum 2010, 131).

Seventh, for the Akan, there are insults that attempt to harm the moral credibility of the addressee. Agyekum reports that a case was brought to the court of the Asantehemma (the Queen Mother of the Ashanti), in which a lady called another lady a villain. He cites the elders as ruling as follows: "This is a serious insulting language (*akoye atennidie bone*). It amounts to driving a person from one's house. A sheep must be slaughtered to atone for this act. The word *busueni*, 'villain' in our Asante dialect means that the person is devilish, dangerous and harmful" (Agyekum 2010, 138). In addition, referring to people as "devil" or "witch" is taboo. The utterer and the addressee would either need to go to a medicineman or medicinewoman where the utterer would take an oath to affirm the veracity of his or her claim, or to the traditional court where the utterer would be severely punished if he or she did not prove his or her claim (Agyekum 2010, 138).

Eighth, it is taboo among the Akan to make derogatory references to an addressee's marriage, occupation, or religion. Also forbidden are derogatory references to body parts, such as *wo nkonto* (bow-legged person), *wonni aninton* (you have no eyelids), *wo se a asaisai* (your displaced teeth), *wo nto trawa* (your flat buttocks), *nsansia* (you six-fingered person), and so on (Agyekum 2010, 132).

Nevertheless, certain forms of verbal aggression are sometimes permitted in certain games (such as a game between peers called *aboreme*, which means "to dig or search"), and in certain festivals. Here I give the example of the *Apoa* ("cleansing" or "exorcising") festivals of the Brong Ahafo area:

During these periods, anybody can hurl insults at the King or chief without any sanctions. It is believed that these are the times when the attention of the rulers can be drawn to some of the faults of their administration, so that they can start to take corrective measures to rectify the shortcomings in the society after the festival (Agyekum 2010, 140).

More generally, insults are permitted in these contexts to enable people to tease one another. These insults are used carefully, as they could lead to real conflicts in which insults would regain their taboo status and punishment would be needed (Agyekum 2010, 139–40). Once the festival or game is over, the taboos are back in place.

The Akan have certain commonly accepted views that form the philosophical foundation of their disapproval of verbal aggression. I have mentioned that one of such views is that the manner of one's speech is just as important as what one wants to say (see Obeng 1994, 41). Let me provide a little more detail of this view. Indeed, they hold that "a person who uses blunt language instead of euphemism (presumably in potentially inflammatory situations) is regarded as not being able to speak well" (Saah 1986, 369; Words in parentheses in the original text). A second view is that the damage inflicted by verbal abuse is psychologically permanent. This is reflected in the popular Akan proverb *"Asɛm tesɛ kutwa, wopepa a, ɛnkɔ* (Speech is like a scar: it never disappears even when wiped or cleaned)". Consequently, the Akan avoid verbal attacks (possibly even more than they would avoid physical ones). Regarding this Obeng observes:

> So powerful and 'deadly' is the spoken word that conversational participants adopt various strategies in order not to step on one another's toes or threaten each other's faces. . . . conversational participants use, singly or conjointly, such effective communicative strategies as displaying reluctance, hesitation, or

delay with 'well', to signal that a forthcoming move is face-threatening. (Obeng 1994, 40)

The Akan have also created several instruments to blunt the acidity of a criticism if one must render it. Such expressions include "*mepa wo kyɛw* (I beg you)", or "*mesere meka* (I beg to say)". The belief is that begging before criticising shows the addressee that the utterer means well. These expressions could also be used to warn the addressee of an impending profanity or indecent use of language, in order to placate him or her in advance, and, at the very minimum, to give him or her the impression that the language is not malicious (see Yankah 1991, 56 and Obeng 1994, 41). Akwasi Gyan-Apenteng makes a similar point when he remarks: "In all Ghanaian cultures, we have expressions that precede the use of 'bad words' as prior detoxification for bad behaviour" (Gyan-Apenteng 2016, par 3). The Akan also recognise that in certain situations we need to be direct and candid with our views (as seen in Buss 1961 and Berkowitz 1962) but believe that if we judge those views to be face-threatening, we ought to be a bit indirect with language (Obeng 1994, 64). Such indirect language includes using metaphors, proverbs, euphemisms, circumlocutions, hyperboles, innuendos, among others (Obeng 1994, 64).

It is therefore evident that the Akan have created a whole system of rules to constantly keep verbal aggression in check. They understand that verbal aggression "compels the target to retaliate with more offensive words" (Agyekum 2010, 111). Agyekum cites Clyne thus: "Words chosen from the 'strong' end of the lexical field are likely to be responded to with other words from that end, with one interlocutor trying to undo the other" (Clyne 1987, 90; cited in Agyekum 2010, 111). This is why verbal aggression leads to verbal conflicts (see for instance Grimes 1977).

THREE PRINCIPLES OF DEMOCRATIC VERBAL DISCIPLINE

In this section I seek to draw out three principles that, in my observation, underlie the Akan attitude towards verbal aggression in the social context. The first principle is what I would call the *affective neutral approach to disagreement*. According to this principle, the argument of one's opponent is the target of one's criticism, not the opponent himself or herself. The idea behind this principle is to combine the project of a rejection or revision of an opponent's position with the attitude of full respect for him or her. This principle teaches that we ought to separate the two, and never conflate them. The principle is vital in keeping a society healthy even in the midst of the most passionate disagreements.

There is a Western parallel to the principle that it is our opponent's argument rather than our opponent's person that matters for debating positions. The Western version of the principle is not clearly outlined, but we see it in the form of 'tabooing' a violation of the principle. This taboo is seen in logic, when we define ad hominem as a fallacy of attacking an opponent's person rather than his or her argument. One could observe that the Akan go beyond Western logic, in the sense that they actually elaborate and categorise personality attacks in order to leave no doubt about the various ways in which they could occur (see the previous section).

The second principle is that the most candid criticisms (where they need to be sharp) could be delivered without the impression of being insulting or denigrating. This is undoubtedly a difficult task by itself, but the Akan have come up with an easy way to be candid with one's opponent without coming across as disrespectful. This is simply by beginning with the respectful clauses we know (some of which we have already seen in the Akan culture), such as "Forgive me . . .", "If I may, . . .", or "Pardon me . . ." To see how effective these clauses could be, we could consider them in practice. Let us take any expression that has the potential to hurt the feelings of an addressee's sensibility, then simply prefix it with one of these clauses, and it becomes clear that the presence of the clause takes away some of the acidity in the criticism. We are all familiar with the Western version of this approach to delivering a criticism. According to the Western version, we begin with a clause such as "With due respect, . . ." or "I hope you will excuse me if I say . . ." Such clauses are tension neutralisers. One learns how and when to use them, as they enable one to express one's opinions candidly without losing the collegiality of the recipient.

The third principle is that collective peace takes precedence over individual victory. When the Akan worry about how to talk to one another (as they evidently do courtesy of their verbal taboos), it indicates that they are more concerned about collective peace than individual victories in debates or verbal conflicts. Let me, at this point, add that it is not only the vanquished who bears the responsibility for promoting collective peace when considering further options: the victor also shares the obligation to promote public peace by resisting the temptation to gloat in his or her victory. This makes it easier for the vanquished to refrain from actions that may further strain the peace. The general idea behind this principle, then, is that we ought to let go of certain arguments if we know that they have the potential to interfere with the public peace. A recent modern expression of this principle was presented during the Ghana 2012 Presidential Election Petition, in which the New Patriotic Party (NPP) accused the ruling National Democratic Coalition (NDC) of rigging the 2012 Presidential elections. The popular sentiment then was that the NDC could not have won the election and used the power of Presidential incumbency to manipulate it, but the court ruled in favour of the NDC. This was the closest that Ghana came to a civil conflict in its history. However, the NPP (which is an Akan-dominated party) told its supporters that the country's peace was more important than their grievances. They reminded their supporters of their love "for Mother Ghana". Their presidential candidate, Nana Addo Danquah Akufo Addo, said in a highly publicised speech that although he did not agree with the ruling, he accepted it for the sake of the peace of the country.[2] He won the next presidential election (in December 2016) with an emphatic majority.

APPLYING THE GENERAL PRINCIPLES OF VERBAL DISCIPLINE TO CONTEMPORARY POLITICAL LIFE

It is apparent that the Akan system of verbal taboo is a bit antiquated. Indeed, many of the invectives used today are much more sophisticated, as the cases we earlier cited from contemporary Ghana and the United States illustrate. As we have seen, most of the insults that worried the Akan were those that emerged from interpersonal communication between individuals. However, the insults of concern today are those delivered on traditional and social media. The type of channel usually determines the kinds of insults. In the case of contemporary media, verbal aggression has expectedly become more sophisticated, less crude, but equally damaging.

An example of one of the most commonly used abusive words in the context of today's multi-party adversarial democracy is to describe a public officeholder as "incompetent". This word is common because members of opposition parties are conditioned by their desire for power to present members of the ruling party as inadequate for the task of governing, while those in the ruling party are equally compelled by their desire to remain in power to present opposition parties as non-viable alternatives. The word "incompetent" is itself not necessarily offensive, since its target could indeed be incompetent. What is offensive is to describe one's opponent as incompetent *without* offering *any* evidence to support the claim. Most politicians think that they can get away with subjecting their opponents to character assassination.

To illustrate the point in the previous paragraph, let us move away from state politics to university politics for a moment: suppose that, in a departmental meeting, a faculty member describes a conference recently organised by a colleague as "incompetently organised". Sensing foul play, someone in the meeting asks him to provide evidence for his claim. At first, he is lost for words, but a little later in the meeting offers manifestly implausible grounds for his claim. To make a damaging claim and support it with plausible reasons is to criticise, but to do so without credible grounds is to simply *attack* a person rather than his or her position or action. Suppose further that on reflecting on the possible motive behind the attacker's claim, we remember that the attacker had, prior to the latest conference, been the only one who had organised conferences in the department in recent times. Consequently, we could infer that the attacker's motive was probably the desire to be seen as the only person in the department who could competently organise conferences.

The example above illustrates that criticism can arise out of impure motives. In the context of modern multi-party democracy, criticism of an opponent's performance could be legitimate, but with two provisos.

First, claims must be *substantiated*. A criticism is usually an argument, and an argument contains a claim (conclusion) and the presentation of evidence to support the claim in at least one premise. Making a claim without providing evidence to support it is *not* an argument; and if a claim is not supported, it is particularly unfair if it is also denigrating. Examples of premises supporting a charge of incompetence could be that the government in question has failed to improve the economy (with relevant statistics as part of the premises), has not improved security (with examples), did not handle an international crisis effectively, and so on. These premises enable the audience to determine if the charge of incompetence has any merit. Indeed, it is sometimes more honourable to offer premises without offering any conclusions, letting the audience infer the conclusions for itself! In other words, it is more appropriate to criticise specific actions and programs rather than call one's opponent names.

Second, a criticism ought not to be accompanied by any insulting expressions. Here, I need not add to the elaboration that the Akan have already provided. During the administration of the Nigerian president Goodluck Jonathan, his predecessor, Olusegun Obasanjo, criticised the government in an open letter for failing to deal effectively with Boko Haram (Obasanjo 2013). President Jonathan fired back with a letter, also made available to the public, in which he referred to Obasanjo's "hardly original idea of carrot and stick" in dealing with Boko Haram (Jonathan 2013, par 20).

It is important that we do not resort to insults even when we feel seriously offended. A Makerere University Research Fellow, Dr. Stella Nyanzi, was in the news a while ago for referring to the Ugandan President Yoweri Museveni on her Facebook page as "a pair of buttocks" (Shaban 2017). One may feel that the Ugandan head of state deserves this appellation because of his long and draconian rule. Nevertheless, two wrongs do not make a right: it is quite possible to effectively criticise him without recourse to such language.

CONCLUDING REFLECTIONS

We have seen the elaborate system of verbal taboos built by the Akan to moderate interpersonal interactions in their society with a view to making it peaceful. Since peace is a prerequisite of progress, one wonders if this is not one of the crucial factors behind the historical greatness of the Ashanti kingdom. The obvious question now is whether or not the system of verbal taboos is still effective in contemporary Akan society. Having lived and worked in Ghana for several years now, I think that its effectiveness has been somewhat diminished by the vagaries of Western civilisation. However, at the same time, one notices attempts to restore the sanctity of traditional values, especially when things are going terribly wrong in contemporary society. For example, tradition appears to have inspired some watch bodies (such as the Media Foundation for West Africa) to begin compiling lists of the most abusive politicians during each elective season in Ghana (as we see in Nyabor 2016), politicians who have made insulting and offensive comments (Media Foundation for West Africa 2016, 5–6), provocative remarks (Media Foundation for West Africa 2016, 6), remarks endorsing violence (Media Foundation for West Africa 2016, 6), and unsubstantiated allegations (Media Foundation for West Africa 2016, 4–5).

In conclusion, there is need to accomplish by policies and laws what tradition accomplished by norms. Where the Akan used the loss of face as a punitive instrument, we could punish with our usual fines and jail terms. People may not lose face these days for being verbally aggressive, but it hurts to lose money and time, and going to jail could produce a modern loss of face. Democracy permits vigorous debate. The point, however, is that citizens ought not to resort to verbal aggression, that is, statements intended to humiliate or offend the addressee. These come in the general forms of either outright insults or damaging claims made without being accompanied by substantiating premises. Countries ought to formulate policies to restrain such verbal aggression. The usual challenge with formulating policy for this purpose is to avoid constraining the freedom of expression, as this freedom is central to the practice of any democracy. Nevertheless, I think that these kinds of verbalisation could be isolated and proscribed with no such threat to the freedom of expression. It is encouraging that there already exist forms of verbalisation that are criminalised, yet we do not consider their criminalisation to curtail our freedom of expression. Such verbalisation includes criminal intimidation, slander and libel. More specifically, in formulating these policies, we ought to be guided by an acute awareness of the potential of verbal aggression to cause grievous harm to individuals and to society.

NOTES

1. NDC (National Democratic Coalition) and NPP (National Patriotic Party).
2. Available for watching at this YouTube link: https://www.youtube.com/watch?v=rFzjGGpqOUs.

REFERENCES

Agyekum, Kofi. 2010. *Akan Verbal Taboos*. Accra: Ghana Universities Press.

Ajei, Martin. 2016. "Kwasi Wiredu's Consensual Democracy: Prospects for Practice in Africa". *European Journal of Political Theory*, Vol.15 No.4, pp. 445–66. http://journals.sagepub.com/doi/full/10.1177/1474885116666451.

Ani, Emmanuel I. 2015. "Conflict and Dialogue Perspectives to Social Change: Insights from an African Culture". *Philosophia: International Journal of Philosophy*, Vol. 16 No. 2, pp.140–57. https://www.researchgate.net/profile/Emmanuel_Ani/publication/286463808_Conflict_and_dialogue_perspectives_to_social_change_Insights_from_an_African_culture/links/5847caf708ae8e63e632388e.pdf.

Baffoe, Michael. 2010. "Ghanaian Politics and Personal Insults". *Ghanaweb*, 2 November 2010. http://www.ghanaweb.com/GhanaHomePage/NewsArchive/Ghanaian-Politics-and-personal-insults-196510.

Berkowitz, Leonard. 1962. *Aggression: A Social Psychological Analysis*. New York: McGraw-Hill.

Buss, Arnold. H. 1961. *The Psychology of Aggression*. New York: John Wiley and Sons.

Clyne, Michael. 1987. "The Role of Linguistics in Peace and Conflict Studies". *Australian Review of Applied Linguistics*, Vol. 10 No. 1, pp. 76–97. http://www.jbe-platform.com/content/journals/10.1075/aral.10.1.05cly.

Dahl, Robert A. 1971. *Polyarchy: Participation and Opposition*. New Haven: Yale University Press.

Dryer, Sand. 2017. "Political profanity and crude creativity on the US election campaign trail". *Oxford Word Blog (In) Oxford Dictionaries*. http://blog.oxforddictionaries.com/2016/02/political-profanity/.

Fagan, Jeffrey. A., Douglas K. Stewart and Karen V. Hansen. 1983. "Violent men or violent husbands? Background factors and situational correlates". Finkelhor, David, Richard J. Gelles, Gerald T. Hotaling and Murray A. Straus eds. *The Dark Side of Families: Current Family Violence Research*. Beverly Hills, CA: Sage, pp. 49–67.

Flegenheimer, Matt, and Maggie Haberman. 2015. "Foul-mouthed and proud of it on the '16 campaign trail". *New York Times*, 27 November 2016. https://www.nytimes.com/2015/11/28/us/politics/2016-candidates-are-cursing-more-and-on-purpose.html?_r=0.

Grimes, Larry M. 1977. "The Linguistic Taboo: Examples from Modern Mexican Spanish". *The Bilingual Review*, Vol. 4, pp. 69–80. http://www.jstor.org/stable/25743710?seq=1#page_scan_tab_contents.

Gyan-Apenteng, Akwasi. 2016. "Insults and Lies don't Win Elections". *Graphic Online*, 21 February 2016. http://www.graphic.com.gh/features/opinion/insults-and-lies-don-t-win-elections.html.

Huntington, Samuel P. 1984. "Will more countries become democratic?" *Political Science Quarterly*, Vol. 99 No. 2, pp. 193–218. http://www.jstor.org/stable/2150402?seq=1#page_scan_tab_contents.

Kukubor, Kofi B. 2011. "Demagoguism: An Analysis of Politics of Insult in Ghana". *MC Modern Ghana*, 29 December 2011. https://www.modernghana.com/news/369413/demagoguism-an-analysis-of-politics-of-insults-in-ghana.html.

Lang, S., Britt Af Klinteberg and P.O. Alm. 2002. "Adult psychopathy and violent behavior in males with early neglect and abuse". *Acta Psychiatrica Scandinavica*, Vol. 106 No. 412, pp. 93–100. https://www.researchgate.net/profile/Britt_Klinteberg/publication/11302927_Adult_psychopathy_and_violent_behavior_in_men_with_early_neglect_and_abuse/links/09e4150e830b082660000000.pdf.

Larbi-Odei, Abigail. 2016. "Insults, False Claims dominated political discourse in 2012 elections: will 2016 be different?" *Joy Online*, 7 March 2016. http://www.myjoyonline.com/opinion/2016/April-7th/insults-false-claims-dominated-political-discourse-in-2012-elections-will-2016-be-different.php.

Obasanjo, Olusegun. 2013. "Before it is Too Late". *Vanguard* (Headlines), 12 December 2013. https://www.vanguardngr.com/2013/12/obj-blasts-jonathan-in-18-page-letter/.

Obeng, Samuel. 1994. "Verbal Indirection in Akan Informal Discourse". *Journal of Pragmatics*, Vol.21, pp.37–65. https://www.researchgate.net/profile/Samuel_Obeng/publication/222863102_Verbal_indirection_in_Akan_formal_discourse/links/53ff46f50cf21ac8791d45e9.pdf.

Media Foundation for West Africa. 2016. "Monitoring of Indecent Campaign Language on Radio: Findings for the Period May 16–31, 2016". http://www.mfwa.org/wp-content/uploads/2016/06/MFWA-Language-Monitoring-Report-for-May-16-31-2016.pdf.

Nyabor, Jonas. 2016. "NDC, NPP top list of most abusive political parties". *City 93.3 fm: citifmonline*, 25 October 2016. http://citifmonline.com/2016/10/25/ndc-npp-top-list-of-most-abusive-political-parties/.

Rothman, Lily. 2016. "A brief history of cursing in American politics". *Time* (Magazine Online) History Feature, 16 February 2016. http://time.com/4225553/donald-trump-cursing-swearing-president/.

Saah, Kofi K. 1986. "Language use and attitudes in Ghana". *Anthropological Linguistics*, Vol. 28 No. 3, pp. 67–77. http://www.jstor.org/stable/30027963?seq=1#page_scan_tab_contents.

Stets, Jan. 1990. "Verbal and Physical Aggression in Marriage". *Journal of Marriage and Family*, Vol. 52 No. 2, pp. 501–14. http://www.jstor.org/stable/353043?seq=1#page_scan_tab_contents.

Shaban, Abdur Raman Alfa. 2017. "Ugandan Government wants Psychiatric Checkup for Varsity Don who Insults President". *Africanews* (Uganda), 10 April 2017. http://www.africanews.com/2017/04/10/uganda-gov-t-wants-psychiatric-checkup-for-varsity-don-who-insulted-president//.

Schumpeter, Joseph A. 1976. *Capitalism, Socialism and Democracy*. London: George Allen & Unwin.

Weiler, Barbara Luntz and Cathy Spatz Widom. 1996. "Psychopathy and violent behavior in abused and neglected young adults". *Criminal Behaviour and Mental Health*, Vol. 6, pp. 253–57. http://onlinelibrary.wiley.com/doi/10.1002/cbm.99/full.

Wiredu, Kwasi. 2011. "State, Civil Society and Democracy in Africa". Lauer, Helen and Kofi Anyidoho eds. *Reclaiming the Human Sciences and Humanities through African Perspectives*, Vol. II. Legon-Accra: Sub-Saharan Publishers, pp. 1055–66.

Yankah, Kwesi. 1991. "Oratory in Akan society". *Discourse and Society*, Vol. 2, pp. 47–64. http://journals.sagepub.com/doi/abs/10.1177/0957926591002001003.

Chapter Nine

An Appeal for a Communitarian Model of Democracy

Munamato Chemhuru

Western liberal democracy is now very frequently taken to be another expression for civilisation and political decency (Offor 2006, 120). However, in post-colonial Africa, attempts to implement it have resulted in a myriad of social, political, and economic problems, including poverty, corruption, dictatorship, vote-rigging, disputed elections, civil wars, genocide, coups d'état, as well as exclusion and alienation of ethnic minorities through multi-partism. Countries such as Nigeria, Kenya, the Democratic Republic of Congo, Uganda, Sudan, Rwanda, and Zimbabwe have experienced many of these challenges.

My contribution to the discourse on the quest for indigenous African models of democracy for the twenty-first century entails a proposal for a political paradigm which resonates with the continent's political history and cultural context. I argue that if the current social, economic and political problems facing post-colonial Africa are to be adequately addressed, there is need to revisit African traditional communitarian systems of democracy rather than continuing to rely on Western liberal democratic principles that are not only alien to the continent's social and political conditions, but that have also largely failed in much of contemporary Africa because they do not serve the aspirations of the majority of the citizenry, and are therefore reminiscent of the colonial legacy. As Kwasi Wiredu laments "the apparently willing suspension of belief in African political traditions" among Africans, he comes to the conclusion that "it is equally obvious that Africa has suffered unspeakably from the political legacies of colonialism. Unhappily, she continues in this sphere to suffer, directly or indirectly, from the political tutelage of the West" (Wiredu 1996, 143).

My submission in this chapter is an interpretation of African communitarian democracy, which, except for the recent critical work by Bernard

Matolino (2018), has received minimal attention in current discourse on indigenous African models of democracy—a notion that was ignited by Kwasi Wiredu. This could perhaps address Kenyan philosopher Reginald M. J. Oduor's concern that "it is time we looked at our indigenous political heritage and utilised it to build a society whose values strike resonance with our peoples" (Oduor 2017).

Accordingly, I first set out by examining some of the shortcomings of Western liberal democracy in the post-colonial African context. I then proceed to argue for the appropriateness of African communitarian democracy as a reasonable basis for good governance and peace-building in Africa, as I critically compare it with Western liberal democracy. Overall, my argument in this chapter is premised on what Martin Odei Ajei (2016, 447) sees as "the on-going process of conceptually decolonising African thought and practice".

LIBERAL DEMOCRACY AND THE AFRICAN POST-COLONIAL CHALLENGE

In most of the world today, Western liberal democracy is presumed to be the only means to political salvation for countries that seek to uphold political ideals such as human rights, justice, equality, fairness, and good governance. Towards the end of the last millennium, Francis Fukuyama asserted that "as mankind approaches the end of the millennium, the twin crises of authoritarianism and socialist central planning have left only one competitor standing in the ring as an ideology of potentially universal validity: liberal democracy, the doctrine of individual freedom and popular sovereignty" (Fukuyama 1992, 42). Similarly, Francis Offor observed that "more than two-thirds of all the sovereign independent states in the world have come to accept . . . liberal democracy and have embraced this form of government as the best route to the resolution of the problems of economic development and political organisation" (Offor 2006, 124).

Post-colonial African states have not been spared from this apparently triumphant march of liberal democracy, "given the fact that by 2004 most African states [had] adopted liberal democracy as their system of governance" (Lumumba-Kasongo 2005, 1). Thus democracy, as understood from the Western liberal tradition, has been taken as the measure of good governance in most African countries. It is therefore not surprising that when African states fail to conform to some Western liberal democratic principle such as the holding of periodic multi-party elections or fail to uphold fundamental human rights of *individuals*[1] within their constitutions, they are excluded from critical economic, medical, and military aid, and subjected to other stringent political and economic sanctions from the powerful nations of the West. As a result, most post-colonial African states try to shun indigenous forms of governance emanating from the communitarian[2] worldview typical of pre-colonial African cultures, and to replace them with alien liberal democratic systems of governance prescribed by their former colonial masters.

Besides, the widespread belief that pre-colonial African societies were not democratic is a narrative popularised to justify the perpetuation of Western liberal democracy in the post-colonial African state. This is why Ernest Wamba-dia-Wamba thinks that "we must de-construct colonial legacy and the rigidity of *traditions* (traditions invented or imagined by colonialists while claimed to be African and adopted as such by Africans); these *traditions* are used to justify and enforce the post-colonial state which we have to de-imperialise" (Wamba-dia-Wamba 1992, 32). Indeed, Ali Mazrui acknowledges the centrality of democracy in pre-colonial Africa, and blames Western liberal democracy in post-colonial Africa for killing African democracy. Mazrui even coins the term "democracide" (Mazrui 2016, 17–35).

A number of first generation African political thinkers in the first decades of independence, such as Kwame Nkrumah, Léopold Sédar Senghor, and Julius Nyerere, argued for the need to revisit the African traditional political heritage in the form of African communitarian democracy. Although some of their arguments in support of one-party polities cannot be taken as viable alternatives to liberal democracy, these thinkers wanted newly established post-colonial African states to recognise and respect the communitarian structures of traditional African societies. However, their calls fell on deaf ears, as most post-colonial African states wanted to find a suitable place in the envisaged global village under the umbrella of Western liberal democratic principles.

The more than half a century of political independence in most African countries has been mainly characterised by alien models of governance, and chiefly by Western liberal democracy, which is antithetical to the traditional African democratic principles that Gyekye (1992, 241–55) has in mind. It is in this period that we see newly established Western type democracies degenerating into civil and military dictatorships. For example, as he takes stock of the history of military coups in the post-colonial era in Africa as a result of the failure of Western liberal democracy, Ali Mazrui observes that "by 1966, Nigeria, Africa's giant, had its first coup. A month later Kwame Nkrumah, the icon of Pan-Africanism, was overthrown in Ghana. A string of other coups followed" (Mazrui 2016, 23). These and other forms of dictatorships, bad governance, and corruption in post-colonial Africa, leave a lot to be desired with regard to liberal democracy in Africa. Consequently, Gyekye correctly observes that "the political institutions that were bequeathed to the African people by their colonial masters—institutions that were modelled on those of their rulers—did not function properly" (Gyekye 1992, 241).

Lumumba-Kasongo (2005, 7) correctly observed that "liberal democracy is primarily the product of western political thought and the evolution of western societies through bourgeois and technological revolutions in England, France, and the United States". Consequently, I concur with Oduor (2017) that "liberal democracy is not synonymous with democracy", and, in the rest of this section, highlight some of the shortcomings of liberal democracy as it has been understood and practiced in post-colonial Africa.

From its origins, the Greek *demos* ("the people") and *krateia* ("rule"), *demokratia* (democracy) has been accepted to mean the power of the people (Gyekye 2013, 240). Over time, democracy has been almost universally understood to refer to a "government of the people, by the people, and for the people". This traditional Western view of democracy, from the American founding father and the sixteenth U.S. president, Abraham Lincoln, has significantly shaped the understanding and application of democracy as a form of government mainly informed by the general populace, and oriented towards the promotion of the interests of this general populace. Indeed, democracy ultimately has to do with safeguarding the interests of the people, enhancing, rather than limiting their liberty to determine their own destiny through political action.

However, in the post-colonial African context, democracy has often been understood to mean liberalism (the doctrine of the supremacy of the individual and his/her rights over the demands of society). This explains why the idea of liberalism has, and continues to be, taken as a measure of democracy in post-colonial Africa. Yet these two concepts are evidently not identical: it is quite possible to have a democracy which does not subscribe to doctrinaire Western liberalism. This is why I take as reasonable the view that although pre-colonial African communities were inherently democratic, they were essentially communitarian rather than liberal.

In making a distinction between liberalism and democracy, Fukuyama correctly highlights the individualist character of the idea of liberalism as opposed to democracy:

> Liberalism and democracy, while closely related, are separate concepts. Political liberalism can be defined simply as a rule of law that recognises certain individual rights or freedoms from government control . . . [while democracy] . . . is the right held universally by all citizens to have a share of political power, that is, the rights of all citizens to vote and participate in politics. (Fukuyama 1992, 42)

I object to Western liberal democracy in Africa on at least five grounds.

First, liberal democracy is mostly advocated as the appropriate system of governance for the continent by powers that formerly colonised large swathes of Africa, namely, Britain, France, Portugal, Germany, and Italy. Yet the success of democracy today is more easily seen in social democracies such as Denmark, Norway, and Sweden—countries that did not participate in colonialism—than in these imperialist powers. In addition, social democracy is more compatible with, and closer to, the communitarian social arrangements characteristic of pre-colonial African polities than liberal democracy.

Second, liberal democracy lays a disproportionate emphasis on individual liberties—an emphasis that downplays the social nature of the human person. Although his focus is contemporary Western liberal societies, Michael Walzer's observation is relevant in this regard, namely that liberal societies are "the home of radically isolated individuals, rational egoists, and existential agents, men and women protected and divided by their inalienable rights" (Walzer 1990, 7). In contrast to communitarian democracy, liberal democracy lays emphasis on the freedoms of the individual such as the freedoms of association, movement, and worship, some of which are in conflict with African communitarian values. Because it is based on the political ideals of human equality and human rights, liberal democracy commits what I would call the universalist fallacy, that is, the error of assuming that all human beings share the same social, ethical, and political values. As Lumumba-Kasongo puts it, "universalism projected by liberal democracy, as fully expanded by the western-supported human rights organisations, is indeed Eurocentric" (Lumumba-Kasongo 2005, 20).

Besides, in the African context, the idea of the freedom of the individual as espoused by Western liberal democracy has, in practice, given more liberties to individual politicians than to the general populace. Consequently, a culture of impunity[3] has been the defining characteristic of post-colonial African leaders, as they seek to consolidate their individual power, wealth, and military might. In this endeavour, they manipulate various democratic processes. For example, under Robert Mugabe, Zimbabwe made several amendments to its independence constitution before it replaced it with a new one in 2013. Thus, Fukuyama is vindicated for his assertion that "democratic procedures can be manipulated by elites, and do not always accurately reflect the will or true self interests of the people" (Fukuyama 1992, 43).

Third, liberal democracy in post-colonial Africa places an inordinate emphasis on multi-party politics and periodic elections to choose representatives in various institutional structures such as local government, parliament, and the presidency or premiership. The rationale for such a political structure is that those chosen to hold the said offices will represent the will of the people in these various institutions. However, it is difficult to imagine grounds on which the will of the people could be expressed and effected in "real and concrete terms" (Gyekye 1992, 244). For example, in certain circumstances, the chosen representatives may not be well acquainted with the challenges that confront the people from day to day. This is why the people ought to actively and directly participate in identifying the best possible course of action on any given fundamental issue through communitarian democracy.

In addition, while multi-party politics and periodic elections are requisite ingredients of liberal democracy, they remain alien to the fundamentally communitarian African context. As he argues for a non-party consensual democracy, Kwasi Wiredu correctly observes that "to many democracy seems to be synonymous with the multi-party system. . . . Yet that political doctrine seems clearly antithetical to the philosophy of government underlying traditional [African] statecraft" (Wiredu 1996, 143). Furthermore, multi-party politics has perpetrated and continues to perpetrate intolerance between citizens in competing political parties. Such intolerance has often been expressed through smear campaigns and even violent clashes, and in some instances military overthrows of sitting governments. This is why Ali Mazrui sees Western liberal democracy in post-colonial Africa as porous to the extent that it has exposed African countries to political instability (Mazrui 2016, 24).

Fourth, liberal democracy is, in most cases, based on the opinion of the majority on any given issue, especially when it comes to voting for political leaders or making crucial decisions through referenda. Consequently, liberal democracy in post-colonial Africa has been interpreted to mean rule by the majority. However, as Wiredu observes, "majority opinion in itself is not a good enough basis for decision making, for it deprives the minority of the rights to have their will reflected in the given decision" (Wiredu 1996, 186).

Fifth, in the post-colonial African context, liberal democracy and political corruption seem to be intertwined, so that one tends to wonder what could be the relationship between the two. According to Gyekye, political corruption refers to "the illegal, unethical, and unauthorised exploitation of one's political or official position for personal gain or advantage. . . . political corruption is thus an act of corruption perpetrated against the state and its agencies by a person holding an official position in pursuit of his private or personal gain" (Gyekye 1992, 83). Some examples of such corruption are theft from state coffers, fraud, nepotism, and favouritism on other grounds, all of which are characteristic of most post-colonial African states in the twenty-first century. According to Gyekye, "post-colonial Africa is undeniably among the worst victims of political corruption" (Gyekye 1992, 82).

One of the consequences of political corruption in the post-colonial African state is the suffocation of liberal democratic principles. According to Gyekye, political corruption "is undoubtedly the most common cause of the military overthrow of civilian governments in Africa, with the consequent disruption of the democratic process: thus, it is the greatest and most serious disease of governments in Africa" (Gyekye 1992, 82). As he addressed the National

Foundations Dialogue Initiative in Johannesburg, South Africa, former South African president Kgalema Motlanthe considered the history of post-colonial African democracies and came to the conclusion that "at the heart of democracy deficiency is lack of accountability to the people" (Motlanthe 2017).

A CASE FOR THE AFRICAN COMMUNITARIAN MODEL OF DEMOCRACY

Communitarianism has generally been understood to have been the way of life of indigenous or traditional African communities during the pre-colonial era. However, its potential contribution to the development of practicable systems of governance for post-colonial African states has not been given much thought. Yet as Kwame Gyekye correctly observes, "the traditional system of government did have some democratic features from which a new political system can profit" (Gyekye 1992, 241). Consequently, in what follows, I argue that traditional African communitarianism is a solid foundation for models of democracy in post-colonial Africa.

Generally, African communitarian philosophy is mainly influenced by a number of thinkers, including Léopold Sédar Senghor (1964), Kwame Nkrumah (1964), Julius K. Nyerere (1968), John S. Mbiti (1969), Ifeanyi Menkiti (1984; 2004), Kwame Gyekye (1992), and Kwasi Wiredu (1996), among others. Despite their exposure to varied social and political conditions, all these thinkers hold the view that African traditional societies generally lay great emphasis on a shared existence among members of their group. John S. Mbiti famously expressed this confidence in the metaphysical and ethical sense of collective existence in his dictum that "I am because we are, and since we are, therefore I am" (Mbiti 1969, 106). Similarly, Menkiti references the communitarian orientation in his assertion that "as far as Africans are concerned, the reality of the communal world takes precedence over the reality of the individual life histories, whatever these may be" (Menkiti 1984, 171).

Understood from an African communitarian perspective, Lincoln's famous saying that "democracy is government of the people, by the people, and for the people" would be revised to state that democracy is rule of the community, by the community, and for the community. The implication is that the quality of governance ought to be judged by the extent to which values of solidarity such as the collective benefits of culture and human rights are guaranteed in a given social and political context. In other words, the focus is much more on the welfare of the community rather than on the liberties of the individual *qua* individual. Unlike the Western liberal tradition, the assumption is that if the welfare of the community is promoted, the interests of the individual will also be catered for. From this perspective, the space for individual human liberties as espoused by the Western liberal view of democracy is significantly reduced. Nevertheless, while African communitarian democracy might be incorrectly perceived as "reluctant to accept the individualistic justification for the human rights protection" (Hellsten 2004, 69), it is based on collective democratic ideals from which the individual stands to benefit alongside all other individuals.

An important feature of African communitarian democracy is the emphasis on the people's participation in decision-making on matters that have an impact on their welfare. On the other hand, in Western liberal democracy, mainly based on electioneering and majoritarianism, there is little room for meaningful citizen participation in the day-to-day decisions. For this reason, Ajei observes that "a political challenge facing constitutional democracies in Africa is the lack of adequate representation and participation in the democratic processes and institutions" (Ajei 2016, 445). The only time that individuals participate in the political process is during elections, where they choose a few individuals in the name of representation. Thus, Gyekye correctly asserts that "it is not enough, surely, for people to be included—and to participate—only in the periodic elections of those who are to govern and to make laws for the state" (Gyekye 2013, 238).

In contrast to Western liberal democracy which is by and large majoritarian, African communitarian democracy is based on decisions mainly arrived at by consensus of all the individuals. According to Wiredu, "the pursuit of consensus was a deliberate effort to go beyond decision by majority opinion" (Wiredu 1996, 186). In other words, even the 'minority', who may not initially agree with the majority, would be persuaded to accept a view through consensus-building. In effect, this kind of approach to decision-making facilitates compromise, contrary to the winner take all approach in majoritarian democracy. Accordingly, although Matolino sees some serious problems in *Consensus as Democracy in Africa*, he observes that "majoritarianism has led to political disaffection of the losers and has caused enduring divisions between and among different political parties" (Matolino 2018, p.xi).

It is important to emphasise that communitarian democracy respects the rights of the individual as well. It proffers a collectivist view of fundamental human values such as the rights to life, property, and expression. According to it, if these fundamental values are understood and respected from a collectivist perspective, they will almost always cascade to the individual. This contrasts with the Western liberal notion of democracy, in which such fundamental values are understood almost solely from the perspective of the individual person. Thus Walzer (1990, 9) correctly points out that liberal society "is fragmentation in practice, and community is the exact opposite, the home of coherence, connection, and narrative capacity".

In sharp contrast to a liberal democracy, there are no clear distinctions between and among the state, the rulers, and the general citizenry in a communitarian democracy. For this reason, a communitarian model of democracy promotes a sense of responsible citizenship among individuals. Gyekye succinctly expresses this point, as he compares the traditional African communitarian political attitudes with those characteristic of liberal democracy in Africa after colonialism:

> It must be noted that both colonial and post-colonial governmental systems in Africa created a distance between the government and the governed. This, in turn, engendered attitudes of unconcern and insensitivity to the affairs of the state on the part of the governed. Consequently, the general attitude of the citizen was that it was possible to injure the state without injuring oneself, an attitude that opened the floodgates of bribery, corruption, carelessness about state property or state enterprises, and other antisocial acts. Traditional ideology, however, positively maintained that any injury done to the community as a whole directly injures the individual. (Gyekye 1992, 254)

One possible objection to my advocacy for African communitarian democracy is the question as to whether or not it is possible to separate liberalism from democracy. My response to this question is in the affirmative, because democracy, properly understood, is not alien to Africa: what is alien are Western liberal ideas that are not compatible with African political history and culture. Even Francis Fukuyama, that renowned advocate of liberal democracy, echoes the same sentiment as he observes that "while liberalism and democracy usually go together, they can be separated in theory" (Fukuyama 1992, 43). Although Fukuyama thinks that a non-liberal democracy does not protect the rights of individuals and minorities, his position concurs with my own in asserting that there is a possibility for a country to be democratic without necessarily being liberal and vice versa (See also Fukuyama 1992, 44). For example, the pre-colonial traditional African forms of governance were inherently thoroughgoing communitarian democracies that could not be taken to be liberal in the Western sense. At the same time, contrary to what Fukuyama would have us believe, such democracies did not necessarily trample on the rights of the individuals and minorities. Indeed, in his presentation of his moderate view of communitarianism, Gyekye observes:

> [African communitarianism] gives accommodation to communal values as well as to values of individuality, to social commitments as well as to duties of self attention. Even in its basic thrust and concerns it gives prominence to duties toward the community and its members, it does not—cannot—do so to the

detriment of individual rights whose existence and value it recognises, or should recognise, and for a good reason. (Gyekye 1992, 121)

CONCLUSION

Oduor (2017) challenges us not to limit our understanding of indigenous African knowledge systems to areas such as agriculture and health, but to apply them to the social and political spheres as well. This is what I have attempted to do in this chapter. While some of the frameworks that provided the basis for traditional African systems of governance no longer exist, it is not too late to reconfigure the pre-colonial African traditional political heritage for our post-colonial contexts without necessarily being anachronistic. While the focus of Samkange and Samkange (1980, 10) is the philosophy of *hunhuism* or *ubuntuism*[4], their caution against anachronism is relevant here: "We must . . . not lose sight of the fact that we live today, not in the Iron Age of our grandfathers but in a shrunken age of multi-national companies, supersonic travel and satellite communication". Nevertheless, it is my considered opinion that unless post-colonial African states adopt essentially indigenous and/ or traditional African systems of governance, they will continue to face the kind of problems that they have grappled with since the attainment of political independence to date.

ACKNOWLEDGEMENTS

This chapter was written during my sabbatical from Great Zimbabwe University while I was a GES Post-doctoral Fellow at the University of Johannesburg's Department of Philosophy, Faculty of Humanities (2017). I wish to thank Professors H. P. P. [Hennie] Lottër and Thaddeus Metz for their useful comments to earlier drafts of this chapter. I also thank the two anonymous reviewers and the editor, Reginald M. J. Oduor, for their useful suggestions.

NOTES

1. The emphasis on 'individuals' is meant to highlight the orientation of human rights towards the individual person when understood from the Western liberal perspective, while the African view is largely communitarian, laying greater emphasis on the collective good.

2. 'Communitarianism' and 'communalism' are often used interchangeably in reference to 'communitarian thinking' or 'communitarian philosophy'. However, in this chapter I make use of 'communitarian thinking', 'communitarian philosophy', or 'communitarian model'. I do this in order to avoid the extremist view that is normally denoted by the usage of 'isms' as in 'communitarianism' and 'communalism' (See also Ramose 2004, 150).

3. Erasmus Masitera (2011) also articulates this pertinent issue affecting the postcolonial African state, with special reference to the Zimbabwean context.

4. I have used the terms *hunhuism* or *ubuntuism* in the way in which they are used by Samkange and Samkange (1980) to refer to the African philosophy of *unhu/ubuntu*. The terms, derived from the Nguni languages, basically refer to the African conception of humane and relational existence which is mostly shaped by the understanding of the person as an integral part of the community.

REFERENCES

Fukuyama, Francis. 1992. *The End of History and the Last Man*. New York: The Free Press.

Gyekye, Kwame. 1992. "Traditional Political ideas: Their relevance to Development in Contemporary Africa". Wiredu, Kwasi, and Kwame Gyekye eds. *Person and Community*. Washington D.C.: The Council for Research in Values and Philosophy, pp.241–55.

———. 2013. *Philosophy, Culture and Vision: African Perspectives*. Accra: Sub-Saharan Publishers.

Hellsten, Sirkku Kristiina. 2004. "Human Rights in Africa: From Communitarian Values to Utilitarian Practice". *Human Rights Review*, Vol. 5 No. 2, pp. 61–85. https://doi.org/10.1007/s12142-004-1003-7.

Lumumba-Kasongo, Tukumbi. 2005. "The Problems of Liberal Democracy and Democratic Process: Lessons for Deconstructing and Building African Democracies". Lumumba-Kasongo, Tukumbi ed. *Liberal Democracy and its Critics in Africa: Political Disfunction and the Struggle for Social Progress*. Pretoria: University of South Africa Press, pp. 1–25.

Masitera, Erasmus. 2011. "Creating a Culture of Impunity in Zimbabwe: A case for Philosophical Input in Development Issues". *Africana*, Vol. 5 No. 2, June/July 2011, pp. 98–122. http://africanajournal.org/wp-content/uploads/AFRICANA-Vol5-No2.pdf.

Matolino, Bernard. 2018. *Consensus as Democracy in Africa*. Grahamstown: NISC (Pvt) Ltd.

Mazrui, Ali Alámin. 2016. "Democracide: Who Killed Democracy in Africa? Clues of the Past, Concerns of the Future". Mazrui, Ali Alamin and Francis Wiafe-Amoako eds. *African Institutions: Challenges to Political, Social, and Economic Foundations of Africa's Development*. Lanham: Rawman and Littlefield, pp. 17–35.

Mbiti, John S. 1969. *African Religions and Philosophy*. New York: Doubleday.

Menkiti, Ifeanyi. 1984. "Person and Community in African Traditional Thought". Wright, Richard ed. *African Philosophy: An Introduction*. Lanham: University Press of America, pp. 171–80.

———. 2004. "On the Normative Conception of a Person". Wiredu, Kwasi ed. *A Companion to African Philosophy*. Malden: Blackwell, pp. 324–31.

Motlanthe, Kgalema. 2017. "Opening remarks", The National Foundations Dialogue Initiative, Johannesburg, 5 May 2017.

Nkrumah, Kwame. 1964. *Consciencism: Philosophy and Ideology for De-colonisation*. London: Panaf Books.

Nyerere, Julius. 1968. *UJAMAA: Essays on Socialism*. New York: New York University Press.

Oduor, Reginald M. J. 2017. "Democracy Free from Hegemony". Opening Remarks at the International Conference on "Beyond Liberal Democracy: The Quest for Indigenous African Models of Democracy for the Twenty-First Century", Nairobi, Kenya, organised by the Department of Philosophy and Religious Studies, University of Nairobi, Kenya, and the Council for Research in Values and Philosophy, Washington, D.C., U.S.A., 22–23 May 2017.

Offor, Francis. 2006. "Democracy as an Issue in African Philosophy". Oladipo, Olusegun ed. *Core Issues in African Philosophy*. Ibadan: Hope Publications, pp. 120–34.

Ramose, Mogobe Bernard. 2004. "In Search of an African Philosophy of Education". *South African Journal of Higher Education*, Vol. 18 No. 1, pp.138–60. https://www.ajol.info/index.php/sajhe/article/view/25487.

Samkange, Stanlake, and Tommie Marie Samkange. 1980. *Hunhuism or Ubuntuism: A Zimbabwean Indigenous Political Philosophy*. Salisbury: Graham Publishing.

Senghor, Léopold Sédar. 1964. *On African Socialism*. Cook, Mercer trans. New York: Praeger.

Walzer, Michael. 1990. "The Communitarian Critique of Liberalism". *Political Theory*, Vol. 18 No. 1, pp.6–23.

Wamba-dia-Wamba, Ernest. 1992. "Beyond Elite Politics of Democracy in Africa". *Quest: Philosophical Discussions*, Vol. 4 No. 1, pp.28–43.

Wiredu, Kwasi. 1996. *Cultural Universals and Particulars: An African Perspective*. Indiana: Indiana University Press.

Chapter Ten

Elements of an Indigenous African Model of Democracy

Joseph Situma, Kisemei Mutisya, and Christine Buluma

Are we at the end of history? Francis Fukuyama (1992) famously contended that in the aftermath of the Cold War, the world was at the end of history. His contention was born out of the assumption that history, in the substantive sense of the word, only happens where there are contradictions at the ideological level. This conception of history echoes Kant, Hegel, and Marx. For Fukuyama, "the last man standing," after millennia of conflict, is liberal democracy and capitalism. Fukuyama affirms this in his assertion that "The state that emerges at the end of history is liberal insofar as it recognises and protects through a system of laws man's universal right to freedom, and democratic insofar as it exists only with the consent of the governed" (Fukuyama 1992, 20). In this sense, therefore, once there is only liberal democracy, that is, once there are no alternative systems to challenge liberal democracy, all contradictions are resolved.

Fukuyama (1992) follows Kojeve (1969) in contending that post–Cold War Western Europe is the embodiment of liberal democracy as conceived in the French Revolution and Hegel's *Phenomenology of Spirit* (Hegel 1807). Other parts of the world are also allegedly on the path to the realisation of liberal democracy, that, according to Fukuyama, is the most perfect mode of human existence. So, for Fukuyama, developing countries in Africa and elsewhere will eventually arrive at the inevitable destination of humankind—liberal democracy and capitalism.

In this chapter, we propose certain elements drawn from indigenous African modes of governance that can be utilised by post-colonial African states to make them more viable than they are at present. In the next section, we offer a critique of Francis Fukuyama's thesis. thereafter, we analyse the relationship between liberal democracy and capitalism and contend that liberal democracy is fundamentally at variance with human fulfilment. This leads to the fourth section, in which we offer tentative socio-political elements drawn from indigenous African notions and practices for incorporation into the governance structures of post-colonial African states. The thesis of the chapter is that these elements, utilised together with certain elements of Western thought, offer an alternative that is more viable for present-day Africa than liberal democracy and capitalism.

CRITIQUE OF FUKUYAMA'S THESIS

Francis Fukuyama's assertions are contentious in a number of respects. Is it plausible to speak, as Fukuyama does, of a universal culture and a universal set of values? How can the thesis be reconciled with the reality of a multicultural world? Is it not the case that Western civilisation is simply one among many in the world? One also wonders whether developing countries, such as African states, have no other option except to pursue both liberal democracy and capitalism. Thus Lewin (2011, 85) poses: "Is democracy a positive factor for economic growth and development?" In view of the economic growth and development trajectories of the East Asian tigers, India and Chile, Lewin asserts that "democracy is neither sufficient nor necessary for growth and development" (Lewin 2011, 85). Yet it is highly probable for a dictatorial regime to engage in predatory exploitation of national resources and skewed budgetary allocations, in the event of which economic growth would be asymmetrical to human development (Lewin 2011, 85; Conceicao and Kim 2009, 2).

Huntington's *The Clash of Civilisations and the Remaking of World Order* (1993) is a robust response to Fukuyama's audacious assertions and an enlightening exploration of civilisations. Huntington not only presents plausible arguments and accounts of historical events after the Cold War to challenge Fukuyama's apocalyptic conclusion, but also warns against the tendency of thinkers to interpret reality simplistically. Furthermore, pertinent to our quest for indigenous models of democracy is his view that "Throughout Africa tribal identities are pervasive and intense, but Africans are also increasingly developing a sense of African identity, and conceivably sub-Saharan Africa could cohere into a distinctive civilisation" (Huntington 1993, 47). Equally plausible is Huntington's general view of civilisations in his assertion that "While civilisations endure, they also evolve. They are dynamic; they rise and fall; they merge and divide; and . . . they also disappear and are buried in the sands of time" (Huntington 1993, 43).

LIBERAL DEMOCRACY AND CAPITALISM

Whether liberal democracy is the ultimate destination of all societies or simply a stage in the evolution of Western civilisation, it is imperative to spell out its tenets and the economic system in which it has developed. Liberal democracy aims to safeguard the basic rights of citizens through checks and balances that hold the leadership to account, and through the holding of regular elections (Plattner 2010, 84). In addition, for liberal democracy, the rights of the individual take priority over common goods, and hence Rawls's view that justice transcends other values and takes precedence over them (Rawls 1985, 235). Liberal democracy's individualistic view of human beings presumes that society ought to be a subsidiary dimension of human life, or else it will tend to be repressive. It holds that the greatest need of the individual is to be protected from societal encumbrances, and that this is the state's primary function. Entwined with personal liberty is the necessity of tolerance, which arises from the modern emphasis on roles rather than character, to the extent that most human beings within liberal society have no character in the real sense of the term (MacIntyre 1981, 23–35).

Conceptually, liberalism balances liberty and equality, but in reality, there is always tension between the two, because the pursuit of liberty upsets equality and vice versa. Even more pertinent is the fact that liberty's balance with tolerance is always in jeopardy. Popper captures the essence of this imbalance in his paradox of tolerance: "Unlimited tolerance must lead to the disappearance of tolerance. If we extend unlimited tolerance even to those who are intolerant, if we are not prepared to defend a tolerant society against the onslaught of the intolerant, then the tolerant will be destroyed, and tolerance with them" (Popper 1945, 226). The reality and problematic of this paradox are at the root of current intolerance of non-European immigrants in Europe and the USA. Even Fukuyama's prediction of a Europe composed of states that are less concerned with sovereignty and ideology has not been borne out: now, more than ever, the idea of universality of human rights is deemed questionable (Namli 2018; Hopgood 2014; Posner 2014; Brown 2007).

In fact, history is here with us in "the trends and practices many believed had been erased: arbitrary executions, attempts to annihilate ethnic and religious minorities, the annexation of territory, and mass movement of refugees and displaced persons" (Welsh 2016). Fukuyama simply faithfully follows in the footsteps of Hegel in categorising Africa to suit his thesis. Whereas in Hegel's account Africa was not part of history because for him nothing significant happened there and Europe was the hotbed of history (Hegel 1956, 99), Fukuyama holds that in the post–Cold War era Africa (and Third World countries at large) are "mired in history", and Europe is beyond history

(Fukuyama 1989, 16). Presumably, for Fukuyama, it is a sign of progress for a society to be beyond history as Western Europe and the United States allegedly are. Hegel's and Fukuyama's positions are examples of theorists interpreting reality to suit their parochial interests.

Interestingly, Fukuyama concludes that "The end of history will be a very sad time. The struggle for recognition, the willingness to risk one's life for a purely abstract goal, the worldwide ideological struggle that calls forth daring, courage, imagination, idealism, will be replaced by economic calculation, endless solving of technical problems, environmental concerns, and the satisfaction of sophisticated consumer demands" (Fukuyama 1989, 17). He goes on to assert that in the aftermath of realising full-fledged liberal democracy, the existential condition of human beings is one of boredom and sadness (Fukuyama 1992, 21). Now, if that is the progress that the Western world has realised, then societies in Africa and elsewhere had better try to salvage and consolidate their cultures in order to use them as vehicles for getting to better destinations.

In any case, African nation-states have been rocked by military coups, political oppression, ethnic strife, and economic degradation (Skinner 1998, 20). This is because, regardless of the ideologies that African states adopted at independence, their economies have tended to be in deterioration mode, resulting in widespread disaffection. Scholars attribute the failure of post-colonial African nation-states to the following factors, among others: the persistence of primordial bonds (Gertz 1963); marginalisation of communities (Horowitz 1985); the alien nature of the state (Skinner 1998); superficial adoption of liberal democracy and ideologies (Sardan 1999; Situma 2010); the politics of ethnicity, clientelism and patronage (Bayart 1989; Berman, Eyoh & Kymlicka 2004; Njeru 2007). These factors have nurtured political environments in which vices thrive at all levels of society[1], and apathy and despair inundate citizenry[2].

Responses to the crises of the post-colonial African state have been varied. On one hand, African leaders have belatedly tried to heed Peter Llyod's advice "to turn the allegiance of the masses from ethnic groups to the state, and from their traditional rulers to the parliamentary leaders" (cited in Skinner 1998, 19). Yoweri Museveni's restoration of traditional monarchies in Uganda appears to do the reverse, but it is calculated to ensure reliance of the traditional leaders on the national government. In Kenya, political leaders have developed a knack for seeking blessings from traditional leaders of ethnic groups in a bid to win or retain political offices during elections. Yet the politicians have merely used such leaders for symbolic purposes, and have consequently destroyed the prestige of such leaders, just as the colonial administration used some traditional ethnic leaders and thereby destroyed them (Skinner 1998, 19).

On the other hand, there have been institutional and legislative responses to the failure of post-colonial African nation-states. A case in point is Kenya, which promulgated a new constitution in 2010, heralding the establishment of the Office of the Ombudsman, greater separation of powers between the executive, judiciary, and legislature, a provision for public interest litigation, and an enhanced bill of rights, among others. The Constitution of Kenya 2010 also laid down the legal framework for devolution in the establishment of forty-seven county governments. Many in the country hoped that the constitution would be an antidote to oppression and injustice, an imperial presidency, inequitable distribution of state resources, and marginalisation. However, more than ten years after the euphoric promulgation of the constitution and the attendant establishment of new institutions, it appears that the words of Berman, Eyoh and Kymlicka (2004, 2) are still applicable to Kenya: "The material preoccupations and personalistic nature of patronage networks that are the conduit of ethnic politics continue to eliminate the relevance of formal institutions, ideology and policy differences in the organisation of the wider civic political arena".

Generally, citizens' perceptions of outcomes of institutional, legal, and political transformations tend to be divided along ethnic fault lines, with those who are predominant holders of power and determiners of distribution of national resources on one side, and those who are marginalised on the other. Thus, while perceptions are helpful indicators of outcomes of social, political, and economic interventions, they are limited (Nouvet 2016). Furthermore, there is hardly "agreement among Africans about the meaning of democracy" (Skinner 1998, 21). Indeed, even in Western discourse, liberal democracy is just one of the various versions of democracy (Smit and Oosthuizen 2011; Coppedge and Gerring 2011; Nussbaum 1997). However, "Increasingly, African scholars insist that whereas western ideas about democracy are specifically rooted in the notion of political and social rights for individuals, the reality of Africa is one in which 'collectivities' or 'ethnic' groups, rather than individuals are demanding social justice" (Skinner 1998, 21).

It is also worth noting that liberal democracy and capitalism have subverted several aspects of indigenous African values, including hard work, generosity, honesty, and respect. A glimpse into the subversion of these aspects was captured in a survey of the personal convictions of Kenyan youth in 2016: "50 percent of youth surveyed believe it doesn't matter how one makes money as long as one does not end up in jail; 47 percent admire those who make money through hook or crook (including hustling[3]); 30 percent believe corruption is profitable" (Awiti and Scot 2016, 2). The report concluded that the youth's expressed desire for entrepreneurship is incompatible with high tolerance for corruption, tax evasion, and the desire to make money by any means. In contrast to the findings of the survey, in indigenous African societies, hard work is valued as the proper way of earning a livelihood and addressing poverty.

It is against the foregoing backdrop that we turn to indigenous African modes of social existence, with the aim of considering what can be recovered from them for purposes of constituting more viable socio-political entities in place of the current ones that are largely modelled on alien traditions, and partly the outcome of distortions that arose from, among others, the violent and degrading constructs of slave trade and colonisation.[4]

TENTATIVE ELEMENTS FOR DEMOCRACY FROM INDIGENOUS AFRICAN MODES OF SOCIO-POLITICAL EXISTENCE

In considering elements of an indigenous African model of democracy other than citizens' participation in the writing of their country's constitution and in electing their leaders, we partially concur with Campbell's formula for determining the quality of democracy: "Quality of democracy= (freedom + other characteristics of the political system) + (performance of the non-political dimensions)" (Campbell 2008, 3). Our concurrence is partial because liberal democracy gives the non-political aspects of the human condition less weight than the political ones. It gives less weight to such non-political aspects as morality, community, and culture, considering them as supererogatory.[5] Indeed, liberal democracy does not assign any significant value to these aspects that are fundamental to indigenous African thought. Campbell's democratic ranking identifies six individual dimensions (rule of law, participation, accountability, equality, freedom, and performance), and scores each of them on a range of 1 to 100, without taking into account the impact of the ideological framework (Campbell 2008, 5). Campbell's survey instrument is a logical outcome of liberalism's presumption that ideology has less significance in free societies, as evident in Rawls (1971) and Fukuyama (1992).

George Ayittey (1991) and Elizabeth Isichei (1997) studied indigenous African institutions in their diversity, and concluded that Africa was complex and diverse, with both democratic and despotic legacies of leadership. Indigenous African institutions, therefore, offer both desirable and undesirable practices. In the present section, we aim to identify desirable practices from those institutions for incorporation into the governance systems of contemporary African polities.

African cultures were diverse during the pre-colonial era, and they continue to be varied today. Nevertheless, there are certain common elements in their political practice that have great potential to enhance the quality of governance in contemporary African polities.

LEADERS AS PARENT FIGURES

In pre-colonial Africa, there were segmented or decentralised communities as well as centralised ones. The latter had well-developed political, social, and economic systems, with the king or chief together with elders maintaining law and order. The leaders in such political formations were responsible not only for security, but also for facilitating the prosperity of the community by promoting trade and agriculture. Decentralised communities did not have a standing army, but as Cobbah observes, in times of war, members of extended families fell "into a hierarchy to assure the smooth running and survival of the community" (Cobbah 1987, 324). Elders in these kinds of communities were accorded respect because they were responsible for caring for all the members of the clan. This overarching responsibility was mirrored in the elder who was the father/guardian of all, rather than simply the patriarch of his homestead. Even in centralised communities, kings, queens, and chiefs were (in a fairly strong sense) paternal/maternal figures beyond the confines of their homesteads. This is a significant element which can constitute one of the pillars of indigenous African models of democracy for the twenty-first century, instead of the impoverished model of liberal democracy—in which the leaders behave as though they were executive directors of impersonal utility providers (Knight 1998, 227).

Generally, on the aspect of compassion for those whom they lead, contemporary African leaders compare unfavourably with traditional ones, whether in centralised or decentralised traditional communities. Contemporary African leaders manifest egocentric and narcissistic tendencies that destroy all lives except those of their homesteads. There are cases of leaders who extend their care to the members of their clans, which in the pluralistic states amount to nepotism. If this indigenous element is to be used as a pillar for democracy in the current multi-ethnic states, we ought to heed Emeakaroha's counsel:

> The African should carry the ideals of his community into the wider community ... The values cherished in his community should enable him to know that the other man is brother as a human being. Therefore the Igbo proverb which says that: "Don't laugh at a distant boat being tossed by the waves, your brother may be in it"; should now be: "Don't laugh at a distant boat being tossed by waves, a human being is in it." (Emeakaroha 2002)

In other words, there is need for expansive compassion that would enable citizens and leaders to have a sense of compatriotism,[6] even as they remain aware of their ethnic identities. Compatriotism would directly necessitate commitment to justice which precludes violations such as those that have been witnessed in African nation-states under liberal democracy.

COSMOPOLITANISM WITH A COMMUNITARIAN UNDERPINNING

Granted that the perpetrators of the greatest injustices in African nation-states are leaders, cultivation of the indigenous notion of fatherland or motherland would definitely reorient citizens' outlook of their obligations and rights. It is worth noting that the indigenous African notions of fatherhood, motherhood, brotherhood, and sisterhood were broader than the atomistic notions of liberalism. The great challenge that has to be addressed in this respect is how to justify and exercise kinship partiality within a national framework, and even further how to justify and exercise compatriot partiality within the cosmopolitan framework (Bascara 2016). As a point of departure, the widespread notion of justice, according to which "the killing of a kinsman . . . is a crime but also an abomination. . . . But if an outsider is killed, the offence takes a different dimension and is viewed with lesser degree of gravity" (Emeakaroha 2002), must be reconfigured to accord with the reality of nation-states.

Could *ubuntu*[7] provide the key for reconfiguring the indigenous African notion of justice to the national and even global levels? The salient notion of *ubuntu* is that a person is a person through other persons. Desmond Tutu expresses this pertinently in his assertion that "Ubuntu says I am human only because you are human. If I undermine your humanity, I dehumanise myself" (cited in Wilson 2001, 9). The notion of humanity is at its fullest, not in uniformity of human activities and choices, but rather in recognition of diverse human values and norms, and the accessibility of these for our appropriation through adoption or adaptation. Besides, Tutu's assertion means that authentic human fulfilment is the fruit of compassionate aspirations and endeavours. On this matter, there are the contrasting mien of two persons: Person X is steeped in virtues and remains committed to a virtuous life even when dealing with the most insurmountable tasks, while person Y is not committed to anything and, therefore, is strongly inclined to abandon any of his or her pursuits at the slightest encounter of difficulty. Person Y is Fukuyama's post-history man or woman; for as we earlier noted, Fukuyama asserted that the noble aspects of courage, imagination, and idealism would be supplanted by economic calculation, preoccupation with technical aspects, environmental concerns, and consumerism (Fukuyama 1992, 17). The humanistic view of human beings is that they are the products of their choices and actions individually and collectively. Inhuman endeavours by individuals, ethnics, and classes inevitably lead to unhappiness, frustration, and wastage. The communitarian plank in human fulfilment means that liberal democracy, with its emphasis on the almost unbridled freedom of the individual, is not a viable model.

Other elements that would be at the core of an indigenous African model of democracy for the twenty-first century include decentralised political systems and participatory democracy, but these cannot deal with the problems bedevilling African countries without the cultivation of communitarian civic virtues and a consensus approach to conflict resolution, both of which would be useful in instances where the interests of the minority could be swamped by a majoritarian approach (Norris 1997, 6). While most African countries transited from colonial rule to independence with majoritarian electoral systems, there is evidence that this approach alienates some ethnic groups, thereby sparking instability and stoking the clamour for secession. The fact that liberal democracy presumes the justification of the status quo compounds the problem, since the ethnic group which has control of state machinery also has the resources to manipulate political processes and outcomes. Indigenous African models of democracy do not offer a quick fix to this liberal conundrum, but if adopted, would provide a gradual way out of it. The political elite who alienate, oppress, and exploit some groups are heirs of liberal democracy. They do not think there is anything wrong with some people being at the margins of capital and state, considering that to be simply a stage that will be surpassed later in history. The problem is that the marginalised do not read from that script, but instead question the legitimacy of the state. Devolution or decentralisation without moral and cultural transformation is not the solution, because then marginalisation is devolved to the counties. There has to be an overhaul of people's outlook, values, and norms; and that is a conceptual revolution.

HIGH PREMIUM ON THE AFRICAN VIEW OF THE FAMILY

Directly interwoven with the African communal orientation is the place of the family in the general African conception of life. The fact that "the Africans prize life above every other thing," and that "the African worldview places the individual within a continuum of the dead, the living, and the yet to be born" (Emeakaroha 2002), means that political processes informed by African worldviews would be imbued with greater import than can ever happen in liberal democracy. There is a stark contrast between the view and actions of a "hollow" person and a person who has to weigh his or her conduct against the view of the living dead and the yet to be born, let alone the living. The African family, the most important institution in the African worldview, is actually a community of valued relationships that is highly conscious of its history, and also extends into posterity. In a model of democracy that highly values the family, citizens are more likely to exercise due diligence when electing their leaders, as well as when making other decisions. This contrasts with the brinkmanship, as well as with the mercenary and predatory conduct of both citizens and leaders, in a liberal democracy.

Furthermore, the significance of the community occupies a much higher rank than the autonomy and dignity of the individual. Thus, Cobbah observes that "In a society like the Akan, the pursuit of human dignity is not concerned with vindicating the right of any individual against the world. The African notion of family seeks a vindication of the communal well-being. The starting point is not the individual but the whole group including the living and the dead" (Cobbah 1985, 322). This is encapsulated in the African adage that "The prosperity of a single person does not make a town rich. But the prosperity of the town makes persons rich" (Emeakaroha 2002). In economic terms, African nation-states ought to include measures of prosperity that are inclusive of all citizens, even as they churn out calculations of GDPs.

INDIGENOUS AFRICAN MORALITY

In an extensive study of the Swahili of the eastern coast of Africa, Kai Kresse observed that a central aspect of their moral outlook is "the saying *Mtu ni watu*, 'A human being is humanity'". The Kiswahili saying reflects the pervasiveness of *ubuntu* in Africa, to which van Binsbergen (2001, 53) attests. Of great relevance to our reflections on morality is Kresse's observation that "In Kiswahili, the conception of humanity is semantically linked to morality, which is an exclusively human quality" (Kresse 2007, 139). If indeed it is the case that "*utu*" [Kiswahili for 'humanity'] has morality and goodness as primary connotations" (Kresse 2007, 139), then this probably is the crucial element that can banish brazen looting and destruction of public institutions.

The importance of *utu* (Kiswahili for "humanity") in indigenous African models of democracy is also due to the fact that there is no such condition as 'bad humanity' (Kresse 2007, 145). When people have lost their humanity, they are relegated from "the realm of humanity (*utu*) to the sphere of animals, bestiality (*unyama*)" (Kresse 2007, 145). It would appear that the dynamics of liberal democracy have undermined the humane aspects of people from the West. Liberal democracy and its moral theory and sociology have accomplished this by obliterating "any genuine distinction between manipulative and non-manipulative social relations" (MacIntyre 1981, 23). In the liberal democracy of the post–Cold War era, the distinction between *mtu* (Kiswahili for "human being") and *kitu* (Kiswahili for "a thing") is erased, and with the erasure has come the loss of humanity. Indigenous African models of democracy for the twenty-first century must therefore recover and guard this distinction.

THE CRUCIAL PLACE OF SOCIALISATION

In view of our proposals in the preceding paragraphs, the question arises: how can African states cultivate these indigenous elements to levels that can translate to a shift from liberal democracy to indigenous African models of democracy? Kohlberg (1981), MacIntyre (1999), Kresse (2007), Situma (2015), and Situma, Odiemo, and Mutisya (2017) argue that socialisation is crucial to moral development, and that moral development is the acquisition of virtues. In addition, Adjibolosoo asserts that "in many cases, productivity and quality enhancement programs fail because they ignore the fact that for continuing success, human factor engineering must be made the primary core of these programs" (Adjibolosoo 1996, 83; see also Adjibolosoo 2004).

CONCLUSION

From the foregoing reflections, it is evident that cultures are dynamic, and in view of the African encounter with other cultures, the task of determining and recovering viable elements of democratic governance from indigenous African cultures is an onerous one. Praeg points out that one of the challenges to constituting political processes on humanism is the occurrence of hazardous events that neuter valuable foundational aspects such as happened in South Africa in 2012, when, in spite of its professed commitment to *Ubuntu*, the government unleashed security agents on demonstrators, killing dozens of them. Praeg rightly characterises that event as a moment when "Existence is reduced to the random outcome of the calculation of fleeting interests ... Of course, there is a real sense in which the political is always precisely such a calculation" (Praeg 2014, xii). In other words, even when a people commits itself to humanism, it must constantly confront the temptation to resort to expedience. Humanism, expressed in various cultures, demands continuous self-interrogation in a bid to understand what being human entails. This is what Praeg conceives as "a lasting iteration of the founding intent, a determination to remain anchored to the sense of purpose that first unified the collective as 'We'" (Praeg 2014, xii).

Moreover, the process of recovering Africa's communal values can only effectively address the cognitive crises that colonisation and the inheriting of liberal democracy triggered if school curricula incorporate such values progressively and systematically. This proposal arises from our earlier argument for the cultivation of the indigenous notion of fatherland or motherland in order to reorient citizens' outlook towards their obligations and rights, reconfiguring their notions of justice in order to align them with the reality of living in a multi-cultural state, and entrenching in them the idea of *utu* (Kiswahili for "humaneness,") namely, that if they undermine other people's humanity, they dehumanise their own selves. The inculcation of these and other values ought to be continuous throughout learners' progression in the education system, and should be structured to be coherent. This is the human engineering dimension which Adjibolosoo (1996; 2004) proposes. In view of the fact that the colonial state was, by definition, imposed on African societies (Young 1994, 3), and because institutions and practices are multifaceted, the process of recovering indigenous African values and practices must be multi-disciplinary. Only after identifying and re-conceptualising appropriate indigenous African values and practices can the project of nurturing citizens with patriotism instead of parochialism be undertaken.

NOTES

1. For a detailed explication of corruption, see Sardan, J. P. Olivier de, 1999. "A Moral Economy of Corruption in Africa," *The Journal of Modern African Studies*, Vol. 37 No. 1 and U4Expert Answer, Transparency International: The Global Coalition against Corruption, www.transparency.org.

2. See Berman, Bruce J. 2010. "Ethnicity and Democracy in Africa". JICA-RI Working Paper No. 22, November 2010, JICA Research Institute.

3. This is slang for using illicit or informal means to achieve an outcome.

4. This endeavor does not preclude harnessing some valuable aspects from other traditions, including Western and Eastern ones.

5. "Supererogation" refers to the act of exceeding what is morally required of an individual or institution.

6. Compatriotism is the sense of fellowship among people who are citizens of one country. On the other hand, patriotism is the sense of being strongly identified with the interests of one's country.

7. We use *ubuntu* in the same sense as Praeg (2004) "to refer to the living practice (the 'unadulterated forms of African social life')," but also to refer to the African outlook.

REFERENCES

Adjibolosoo, Senyo. 1996. "Education and Training for Effective Leadership Development and Productivity and Quality Management in Africa". Adjibolosoo, Senyo ed. *The Human factor in Developing Africa*. Westport: Praeger Publishers, pp. 83–98.

———. 2004. "The Human Factor Engineering Process: Preparing People for the Tasks and Challenges of Management". *Problems and Perspectives in Manage-*

ment, Vol. 2 No. 2, pp. 149–64. https://businessperspectives.org/component/zoo/the-human-factor-engineering-process-preparing-people-for-the-tasks-and-challenges-of-management.

Awiti, Alex O. and Bruce Scott. 2016. *The Youth Survey Report*. Nairobi: Aga Khan University.

Ayittey, George. 1991. *Indigenous African Institutions*. Leiden: Martinus Nijhoff.

Bascara, Rachelle. 2016. "Compatriot Partiality and Cosmopolitan Justice: Can we justify Compatriot Partiality with the Cosmopolitan Framework?" *Etikk I Praksis: Nordic Journal of Applied Ethics*, Vol. 10 No. 2, pp. 27–39. http://dx.doi.org/10.5324/cip.u10i2.1921.

Berman, Bruce J. 2010. "Ethnicity and Democracy in Africa". JICA-RI Working Paper No. 22, November 2010. JICA Research Institute.

Berman, Bruce, Dickson Eyoh and Will Kymlicka. 2004. *Ethnicity and Democracy in Africa*. Ohio: Ohio University Press.

Brown, Chris. 2007. "Universal Human Rights: A Critique". *The International Journal of Human Rights*, Vol. 1 No. 2, pp. 41–65. https://doi.org/10.1080/13642989768406666.

Campbell, David F. J. 2008. "The Basic Concept for the Democracy Ranking of the Quality of Democracy". Democracy Ranking, Vienna. http://democracyranking.org/downloads/basic_concept_democracy_ranking_2008_A4.pdf.

Cobbah, Josiah A. 1987. "African Values and Human Rights Debate: An African Perspective". *Human Rights Quarterly*, Vol. 9 No. 3, pp. 309–31. http://www.jstor.org/stable/761878.

Conceicao, Pedro, and Namsuk Kim. 2009. "The Asymmetric Impact of Growth Fluctuation on Human Development: Evidence from Correlates of Growth Decelerations and Accelerations". *Journal of Developing Areas*, Vol. 48 No. 3, pp. 31–45. https://papers.ssrn.com/sol3/papers.cfm?abstract_id=2001534.

Coppedge, Michael, and John Gerring et al. 2011. "Conceptualising and Measuring Democracy". *Research Articles*, Vol. 9 No. 2, pp. 247–67. http://128.197.153.21/jgerring/documents/MeasuringDemocracy.pdf.

Emeakaroha, Emeka. 2002. "African Cultural Values". www.emeka.at/african_cultural_vaules.pdf.

Fukuyama, Francis. 1989. "The End of History?" *The National Interest*, No. 16, pp. 3–18. http://www.jstor.org/stable/24027184.

———. 1992. *The End of History and the Last Man*. New York: Free Press.

Hegel, Georg Wilhelm. 1807. *Phenomenology of Spirit*. Miller, A.V. trans. Oxford: Oxford University Press.

———. 1956. *The Philosophy of History*. Sibree, John trans. New York: Dover Publications.

Hopgood, Stephen. 2014. *The Endtimes of Human Rights*. Ithaca, NY: Cornell University Press.

Huntington, Samuel. 1996. *The Clash of Civilisations and the Remaking of World Order*. New York: Simon and Schuster.

Isichei, Elizabeth. 1997. *A History of African Societies to 1870*. Cambridge: Cambridge University Press.

Kohlberg, Lawrence. 1981. *Essays on Moral Development, Vol. 1: The Philosophy of Moral Development*. San Francisco, CA: Harper & Row.

Kojeve, Aexandre. 1969. *Introduction to the Reading of Hegel: Lectures on Phenomenology of Spirit*. Ithaca: Cornell University Press.

Kresse, Kai. 2007. *Philosophising in Mombasa: Knowledge, Islam and Intellectual Practice on the Swahili Coast*. London: Edinburgh University Press.

Lewin, Michael. 2011. "Botswana's Success: Good Governance, Good Policies, and Good Luck". Chuhan-Pole, Punam and Manka Angwafo eds. *Yes Africa Can: Success Stories from a Dynamic Continent*. Washington, DC: The World Bank.

MacIntyre, Alasdair. 1981. *After Virtue: A Study in Moral Theory*. Notre Dame: Notre Dame University Press.

Namli, Elena. 2018. "Critique of Human Rights Universalism". Stenmark, Mikael, Steve Fuller, Ulf Zackariasson eds. *Relativism and Post-Truth In Contemporary Society: Possibilities and Challenges*. N.P.: Palgrave Macmillan.

Norris, Pippa. 1997. "Choosing Electoral Systems: Proportional, Majoritarian, and Mixed Systems". *International Political Science Review*, Vol. 18 No. 3, pp. 297–312.

Nussbaum, Martha. 1997. *The Feminist Critique of Liberalism: The Lindley Lecture*. Kansas City: University of Kansas.

Plattner, Marc. 2010. "Populism, Pluralism, and Liberal Democracy". *Journal of Democracy*, Vol. 21 No. 1, pp. 82–92.

Popper, Karl. 1945. *The Open Society and Its Enemies*. https://www.andrew.cmu.edu/user/jksadegh/A.

Posner, Eric. 2014. *The Twilight of Human Rights Law*. Oxford: Oxford University Press.

Praeg, Leonhard. 2014. "Preface". Praeg, Leonhard and Siphokazi Magadla eds. *Ubuntu: Curating the Archive*. Pietermaritzburg: University of KwaZulu-Natal Press.

Skinner, Elliot P. 1998. "African Political Cultures and the Problems of Government". *African Studies Quarterly*, Vol. 2 No. 31, pp. 16–25. http://www.africa.ufl.edu/asq/v2/v2i3a3.pdf.

Smit, Marius H. and Izak Oosthuizen. 2011. "Improving School Governance through Participative Democracy and the Law". *South African Journal of Education*, Vol. 31 No. 1, pp. 55–73.

Van Binsbergen, Wim. 2001. "Ubuntu and Globalisation of Southern African Thought and Society". *Quest: African Journal of Philosophy*, Vol. XV No. 1–2, pp. 50–90. https://www.researchgate.net/publication/270013273_The_Bewaji_Van_Binsbergen_and_Ramose_debate_on_'Ubuntu'.

Welsh, Jennifer. 2016. *The Return of History: Conflict, Migration, and Geopolitics in the Twenty-First Century*. Toronto: House of Anansi Press.

Wilson, Richard A. 2001. *The Politics of Truth and Reconciliation in South Africa: Legitimising the Post-apartheid State*. Cambridge: Cambridge University Press.

Young, Crawford. 1994. *The African Colonial State in Comparative Perspective*. New Haven, CT: Yale University Press.

Chapter Eleven

Democracy and the Right of the Minority in Africa

Moses Oludare Aderibigbe

In the contemporary world, democracy has become the most acceptable form of government, mainly because of its ideals that affirm the right of people to participate in the social, economic and political affairs of their countries. Nevertheless, the principle of the supreme right of the majority, which is the basis of elections in the Western liberal democratic tradition, amounts to the majority imposing its will on the minority, thus legitimising the disempowerment of minorities in the state. In this chapter, I argue that given the tendency of a sizeable proportion of Africans to vote according to their ethnic, cultural and/or religious identities, democracy will need to mean much more than voting at elections. Consequently, I concur with the position of Prempeh (2005, 814) that the globalised democracy and human rights require reinterpretation and application in diverse cultural contexts beyond the narrow limits of Western liberal values. I advocate the value of rational consensus which respects diversity, thereby ensuring that all voices are heard through 'dialogic confrontation' in a bid to arrive at unanimous decisions on matters that affect the whole society. The ethos of tolerance, which allows citizens with diverse opinions to soberly deliberate on issues of common interest, would contribute to solving our multifaceted problems. My goal is to highlight the need to allow the process of decision-making to move down to the local units such as lineages and extended families. This would promote social stability by getting those that would otherwise have been excluded from a share in power and its attendant benefits to be involved in charting the political direction of their countries, thereby securing their good will.

I have divided the chapter into three main sections: the first section presents a general overview of the concept and ideals of democracy. In the second, I contend that since liberal democracy is only one model of democracy among others, the West has no right to impose it on Africa. In the third, I follow Kwasi Wiredu (1995) in advocating for a no-party, consensual democratic system of government in contemporary African states.

DEMOCRACY AND ITS IDEALS

It is now almost common knowledge that democracy comes from two Greek words, *demos* ("people") and *kratein* ("rule"), so that it literally means "people rule". However, "the people," in the understanding of the ancient Athenians usually associated with the origins of Western democracy, referred to the body of citizens, which consisted mainly of adult free males of indigenous birth. As such, foreign residents, women, children and slaves were denied the right to participate in the affairs of the *polis* ("city-state"). Rule by the people was direct, in that legislative decisions were taken by the people at mass assemblies (Irele 1998, 83). In addition, as Frederic Kenyon explains, elective offices were filled by lot:

> There was . . . to be a council, consisting of four hundred and one members, elected by lot from among those who were over thirty years of age; and no one might hold office twice until everyone else had his turn, after which they were to cast the lot afresh. If any member of the council failed to attend when there was a sitting of the council or of the assembly he paid a fine . . . The council of Areopagus was guardian of the laws and kept watch over the magistrates to see that they executed their offices in accordance with the laws. (Kenyon 1952, 554)

Besides, all male, freeborn Athenians were equal before the law, and enjoyed freedom as stipulated by the law. They had equal right to be heard in the sovereign assembly of the state before it could arrive at decisions. Besides, all important trials were held before popular courts whose members were chosen by lot (Irele 1998, 83).

Thus, in essence, Athenian democracy allowed the people to make their own decisions about the way they were to be governed rather than having a small group of people making decisions on their behalf.

However, over the centuries, the concept of democracy has acquired a variety of interpretations. For example, during the Cold War, both leading Western and Eastern powers and their satellites laid claim to being the ones practising genuine democracy. There is therefore evident difficulty in arriving at a scholarly consensus on a precise definition of 'democracy'. We also need to take seriously George Orwell's caution:

> A word like democracy not only [has] . . . no agreed definition, but the attempt to make one is resisted from all sides. It is almost universally felt that when we call

a country democratic we are praising it: consequently the defender of every kind of regime claims that it is a democracy and fears that they might have to stop using the word if it were tied down to any one meaning. (Orwell 1968, 132–33)

Nevertheless, in pursuit of a degree of clarity, let us consider some definitions of democracy that scholars have offered.

Following Robert Dahl, Okunade (1998, 129) defines democracy as a system of government in which the authority to exercise power derives from the will of the people. According to him, democracy "maximises opportunities for both political contestation and political participation". Going by this view, democracy is highly responsive to all citizens. Similarly, Irele follows Durkheim's conception of democracy in a dialogic framework (Irele 1998, 16; Durkheim 1957, 91). Durkheim's analysis of democracy is premised on the conviction that issues that concern the democratic political community ought to be subject to collective debate and scrutiny (Durkheim 1957).

Claude Ake (1992, 1) views democracy as popular power, that is, rule by the demos:

> This was the conception of the Greeks who 'invented' the theory and practice of democracy. That was the meaning of democracy during the French revolution, which is the midwife of modern democratic practice. It remains the classic definition of democracy, rephrased with poignant simplicity by a famous American as "government of the people, by the people and for the people." (Ake 1992, 1)

One may well ask: have these democratic ideals become social practice? Take, for example, the ideal of democracy as a government by the people: are there states in which all the people govern themselves by actively participating in the day-to-day management of the affairs of their polity? It appears that the answer to this question is negative. Among states that are often considered to be highly democratic, it is hardly possible to find one in which the people govern themselves directly. As I earlier noted, the only state which approximated this ideal to a significant degree was the ancient Athenian city-state, with its form of direct democracy by a minority, namely, the freeborn male adult citizens. However, in most liberal democracies, there is a form of indirect system of governance, in which representatives are chosen through periodic elections.

Nonetheless, there are some principles and ideals that are necessary features of democracy. They are given practical expression in the laws and institutions of society and provide directions on how members of society ought to work towards its betterment. According to Busia (1975, 453), democracy is founded on respect for every human being, implying subscription to racial equality. The wide agreement on this principle was evident in the unanimous condemnation by African states of minority Caucasoid governments in South Africa, the former Southern Rhodesia (now Zimbabwe), and the Portuguese colonies of Angola and Mozambique, in all of which there were tensions between those who enjoyed full rights and those whose rights were denied (Busia 1975, 453).

In addition, there ought to be freedom of speech in a democracy, with citizens at liberty to express their views on government policies, and on whatever else is of concern to them as individuals, and to their society at large. There also ought to be freedom of press and religion. All these liberties presuppose the equality of all citizens. However, the notion of equality entails a set of ideas that apply to various contexts, and include political equality, equality before the law, equality of opportunity, economic equality, and social equality. The most important among these is equality in the voting system, which requires that each vote is given the same weight, without discrimination against any one on grounds such as gender, race, religion, or economic status (Irele 1998, 86). Furthermore, it is an imperative of democracy that the government be answerable to the people: those holding public offices are required to account for their policies and programs.

In the light of the ideals of democracy listed above, it may be concluded that although, as I earlier noted, it is difficult to arrive at a universally acceptable definition of democracy, any governance system committed to the pursuit of these ideals can be considered to be democratic.

LIBERAL DEMOCRACY: A MODEL AMONG OTHERS

At the present time, the most popular form of democracy in a significant part of the world is liberal democracy. According to Wingo (2004, 451), in the United States, and in many European countries, the wedding between liberalism and democracy took place about two hundred years ago. In that union, there were some concessions by democracy to political liberalism, and liberalism to democracy. Thus, in the United States, political liberalism and democracy form an organic whole to such an extent that we do not even see the two as being distilled from different traditions (Wingo 2004, 452). Liberal democracy emphasises the rule of law, separation of powers, and the guarantee of the rights of individuals to pursue happiness as they deem fit.

In addition, Macpherson (1965, 29) highlighted the birth, in the West, of the possessive individual of Thomas Hobbes, and the articulation of two complementary concepts of the human person, namely, the atomic individual as (a) a consumer of utilities, and (b) the maximiser of his or her capacities. In the West, the human person began to be seen as an individual endowed with the right to accumulate property in freedom. Iwuchukwu (1997, 87) explains that this view gave birth to a new form of government with strong emphasis on: (a) popular participation, even if by means of representation, and (b) class/party politics which reflects the underlying class struggle, and this form of government came to be known as liberal democracy. It was liberal because of its emphasis on the rights of the individual, and democratic because it contained elements that promoted self-government, and that had been present in ancient Greek democracy.

However, there are forms of democracy that stand in opposition to the liberal model. For example, there is the Marxist model, which, as Macpherson explains, "contains an ideal of human equality, not just equality of opportunity to climb a class ladder, but such an equality as could only be fully realised in a society where no class was able to dominate or live at the expense of others" (Macpherson 1965, 24). Thus, the Marxist approach lays emphasis on the economic condition of the citizens. According to Marx, for any society to be democratic, it must be classless, with the means of production under the control of the workers. For Marx, then, without the economic equality of all the citizens through the elimination of economic classes, there can be no true democracy (Marx and Engels 1977, 398).

Yet another model of democracy is one that was highlighted by Macpherson (1965, 28) to be suitable for the developing nations of Africa and the rest of the Third World. This model lays emphasis on freedom from starvation and ignorance, and stresses grassroot participation and collective decision-making in an environment free from class struggle. Central to this model of democracy is a one-party form of government, which, in the view of Western liberal democracy, is undemocratic. However, the assessment by liberal democracy of this governance model fails to take account of the true meaning of democracy. In this regard, Macpherson observed: "a one-party government may properly be called democratic if there is full intra-party democracy, if party membership is open, and if the price of participation in the party is not a greater degree of activity than the average person can reasonably be expected to contribute" (Macpherson 1965, 28).

Furthermore, although due to the history of colonialism in Africa people in the continent are mostly familiar with liberal democracy, Western Europe has also produced social democracy which is found in Scandinavian countries (Finland, Denmark, Norway, Sweden, and Iceland). Those countries have constitutional monarchs as ceremonial heads of state, and prime ministers vested with executive authority. They have unicameral parliaments and use proportional representation in their electoral systems. Besides, each of them operates a multi-party system, and has numerous political parties. As a result, quite frequently no one party has a chance of gaining power alone, making coalition governments necessary, which in turn leads to co-operation among parties.

Although there are some differences among the governance models of the Scandinavian countries, they all lay a high premium on social welfare with the aim of promoting equality and solidarity. Their governance models are underguarded by sets of values that are actualised through public policy. As a result, the differences among classes and regions in each of the countries have been significantly reduced. As Torben Inverse (1998, 59) noted, Scandinavian social democracy represents one of the most systematic attempts to shape economic institutions and policies in pursuit of equality and employment. Thus, Noralv Veggeland (2020, 135) observes that the Scandinavian countries have a long history and have experienced similar social and economic developments. Veggeland goes on to observe that the most common feature of their systems is a well-developed welfare state characterised by its universalism, meaning that all citizens are entitled to basic social benefits and job protection, and each of the countries' public policies are characterised by high social spending, high taxes, and a large public sector.

In the light of the variety of models of democracy, the former Western colonial powers are not justified to impose liberal democracy on Africa. It is for this reason that we now go on to explore an indigenous model of democracy suitable for twenty-first-century African states.

DEMOCRACY BY CONSENSUS FOR AFRICA: ITS JUSTIFICATION AND CORE VALUES

One of the reasons for the failure of democracy in Africa today is the fact that the Western-style multi-party model of democracy being practiced in the continent is not in conformity with the cultural orientation of her peoples. Liberal democracy may be appropriate for some cultural contexts, but it does not guarantee socio-political and economic progress to the peoples of Africa because, contrary to the indigenous African outlook, it marginalises and disempowers minorities instead of facilitating exhaustive deliberations with a view to arriving at consensus. One step in the right direction would be to re-examine indigenous African values, with a view to appropriately incorporating them into existing political structures in order to address contemporary problems of governance.

The question then arises as to whether or not there were any systems of political parties in indigenous African political formations. Over the years, scholars have made several attempts to respond to this question, but each response has largely depended on the ideological leaning of each thinker.

Thus, on one hand, going by Julius Nyerere's view, Africans operated party systems, but they were not multi-party systems like those in the West where parties came into being as a result of existing social and economic divisions, and from the need to challenge the monopoly of political power by aristocratic or capitalistic groups (Nyerere 1969, 479). Indeed, Nyerere defended the one-party system of governance on the basis that according to the African worldview, "society" is an extension of the basic family unit to which we all belong. For him, this outlook is a firm foundation for both socialism and democracy in Africa:

> We, in Africa, have no more need of being "converted" to socialism than we have of being "taught" democracy. Both are rooted in our own past in the traditional society which produced us. Modern African socialism can draw from its traditional heritage the recognition of "society" as an extension of the basic family unit. (Nyerere 1977, 12)

On the other hand, according to Sithole (1959, 459), if African political institutions of the past tell us anything at all, it is that they were no-party systems. Similarly, Wiredu (1995, 59), judging from the Ashanti political system, asserted that there was no party system in the sense of the word "party" which is basic to majoritarian democracy. However, for Wiredu, what could be termed as parties were the lineages to which people belonged, which were parties to the project of good government. The youth, for example, constituted themselves into an organised party under a recognised leader, and the party was entitled to make representations directly to the relevant council on all matters of public interest, much as the party was not a member of the council. The only difference was that none of the groups organised themselves for the purpose of gaining power and thereby depriving others of it. For Wiredu, this is the aspect of the traditional African political systems to which the advocates of the one-party system appealed in their attempts to prove its African ancestry and authenticity. Wiredu therefore advocates for a no-party system of governance formed through the consensus of elected representatives who become a kind of coalition—not of parties, but rather of citizens (Wiredu 1995, 61).

Following Wiredu, I hold the view that for democracy to flourish in Africa, there is need to return to a no-party system of governance. The fact that traditional African chiefs assumed leadership without elections is evidence that a no-party system can flourish in Africa. According to Teffo (2004, 445), it is shortsighted to insist that the only way kings and chiefs and anyone else can attain political power legitimately is through elections. Over the millennia, and even up to our day, monarchs (kings and queens) all over the world have not, as a rule, acquired their constitutional status through elections. Nevertheless, their status has not been viewed as necessarily antithetical to the authenticity of democratic modes of governance. For example, the monarch of England is not elected, and yet advocates of democracy do not treat British democracy with contempt. Consequently, it is possible, even in contemporary Africa, to develop a democratic system of governance where legitimate political power is attained without elections.

I also share Wiredu's view that consensus is the answer to the political woes of contemporary African states. This is due to the fact that indigenous African social organisation was undergirded by the principle of solidarity, which is to say that it was characterised by a communal spirit and was therefore people-centred. As such, decision by consensus was often the order of the day. According to Wiredu (1995, 62), consensus is not simply an optional bonus; rather, it is essential for securing substantive, or what might also be called decisional, representation for the people's representatives and, through them, for the citizens at large, and this is nothing short of a fundamental human right.

Furthermore, Wiredu maintains that at the very minimum, efforts ought to be made to persuade each representative of the practical necessity of every decision. For Wiredu, if discussion has been even moderately rational, and if the spirit has been one of respectful accommodation on all sides, surviving reservations on the part of a momentary minority would not prevent the recognition that if the community is to go forward, a particular line of action must be taken. This, for Wiredu, must not be confused with decision-making on the principle of the supreme right of the majority: in this case the majority prevails not *over*, but rather *upon*, the minority—they prevail upon them to accept the proposal in question, not simply to live with it, the latter being the basic plight of minorities under majoritarian democracy (Wiredu 1995, 62).

Moreover, on the issue of consensus, Wamala (2004, 439) convincingly avers that the traditional African consensual system of government was efficient and effective. According to him, the Baganda had a monarchical system of a limited rather than an absolute sort. The monarch ruled through a council of heads of clans, and there were heads, sub-heads, and chiefs at the various levels of society. In any debate, the aim was to reach a consensus. If, after due deliberations, the council reached consensus, it was taboo for the monarch to oppose or reject it. This, for Wamala, is why the monarchy was of a "limited" variety; it is also why the monarchical character of the system was compatible with its being democratic.

In view of the reflections above, I opine that what African states need are democratic systems based on decision-making by consensus rather than the current majoritarian ones. To be sure, a consensual system has its own challenges, especially where a crucial decision has to be taken without unanimity. In such instances, deliberations would be undertaken on the basis of commitment to respect diverse and divergent opinions with the aim of arriving at a decision which those holding a minority opinion would be able to live with.

One value which could make democracy sustainable in Africa is tolerance. The English word "tolerate" is derived from the Latin terms *tolerare* and *tolerantia*, which imply enduring, suffering, bearing, and forbearance. Ancient Greek terms that may also have influenced Western philosophical thinking on toleration include *phoretos* ("bearable" or "endurable"), *phoreo* (literally "to carry"), and *anektikos* ("bearable," "sufferable" or "tolerable") from *anexo* ("to hold up") (Fiala 2017, 1). Appadorai (1975, 21) identified imperative conditions for the viability of any democracy, namely, the widespread habit of tolerance and compromise among members of a community, a sense of "give and take," the provision of adequate opportunities for the individual to actualise his or her potentialities, and proper organisation and leadership. Members of ethnically or religiously plural societies, such as those in most post-colonial African states, ought to learn to tolerate one another.

With regard to tolerance, Busia (1975, 453), while comparing the challenges of democracy in traditional and modern African societies, suggested that democracy cannot work unless those who seek to exercise the liberties befitting the dignity of the human person recognise the equal rights of others to exercise them too. In other words, they ought to affirm the right of others to think and choose differently. In traditional African societies, a large proportion of members subscribed to the same religious beliefs, shared in the same rituals, and held the same views about the universe. Thus, the highly valued solidarity of those societies was based on conformity. Nevertheless, in contemporary pluralistic African societies, it is unrealistic to hope to achieve solidarity on the basis of conformity. As such, one of the most important characteristics of a pluralistic democratic society is tolerance. Furthermore, as I earlier noted, Western-style party politics, with its attendant one-person-one-vote, coupled with its majoritarian orientation, leads to domination of minorities by majorities, causing tensions in contemporary African polities. As such, adopting the ethos of tolerance would enable the various groups to endure one another in the course of deliberation until consensus is reached. This would ensure that all groups meaningfully participate in the affairs of the polity.

The prospect of living together as cohesive societies and building stronger political structures than what we have had to date is not an illusion. We shall be firmly on the path to achieving this when we re-examine our value systems with a view to restructuring our political systems in such a way that everyone is included in drawing the road map to our collective well-being. For this to happen, we ought to rededicate ourselves to virtues such as honesty, respect for one another, the upholding of human dignity, the sanctity of human life, integrity, justice, and the conception of the polity as a large family, which is the central nerve of our communalism.

CONCLUSION

In its traditional cultural heritage, Africa has what it takes to be independent and self-reliant. In the preceding reflections, I have advocated for a model of democracy which draws from the African political heritage to guarantee the rights of minorities, thereby addressing their fear of perpetual domination. The supreme right of the majority upheld in the present Western-type political systems deprives minorities of their civil rights. Consequently, I agree with Wiredu that the value of rational consensus undergirded by the principle of solidarity, which characterised indigenous African social organisation, was people-centred, and is the answer to the political woes of contemporary African states.

In the same vein, the value of tolerance, which promotes a sense of "give and take" among members of a society, makes provision for the individual to actualise his or her potentialities, and ensures adequate organisation and leadership among members of ethnically or religiously plural societies such as those in most post-colonial African states. Finally, the values of justice, integrity and respect for one another, which are core to a democratic culture, would go a long way in laying the foundation for sustainable democracies in twenty-first-century Africa.

REFERENCES

Ake, Claude. 1992. *The Feasibility of Democracy in Africa*, No. 1. Ibadan: Centre for Research Documentation and University Exchange.

Appadorai, Angadipuram. 1975. *The Substance of Politics*. Oxford: Oxford University Press.

Busia, Kofi Abrefa. 1975. "Democracy and One-Party System". Mutiso, Gideon-Cyrus & S. W. Rohio eds. *Readings in African Political Thought*. London: Heinemann, pp. 462–67.

Durkheim, Émile. 1957. *Professional Ethics and Civic Morals*. London: Routledge and Kegan Paul.

Fiala, Andrew. 2017. "Tolerance". Fieser, James and Bradley Dowden eds. *Internet Encyclopedia of Philosophy*. www.iep.utm.edu/tolerati/.

Irele, Dipo. 1998. *Introduction to Political Philosophy*. Ibadan: Ibadan University Press.

Iversen, Torben. 1998. "The Choices for Scandinavian Social Democracy in Comparative Perspective". *Oxford Review of Economic Policy*, Vol. 14 No. 1, pp. 59–75.

Iwuchukwu, Oliver. 1998. "Democracy and Regional Ontologies". Oguejiofor, J.Obi ed. *Africa Philosophy and Public Affairs*. Enugu: Delta Publications, pp. 82–93.
Kenyon, Frederic. 1952. "The Athenian Constitution". Hutchins, Robert ed. *The Works of Aristotle*, Vol. II. Oxford: Oxford University Press.
Macpherson, Crawford B. 1965. *The Real World of Liberal Democracy*. Toronto: CBC Publications.
Marx, Karl, and Frederick Engels. 1977. *Selected Works*, Vol. 3. Moscow: Progress Publishers.
Nyerere, Julius K. 1977. *Ujamaa: Essays on African Socialism*. Oxford: Oxford University Press.
Okunade, Bayo. 1998. "Democracy and Human Rights in the Context of Twenty First Century Africa". Oladipo, Olusegun ed. *Remaking Africa: Challenges of the Twenty-First Century*. Ibadan: Hope Publications, pp. 127–44.
Orwell, George. 1968. "In Front of Your Nose: 1945–1950". Orwell, Sonia and Ian Angus eds. *The Collected Essays, Journalism and Letters of George Orwell Vol. 4*. New York: Harper & Row, pp. 132–33.
Prempeh, Edward Osei Kwadwo. 2005. "Globalising Democracy and Human Rights". *Canadian Journal of Political Science*, Vol. 38 No. 3, pp. 814–15. https://www.cambridge.org/core/journals/canadian-journal-of-political-science-revue-canadienne-de-science-politique/article/div-classtitleglobalizing-democracy-and-human-rights-div/EDC53FA9C145BBC8DEA3E574908B12A4.
Sithole, Ndabaningi. 1959. "The One/Two-Party System". Mutiso, Gideon-Cyrus & S. W. Rohio eds. *Readings in African Political Thought*. London: Heinemann, pp. 459–61.
Teffo, Joe. 2004. "Democracy, Kingship, and Consensus: A South African Perspective". Wiredu, Kwasi ed. *A Companion to African Philosophy*. Oxford: Blackwell Publishing, pp. 443–49.
Veggeland, Noralv. 2020. *Democratic Governance in Scandinavia: Developments and Challenges for the Regulatory State*. Switzerland: Springer Nature Switzerland.
Wamala, Edward. 2004. "Government by Consensus: An Analysis of a Traditional Form of Democracy". Wiredu, Kwasi ed. *A Companion to African Philosophy*. Oxford: Blackwell Publishing, pp. 435–42.
Wingo, Ajume. 2004. "Fellowship Association as a Foundation for Liberal Democracy in Africa". Wiredu, Kwasi ed. *A Companion to African Philosophy*. Oxford: Blackwell Publishing, pp. 450–59.
Wiredu, Kwasi. 1995. "Democracy and Consensus in African Traditional Politics: A Plea for a Non-Party Polity". *Conceptual Decolonisation in African Philosophy: 4 Essays*. Selected and Introduced by O. Oladipo. Ibadan: Hope Publications, pp. 53–63.

Chapter Twelve

Critical Reflections on the Quest for a Monolithic Democratic Alternative to Liberal Democracy for Africa

Tayo Raymond Ezekiel Eegunlusi

Many scholarly works conceptualise democracy as being universal in nature. The confusion emanating from the use of the word "universal" derives from ambiguous conceptualisations. One of these is the notion of an ideal democracy, which suggests an esoteric universalism, as in Plato's conception of the universal in his theory of Forms (Plato 1997, 363–70), in which he conceives of ideas as permanent and invisible entities from which material things in the world derive their nature.

Despite Plato's denunciation of democracy, his conceptualisation of the Forms does not exclude democracy. This implies that there exists a universal (monolithic) democracy as well as particular democracies, that is, globally applicable democracy versus culture-bound democracies. Liberal democracy has become the most well-known version of particular democracy. Regrettably, it is taking on a seemingly monolithic character, and is in effect being imposed on the rest of the world. Furthermore, some of the cultures that have tried to adopt it lack the prerequisite ethical and epistemological orientation to promote its practicability. As such, liberal democracy frequently fails in non-Western regions of the world such as Africa and Asia.

In the light of the foregoing observations, I raise doubts about the possibility of a monolithic (universal) alternative African (cultural) conception of democracy as is suggested by the search for an alternative democratic model for Africa. I argue in this chapter that three considerations are important with regard to the quest for alternatives to liberal democracy by African and Africanist scholars. *First*, there is the (ontological) debate relating to universal democracy versus particular democracies. Essentially, democracy is peculiarly culture-bound: it cannot be practiced in isolation from people's cultures, and whatever conceptualisation each culture has cannot be said to be universal but particular. Consequently, to suggest an overarching democratic model for Africa is illusory. *Second*, in their discussions, scholars of democracy often take Africa's multivalent identities for granted. Considering the diverse identities and experiences of African peoples, preference for any conceptualisation of democracy from any region may be perceived by other African societies as a culture-imposition. *Third*, while Western imperialism is often correctly blamed for the failure of liberal democracy in Africa, the moral deficiencies that caused the breakdown of the governance systems of pre-colonial African societies have also contributed to the failure of liberal democracy in contemporary African polities. In the past, various vices affecting the socio-political and economic dealings in African communities shaped traditional governance structures and gave rise to people's outcries against despotic rule (Owusu 1992, 377–96; David and Ugochukwu 2013, 2). These same deficiencies are some of the reasons for the failure of liberal democracy in Africa today.

Reflecting on the issues above utilising conceptual and historical methods, I debunk the quest for a universal democratic model for Africa, given the continent's cultural diversity, and argue that different African states ought to look within their cultures to determine and particularise democracy in ways that suit them. In the next section, I outline the key elements of liberal democracy within the broad framework of the Western liberal tradition. Next, I reflect on the debate between universalist and particularist approaches to democracy in Africa. That is followed by a section in which I assess well-known African perspectives on the failure of liberal democracy. Thereafter, I focus on the diversity of African identities in relation to liberal democracy. I then discuss the importance of particularising democracy in Africa, after which I recapitulate my basic arguments.

CONCEPTUALISING LIBERAL DEMOCRACY

Several societies have practiced liberal democracy since the eighteenth century C.E. Writers such as Dewey (2001), Macpherson (1977), Held (2006), McGrew (2003), Cunningham (2002), and a host of others have examined different models of democracy from the Athenian democracy through to the advent of liberal democracy. While many of these contemporary writers discuss perspectives that conceptualise democracy as having a universal nature, others highlight the pivotal role of its cultural context. Macpherson gives democracy a particularistic inflection by recognising communist democracy, liberal democracy, and Third World democracy as the three models of democracy during the Cold War era. Although events have largely overtaken Macpherson's categorisation as far as communist democracy is concerned, liberal democracy and Third World democracy continue to flourish, and I will pay considerable attention to them.

Liberal democracy springs from *liberalism*—the view that individuals have the right to freely pursue objectives aimed at self-realisation without hindrances from others in society. For liberalism, individual freedom and social progress take precedence over any form of authoritarianism. Classical liberalism has three fundamental aspects—the political, moral, and economic (Locke 1980, 9–51; Smith 2008, 359–62).

Classical liberalism lays emphasis on the freedom of the individual, and the implicit freedom in the fields of politics and economics. Deriving from reflections on classical liberalism, welfare liberalism maintains that although people have the right to pursue their objectives, priority ought to be given to taking care of the interests of the less privileged members of society. On its part, economic liberalism focuses on the principles of free markets and the right to private property (Friedman 1962, 132–36; George 1980, 45–46, 286–87; Rawls 1972, 55–65; Donaldson 1989, 80–86). While the economic core of liberalism emphasises the right of the individual to own property and to make choices about his or her property without obstacles from the state, and while the moral core underscores the importance of basic human rights and dignity, political liberalism holds that the freedom of the individual ought to be the focus of governmental actions. As such, basic human rights, such as the right to life, free speech, free association, and the right to own property underpin the conviction that governments ought to exist to protect individual liberty by limiting restrictions to it. Thus, based on the ideal of the right of individuals to constitute a government which protects their liberties as individuals based on the collective will of the members of their society, liberal democracy is the culmination of political liberalism.

Macpherson (1977) argues that liberal democracy possesses the characteristics requisite for promoting self-governance and the ideals of a liberal capitalist economy. This implies that the ideals of liberal democracy and liberal capitalism are interwoven. Held (2006) perceives liberal democracy as a model that thrives through arrangements that protect the rights of individuals, having developed as a reaction against "absolutism" in Europe. In view of the principles of liberal political theory, free trade, and the right to self-determination, Held asserts that liberal democracy has two strands, namely, protective liberal democracy and developmental liberal democracy. The former, following Hobbes's and Locke's views, is that under which individuals, by their consent, gave up their rights of self-governance and formed a government to guard their liberty, while equally empowering the government to protect "social and political order" (Held 2006, 60). The latter, in line with the views of John Stuart Mill (1994, 11–21), is that in which participation in politics is essential for protecting the interests of the individual, as well as for ensuring his or her development and enlightenment.

Liberal democracy has benefitted from various models of democracy since the Athenian democracy over two thousand years ago. The writing of the *Magna Carta*, as well as the American, French and English Revolutions heightened agitations for personal freedom, thereby popularising liberal democratic ideas. Indeed, the rise of liberal democracy was motivated by the desire for the actualisation of the rights to self-determination, and these were prioritised over hereditary rights of royal families that undermined the participation of the masses in governance (Locke 1980; Montesquieu 1914, 71–95; Paine 2003, 8–35; de Tocqueville 1994, 41–52; Wollstonecraft 2011, 1–48).

Furthermore, liberal democracy is often conceptualised as (i) universal in nature, or (ii) having universal applicability. In the first sense, cultural overtones seem to be glossed over, while ideals such as toleration, equality, justice, and human rights (such as the right to life, as well as religious, economic, and political freedom) are prioritised as capturing the universal essence of liberal democracy. The second sense, which depends on the first, considers liberal democracy as an overarching or monolithic system of governance that eliminates all cultural barriers, and which everyone therefore ought to practice. This line of thought seems to overlook the fact that democracy is culture-bound.

African political theorists often give the impression that the substitute to liberal democracy ought to be universal (monolithic). Is such an alternative attainable? In doubting its attainability, I put the above issues concerning the conceptualisation of liberal democracy in perspective in the reflections below.

UNIVERSAL DEMOCRACY VERSUS PARTICULAR DEMOCRACY

As I intimated at the end of the previous section, it is common in writings of a substantial number of African political thinkers to talk of arriving at an African theory of democracy (Fayemi 2009, 103), or an African alternative to democracy (Wiredu 1995, 62–63). In the first sense, Africans see hope in reforming liberal democracy, while in the second, they seek for its complete replacement. It is with regard to these two positions on liberal democracy that Fayemi (2009, 104) noted that questions concerning democratic sustainability, democracy as essential for development in Africa, and the desirability of liberal democracy or an African substitute for it is divisible into three schools of thought: universalism, traditionalism and eclecticism.

Universalists are of the view that liberal democracy is the best form of government because of its tendency to unite all humankind without seriously considering their cultural backgrounds and other divisive factors. One of its major proponents, Francis Fukuyama, stated that the post–Cold War period marked "the end point of mankind's ideological evolution and the universalisation of Western liberal democracy as the final form of human government" (Fukuyama 1989, 4). He further maintained that the emerging post–Cold War liberal state, a "universal homogenous state" (Fukuyama 1989, 8, 10, 11, 17), heralded the end of history, and would legally and universally protect freedom, human rights, dignity, and democratic ideals by allowing people's consent to prevail, and was confident that the liberal democratic ideology would govern the material world in the long run (Fukuyama 1989, 4).

On its part, traditionalism, following scholars such as Wamba (1990, 127–30), Eboh (1990, 167–68), Offor (2006, 121–22), and Wiredu (1995, 57–61) holds that liberal democracy cannot solve many of the problems of the African continent, and that there is need for "an indigenous democratic system . . . more natural to African culture" (Fayemi 2009, 109). In this sense, Wamba sees a dichotomy between "democracy in Africa and democracy for Africa" (cited in Fayemi 2009, 114). Going by this distinction, "democracy for Africa" is an unsuitable colonial imposition, while "democracy in Africa" allows for emancipation, self-determination and the promotion of the people's welfare.

As for eclecticism, it advocates a merger of universalism and traditionalism so as to harness useful ideas and ideals within different cultures to promote sustainable development in Africa (Gyekye 1997, 43–120; Owolabi 2003, 431–44).

On a critical note, are the views of the authors in each of the three schools of thought above not intended to be regarded as applicable to the whole of Africa ("universal")? If so, what do such African scholars really have in mind when they talk about a universal African democracy as against democratic particularities? What is the nature of the universal African democracy to substitute liberal democracy? Regarding these questions, a number of perspectives are relevant.

First, what is the basis of the view that liberal democracy is universal? Generally, one of the points on which liberal democracy's claim to universality hinges is that of the ontology of personhood as sacrosanct. Being based on the conviction that human rationality is universal, the idea of the dignity of the human person is fundamental to liberal democracy and forms the basis of arguments in its favour to achieve citizen participation, consensus, respect for others, formation of social organisations, fulfilment of civil obligations, and holding government officials accountable (Rawls 1999, 56).

One description of the ontology of personhood in the African context can be found in the work of Gbadegeshin (1998) on the social, moral and metaphysical conceptions of *eniyan* (person) in Yoruba culture. Gbadegeshin described the sacredness of personhood in the Yoruba worldview, manifested in the rousing approval that greets the birth of a child, which is a celebration of the baby's individuality, as society recognises his or her personhood as a "little thing of great joy" (Gbadegeshin 1998, 292). Since the Yoruba do not make strict distinctions between physical and spiritual entities, by regarding a baby as *eniyan* ("person"), this approval is considered significant both ontologically and physically (the universal sacredness of all human beings). In applying this to the idea of democratic universality, humans are entitled to the leverage to contribute to the overall development of society through association, cultivation of values of dignity and other-regarding virtues that favour common causes, respect for others' right to exercise their freedom and pursue their personal development based on the fear of the deities, fear of elders, fear of what the society will say, and a general consideration of the humanity of others.

Onyibor (2008, 169) argues that liberal democracy is abused because it is not "built on African ontology and worldview and there was little or no attempt to adapt it to African realities and experience [sic]". Concerning the nature of this African ontology, Onyibor wrote: "An African traditional ontology" is based on "adherence to natural law principle" and the observation that leaders in "traditional African community ... are called by the gods and ancestors to lead their people", having received "ritual objects symbolising truth, justice and fair play" as their proofs of authority. Further taking the significance of these objects into consideration, he expects "political office holders" to "exercise political authority" through the "highest degree of purity of life, truth and justice, and that political leader [sic] should possess a high degree of humility, patience, tolerance, and spirit of forgiveness" so as to guard against retributive justice (Onyibor 2008, 169–70). On a closer examination, Onyibor's generalisation for the whole of Africa depicts what may be termed a universal African democratic perspective as against the reality of cultural relativity in African societies.

Second, are considerations of a universal African democracy to be construed in terms of Plato's understanding of universality and particularity (Plato 1997, 363–400)? Are they to be conceptualised in line with the views on democratic universalism espoused by Francis Fukuyama (1989) and Amartya Sen (1999), respectively?

For Fukuyama (1989), the end of the Cold War gave liberal democracy political dominance as the only universal political system left for humanity. Although Huntington (1993) considered this view unrealistic, ambitious, and lacking correspondence to actual events, the meaning of Fukuyama's assertion of the universality of democracy is that it is dominant or widespread.

On his part, Sen (1999) thinks that the universal appeal of democracy depends on its being perceived as valuable to all. He argues for the "*instrumental* importance of political incentives in keeping governments responsible and accountable" and "the *constructive* role of democracy in the formation of values and in the understanding of needs, rights, and duties" (Sen 1999, 8–9). He thereby denies the necessity of consent in defining the basis for accepting democracy as universal, and considers the basis of democracy's universality to be that it is generally perceived as an ideal which people aspire for in their recognition of the fact that it is needed by all. Although Sen's account touches on a number of important points, it captures only one side of the argument for the universality of democracy, namely, the widespread desire among the peoples of the world to have democracy. He neglects the fact that certain events (some as old as colonialism, and others as recent as America's triumph over the Soviets after the Cold War and the attendant spread of its ideology through information and communication technology coupled with the show of military might), led to the imposition of liberal democracy on a sizeable proportion of the world.

However, both Sen's and Fukuyama's conceptualisations differ from Plato's argument concerning the universal existence of things. In Plato's view (Plato 1997, 363–400), there are models or archetypes of every existing thing in the world of Forms. These models differ markedly from the things that imitate them in the world of everyday life. Although Plato contested the idea of democracy as that which promotes tyranny in a state by empowering the majority to suppress the interest of the minority, the implication is that there is an ideal democracy and its corresponding practices, with such practices imitating this ideal democracy. We can then reasonably infer that the conceptualisation and the practise of democracy are distinct, with the latter deriving its nature from the former. The sense in which this account differs from Sen's and Fukuyama's conceptualisations is that Sen's and Fukuyama's seek a realistic democratic structure in contrast to the rational but unattainable ideals of Plato's Forms.

Since the practice of democracy is more meaningful to humans than its conceptualisation even though it (the practice) derives from the conceptualisation, I shall construe the ideal democracy as that which the human mind can conceptualise, and the real as that which we deal with in practice. As such, I will treat universal democracy as widespread in the world around us rather than as Plato's universal Form. This is against the background of the fact that both African and non-African writers often use the term "universal" without the requisite clarification.

Scholars ought to make a distinction between universal democracy on the one hand and particular democracies on the other, in the sense of the former being treated as either an ideal that is unattainable in terms of Plato's esoteric theory of Forms, or as a prevalent or widespread ideal that is subject to adaptation in practice in every culture, the latter focusing on culture specific models of governance. The trend of expecting African specific issues to become "universal" was manifest in Wiredu when he referred to the need to synthesise African "traditional philosophies" with the knowledge of modern philosophies as a means through which "African philosophers can contribute to the flourishing of our peoples and, ultimately, all other peoples" (quoted in Oladipo 2002, 337). This is similar to Kant's categorical imperative: "Act as if the maxim of your action were to become through your will a universal law of nature" (Kant 1997, 31).

Furthermore, in line with indigenous Akan practice, Wiredu (1995, 57–61) argued for consensus and non-party democracy in post-colonial African states as a means of transcending majority opinion and taking care of minority views in order to avoid the "tyranny of the majority" and "institutionalised disaffection" among the people. Wiredu (1995, 55–56) viewed elections[1], in the model of democracy practiced by the Akan, as a mere formality rendered unnecessary by consensus in decision-making and adjudicative procedures. According to Wiredu, even though there may be a monarch making decisions, he or she does not do so alone, but rather in the company of chiefs or council of advisers, so that when the decision is eventually communicated to the community, it is taken as the king/queen-in-council's decision rather than the sole decision of the monarch. It is apparent that by advocating this idea, Wiredu thinks that it can be put into practice throughout the continent. In other words, considering his strong and lengthy arguments in favour of consensual democracy and non-party politics, he treats his prescription as a monolithic democratic substitute to liberal democracy.

LIBERAL DEMOCRACY: FAILURES, TRADITION AND CONTRADICTIONS

It is common for African scholars to argue that liberal democracy has failed in Africa. Although liberal democracy is based on ideals that make it laudable in principle, like every other system, its shortcomings arise in the course of its being implemented. Thus, besides acknowledging liberal democracy's defect of promoting majoritarianism, Onyibor (2008, 169) asserts that "Liberal democracy in Africa is a mere ideological slogan used to foster the views and ideas of the major ethnic groups and the economic interests of the few godfathers". From this we can infer that for Onyibor, it is not the theory of liberal democracy per se which has failed, but rather its implementation. Since people are responsible for the outcomes of the practice of liberal democracy, the theory of liberal democracy in itself cannot be said to have failed. Indeed, theoretical positions are ideals that people aspire to, and that they may attain or fail to attain. This is true of both liberal democracy and the many African political systems of the past regarded as democratic by their proponents. For instance, by their conceptions, the Oyo Mesi[2] monarchical system and the Igbo acephalous political system were generally regarded as having elements of democracy, the former because of its system of administration that involved some level of separation of powers, the latter for operating on the basis of strong consensus in decision-making (Eze, Omeje and Chinweuba 2014, 1315–17). With regard to the former, the Alaafin (palace owner or the king/ruler/emperor), also referred to as the Oba (king), had all executive powers, and was assisted by the palace guards who doubled as part of the policing outfit. He, thus, presided over a system in which formations such as the age grade groups and hunters maintained law and order in the empire. The Aareonakakanfo (Kakanfo for short, which means the generalissimo) was expected to obey the commands of the Alaafin and fight the wars of the empire. As the chief executive, the Alaafin ruled in consultation with the Oyo Mesi, a council of seven men from highly respected families in the Oyo Empire, who constituted the council of state and served as the kingmakers (Johnson 1921, 70).

Theoretically, the Alaafin or Oba (king) was regarded as the Alase Ekeji Orisa (the one who possesses supreme authority, the deputy of the gods) or the Kabiyesi (the unquestionable one, or the one possessing vast authority). However, in practice, the seven members of the Oyo Mesi had the power to check the Alaafin's excesses, while he in turn checked theirs. The Bashorun (leader of the Oyo Mesi, who acted like a modern-day prime minister), performed the annual traditional ritual of determining whether or not the gods were pleased with the Alaafin, which was an indirect way of determining whether or not his rule would continue. What then happens when a Bashorun detests an Alaafin? Does he not recommend the termination of his rule?

The seven members of the Oyo Mesi were ex officio members of the Ogboni (confraternity or secret society)—a powerful group which was regarded as part of the body of strong spiritual stakeholders of the community. The Ogboni, consisting of independent men who worshipped the earth and were considered to be wise in making political and religious decisions, could check the excesses of the members of the Oyo Mesi and the Alaafin. Even though the Alaafin, by tradition, could not be overthrown, in this arrangement, he could be counselled or forced to commit suicide to allow peace to reign in the empire. This could be done by the Bashorun, with the consent of the Ogboni, presenting him with an empty calabash or one containing parrots' eggs with the pronouncement "The gods reject you, the people reject you, the earth rejects you" (Stride and Ifeka 1971, 299)—a way of duly informing him that the only choice opened to him was death, usually through poisoning himself (Johnson 1921, 173).

However, in certain cases, there were intense conflicts between some occupants of the offices of the Alaafin (king) and the Bashorun (leader of the seven-man Oyo Mesi). At other times, there were conflicts between the Kakanfo (generalissimo) and the Alaafin (king). It was, thus, unfortunate that, although all these various individuals and officers of the kingdom played the essential role of maintaining governmental and administrative balance in the overall best interest and stability of the empire, power plays among them culminated in serious conflicts that saw the Oyo governance structure become dysfunctional and epileptic for many years at some points (Johnson 1921, 274–363). In certain cases, the overt and ambitious pursuit of self-interests and power tussles degenerated into grave incendiary conflicts among various towns under the empire that finally led to its collapse, paving the way for British colonial dominance in the region.

On its part, the Igbo acephalous governance system, in what is similar to Western classical democratic practice, depended on the participation of the citizens in administration. Granting the idea of acephalous governance, thoughts of kingship rule was alien to the Igbo community, except in Igbo communities that put kings in place by imitating close non-Igbo neighbouring communities that operated monarchical systems of governance.

The Igbo often deployed dialogue as part of their decision-making processes. Whenever there were pressing issues to decide upon, decisions were first made in each umunna (family). The Ndichie (council of elders or family heads) normally tabled each family's decision at the meeting of the Oha na Eze (village assembly), for further deliberations or ratification. Since every citizen was a member of an umunna, the decisions at the meetings of the family heads or the village council were considered to belong to everyone. Consisting of all physically fit males, the Oha na Eze was the most powerful body, because its members were skilled at prosecuting wars and keeping peace. With the Ndichie maintaining law and order by performing legislative, executive, and judicial functions, the spokesman of the Ndichie was usually also the spokesman of the Oha na Eze. The age grades, ranging from junior to senior grades, implemented administrative and judicial policies of the community (Ayittey 2006, 116–18).

However, despite its laudable representative nature, the acephalous Igbo political system was defective due to its overriding majoritarian approach to decision-making. Suffering the same shortcoming as liberal democracy with its emphasis on majoritarianism, it sometimes left room for intense infighting and clamour for self-expression, which, coupled with the absence of a centralised administrative structure, exposed the system to the subjugation of Western imperialism. Due to the Igbo's promotion of self-expression, personal pursuits and outstanding personal achievements, strong and over-ambitious individuals emerged who perpetrated activities that were contrary to the common good. This culminated in the acceptance by such people to act as colonial warrant officers, thereby weakening the acephalous administrative system (Achebe 2012, 1–11).

Thus, granting that whatever political system humans operate will be susceptible to flaws deriving from human character, the clamour for either a reformation or a complete substitution of liberal democracy is at the level of the contradiction between the theory and the practice of liberal democracy. As derived from Locke's and Montesquieu's views, the theoretical provisions of liberal democracy include the separation of powers among the legislative, executive, and judicial arms of government, with the constitution being supreme (Hague and Harrop 2001, 185–98). Consequently, a comprehensive constitution of the liberal state essentially recognises the rights of persons to participate in government without external compulsion, the protection of the individual's rights, as well as the recognition of the individual's responsibilities to the liberal democratic state of which he or she is a citizen. However, in practice, in most African states operating governments based on liberal democratic ideals, voting rights are vetoed, voting processes violated, extensive corruption perpetrated to subvert the system, and many other severe illegalities committed.

More often than not, humans act out of self-interest. This accounts for the way many African regimes, despite their formal subscription to liberal democracy, endeavour to retain power by violating the rights of their compatriots through political assassinations and other unethical acts. They use the instruments of state to steal public funds, intimidate the people, and perpetrate other forms of injustice. It is for the purpose of dealing with abuse of power that Locke (1980, 68–113) made provisions for the citizens to recall members of the legislature. In one or two instances, the power of recall has received recognition from writers of constitutions, as in sections 69a and 69b of the Constitution of the Federal Republic of Nigeria of 1999.

However, in many of the African states in which the power of recall is entrenched in the constitution, it appears to be a mere fanciful decoration, since, in practice, citizens have not been able to remove officeholders and to replace them with those who will cater to their interests. There are at least four reasons for this.

First, the provision for the power of recall is limited to the legislature, with those in the executive being protected. In many cases, the legislators who could have impeached members of the executive have been bribed by those they ought to oversee, hence weakening the meaningful exercise of their legislative powers.

Second, illiteracy is prevalent in most African countries, keeping citizens ignorant of the provisions of their countries' constitutions and the changes required in them for effective governance. Indeed, it is not an exaggeration to say that many Africans have never read the constitutions of their countries. How then would they understand the provisions of these constitutions?

Third, holders of public offices, in their determination to pursue their interests without hindrances, either buy the people over, or put schemes in place to keep them ignorant of the reasons why they (the officeholders) ought to be removed from power. In many cases, most of the people are too concerned about how to make a living to focus on who governs them, thereby limiting their participation in decision-making.

Fourth, these societies prioritise communal solidarity over values such as justice, accountability, integrity, and dependability. Consequently, communal ties constitute a great hindrance to the use of the power of recall in Africa: those who wish to counteract the exploitative activities of their representatives are warned by their ethnic communities, as their actions are construed to be hindrances to their kinsfolk's interests, or to result in the ridiculing of their community.

LIBERAL DEMOCRACY, AFRICAN DIVERSITY, AND AFRICAN IDENTITY

It is difficult to determine the kind of model of governance to substitute for liberal democracy because of different cultural, social, historical, political, and moral identities and orientations of the African peoples. A wide range of external influences have had an impact on the outlook of various African peoples. These influences cut across the lines of politics, education, and trade. On the surface, one may be tempted to consider Africans as a homogenous people, but, in reality, the peoples are diverse (Kanneh 1998, 1–93). With Europeans' and Asians' influences, combined with a wide range of traditional practices, the orientations of various peoples in different parts of the continent are shaped differently. We can only offer a brief sketch of Africa's diverse identities by examining them as four regions: North, South, East, and West.

Being dominated by Berbers and also comprising of Jews and Arabs, the majority of the peoples of North Africa practice Islam, speaking Arabic and many dialects of Berber (Marçais et al. 1955, 21–29). The Berber culture itself was impacted by interaction with Roman, Arab, Greco-Phoenician, Nubian, Vandal, and European cultures over many centuries. Although the people combine their own traditional cultural elements with aspects of these cultures, many of them mainly consider themselves as Arabs, and are sympathetic towards Arab causes.

The West African peoples have conflicting cultural, political, and ideological orientations. Prior to the advent and spread of Christianity and Islam, they practiced various traditional religions, and many of them still do. While Islam dominates most parts of Northern West Africa, having spread through the trans-Sahara trade routes characterised by interaction with North Africans, Christianity dominates most parts of Southern West Africa due to the Western imperialist expansion, manifesting first as the trans-Atlantic slave trade, and then as colonialism. Furthermore, there are conflicts of values in both West African sub-regions, as their peoples mix indigenous African religions with Islam and Christianity respectively. Besides, the colonial masters ruled the region with different tactics and ideological orientations. One of these was the indirect rule system in Northern West Africa, deployed because the colonial masters found the peoples in that area difficult to dominate, while the Southern West Africans were ruled directly (Mamdani 1996, 145–50; 2000, 43–45). The aftermath of this is that the various peoples of the region hold divergent views about socio-cultural, economic, and political issues, with harmonisation of values remaining elusive, as ethnic and political interests polarise them, creating non-homogenous societies, even though they are all referred to as "West Africans" (Eegunlusi 2013, 127–36).

Similarly, the peoples of Southern Africa are culturally heterogeneous, spreading across many countries such as Botswana, Zimbabwe, Namibia, Angola, and the Republic of South Africa (Vail 1989, pp. xv–xxii, 1–15). The Bantu expansion several centuries ago edged the previous native African peoples to the more remote areas of the region, so that the majority of African ethnic groups in this region are now Bantu (Mufwene and Vigouroux 2009, 6, 22, 26). European colonialism further segmented the peoples. During the apartheid era in South Africa, the most prominent of the Southern African countries, the ruling European elite, espousing a white supremacist ideology, subjugated indigenous African peoples, as well as peoples of Asian origin ("Indians"), and people of mixed-race descent ("Coloured") (Mathabane 1986, 6–55; Adam and Moodley 1993).

The Eastern African peoples, partly influenced by the North and partly by the South, were equally initially exposed to European and Arab cultures due to trade. With colonial domination following the slave trade, seeds of conflicts that were to manifest in later years were sown, as conflicting ideologies of British, French and German imperial interests dominated the region (Eegunlusi 2017, 15).

All over Africa, conflicts of values and identities abound due to the encounter between local and external cultures, resulting in severe disruptions of social orders. After political independence, many African countries were embroiled in a series of inter-ethnic violence and coup d'états. Despotic leadership in many of the countries, coupled with the influence of Western media, resulted in many people embracing liberal democratic values. However, as is common with revolutions, attempts to get rid of repressive governments occasioned the rise of new regimes that were more deceptive and corrupt than the former ones, leaving the people worse off, and their so-called leaders and representatives better off. To make matters worse, various ideological orientations and conceptions of liberty that manifest in forms such as Islamic fundamentalism and ethnic militia are the results of the long-term external influences. Consequently, one wonders what African unity is in reality.

The challenge of cultural diversity in Africa has been aggravated by post-independence crises of identity that have been an obstacle to good governance. One of the angles to these crises is the challenge of personal identity. My conception of this type of identity differs from the biological identity[3] often debated by philosophers wishing to comprehend the essential nature of the human mind, or to investigate what constitutes mind-identity in relation to the functionality or development of the human body, among whom are Jerome Shaffer (1968, 42–48), George Graham (1993, 3–132), and Charles Taylor (1970, 231–41). Embroiled in body-soul/body-mind/brain-mind identity arguments,[4] these scholars debate the existence of the mind, and how one could attribute different identities to the same person or thing at different times.

In contrast to the kind of studies cited in the previous paragraph, I conceptualise personal identity as individual self-awareness and self-recognition (consciousness of a sense of self-/moral worth, development of natural abilities, and cultivation of intelligence) which promotes the good life, ultimately enhancing the welfare of the community. Many Africans appear to be unable to achieve this level of recognition of self-worth that can guarantee a purposeful existence. Thus, they become disenchanted as they relate with national and international political actors. Regrettably, in certain cases, sometimes as a reaction to the political actors and sometimes due to a loss of restraint which makes them team up with the political actors, they engage in corrupt practices and live without thinking about real protection of long-term interests for them and for the continent (Achebe 2012, 244–50).

Personal identity is prior to other forms of identity because it concerns the individual's own self-awareness, and this precedes awareness of other things.

Gaining self-mastery through understanding personal identity and leading a life that contributes to the development of society eliminates the crisis of personal identity. Personal identity crises have led to social identity crises in many African nations. Each individual's discovery of his or her personal identity and development of other-regarding virtues that promote viable interpersonal relations can contribute to the integrating of societies, and can make individuals really profitable (Fanon 1986, 96–98).

Furthermore, personal identity crises often result in situations in which conflicts are induced by individuals who are bent on achieving personal goals, but who make those pursuits appear as common causes, with detrimental effects on communities. For instance, during the Action Group crisis of 1962–1966 in the Yoruba-dominated Western part of Nigeria, conflicts between two dominant personalities, namely, Chief Jeremiah Obafemi Awolowo and Chief Samuel Ladoke Akintola, had detrimental effects on the Yoruba. Chief Awolowo was the premier of the western region before Chief Akintola. Conflicts between the two became an issue of national concern in Nigeria, and crippled activities in the Southwestern part of the country for some time. As a result of tensions between factions in the Action Group, the Yoruba were divided, thus undermining their traditional values of (relational) integrity, mutual trust, and communal tolerance (Sklar 1967, 210). The aftermath of the crisis was that apart from political uncertainty in the region, it caused anxiety throughout Nigeria. To date, the cultural imbalance that resulted from the crisis has made it difficult for many Nigerians to share important values such as loyalty and sincerity, even though they pay lip service to them. As such, many of the people find it difficult to identify with what is good for the nation and its corporate image. Regrettably, there are ripple effects on the socio-economic structures of the nation that also become corrupt, redundant, or utterly dysfunctional (Tuathail et al. 1998, 610–40).

Besides, it is evident that Nigeria's social institutions have fallen far short of the ideal, highlighted by Rawls (1972, 7–12), that justice is basic to the running of social institutions. As part of a complete systemic failure which hinders national development and patriotism, the country's leaders and peoples abdicate their roles, deepening a crisis resulting from a deficiency of national integrity[5]. In line with the observations of Martin Buber (1937, pp. vi–x, 3–34) and Simone de Beauvoir (1994, 790), an I-Thou/We-Thou mentality which amplifies the crises of inter-personal or inter-group identities consumes Nigerians in various spheres of existence. Thus, based on a divisive orientation, different persons or groups act according to what they perceive to be in their best interest, while ignoring or working against the interests of other persons or groups that they perceive as different and distinct from them.

In the light of the foregoing observations, for any one area or region of Africa to prescribe its preferred substitute to liberal democracy for the whole continent could easily be viewed as an imposition. As I have illustrated above, there are numerous conflicts in Africa, even within specific states. Regrettably, internal conflicts in African states are more intense than they were during the colonial period. Although the causes of these conflicts are diverse, African identity crises play a significant role in them. The manipulative and high-handed pre-independence colonial governance strategies and policies created volatile situations in most African countries, thereby sowing seeds of intense future conflicts (Fanon 1964, 84–85). However, these awkward situations were aggravated by our cultural, historical, and personal differences to so afflict the continent that no political system has worked to promote the people's interests. Thus, as different ethnic groups and individuals strive to protect what they consider to be their own group and personal identities, Africa further degenerates into corruption and anarchy, so that human life is threatened, and true pan-Africanism remains elusive. It is therefore inconceivable for Africans to embrace an alternative monolithic system of governance.

DEMOCRACY WITHIN COMMON BOUNDARIES: TOWARDS PARTICULARISING DEMOCRACIES IN AFRICA

I have contended that the idea of a universal African democracy is unrealistic, even though scholars seeking African alternatives to liberal democracy often write as if they intend their views to be adopted by all contemporary African polities in the sense in which Kant expects his categorical imperative to be universalised. For example, I noted earlier that Wiredu favours consensus in decision-making and adjudicative procedures, as well as a non-party democratic alternative for African states (Wiredu 1995, 53–64); but how can Africans achieve this consensus given their cultural diversity, unless they are in smaller polities? The classical Greek model of democracy was successfully consensual and participatory because of the small size of their city states. Besides, how can Wiredu's prescribed governance by consensus be put into practice in contemporary African societies, where people are increasingly consumed by the individualistic outlook of Western modernity? It is evident that Wiredu's prescription, drawn from the Akan experience, points to the fact that democracy is culture bound rather than a universal, monolithic venture. As such, trying to put his prescriptions into practice throughout the continent would be unrealistic.

The proposal to form a United States of Africa graphically illustrates the non-viability of a monolithic model of democracy for Africa's culturally diverse peoples. Proposed in a poem by Marcus Garvey (1924), Africans commenced arguments and activities in favour of the unity of the continent under the umbrella of a United States of Africa. They had intentions of building an African empire-state, like the empires of the past, capable of robustly competing with the other power blocs of the world. They stated their commitment to see the continent's human and material resources utilised for the benefit of its peoples (Dutton 2012, 47). Nevertheless, it cannot be ruled out that politicians who argued for pan-Africanism intended to gain control over a vast African empire that would grant them access to its enormous resources. The project has met stiff opposition from many African leaders who consider it to be unrealistic. One of the arguments against it is based on the fear of loss of national sovereignty (Wapmuk 2009, 660–66).

It is therefore doubtful that any proposal for a unifying democratic idea will be welcomed throughout Africa. Besides, with internal and external violent conflicts in Africa, induced by the divergent ideals of different ideological camps and by the interactions that various parts of the continent have had with alien cultures over many centuries, it is equally doubtful if the peoples can live together under the same democratic umbrella without turning the entire continent into a boiling cauldron of incendiary conflicts (Addison 2001, 1). Given these circumstances, it appears that it is the ambitious nature of philosophical argument that moves African writers to unrealistically search for a unifying continent-wide alternative to liberal democracy. Is it not better then to let each country develop its own democratic system in line with its own social and cultural peculiarities? In other words, ought we not channel our efforts towards particularising democracy in Africa? By overcoming the weaknesses of its current democratic structure and looking within its cultural setting for well cherished ideals that produce a people-sensitive, accountable, and viable alternative to liberal democracy, each country ought to concentrate on developing its own conceptual framework to guarantee its cohesion.

CONCLUSION

My central argument in this chapter is that in view of Africa's diverse history and demography, a monolithic African democratic model as an alternative to liberal democracy is unrealistic. I have contended that scholars arguing for a universal democratic alternative to liberal democracy do so without adequate clarification of the term "universal" as against particularistic references. At the same time, the scholars' posture of universality does not seem to take cognisance of the identities, historical, ideological, and cultural diversities on the African continent that to date have resulted in dysfunctional systems of governance. Consequently, I have argued that since democracy is more culture-bound and particularistic than universal, seeking an alternative to liberal democracy from the viewpoint of democratic universalism will only produce a system that many Africans will consider to be an imposition of a particular African culture on them. As such, each African country ought to have latitude to evolve its own alternative to liberal democracy in line with the cherished social and political ideals peculiar to its culture or diverse cultures.

NOTES

1. Wiredu did not call it "voting" but rather "election". He did not sanction the use of the term "voting" because he argued that it was not originally part of Akan culture, but rather a later coinage resulting from the modern need for the term.
2. The Oyo Mesi was the monarchical system of the Oyo people of Southwestern Nigeria. It was not an absolute monarchy, but rather a sort of constitutional one. The Oyo had no written constitution because they did not learn to read and write until their interaction (first) with the Northern Jihadists (who embraced Islam as a result of interacting with Northern Africans), and (later) with the Europeans. The Alaafin was the Emperor, while the Bashorun, a kind of Prime Minister, was the leader of the Oyo Mesi council, which was expected to defer to the Alaafin, but also to advise him, and to check any autocratic tendencies in him.
3. Here I am referring to thinkers who are concerned about the connection between the physical nature and mental processes. For instance, they are concerned about how the school boy of yesterday could be said to be the Governor today: is he the same person/entity at time T1 and at time T2?
4. I have revised these pairs to have the physical-sounding component precede the apparently non-physical one in each case.
5. By "national integrity", I refer to a situation in which the citizens of a polity are free from corruption, so that they act in a morally upright manner.

REFERENCES

Achebe, Chinua. 2012. *There Was a Country: A Personal History of Biafra*. London: Penguin Books.
Adam, Heribert, and Kogila Moodley. 1993. *The Opening of the Apartheid Mind: Options for the New South Africa*. Berkeley: University of California Press.

Addison, Tony. 2001. "From Conflicts to Reconstruction". UNU-WIDER, Discussion Paper 2001/16, pp. 1–6. https://www.wider.unu.edu/publication/conflict-reconstruction.
Ajala, Aderemi Suleiman. 2009. "The Yoruba Nationalist Movements, Ethnic Politics and Violence: A Creation from Historical Consciousness and Socio-Political Space in South-Western Nigeria". The Guild of Independent Scholars and the Journal of Alternative Perspectives in the Social Sciences. Working Paper No. 1, October 2009, pp. 1–13. https://publications.ub.uni-mainz.de/opus/frontdoor.php?source_opus=2061&la=en. Retrieved 5th Dec., 2018.
Ayittey, George B. N. 2006. *Indigenous African Institutions*. New York: Transnational Publishers.
Beauvoir, Simone de. 1994. "The Political Consequence of Biological Difference". Stumpf, Samuel Enoch ed. *Philosophy: History and Problems*. Boston: McGraw-Hill.
Buber, Martin. 1937. *I and Thou*. Smith, Ronald Gregor trans. Edinburgh: T. and T. Clark.
Cunningham, Frank. 2002. *Theories of Democracy*. London: Routledge.
Dewey, John. 2001. *Democracy and Education*. Manis, Jim ed. Hazelton: Pennsylvania State University.
Dutton, Jacqueline. 2012. "Flipping the Script on Africa's Future in the United States of Africa by Abdourahman A. Waberi". *Spaces of Utopia: An Electronic Journal*, 2nd Series, No. 1, pp. 34–55. http://ler.letras.up.pt/uploads/ficheiros/10636.pdf.
Donaldson, Thomas. 1989. *The Ethics of International Business*. New York: Oxford University Press.
Eboh, Marie P. 1990. "Is Western Democracy the Answer to the African Problem?" Kimmerle, Heinz and Fraz M. Wimmer eds. *Philosophy and Democracy in Intercultural Perspective*. Amsterdam: Rodopi.
Eegunlusi, Tayo R.E. 2013. "Democracy, Federalism and Nigeria's Multi-Ethnic Culture". *Journal of Philosophy and Development*, Vol. 14 Nos. 1&2, pp. 127–46.
———. 2017. "Mental Alienation and African Identity: Exploring Historical Perspectives in Response to the Crises of African Societies". *Open Journal of Philosophy*, Vol. 7 No 1, pp. 1–24. https://file.scirp.org/pdf/OJPP_2017012313371436.pdf.
Eze, Okonkwo C., Paul U. Omeje and Uchenna G. Chinweuba. 2014. "The Igbo: 'A Stateless Society'". *Mediterranean Journal of Social Sciences*, Vol. 5 No. 27, pp. 1315–19. https://www.mcser.org/journal/index.php/mjss/article/view/5212/0.
Eze, R. C., and James E. Agena. 2017. "Xenophobia Attacks: Causes and Implications for Nigeria-South Africa Relations". *American International Journal of Research in Humanities, Arts and Social Sciences*, Vol. 9 No. 1, pp. 20–24. http://iasir.net/AIJRHASSpapers/AIJRHASS17-302.pdf. Retrieved 19th Nov., 2018.
Fanon, Frantz. 1964. *Toward the African Revolution: Political Essays*. Chevalier, Haakon trans. New York: Grove Press.
———. 1986. *Black Skin, White Masks*. London: Pluto Press.
Fayemi, Ademola Kazeem. 2009. "Towards an African Theory of Democracy". *Thought and Practice: A Journal of the Philosophical Association of Kenya*,

Premier Issue, New Series, Vol. 1 No. 1, June 2009, pp. 101–26. https://www.pdc net.org/tap/content/tap_2009_0001_0001_0101_0126.
Friedman, Milton. 1962. *Capitalism and Freedom*. Chicago: University of Chicago Press.
Fukuyama, Francis. 1989. "The End of History". *The National Interest*, Vol. 16, pp. 3–18.
Garvey, Marcus Mosiah. 1924. "Hail! The United States of Africa". https://allpoetry.com/Hail!—United-States-of-Africa. Retrieved 14th Nov., 2018.
Gbadegeshin, Segun. 1998. "*Eniyan*: The Yoruba Concept of Person". Coetzee, P. H. and P. J. Roux eds. *Readings in African Philosophy*. London: Routledge.
George, Henry. 1980 (1886). *Protection or Free Trade?* New York: Robert Schalkenbach Foundation.
Graham, George. 1993. *Philosophy of Mind*. Oxford: Blackwell Publishers.
Gyekye, Kwame. 1997. *Tradition and Modernity: Philosophical Reflections on the African Experience*. Oxford: Oxford University Press.
Hague, Rod, and Martin Harrop. 2001. *Comparative Government and Politics: An Introduction*. New York: Palgrave.
Held, David. 2006. *Models of Democracy*. Cambridge: Polity.
Huntington, Samuel P. 1993. "Clash of Civilisations". *Foreign Affairs*, Vol. 72 No. 3, pp. 22–49. https://www.jstor.org/stable/20045621. Retrieved 19th Nov., 2018.
Johnson, Samuel. 1921. *The History of the Yorubas: From the Earliest Times to the Beginning of the British Protectorate*. Lagos: CMS Bookshops.
Kanneh, Kadiatu. 1998. *African Identities: Race, Nation and Culture in Ethnography, Pan-Africanism and Black Literatures*. London: Routledge.
Kant, Immanuel. 1997. *Groundwork for the Metaphysic of Morals*. Gregor, Mary trans. and ed. Cambridge: Cambridge University Press.
Locke, John. 1980. *Second Treatise of Government*. Macpherson, Crawford Brough ed. Indianapolis: Hackett Publishing Company, Inc.
Macpherson, Crawford Brough. 1977. *The Life and Times of Liberal Democracy*. Oxford: Oxford University Press.
Mamdani, Mahmood. 1996. "Indirect Rule, Civil Society, and Ethnicity: The African Dilemma". *Social Justice*, Vol. 23 Nos. 1&2, pp. 145–62. https://www.jstor.org/stable/29766931. Retrieved 2 July 2013.
———. 2000. "Indirect Rule and the Struggle for Democracy: A Response to Bridget O'Laughlin". *African Affairs*, Vol. 99 No. 394, pp. 43–50. https://www.jstor.org/stable/723546. Retrieved 19 Nov. 2018.
Marçais, Philippe W. 1955. "Peoples and Cultures of North Africa". *The Annals of the American Academy of Political and Social Science*, Vol. 298, pp. 21–29. https://www.jstor.org/stable/1028703.
Mathabane, Mark. 1987. *Kaffir Boy: The True Story of a Black Youth's Coming of Age in Apartheid South Africa*. New York: Penguin.
McGrew, Anthony. 2003. "Models of Transnational Democracy". Held, David and Anthony McGrew eds. *The Global Transformations Reader: An Introduction to the Globalisation Debate*. Cambridge: Polity.

Mill, John S. 1994. "On Liberty". Daly, Markate ed. *Communitarianism: A New Public Ethics*. Belmont, CA: Wadsworth.

Montesquieu, Baron de. 1914. *The Spirit of Laws*. Nugent, Thomas trans. London: G. Bell and Sons Ltd.

Mufwene, Salikoko S. and Cécile B. Vigouroux. 2008. "Colonisation, Globalisation and Language Vitality in Africa: An Introduction". Vigouroux, Cécile B. and Salikoko S. Mufwene eds. *Globalisation and Language Vitality in Africa: Perspectives from Africa*. London: Continuum Press.

Offor, Francis. 2006. "Democracy as an Issue in African Philosophy". Oladipo, Olusegun ed. *Core Issues in African Philosophy*. Ibadan: Hope Publications.

Oladipo, Olusegun. 2002. "Kwasi Wiredu: The Making of a Philosopher (Correspondence with Olusegun Oladipo)". Oladipo, Olusegun ed. *The Third Way in African Philosophy: Essays in Honour of Kwasi Wiredu*. Ibadan: Hope Publications.

Onyibor, Marcel I.S. 2009. "The Changing Application of Democracy". Odimegwu, Ike ed. *Nigerian Democracy and Global Democracy*. Awka: FAB Educational Book.

Owolabi, Kolawole Aderemi. 2003. "Can the Past Salvage the Future? Indigenous Democracy and the Quest for Sustainable Democratic Governance in Africa". Oguejiofor, J. Obi ed. *Philosophy, Democracy and Responsible Governance in Africa*. New Brunswick: Transactions Publishers.

Owusu, Maxwell. 1992. "Democracy and Africa: A View from the Village". *The Journal of Modern African Studies*, Vol. 30 No. 3, pp. 369–96. https://www.jstor.org/stable/161164.

Paine, Thomas. 2003. *The Writings of Thomas Paine*, Vol. II. The Project Gutenberg Literary Archive Foundation. http://gutenberg.net http://promo.net/pg. Retrieved 3rd Apr., 2017.

Plato. 1997. *Complete Works*. Cooper, John M. ed. Indianapolis: Hackett Publishing Co.

Rawls, John. 1972. *A Theory of Justice*. Cambridge, MA: Harvard University Press.

———. 1999. *Law of Peoples*. Cambridge, MA: Harvard University Press.

Sen, Amartya. 1999. "Democracy as a Universal Value". *Journal of Democracy*, Vol. 10 No. 3, pp. 3–17. https://www.unicef.org/socialpolicy/files/Democracy_as_a_Universal_Value.pdf. Retrieved Nov., 2018.

Shaffer, Jerome A. 1968. *Philosophy of Mind*. Englewood Cliffs: Prentice Hall.

Sklar, Richard. 1967. "Nigerian Politics in Perspective". *Government and Opposition*, Vol. 2 No. 4, pp. 524–39.

Smith, Adam. 2008. "Wealth of Nations". Mee, Arthur and John A. Hammerton eds. *The World's Greatest Books 14: Philosophy and Economics*. Salt Lake City: Project Gutenberg Library Archive Foundation. http://gutenberg.net http://promo.net/pg. Retrieved 3rd Apr., 2017.

Stride, George T., and Caroline Ifeka. 1971. *Peoples and Empires of West Africa: West Africa in History 1000–1800*. Lagos: Thomas Nelson.

Tocqueville, Alexis de. 1994. "Effects of Individualism Combated". Daly, Markate ed. *Communitarianism: A New Public Ethics*. Belmont, CA: Wadsworth.

Tuathail, Geraroid, and Susan M. Roberts eds. 1998. *An Unruly World? Globalisation, Governance and Geography*. London: Routledge.

Vail, Leroy. 1989. "Preface". Vail, Leroy ed. *The Creation of Tribalism in Southern Africa*. Berkeley: University of California Press, pp. xv–xxi.

———. 1989. "Introduction: Ethnicity in Southern African History". Vail, Leroy ed. *The Creation of Tribalism in Southern Africa*. Berkeley: University of California Press, pp. 1–15.

Wamba, Ernest Wamba dia. 1990. "Democracy in Africa and Democracy for Africa". Kimmerle, Heinz and Fraz M. Wimmer eds. *Philosophy and Democracy in Intercultural Perspective*. Amsterdam: Rodopi.

Wapmuk, Sharkdam. 2009. "In Search of Greater Unity: African States and the Quest for an African Union Government". *Journal of Alternative Perspectives in the Social Sciences*, Vol. 1 No 3, pp. 660–66.

Wiredu, Kwasi. 1995. "Democracy and Consensus in African Traditional Politics: A Plea for a Non-Party Polity". *The Centennial Review*, Vol. 39 No. 1, pp. 53–64. https://www.jstor.org/stable/23739547?seq=1#page_scan_tab_contents.

Wollstonecraft, Mary. 2011. "A Vindication of the Rights of Men". *The Online Library of Liberty*, pp. 1–148. http://oll.libertyfund.org/title/991. Retrieved 6 April 2017.

Chapter Thirteen

Groundswell

An Unavoidable Democracy, with Special Reference to the Acholi of Uganda

J. P. Odoch Pido

As we reflect on the interaction between African and non-African models of democracy, we may find Western, Asian, South American, Oceanic and African political cultures all having components that are inherent to the human condition. We may also find dimensions of the democratic process that are not recognised in existing, formally identified systems. Some of these are products of innovation that have to be sneaked in or presented in non-confrontational ways. Just as we can contrast de jure and de facto systems, we can also contrast formalised innovations with informal ones. It is one of the latter that I examine, in localised detail, from a design perspective and an indigenous African point of view.

    Governments everywhere and in all times have a vested interest in replicating the status quo and the models that put them in control. School systems and curricula are deliberately designed to perpetuate the status quo. Furthermore, people at the lowest levels of the social hierarchy are usually oppressed and lack the means to assertively or dramatically effect change to the systems in place, and have to be subtly innovative to achieve their goals. For example, looking back through history, we can see the democratic retention of Roman gods in the face of Christian imposition of monotheism: The Roman holidays were translated into Christmas, Easter and Halloween, and transmitted in a seemingly innocuous way through 'child's play'.

    In present-day 'liberal democracies', those who occupy the oppressed stratum (females, the poor and the politically persecuted) can make statements as pushbacks against their oppression through apparently innocuous people, events and settings. Their collective message is the result of the process we call 'groundswell'—change and innovation by unplanned collective consensus. The Garden Wedding throughout East Africa is an example of this process. In their choices of attire, music, food, venue and contents of the ceremony, the bride, and often the groom as well, tell the government, the church and the elders that they are changing the paradigm.

As scholars we must not lose sight of the fact that sticking to textbook definitions can often mask important aspects of realities around us. We must therefore look beyond 'for-scholars-only' definitions and constantly strive to think 'outside the box' in order to extend the boundaries of knowledge. If we define democracy as rule by the people, then we are compelled to admit that collective expression of shared aesthetic preference is a kind of democracy. Sometimes creativity is said to have a liberating effect on us humans because it is about pushing the boundaries of control. Where creativity and innovation are key objectives in any undertaking, players are less constrained by conventions and traditions. At the same time there is a greater tendency to ignore obsolete paradigms, set new precedents and push the horizons of knowledge.

While scholars in several fields including political science are aware of the phenomenon of groundswell, they may not see its manifestations clearly in constrained populations that are under constant threat from those who wield power over them. Dr. Francis Owakah of the University of Nairobi reminds us that Africans living today can recall the status hierarchy established by the colonisers that placed non-African thought and practice at the top and their African counterparts at the bottom. Dr. Owakah further observes that during the colonial period the white dress wedding was seen as representing 'civilisation', while traditional African weddings were not just diminished but demonised (Owakah 2019).

Groundswell is the accumulation of individual choices, made personally and independently, whose result is the establishment of a "common good" without an initial plan or direction from a source in authority. It is the spontaneous, consensual adoption or generation of new ideas and products over a wide area with little or no prior planning. The concept has been particularly relevant in fashion and marketing industries for explaining widespread preferences that cannot otherwise be accounted for (World Bank Group 2018). An example of this phenomenon was the adoption of blue jeans as the de facto national dress in North America from the early 1950s. Eventually the film industry bought into it by costuming leading males and, later, females in jeans. Journalists attributed the jeans phenomenon to Elvis Presley and James Dean without realising that their blue denim costumes had been a response to a groundswell that was already in progress. In spite of many efforts to divert the public, the fashion industry had little choice but to embrace the jeans or blue denim groundswell through the big-name designers by the early 1970s. Jeans became globalised by the early 1980s and persist in every country well into the twenty-first century.

In this chapter, I draw attention to some of the small, apparently innocuous statements of democratic change through the benign channel of a public celebration, namely, the garden wedding. My goal is to describe and elucidate social groundswell, which, though named for a geographical phenomenon (the rise of a huge, widespread wave in the ocean), is metaphorically a democratic force in human societies.

In what follows, I illustrate how Acholi weddings have changed over the last three decades from male-dominated and gerontocratically managed phenomena to female-centred innovations that gently fly in the face of oppression and inequality in society, government and religion. At this point, let me mention two marriage-related Acholi expressions, one showing past oppression, and the other indicating present freedom. The two expressions are "*kel dako ma gwoko gang*" ("marry a wife who takes care of the home") and "*kelo marace ka waci rom*" ("he marries a bad wife arguing that all women are equal".) The first expression is about a tradition that directs, while the second is about freedom to choose and defend one's choice.

A secondary goal of this chapter is to contribute to the study of my own people, the Acholi of Northern Uganda. Over the past century we have been an object of political, social and economic manipulation by a series of governments. In view of the general neglect of Acholi culture in the social scientific literature and a concentration on the worst aspects of our culture and the calamities that have befallen us, it is important to examine Acholi cultural manifestations that are now well documented in social media but have been largely overlooked by scholars. A wedding is a complex designed statement of personal, social, political, economic and religious standing on the parts of the bride and groom, their families and their communities. Very little information on Acholi weddings has surfaced in scholarly publications due, in large part, to our traumatic social and political experience, especially over the last forty or so years. Social scientists and we Acholi have had more pressing matters to attend to. Yet our Acholi weddings tell the world that we are still alive and kicking, and that we are adjusting internally to new paths and paradigms of self-determination.

The thesis of this chapter is that, as humans, no matter what misfortune befalls us, we will act in concert and in simple ways that are democratically assertive. Seeing groundswell as the opposite of "top down" or "trickle down" design, we can be assured that people will "do their own thing" against great odds. Though it may be motivated by greed, ethics, religion, snobbery, aesthetics, economics or any of many other factors, groundswell is an undeniable phenomenon in which we all have a part, operating independently of political systems. Coming, as I do, from a country and a region where the understanding of democracy is not congruent with how it is understood in other places, I find it noteworthy that we Acholi share groundswell with people everywhere in the world.

Following a narrative introduction of my personal observation of groundswell, I go on to describe its manifestation in one Acholi wedding. Through the song that was composed for the wedding party and the guests, we can see many statements of cultural assertion that have arisen over the last fifty years without the initiative of any military, political or administrative force. The cumulative cultural assertions that have become the glamorous Acholi weddings of the twenty-first century are quite different from those of the twentieth and earlier centuries. Violent revolution may be democratic, but accumulated, non-provocative small changes in organisation, dress, food and performance can be equally disruptive with a big smile and lots of fun. To examine the groundswell process manifesting in weddings in Acholiland, we must first look at the transition to 'liberal democracy' which the British colonisers imposed on the Acholi.

POLITICAL PARTY "DEMOCRACY" EVOLVING IN ACHOLI MINDS

Shortly before Uganda's political independence in 1962, the Acholis were introduced to Western-style democracy based on party politics. The 'leaders' who introduced this kind of politics to Acholiland used to passionately discuss their party manifestos instead of clearly articulating what they meant by 'democracy'. Consequently, the Acholi tried in vain to make sense of 'government of, by, and for the people'; and they vaguely understood it as something to do with party politics and voting. The end game was voting to determine losers and to decide which party would "receive independence" and "rule" Uganda. As far as Acholi villagers were concerned, there were three parties in the country, namely, Uganda National Congress formed in 1952, Democratic Party formed in 1954 (Lamwaka 2016, 21), and Independent Party. Although *Kabaka Yekka* (Luganda for "King Alone") and Uganda People's Union also existed, the Acholi were less aware of them because local politicians hardly spoke about them. The question to ask is whether or not many Acholis clearly understood "King Alone" as a party manifesto, and what some of the consequences of their adequate or inadequate understanding of "King Alone" were.

In the 1961 elections, Acholis had to choose one out of five competing male candidates. Each candidate promised to rid Uganda of "colonialism" and to deliver independence and progress if elected. However, it was not easy for Acholi villagers in Northern Uganda to make rational choices during the elections because they did not understand colonialism, independence and progress. Although there was an abundance of political campaigning, it did not help the people to understand democracy because candidates used unfamiliar and complex terms such as "legico" (fashioned from "Uganda Legislative Council"). Almost every candidate said that he would fight and defeat disease and ignorance; and yet it was very difficult for the people to understand how anyone could fight and defeat something as complex, overbearingly powerful and invisible as ignorance.

With inadequate understanding of issues in pre-independence politicking, the Acholi held onto the following thoughts: "We are Uganda National Congress (UNC), the party for Northern Uganda and the Party for the Poor" (Ascherson 1956). By casting votes, the Acholi exercised their "democratic" right, and the UNC's candidate, Akera Ananias, won in my Acholi home constituency. However, the Democratic Party (DP) was the national winner because it had the largest number of elected members of the Uganda Legislative Council. DP's victory broke Acholi hearts, since they had enthusiastically supported UNC. Nonetheless, from the numerical exercise of counting and tallying votes, people learned to associate democracy with numbers and a simple majority victory rather than with governance.

Before Uganda's independence in 1962, casual onlookers in Akara, my home area, believed that Milton Obote had "purchased" Kabaka Mutesa, the King of Buganda (Kituo Cha Katiba Fact-Finding Mission to Uganda 2012). By so doing, he facilitated the union of *Kabaka Yekka* ("King alone") party and his Uganda People's congress (UPC) which was formerly the Uganda National Congress (UNC) (Lamwaka 2016, 22). The thought of Obote "purchasing" Mutesa was unsettling because no one mentioned the currency that Obote used for the transaction. Did he use cash, animals, religion, or the promise of a powerful position? Whatever the case, there was a union that enabled Obote to be the prime minister and Mutesa to be the president. The Obote-Mutesa deal suggested that democracy entails negotiation and "trading". The Acholi metaphorical expression for "trading" is *otwong wile ki otwong* ("a basket trades for a basket"). Many Ugandans saw Obote as a national leader who was an eloquent speaker, persuasive and sometimes witty and cunning. It was from this perception of Obote that we, the Acholi youth of the early 1960s, mistook politics for intrigue. We also mistook negotiation and persuasion for democracy, failing to understand that democracy was about governance of, by and for the people.

In 1966, Obote dismissed Mutesa and made himself the President of Uganda. His action led to the so-called 'Uganda Constitution Crisis' (Musisi and Mahajubu 2018, 14–25). Scholars continue to advance explanations for the disintegration of the Obote-Mutesa union. Some of us in Acholiland believed that Obote sharply disagreed with Mutesa's condescending attitude. In

General, the Acholi agreed with Obote, because in their understanding, *laco pe gudu ter wadi* (Acholi for "a man never touches the buttocks of a fellow man", meaning that no man belittles another man). In addition to removing Mutesa from office, Obote introduced his "move to the left". Western countries did not like the "move" and sought to remove him from office, and they began by accusing him of two crimes, namely, "socialism" and "dictatorship".

Western powers eventually used Idi Amin Dada to remove Obote from office in 1971, not through the ballot, but rather through a military coup. Amin's ascent to power stirred up widespread debate on whether or not elections are a prerequisite for democracy and independence. The fact of Amin's having been a dictator was confirmed by his issuing of many decrees, and ruthlessly dealing with anyone who opposed him. Like Amin before him, Yoweri Kaguta Museveni declared himself President of Uganda after a military coup in 1986. He also has ruthlessly dealt with those who oppose his leadership, and over the past thirty years has been holding what can be correctly described as "elections without choice"; and yet generally, the so-called "democracy advocates" do not refer to him as a dictator.

During Amin's regime in the 1970s, the Ugandan Parliament passed a law banning miniskirts (Mugabe 2015), and advocates of democracy throughout the world protested the ban. As an undergraduate Design student newly transplanted to Nairobi, Kenya, I saw the ban as a knife in the heart of creativity and freedom of expression, that is, the stifling of liberty to make fashion statements. The ban on miniskirts was strictly enforced during Amin's regime. In early 2017, Al Jazeera reported that Father Simon Lokodo, the Minister of Ethics and Integrity in President Museveni's office, was again banning miniskirts in the country. In his words, he was protecting Ugandans from bad Western influences and conserving the country's moral values. Many people thought the Minister was stifling freedom of both personal and artistic expression.

The pre-colonial Acholi political system was a gerontocracy, meaning that elderly males were in charge. Young men and all females had little or no direct part in decision-making. Decisions were not reached by voting, but rather by consensus among the elders, as is the case among the Quakers. As long as one elder did not agree, discussions continued until consensus was reached. To act against the will of one person, they said, *balo laa* ("damages the spittle"), referring to the saliva used in ceremonial contexts to pronounce requisite blessings. Elderly women could be viewed as honorary males and included in consensus-building discussions. Pre-menopausal females stood below the level of honorary males and made their contributions towards consensus through their husbands. Even males below the age of elder-hood made their contributions towards consensus through their fathers or uncles.

Both colonialism and "democracy" disrupted the sternly gerontocratic Acholi socio-political organisation and provided alternatives to it. Besides, Western Christian missionaries aggravated the disruption by proceeding from the assumption that all indigenous African beliefs and practices had to be uprooted and replaced. Consequently, the Acholi gained the leeway to explore new processes of decision-making in their individual and communal lives. They no longer had to accept what was in place when they were born, and they also had several religious systems to choose from, especially Roman Catholicism and the many versions of Protestantism.

The exposure of the Acholi to Europeans, Asians, a new system of government and a new religion introduced a new range of personal choices in life, including education, career and geographical mobility. Ease of movement between geographic locations increased social interactions that, in turn, increase choices of marriage partners and wedding styles. The choices that could be made in the details of a wedding were but the tip of an iceberg of choices that led eventually to paradigmatic changes in the foundations of various institutions. The development of the garden wedding without a unified or imposed plan is but one of many reactions to the variety of experiences and range of choices that history has offered, and is a counterbalance to over fifty years of post-colonial state brutality.

Having presented the foregoing short outline of the advent of Western-style democracy in Acholiland, I now turn to an examination of my personal experience of groundswell.

DISCOVERING GROUNDSWELL: A PERSONAL EDUCATIONAL JOURNEY

In 2015, I attended an International Design Conference in Kampala, Uganda, where two scholars presented a paper on Participatory Design. The authors of the paper attempted to illustrate participatory design using the experiences of Southern African villagers. From the program and from my own misconception, I expected to hear "design of the people, by the people and for the people"—a kind of direct democracy (Kituo Cha Katiba 2012, 23). However, I was somewhat intrigued to find that it was top-down design, because professionals directed it, and the method was largely that of professional design and applied research as described by many authors, notably Spinuzzi in his article on methodologies of participatory design (Spinuzzi 2005, 163). At question time, I asked how the authors' idea of participatory design was different from "design of the professional, by the professional, and for the profession". I no longer remember the answer to my question, but the presentation got me thinking about how we designers could modify what we know as "participatory design" to make it democratic. Ideas of modifying participatory design, to free it from dictates of taste and professional snobbery, continued to nag and inspire me, culminating in the writing of this chapter.

If there is a scale of democratic processes, we can look at it as ranging from deliberate, purposeful and codified ones to informal and consensual ones that are often unaccounted for in constitutions or codified laws. Ideas and preferences can be formally or informally determined and dispersed as top-down, bottom-up, trickle-down, or groundswell. Market forces and legislation determine designs of private automobiles, public transport systems and housing estates, with consumers having to take what is on offer: this is top-down design. Another example of top-down design would be when a government legislates or decrees a form of behaviour for all persons in its jurisdiction. Some contemporary examples of jurisdiction are curfews, lockdowns and quarantines. Historical examples in Kenya are the Hut Tax and de-stocking exercises during the colonial era. We describe behaviour as 'trickle-down design' when it is not decreed but is spontaneous and results from voluntary imitation or unplanned effects of 'top-down design'. Thus, imitating the appearance or lifestyles of movie stars and famous musicians or athletes may count as trickle-down design. An instance of an unplanned result that we can call 'groundswell' is the spontaneous mass movement of people from quarantined or locked down areas of a city.

Some politicians are famous for what they call "trickle-down economics", meaning that the benefits bestowed on the wealthy will also indirectly benefit the poor as the rich spend money. The differences and similarities between "trickle-down design" and "trickle-down economics" is beyond the scope of this chapter. However, when the lower strata of any society imitate the clothing and behaviour of celebrities such as the late Princess Diana, we get "trickle-down design". On the other hand, when the masses force change on the society as a whole, as in a revolution or civil disobedience, that is "bottom-up design". Groundswell is the less adamant but no less noticeable spontaneous generation of novelty through widespread and simultaneous expressions of preferences.

Applying these ideas and observations to my own culture, my focus on a single, exemplary wedding provided a manageable, contained event for analysis, but one that is rich in the number of choices to be made. Long-term experience has yielded some awareness of the design paradigms and of the innovations that take place around a wedding. For example, we already know, although seldom write about, the many choices that are made and the many cultural, family and individual conflicts that arise, in hammering out the pageant of the actual event. To ease the headaches inherent in organising weddings, there are now event designers and managers who do the job on behalf of brides and bridegrooms. In Acholiland, professional involvement is important, but the overall planning is done by the bride and groom.

The twenty-first-century Acholi wedding, organised by brides, grooms and their families, is different from earlier indigenous Acholi weddings, which were usually dictated by parents and older members of the community. In the arranged marriages of the past, parents and their age-mates tightly controlled procedures, from courting the spouse, marriage negotiations, paying dowry, to enjoying the wedding ceremony. All that was left for the bridegroom was to wait for his friends to bring home his bride in the company of her escorts (ideally her younger female relatives). Unlike the traditional Acholi wedding, the new wedding is not *keny den* ("marriage on credit"), because bridegrooms pay the full bride price in cash rather than through instalments over many years. Young people prefer the single payment system because it frees them up from constant demands by their in-laws. The new wedding is also different from church, mosque or temple weddings, where religious institutions set the boundaries within which concerned individuals make choices.

Around 2010, two American friends and I travelled to Northern Uganda intending to reach my home in Akara Muchwini, Kitgum District. We East Africans love to show off our homes to visitors. There we would all see how my people were coping with life after being in Internally Displaced People's Camps for nearly ten years. One of my cousins was getting married on the day we arrived, so I took them to the wedding to see Acholi traditions first hand.

My guests probably did not notice anything strange since that was their first experience of Acholi culture, and were busy absorbing everything that came along. However, for indigenous me, it was a shock to find contemporary music blaring from a disco-type 'high-fi' system, with people dancing heartily. We retired to bed at around 9 p.m., but the party continued through the night. After a few days, my guests left not knowing how different that wedding was from the weddings of my childhood and youth. It also seemed to be a departure from weddings according to the church, mosque or temple. This experience stimulated my curiosity, and led me to study the new style of weddings among the Acholi and other African communities.

After several years of informally following the new wedding style, I confirmed that the music is composed and performed by professional artists. The performances are recorded on DVDs or posted on YouTube for sharing and for preserving records of events (see, for examples, Opiyo 2016; Oryema 2016). Those who cannot afford to hire artists and their bands use such recordings played on powerful music systems. The live performance or disco-style music system is a groundswell phenomenon that appeared, as if from nowhere, in the 1990s throughout Acholiland and elsewhere in Eastern Africa.

I began my formal study by examining many weddings taking place in Uganda. By way of examples, I examined a Basoga wedding (Roo Ya Simba 2019), a Baganda kwanjula/wedding (Next Media Uganda 2017), and a Lango wedding (Obong 2019). After that, I viewed many Acholi weddings on YouTube that served the purposes of comparison and contrast. I eventually settled on one, initially because its music throbbed like drums in the hands of master drummers. The wedding under discussion and similar weddings are influenced in part by colonialism and its structural violence (Maddison 2013; Vaidya 2018). They are shaped by exotic religions, especially church regulations, in the format that would legitimise the marriages in the eyes of various churches. They are also outcomes of authoritarian colonial governments, as well as of post-colonial African ones.

The style of the wedding that I examined embodies and expresses a local social structure into which outsiders are being incorporated, especially since it (the wedding) is cross-cultural. The bride is an Acholi from Lemo, a village nearly six miles north of Kitgum town in Labong'o Sub-District, Northern Uganda. The bridegroom is a German from Berlin. I chose this particular wedding because it is inter-continental, straddling African and European cultural contexts, thereby affording opportunities for numerous and diverse choices. Apart from the Acholi-German wedding, I cite an all-Acholi wedding (Murugut 2012) and a Lango-Acholi wedding (Otim 2015). I use the all-Acholi and Lango-Acholi weddings for purposes of comparison, contrast, and illustration.

AN OVERVIEW OF ACHOLI MARRIAGES AND WEDDINGS

An Acholi marriage is often a choice a couple makes to live as husband and wife, but the choice is normally converted into an agreement between two families (Shahadah 2011, 1). A marriage is a formalisation of the choice and agreement, while a wedding is the celebration and public announcement of the marriage. It is with this understanding in mind that I discuss Acholi traditional marriage and weddings, beginning with the agreement. Arrangement by parents or close relatives (Abadi 2003, 1), and courtship by individuals are the two common ways in which the Acholi and many other peoples of Africa find spouses.

Although rare, *nyom pa ludongo* (Acholi for "arranged marriage") is one-way young men used to, but now hardly ever, find spouses. Internet or face-to-face courtship are two of the current ways of finding spouses. If a girl accepts a suitor's marriage proposal, she gives him a line of beads from her waist, another item of personal adornment (Burite 2007; Ojok 2006), or a handkerchief. The item thus given is a symbol of her unwavering love and readiness to be married. It is important to emphasise that in Acholi expression, a lady does not marry a gentleman: he is the one who marries her. At this point, a wedding should take place. If a wedding does not occur, some girls will elope, and will do so for several reasons. One of the reasons is declaring that they have been indulging in *kwele* (Acholi for "premarital sex"). The second reason is having unprocedurally getting to know the family of the fiancé before proper negotiations have taken place. Both premarital sex and getting to know the fiancé's family without adhering to protocol are equally taboo in Acholi culture (Acaye 2016, 2). Another reason for eloping is for a girl to force her parents to agree to the marriage, especially when she suspects that they do not like her choice of a husband. Lack of bride wealth often stands between a man and his fiancée, so it can also motivate a girl to elope. A father who cannot afford bride wealth for his son will borrow from his relatives or from elsewhere. Borrowing bride wealth is an attempt at avoiding elopement-related stigma.

Where even borrowing fails to raise bride wealth, the two can live as husband and wife in a "come we stay" arrangement (Ogutu 2007, 4). On account of the promise to be true to the marriage, relatives and the community at large usually accept the marriage without the bride wealth being given. In this type of marriage, the indigenous legal position is that the man and woman are married, but their sons cannot marry unless and until the bride wealth for their mother is paid. Besides, if a wife dies before she is formally married, her husband is duty-bound to "marry her posthumously" (*nyomo lyel*, literally "marry the dead"). This is to say that he must still give members of her family the bride wealth due to them, thereby forestalling any spiritual or inheritance problems for her posterity. In general, low-key weddings tend to mark marriages between spouses who have "moved in together" and marriages involving "single mothers".

About eighty years ago, bridewealth among the Acholi consisted of two cows and a few gifts such as a cake of tobacco, an axe, a spear and a chicken. Two male representatives of the bridegroom took the bride wealth to the bride's family, arriving soon after dark because traditional marriage took place at night. Negotiation and acceptance of the bride wealth was followed by celebrations that often began with food and *labwor* (traditional beer), which all the guests enjoyed. One of the two representatives played the *nanga* (a seven-stringed tray zither), while the other one played the calabash to accompany the *nanga* music, with the bride's female representatives singing and dancing to the music. The performance at the party continued into the wee hours of the morning, but never until daybreak since that was socially unacceptable. A few days afterwards, the bride left her home and went to her husband in the company of two or more female escorts. Helping the young wife settle down in her new home was the stated purpose of the escorts, but finding husbands in the clan where she was married was their real mission.

According to oral history, *ajere* (a wedding dance) may have developed between 1940 and 1950 (Niswonger 2010; Opio 2012). Although it is unclear how this happened, one can look at imitation for a possible explanation. Among the Acholi, as in other cultures, adolescents imitate adult behaviour, including dance. However, they modify the dance, and often end up with another dance that is similar in some respects and different in others. Thus, Acholi youth may have developed *ajere* by imitating and modifying existing songs and dances such as the *bwola* (royal dance). Whatever its origin, the popularity of the *ajere* dance grew so much that it became a significant part of Acholi weddings. *Ajere* performers would comprise about five young males from the bridegroom's village, and a matching number of females from the bride's people. The male performers provided music and danced to entertain the guests, but also seduced the girls who danced with them.

Ajere mutated into *myel moko* ("get-stuck dance"), which many people consider to be a courtship tool. It seems that *myel keny* ("wedding dance") was the outcome of mixing a little *ajere* with *myel moko*. Creative picking and dropping of elements and features of various dances continued, and saw wedding dance develop into *bitiri*, *kelalip* and *lakubukubu*[1] of the 1960s and 1970s that were performed immediately after successful marriage negotiations and acceptance of bridewealth (Burite 2007, 1). The performances took place in the bride's mother's house. Most of the female performers were drawn from the bride's family, while most of the male performers came from the bridegroom's family. Singers and instruments supplied music to which performers danced during the party. Alcohol modified the music, dance and codes of conduct, so that wayward behaviour was blamed on alcohol and forgiven. Guests who were not relatives of the two families sat outside the house where they were served food and alcohol and were not expected to enter the house where there were "in-laws", that is, guests from the bridegroom's home. A close look at the wedding that I discuss in this chapter reveals similarities to steps and spirits with *ajere*, *lakubukubu* and *bitiri*.

Around 1996, in the name of security, the Ugandan government drove all people in Acholi sub-region into Internally Displaced People's (IDP) camps (Klein 2012), ostensibly for their own safety. Since no villager was consulted and no clear public explanation was given, some people held the view that forcing people into IDP camps amounted to dictatorship with genocidal intent. Onlookers made many assumptions, among which was that IDP camps were President Museveni's method of "finishing" the Acholis and giving their land to "developers" (Wegner 2012, 2). Hardly anybody thought it was for the safety of the villagers. Squalor, hunger, disease and desperation were so grim that international non-governmental organisations (NGOs) and other humanitarian organisations came onto the scene. Each of them tried to make sense of the senselessness and provide hope for people who had lost hope. It was during the internment period in IDP camps that Acholi weddings changed dramatically, assuming a new style. The widespread adoption of the new style is what is discussed here as groundswell.

One might wonder how life in IDP camps contributed to the change in Acholi weddings. To explain how this happened requires viewing a few selected scenes preceding life in the camps. Soon after Uganda attained political Independence, more Acholis entered formal employment. As a result, more of them became financially wealthier and bought consumer goods, including radios and music systems. The radiogram proved to be most popular because the radio component provided access to news and education, while the gramophone component and the speakers provided loud music for entertainment and for showing-off. Besides, at the time, the dry cells in the gramophone were a mark of "hi-tech". After the Idi Amin regime (1971–1979), generators appeared on the scene, providing electricity for lighting homes and power for music systems. Whereas the radiogram did not significantly enter weddings at that time, generators were later used to provide power for disco-style music systems, and lighting became common in both small and big weddings. By the beginning of 2000, solar energy harvesting and related appliances became common, and provided power for music and lighting during the weddings that took place while people were in the IDP camps. Finally, as already mentioned, foreign NGOs came into Acholiland. They introduced a variety of tents into the region. It is these very tents that now provide shelter and ambience for weddings.

In Uganda access to electric power was associated with "development", good living and membership in the high classes of society. Solar energy harvesting and related appliances were popular before the days of IDP camps because they were a kind of novelty, yet also low cost and convenient. Since a large part of Acholiland was not connected to Uganda's electricity grid, solar energy was a welcome substitute for powering music systems during special occasions, including weddings.

Generally, and for a long time, bridewealth among the Acholi had been fully or partly given in the form of cattle. However, during the camp days, it was only paid in cash because the so-called *Ikaramojong*[2] had raided and de-stocked the Acholi sub-region. In addition, kiosk-style trade thrived in the camps, making cash the most sought-after thing, and a means to a life *labong'o par* (Acholi for "without the need for thinking and planning"), but with plenty of conspicuous consumption. Thus, IDP camps introduced disco-style music, daytime celebrations, conspicuous consumption and a new kind of social freedom.

ANALYSIS OF AN ACHOLI WEDDING IN THE TWENTY-FIRST CENTURY

The type of wedding I examine here is now common in urban East Africa. It is referred to as a "garden wedding", and is a cocktail of cultures—African, European, Asian, Christian, Islamic among others. It may or may not take place in a garden or parklike setting, but certainly not in a church or civil authority office, and it may or may not have a definite religious component. Whatever the name and mixture, today's wedding is like a fashion parade where everyone tries to outdo the rest. The bridal party tends to dress as directed by the bride and bridegroom, but guests dress as they please. Weddings are a display of attractive beauty in the style of *ladagi-ibedi* (Acholi for "you have only yourself to blame if you fail to choose a love partner"). As a fashion statement, the garden wedding is probably influenced by what is happening elsewhere in the world, where young people are experimenting and choosing only what they like.

In this section, I present and analyse the video recording of one Acholi wedding, while also drawing insights from several other Acholi weddings of the last ten or so years. The analysis is guided by my experience, information from other people, and those features of Acholi weddings that have remained unchanged since I last lived in Kitgum over fifty years ago.

In what follows, I focus on the wedding of Atim Jacqueline Michelle, whose video recording is available on YouTube (Obol 2015). The ceremony took place in 2015 in Lemo Village, north of Kitgum town. A central component of the wedding is the "theme song". In the song, the bridegroom's name is not well pronounced, although it sounds like his name is Mr. Vargo. While the visual starts with what seems to be a section of the procession, the song begins with a pronouncement of the bride's place of origin, which can be considered to be a form of spoken heraldry and a cultural way of stamping identity on the wedding.

A large part of the song glorifies the bride as someone very beautiful. It flaunts her as a pledge by her family to the bridegroom's family and the entire community never to let down her husband and his people in any way. Besides being beautiful in the indigenous Acholi aesthetic sense, Acholi society expects the bride to show respect to all, bear many children, and wait on her husband. During the wedding, the bride and her maids dress to complement both external beauty and intrinsic beauty. In general, everyone comes to a wedding well turned out. Dressing well is more than looking right for the occasion: it is also viewed as showing respect to all concerned. It is tempting to think that dressing well for weddings or other special occasions is influenced by European and Christian culture. Euro-Christian traditions suggest that bridegrooms should wear dark-coloured suits or tuxedos, while brides wear white dresses. It is also tempting to think that reserving one's best dress for a wedding is Islamic, since Muslims go to great lengths to adorn themselves for weddings. However, dressing up for a wedding is also part of African traditions, as is evident among the Turkana, Maasai and Samburu of Kenya (Klumpp and Kratz 1993, 195). In the traditional Acholi context, dressing up begins at courtship and continues up to the wedding day, when the bride's parents also put on their best outfits.

During the wedding, all ladies from the bride's clan are highly praised in the song, which is a thinly veiled invitation to young men from far and wide to come and get wives from the clan. Among the Acholi, a bride prefers that her relatives be married in the village where she is married in order to have "someone from whom to get some salt" (a neighbour who is a sister). The long-term strategy is to confront jealousy, rivalry, homesickness, and lack of emotional support during times of adversity. In days gone by, this concept of "neighbours who are sisters" motivated ladies to persuade their sisters to be co-wives and to accept life in polygynous marriages. Recently, I asked a few ladies if they would marry their brothers-in-law. An emphatic "No" was the response most of the time—"one man one wife" was their most frequent explanation. Nevertheless, many of the respondents were of the opinion that they would rather their sisters, not strangers, married their husbands. From our conversations, I think oppression by Western Christianity, classroom education, as well as economic and cultural mobility have resulted in an emphasis on "rights". Individual rights, in particular, appear to undermine the notion of "sisters who are co-wives" and other communalistic practices common among the Acholi and other African peoples.

From the wedding song we learn that the parents-in-law are appreciated for their part in bringing up the bride or bridegroom. Although the task of bringing up children is a responsibility without much of a choice, parents do their part, and whoever marries the product of that effort is expected to show appreciation. Furthermore, the bridegroom's parents are respected not only because they are guests, but especially because they are *welo keny* (wedding guests). One is only allowed to greet them, as inundating them with questions is considered to be despicable (Otim 2017). Normally, only men and women with outstanding decorum are appointed to interact with them.

Blessing is a long-standing Acholi tradition, and elders frequently bless young people. In Vargo and Atim's wedding theme song, the bride's uncles [brothers of her mother] bless her, the marriage and wedding guests. One of the other weddings that I studied was a "born-again" Christian one between Akulu, a bride of Acholi origin, and Orache, a groom of Lango origin (Otim 2015). The wedding theme song, by Otim Lucky Bosmic, emphasises that such a wedding is pure and blessed. Whereas Christian philosophy seems to influence aspects of garden weddings towards the notion that they are "by God for the people", Acholi blessing comes from the people and emphasises *kwo maber* (Acholi for "good living", meaning life with children, relatives, health and happiness). Since Acholi blessing comes from people rather than from God, one could say that it is more "by the people for the people"—a way to express optimism, gain independence, and live positively.

From the YouTube video of Atim Jacqueline Michelle's wedding, it is apparent that the crowd is divided by gender and age, probably because gender and age are the bases of social organisation and behaviour. Indigenous Acholi society assigns women and men different roles, which may be why women and men perform different steps in the wedding dance. However, garden weddings show that gender boundaries are blurring, since one can see women carrying the bride "over the threshold", a practice which may have originated in the forceful abduction of brides by groups of boys. In indigenous Acholi weddings, children were not expected to participate because they might bring their lack of experience to weddings and upset things. Nowadays, however, they are active participants in garden weddings. Besides, none of the parents attended traditional Acholi weddings, but in garden weddings they do; and, as mentioned above, traditional Acholi weddings took place in the house, but tents have replaced the house, probably because they accommodate more guests, require less work, and are therefore more convenient.

Non-Acholi may say that the Acholi wedding dance is sexy because emphasis is placed on women dancing excitedly before men. Nevertheless, a typical Acholi is probably more concerned with performing the dance and enjoying the wedding than with sexual displays. The role of young men and women is to supply the music to which they dance excitedly and vigorously. There are two other groups performing at the same time. One of them comprises middle-aged men and women who are experienced dancers—gentle and mature performers. The other one comprises non-Acholi performers who are grossly inexperienced and "give-it-a-try" dancers, thus giving the wedding a sense of humour. Irrespective of the dancers' competence, they, along with the audience, are more concerned about expressing happiness than showing expertise or offering a critique of dance competency. Freedom from the inhibitions and strict rules of traditional weddings is part of why garden weddings are said to be democratic, and why they are persuasive and soaring in popularity.

The generational groups of musicians and dancers are in many ways overshadowed by the lead musician who brings the wedding together through song. From an examination of the Vargo and Michelle wedding as well as similar weddings, the most popular musician in Acholiland is a man named

Obol. It is clear that he has a team of professionals who travel with him to weddings. The story is that you invite him to perform only if you can afford to pay, but he does not impose himself on anyone. Affording the artist means affording his public address system and performers, suggesting a level of paid professionalism characteristic of Western-style arrangements entailing a "willing buyer willing seller" transaction. The days of informally recruited neighbourhood musicians and unamplified wedding music are gone.

I noted earlier that wedding guests turn out well dressed, as is the case in the Vargo and Michelle wedding. Whereas dressing up is also an outstanding feature of traditional Acholi weddings, the element of choice in garden weddings supports the concept of groundswell because it is both individualised and innovative. The bride chose from a wide range of fashion styles such as European, Asian, African, and a number of permutations of fashion and adornment styles. The wide variety of choices for everyone made the brides, bridegrooms and their sponsors feel that this was democratic in contrast to the limited range of choices of the past. Guests chose from their own wardrobes, from the wardrobes of their friends and/or relatives, or from a carefully selected fashion house. Whereas every wedding guest tried to look well turned out, no guest was a slave to fashion or any formal dress code. Some were dressed in Western style and others in bright West African prints fashioned in to traditional Ugandan outfits.

Another notable departure from the weddings of the past was the absence of rings. Vargo gave Michelle a necklace instead. Apparently, people are no longer bound to the Christian exchange of rings and marriage vows. A groom can now give his bride a necklace instead of a ring, and the couple can write their own ceremonial exchange of vows as long as it includes the statements prescribed by Ugandan law.

To further illustrate the spirit of freedom, let us turn to a second wedding that I studied (Murugut 2012). The bride of this wedding is Lawino, but Sharon is her Christian name, implying that she chose to be Christian and indigenous Acholi at the same time. Her wedding indicates that she has left her maiden home, yet she is still the daughter of Palabek Kal—her maiden home. She is married to Michael Obita, yet she remains the daughter of her parents, namely, Boniface and Susan. Sharon is a Twenty-First Century Acholi—she and her maids are dressed in Gomeses,[3] high heels, "wet look hairdo's", lipstick, and probably carry cell phones in their handbags. However, they are very full figured and perform traditional Acholi wedding dances that focus on the shaking of buttocks as was the case in pre-colonial times. The arena is now the dustless compound of a "permanent house", and there are drumbeats, but from loudspeakers rather than from drums on site. Sharon seems to be closer to Clementine of Okot p'Bitek's poem "Song of Lawino," and a participant in the groundswell that is a part of cultural democracy pervading Acholiland and other parts of Uganda.

Many East Africans, including those from Ethiopia (WBS TV Uganda 2015a), Uganda (WBS TV Uganda 2015b), Rwanda (Simiyu 2013), and Kenya (Watamu Marine Association 2015) nowadays do not want to wed in church. Inquiries revealed that Christian doctrine and practice are waning. This is why divorce is at times viewed as preferable to remaining in a bad Christian marriage. Disease or poverty also separate married couples. Women are no longer comfortable seeing the husband as the head of the family and the wife as his "rib". In brief, many people find church weddings and their implications oppressive enough for them to opt for garden weddings that can be purely secular or can be conducted by clergy.

In a traditional Acholi wedding, females sit on cowhides placed on the floor rather than on chairs. However, in the Vargo and Michelle wedding, we see females sitting on chairs, thereby enjoying enhanced comfort and convenience. Besides, the chairs are a symbol befitting the cross-cultural wedding. At some point bridesmaids are seen kneeling on mats. The bridegroom "searches" among them, and "finds" his soon-to-be wife: the bride ensures that she is found. This is neither traditional Acholi nor Christian but is the practice among some of the other peoples of East Africa, especially the Kalenjin. Lifting and carrying a bride over the threshold is common in European-style weddings, and there is a point in this wedding where the best man picks up the bride, carries her and gives her to the bridegroom. The Acholis adopted this practice, and now use it jokingly as a metaphor for *bedo ki ore*, which means facing life with a sense of humour and optimism.

SUMMARY AND CONCLUSION

In this chapter, I have used the emergence of the garden wedding among the Acholi of Uganda to illustrate the way in which groundswell has found expression in the exercise of freedom to choose in spite of the oppressive formal structures of the post-colonial state and the overbearing demands of African traditions. The fountainhead of groundswell in traditional and contemporary Acholi culture is unmarried youth who often experiment with, change and use traditions as they desire. They do this either in defiance or simply in new and creative ways. A change is on its way to becoming groundswell when an increasing number of youth embrace it, or when it is popularised in other ways. Given its popularity among the Acholi, the garden wedding is indeed a form of groundswell: no one designed it, legislated it or prescribed it. It developed organically and spontaneously during a time of great stress for the Acholi. Despite the genocidal treatment of governments and the patriarchal oppression from the churches and from age-old Acholi customs, Acholi youth have carved out their own consensual customs. When the elderly try to force them into upholding old ways, they are known to respond: "*pe idiya*" ("Don't press me too hard", that is, "Let me do what I please and as I please").

My ultimate conclusion is that in spite of circumstances, rules, laws and traditions, humans will do what suits them and suffer the consequences. Wise leaders will recognise groundswell when it begins to happen and will embrace it and move with it. Those that do not take groundswell into account, or who try to stop it, do so at their peril. There are many kinds of perils, including loss of elections, revolution, widespread defiance and ridicule. However, the most potent peril is the judgment of history. The Acholi of Northern Uganda have rebounded from the abuses of history for over a century, and will continue to do so through the small, cumulative statements of subtle defiance that I identify as groundswell. Such statements are expressed in many ways, but particularly in the multifaceted redefinition of their weddings.

NOTES

1. *Bitiri*, *kelalip* and *lakubukubu* are different terms used in reference to variations of the wedding dance depending on the influence of various Acholi localities. *Kelalip* probably began in the 1960s, when bride price shot up to 1000 Shillings (East African currency). *Bitiri* got its name from the use of saucepans to make musical percussion, while *lakubukubu* got its name from the use of a big calabash to make musical percussion.
2. *Ikaramojong* is derived from the Iteso reference to *Karamojong*, meaning "a weak people".
3. Gomes is the voluminous female dress that a Goan tailor named Gomez introduced to The Basoga in Jinja in the late nineteenth century. Later Christian missionaries and the Baganda introduced it to Acholiland in the early twentieth Century.

REFERENCES

Abadi, Abraha. 2003. "Marriages and Wedding Ceremonies in Ethiopia". http://www.ethiomedia.com/newpress/marriage.html.

Acaye, Genesis. 2016. "Acholi Traditional Marriage". http://www.bmsworldmission.org/news-blogs/blogs/acholi-traditional-marriage.

Ascherson, Neal. 1956. "The History of Uganda National Congress". A paper presented to the East African Institute for Research, Kampala and North-western University, Evanston, Illinois.

Burite, Joseph. 2007. "Traditional Marriages In Uganda: *Nyom*—The Acholi Marriage". http://www.ugpulse.com/heritage/traditional-marriages-in-uganda-nyom-the-acholi-marriage/739/ug.aspx.

Kituo Cha Katiba. 2012. "The Federo Question of Buganda in Uganda within the Context of the East African Political Federation". Mwami, Abunuwasi and Godfrey Muriuki Eds. Kampala: Fountain Publishers.

Klein, Alice. 2012. "Northern Uganda Displaced People are Left to Fend for Themselves". *The Guardian*. https://www.the guardian.com/global-development/poverty-matters/2012.

Klumpp, Donna, and Corinne Kratz. 1993. "Aesthetics, Expertise and Ethnicity: Okiek and Maasai Perspectives on Personal Ornament". Spear, Thomas, and Richard Waller eds. *Being Maasai*. Oxford: James Carrey Ltd, pp. 195–222.

Lamwaka, C. 2016. *The Raging Storm*. Kampala: Fountain Publishers.

Maddison, Sarah. 2013. "Indigenous Identity, 'Authenticity' and the Structural Violence of Settler Colonialism". *Journal of Identities: Global Studies in Culture and Power*, Vol. 20 Issue 3, pp. 288–303. https://www.tandfonline.com/doi/abs/10.1080/1070289X.2013.806267?journalCode=gide20.

Mugabe, Faustin. 2015. "Idi Amin Decrees on Miniskirts, Gonorrhoea and Wigs". *Sunday Monitor*, 31 May. http://www.monitor.co.ug/Magazines/PeoplePower/Idi-Amin-decrees-on-mini-skirts—gonorrhoea-and-wigs/689844-2734504-74yweoz/index.html.

Murugut, O. J. 2012. "*Nyom pa Sharon ki Michael*". https://www.youtube.com/watch?v=8_0PSZ-r2j8.

Musisi, F., R. O. Herbst and A. Mahajubu. 2018. "Unlocking the Mysteries of the Origins of the 1966 Ugandan Constitutional Crisis". *Global Journal of Arts, Humanities and Social Sciences*, Vol. 6 No. 3. www.eajournals.org)14ISSN.

Next Media Uganda. 2019. "Djs Jauharah Shatra and Selector Sulaiman". https://youtu.be/ilWKuZoHNm4.

Niswonger, Kristin. 2010. "Acholi Dance at Gulu SS 2010". https://video.search.yahoo.com/search/video?fr=yfp-.

Obol, Simpleman. 2015. "*Nyom pa Atim Jacqueline Michelle*". https://www.youtube.com/watch?v=ZPJy8rKnlfQ.

Obong, Bonny. 2019. "Lango Traditional Wedding". https://www.youtube.com/watch?v=qdX5C8-OpD8.

Ogutu, Gilbert E.M. 2007. "Luo Leviratic Union: Wife/Husband 'Inheritance' Revisited". Paper read at the 5th Africa Population Conference on "Emerging Issues on Population and Development in Africa", ARUSHA, Tanzania, 10–14 December. http://uaps2007.princeton.edu/papers/70600.

Ojok, Boniface. 2006. "The Justice and Reconciliation Project: Field Notes No. 2". Liu Institute for Global Issues and the Gulu NGO Forum, Gulu. www.northern-uganda.moonfruit.comhttps.

Opio, David. 2012. "*Ajere* Dance". Johannesfilm 83. https://youtu.be/YWzdCnx-8Qo.

Opiyo, Twongweno. 2016. "Miriam Introduces Dennis". https://youtu.be/_R06Rc X1pPM.
Oryema, Geoffrey. 2016. "Acholi Traditional Wedding". https://youtu.be/Vw3Fq6Q LsOo.
Otim, Lucky Bosmic. 2015. "Nyom Pa Jo Mu Ye". https://www.youtube.com/watch?v=SCCb9A7sg4k.
———. 2017. "Nyom Pa Florence ki Opio". https://youtu.be/NJadfPHRBHA.
Owakah, Francis. 2019. "Introducing Mudimbe to East Africa: The Good, The Fun and The Ugly". Paper presented at the International Symposium on "The Philosophy and Literary Work of Philosopher V. Y. Mudimbe: Its Relevance and its Legacy", at the University of Nairobi, organised by IFRA-Nairobi and the Department of Philosophy and Religious Studies of the University of Nairobi, 17 December 2019.
p'Bitek, Okot. 1966. *Song of Lawino*. Nairobi: East Africa Publishing House.
Roo ya Simba. 2014. "Busoga Dance". https://www.youtube.com/watch?v=7e6-3-PthJY accessed 31 December 2019.
Shahadah, Alik. 2011. "African Marriage". http://www.africanmarriage.info/
Simiyu, Hein. 2013. "Rwandese Wedding Ceremony". https://www.youtube.com/watch?v=Nz7B26zBRKY.
Spinuzzi, Clay. 2005. "The Methodology of Participatory Design". *Technical Communication*, Vol. 52 No. 2, pp. 163–74. https://www.researchgate.net/publication/233564945_The_Methodology_of_Participatory_Design.
Vaidya, Ashish A. 2018. "Shadows of Colonialism: Structural Violence Development and Adivasi Rights in Post Colonial Madhya Pradesh". *Journal of South Asia Studies*, Vol. 41 No. 2, pp. 315–30. https://www.tandfonline.com/doi/abs/10.1080/00856401.2018.1428044.
Watamu Marine Association. 2015. "Watamu Wedding: Traditional Kenya Luhya Tribe". https://www.youtube.com/watch?v=HgSIX_lXdGk.
WBS TV Uganda. 2015a. "Ethiopian Wedding, Simply the Best". https://www.youtube.com/watch?v=z2RgfpjQRek.
———. 2015b. "Wedding Moments: Flavia Ayanjula Geogrey". https://www.youtube.com/watch?v=Jlj9VeP9Cy4.
Wegner, Patrick. 2012. "A Genocide in Northern Uganda? The 'Protected Camps' Policy of 1999 to 2006". https://justiceinconflict.org/2012/04/09/a-genocide-in-northern-uganda-the-protected-camps-policy-of-1999-to-2006/.
World Bank Group. 2018. "Groundswell: Preparing for Internal Climate Migration". https://www.worldbank.org/en/news/infographic/2018/03/19/groundswell—-preparing-for-internal-climate-migration.

Chapter Fourteen

In Defence of Ethnically Based Federations in Post–Colonial African States, with Special Reference to Kenya

Reginald M. J. Oduor

At the dawn of political independence in the late 1950s and early 1960s, many African states, under the close supervision of their colonisers, adopted constitutions that stipulated multi-party systems of governance in line with Western liberal democracy, with its vision of an ethnically blind society. Nevertheless, some of them also adopted federal governance systems in a bid to assure minority ethnic groups of a measure of autonomy in the nascent polities. However, within a very few years, civilian autocrats replaced the multi-party systems with one-party rule, and jettisoned the federal structures in favour of strong centralist ones. In other cases, military juntas wrested power from civilian governments and put aside any semblance of constitutional democracy. Consequently, from the late 1980s, there was a second attempt to entrench liberal democracy in these polities through the writing of the so-called second-generation constitutions. Nevertheless, presidents are amending the second-generation constitutions to abolish term limits, engineering the folding up of opposition parties by enticing their leaders with state largesse, and misusing state power to curtail civil liberties and influence outcomes of elections in their favour. In other cases, military juntas are again taking power and abrogating the constitutions.

Most of the manoeuvres outlined above have, and continue to be, augmented by politicians who mobilise support on the basis of ethnicity, all the while professing to be committed to the liberal ethnically blind vision of a polity. In Kenya, for example, most of the highly prestigious and influential cabinet positions, heads of parastatal corporations, and other appointive public offices—such as heads of the military, police, intelligence, central bank, treasury and auditor general, among others—go to the ethnic group to which the president belongs. This situation once prompted some Kenyan politicians to tell their ethnically based followers that they needed to elect their own to the Presidency because "It is our turn to eat"—a remark that inspired Michela Wrong's book under the same title (Wrong 2009). Thus Lentz (1995, 303) has been vindicated in his prediction that in the years to come, ethnicity, in whatever concrete forms and under whatever name, would be so important a political resource and an idiom for creating community, that social scientists and anthropologists had no choice but to confront it: clearly, this imperative equally applies to political philosophers. As such, we can no longer ignore the fact that ethnicity will remain a crucial factor in the politics of ethnically plural African states, and must instead explore ways of factoring it into the socio-political engineering of these states.

It has often been said that doing the same thing over and over again and expecting to get different results is insanity. While the symptoms of mental illness are much more diverse than this, common sense demands that instead of preparing for a third attempt at entrenching liberal democracy in African polities, African and Africanist socio-political theorists ought to explore alternative models of democracy that draw from the rich and diverse indigenous African political thought and practice, while also utilising the truly emancipatory elements of other political traditions. In view of the fact that I have already offered my objections to Western liberal democracy from an African perspective (Oduor 2019a), here I will go ahead to explore an alternative to it.

Consequently, in what follows, I offer a rationale for ethnically based federations in ethnically plural post-colonial African states, with special reference to my country, Kenya. My assumption is that each post-colonial African country would have to formulate its own model of governance that adequately responds to its peculiar circumstances. However, this does not preclude people from various countries learning from one another. I present this proposal as an alternative to Western liberal democracy with its vision of ethnically-blind polities. My proposal is informed by the fact that despite globalization, ethnocentrism continues to be a potent influence in societies in many parts of the world, a sizeable number of African countries included. *Ethnocentrism* is the tendency to see the world from our cultural group's point of view, and therefore to judge the rest of the world on the basis of our customs and values (Johnson 2001, 216–17).

This chapter is a work in political philosophy. Like all other branches and sub-branches of philosophy, the core method of political philosophy is reflection, entailing techniques such as criticism, conceptual and linguistic analysis, and systematic speculation (Oduor 2010). According to Miller (2003, 3–4), among the questions that political philosophy asks are the following:

- Does it really make a difference to our lives what kind of government we have?

- Do we have any choice in the matter, or is the form of our government something over which we have no control?
- Can we know what makes one form of government better than another?

In the next section, I put forward three arguments for the inclusion of the principle of the recognition and protection of ethnic identities and interests into the constitutions of ethnically plural post-colonial African states, namely, the right to ethnic identity as part of the right to freedom of association, the need for an antidote to perpetual cultural and economic domination, and the need to mitigate the deleterious effects of the discourse on the nation-state. That is followed by three sections that focus on the Kenyan situation, the first examining the demographic and legal dimensions of inter-ethnic relations in the country, the second presenting a synopsis of the history of the struggle for ethnically based federalism in the country, and the third proposing the outlines of an ethnically based federal system of government with a communalistic orientation for the country. In the penultimate section, I briefly examine the experiences of Botswana and Ethiopia, the former reputed for a stable unitary liberal democratic system, the latter unique for its experiment with ethnically based federalism, and argue that the former actually strengthens my case for ethnically based federalism, while the latter's effect on my argument is indeterminate because of the highly authoritarian character of the Ethiopian People's Revolutionary Democratic Front (EPRDF) regime for almost three decades.

THREE ARGUMENTS FOR THE CONSTITUTIONAL RECOGNITION AND PROTECTION OF ETHNIC IDENTITIES AND INTERESTS IN ETHNICALLY PLURAL POST-COLONIAL AFRICAN STATES

The gist of the Western prescription for post-colonial African states is that they minimize, if not entirely get rid of, the multiplicity of ethnic identities and loyalties, with a view to promoting a liberal democratic culture. For example, Lynch (2006, 54) laments the fact that different Kenyan communities such as the Sengwer, Endorois, Tharaka, Suba and Giriama have been asserting their ethnic identities. Lynch seems to ignore the fact that many of these ethnic identities predate colonial times, while the Kenyan identity is an artificial colonial creation only dating back to 1920 (see Oduor 2011, chapter 2). In support of an ethnically blind society, Western liberals cite several undesirable effects of ethnocentrism. For example, Johnson (2001, 217) asserts that high levels of ethnocentrism can lead to the following negative consequences:

- Inaccurate attributions about the behaviour of strangers (we interpret their behaviour from our point of view, not theirs).
- Expressions of disparagement or animosity (ethnic slurs, belittling nicknames).
- Reduced contact with outsiders.
- Indifference and insensitivity to the perspectives of strangers.
- Pressure on other groups to conform to our cultural standards.
- Justification of violence, including all-out war, as a means of expressing cultural dominance.

Yet a major factor in the politics of a sizeable number of contemporary African states is the use of ethnic identity for political mobilisation—what has often been referred to as 'politicised ethnicity' or 'ethnicised politics'. Nevertheless, many regimes in African countries continue to preach the liberal democratic vision of an ethnically blind society, while at the same time pursuing policies that are manifestly to the advantage of the ethnic elite in power, with a few crumbs for their followers and impoverishing exclusion for 'outsider' ethnic groups, aggravating the tensions and uncertainties in these polities. It is therefore evident that scholars ought to explore ways of incorporating the fact of ethnic identity into the socio-political engineering of these polities rather than to vilify it.

Consequently, in the subsequent paragraphs of this section, I shall show that there are at least three grounds for including the principle of the recognition and protection of ethnic identities and interests in the constitutions of ethnically plural post-colonial African states.

The Right to Cultural Identity as Part of the Right to Freedom of Association

By *identity* we normally refer to both a person's own and other people's understanding of his or her fundamental defining characteristics as a human being. A similar outlook pertains with regard to a person as a member of a group, whether it be an economic, political, religious or ethnic group. Individuals often greatly value their membership in a group, viewing their group as endowed with dignity and distinct from all other groups, and an essential component of their sense of self-respect. It is in this light that I speak here of 'ethnic identity'. Indeed, one of the most powerful bases for group identity is ethnicity. Thus, people often consider respect for their ethnic identities as part and parcel of respect for them as individuals. Consequently, as Taylor (1994, 25) stated, a person or group of people can suffer real damage if the people around them mirror back to them a demeaning picture of themselves, imprisoning them in a false, distorted, and reduced mode of being.

Besides, studies in the social sciences attest to the fact that the individual's point of view is significantly influenced by his or her social environment whose major feature is often ethnicity (Jenkins 1997; Kellas 1998). As such, a model of democracy which disregards the right of an individual to identify with his or her ethnic group and to pursue political aspirations in this context unduly limits the right to free association. As Narang (2002, 2698) correctly noted, both individual and collective human rights derive from the fundamental nature of humankind. On the one hand, individual human rights represent the principle of biological unity, the oneness of all human beings as members of humankind. On the other hand, collective human rights represent the principle of cultural diversity, that is, the distinctiveness of various ethno-cultures developed by different ethnic groups among humankind.

Each ethnic group typically traces its origin to a single ancestor or group of ancestors, as the Kikuyu with Gikuyu and Mumbi, the Luo with Ramogi, and the Maragoli with Logoli. As such, members of an ethnic group view each other as kinsmen and kinswomen, that is, as fellow members of an extended family. Indeed, among the Kenyan masses, the deep sense of kinship, with all it implies, is one of the strongest forces governing social life. As Mbiti (1969, 104) put it, "Almost all the concepts connected with human relationship can be understood and interpreted through the kinship system. This it is which largely governs the behaviour, thinking and whole life of the individual in the society of which he is a member". Consequently, it is inconsistent for African postcolonial states to profess to support marriage and the family, while castigating loyalty to ethnic groups that are seen by the vast proportion of their citizenry as constituting their extended families. Just as it is necessary for one to accept and to have a degree of pride in one's ancestors, so it is desirable to draw strength from association with an ethnic group whose traditions enrich one's life (Okondo 1964, 37; Hunt and Walker 1974, 442). Thus, while many view ethnic consciousness as being antithetical to Africa's democratisation, it can actually catalyse it by complementing other forms of representation in multi-ethnic African states (Hameso 2002).

When ethnic consciousness is ignored or castigated in the name of "nation-building", resentment develops among those who value their ethnic identities. In this regard, Narang (2002) has written:

> People invariably retain an attachment to their own ethnic group and the community in which they were brought up. There is an interdependence between the individual and collective processes of identity formation. Thus individuals expect to recognise themselves in public institutions. They expect some consistency between their private identities and the symbolic contents upheld by

public authorities, embedded in the social institutions, and celebrated in public events. Otherwise, individuals feel like social strangers, they feel that the society is not their society. (Narang 2002, 2696)

Thus, in our efforts at democratisation in Africa, we ought to ensure that the political environment is not threatening to the security and well-being of non-dominant ethnic groups. If, in our Bills of Rights, zealous support is given to the protection of the rights of an individual, then that individual's right to promote his or her ethnicity ought also to be recognized (Hameso 2002). As Preece (2001) cautioned, "our fundamental human desire for a language, culture and value system which is an expression of ourselves means that political attempts to forcibly suppress or alter these hallmarks of identity are unavoidably destructive of both human freedom and creativity". The most effective way to protect the rights of non-dominant ethnic groups is to develop and adopt institutional arrangements that enhance the ability of such groups to have significant input into policies that affect their lives, and to ensure that such policies draw from their understanding of their reality (Mbaku 2000; Okondo 1964, 38).

Ultimately, proscribing the free expression of ethnic loyalty amounts to a violation of the right to free association, and is a case of liberalism itself being illiberal in practice. This fact has now been partly recognised by the United Nations despite its intensely liberal orientation. Indeed, the United Nations' *Universal Declaration of Human Rights* (United Nations 1948) had a distinctly liberal democratic orientation, envisaging rights as strictly belonging to individuals. However, due to pressure from non-Western cultures, current discourse on human rights within the United Nations framework acknowledges three categories of entitlements, referred to as "generations of rights".

First, there are the entitlements that constitute free and equal citizenship and include personal, political, and economic rights, usually jointly referred to as "civil rights". These have been advocated most articulately by the Western liberal tradition and espoused in numerous political documents such as the constitutions of many countries, including both Kenya's independence and 2010 constitutions.

Second, there are economic welfare entitlements, including rights to food, shelter, medical care, and employment. Thus, the United Nations *International Covenant on Economic, Social, and Cultural Rights* provides that the state parties to the agreement "recognize the right of everyone to an adequate standard of living for himself and his family, including adequate food, clothing and housing, and to the continuous improvement of living conditions" (United Nations 1966a, Art.11 (1)). The increasingly dominant view is that such welfare rights are preconditions for promoting free and equal citizenship envisaged by the first-generation rights described above (Waldron 1993; Sunstein 2001).

Third, there are what may be broadly termed "rights of cultural membership". These include language rights for members of cultural minorities and the rights of indigenous peoples to preserve their cultural institutions and practices, and to exercise some measure of political autonomy (Kymlicka 1995). There is some overlap between this category of rights and the first-generation rights above, as is evident with regard to the right to religious freedom, but rights of cultural membership are broader. The United Nations' *International Covenant on Civil and Political Rights* declares that third-generation rights ought to be protected:

> In those States in which ethnic, religious or linguistic minorities exist, persons belonging to such minorities shall not be denied the right, in community with the other members of their group, to enjoy their own culture, to profess and practice their own religion, or to use their own language. (United Nations 1966b, Art.27)

THE NEED FOR AN ANTIDOTE TO PERPETUAL CULTURAL AND ECONOMIC DOMINATION

During the era of single-party rule, African states combined the free trade policies of Western countries with the centralist political framework of the former European communist block to produce an oppressive monstrosity that perpetuated the subjugation of those ethnic groups that did not have a grasp of state power: this is what Hellsten (2009) refers to as Afro-libertarianism. By the time multi-party politics was re-introduced in the early 1990s, many ethnic groups were so politically and economically disadvantaged that it was relatively easy for the single-party rulers to retain power. The win-lose nature of multi-party competition continues to act as an important element in reducing the willingness of those in power to concede electoral defeat to the opposition (Hameso 2002). This is reason enough for African political theorists to invest their efforts on identifying strategies for promoting social cohesion through the constitutional recognition and protection of ethnic identities and interests in multi-ethnic post-colonial African polities.

Furthermore, politics is an integral part of culture. As such, to impose the Western liberal vision of an ethnically blind polity on ethnic groups wishing to assert their identity in the political realm is actually cultural imperialism. Michael Walzer correctly observed that one of the criteria by which human beings can be said to be equal and to deserve equally respectful treatment is the fact of their being creators of culture:

We are (all of us) culture-producing creatures; we make and inhabit meaningful worlds. Since there is no way to rank and order these worlds with regard to their understanding of social goods, we do justice to actual men and women by respecting their particular creations. And they claim justice, and resist tyranny, by insisting on the meaning of social goods among themselves. Justice is rooted in the distinct understandings of places, honours, jobs, things of all sorts, that constitute a shared way of life. To override those understandings is (always) to act unjustly. (Walzer 1983, 314)

In addition, as Kymlicka (1995, 126) noted, our capacity to form and revise a conception of the good is intimately tied to our membership in a societal culture, since the context of individual choice is the range of options passed down to us by our culture. Consequently, non-dominant cultures in multi-ethnic states need protection from the economic or political decisions of dominant cultures if they are to provide this context for their members.

Besides, what is called 'common citizenship' in a liberal democratic multi-ethnic state, where the citizens' ethnicity is officially ignored, in fact involves supporting the culture of the majority ethnic groups (Taylor 1994, 43; Kymlicka 1995, 110–11). Thus, in Western countries, the official languages are the languages of the cultural majorities, the religious holidays of the majorities are public holidays, and the economic activities of dominant cultures enjoy the support of the state while those of non-dominant ones are neglected or even overtly discouraged. Similarly, in Kenya, the government's policies on culturally related economic activities (agriculture, pastoralism, and hunting-gathering) have a direct negative impact on non-dominant cultural groups, namely, pastoralists, and hunter-gatherers. Indeed, a consideration of the interaction among various ethnic groups in Kenya reveals that a hierarchy has developed based on unequal political power which translates into unequal access to, and control over, land. From colonial times, alien Western capitalism has encroached on land, whether it belongs to agriculturalists, pastoralists, or hunter-gatherers; agriculturalists have moved into pastoralist lands, and agriculturalists and pastoralists have taken over hunter-gatherer territories (see Campbell 2004, 7–8; Oduor 2011, chapter 2). Except for alien Western capitalist encroachment, numerical strength or weakness has been pivotal to this hierarchical process of economic dispossession, as the agriculturalists are more numerous than the pastoralists, and the latter have a demographic advantage over the hunter-gatherers.

Moreover, it is becoming increasingly accepted in many countries that some forms of cultural difference can only be accommodated through special legal or constitutional measures above and beyond the common rights of citizenship classically recognised by Western liberal democracy (Kymlicka 1995, 26; Mute 2002, 145). For example, the upholding of the rights of ethnic minorities entails the protection of their existence, non-exclusion, non-discrimination, and non-assimilation (Narang 2002, 2699). This is usually achieved through ethnic-differentiated rights such as territorial autonomy, veto powers, guaranteed representation in central institutions, land claims, and language rights, all of which are intended to minimise or eliminate the vulnerability of such groups to majority decisions (Kymlicka 1995, 109).

It is noteworthy that a number of countries in different parts of the world have factored their ethnic diversity into their governance structures, yet they have not fared any worse than those which have not. For example, the Lebanese constitution predetermines the ethnic composition of the entire parliament, and of key positions such as the president and the prime minister (Reilly and Reynolds 1999). Indeed, there are indications that the recognition of group political rights reassures non-dominant ethnic groups about their liberties and security, reducing the incentive for civil war, secession, and the defence of co-ethnic across the borders of states in which such groups are distributed (Rothchild 2000, 6; Talbott 2000, 160).

Thus, while I concur with the argument of Amartya Sen (2006) for a rational awareness of our multiple identities in combination with policies promoting such awareness to mitigate ethnic hatred, Sen's position does not necessarily imply an ethnically blind public policy. Indeed, it is because human beings frequently choose to highlight one of their identities above others that politicised ethnicity has thrived in many African countries. Simply preaching against negative ethnic consciousness while allowing the flourishing of ethnically based politics has not averted, but has actually stoked, the numerous political upheavals in Africa over the past six decades or so. Indeed, those who doubt the necessity of catering for ethnic diversity need to consider that in 2002, in about 190 countries, there were 3,000 ethnic groups who were engaged in one or other form of struggle for their identity (Narang 2002, 2696). As such, an ethnically plural state ignores the aspirations of ethnic groups to its detriment.

Consequently, in spite of incessant calls for the integration of various ethnic groups in each multi-ethnic African state, I concur with Ake (1993) that Africa's problem is *not* ethnicity, but rather socio-political conditions conducive to its being abused:

> ethnicity supposedly epitomizes backwardness and constrains the development of Africa. This presupposition is misleading, however, for it is development rather than the people and their culture which has to be problematized. Development has to begin by taking people and their culture as they are, not as they might be, and proceeding from there to define the problems and strategies for development. Otherwise, the problematic of development becomes a tautology. The people are not and cannot be a problem just by being what they are, even

if part of what they are is ethnic consciousness. Our treatment of ethnicity and ethnic consciousness reflects this tendency to problematize the people and their culture, an error that continues to push Africa deeper into confusion. . . . The point of course is not to romanticize the past and be captive to it but to recognize what is on the ground and strive to engineer a more efficient, less traumatic, and less self-destructive social transformation. (Ake 1993)

Ake (1993) went on to warn that the usual easy judgments against ethnic consciousness were a dangerous luxury at a time when long-established states were decomposing under pressure from ethnic and nationalist assertiveness, and when the community of independent states was shrugging off their demise. For him, the enormous implications of this for Africa, where hundreds of ethnic groups are squeezed chaotically and oppressively into approximately fifty states, are easy enough to imagine.

According to Curry and Wade (1968, 2), a political decision is often an exchange decision in which one has to balance what one can get against what one has to forego in order to get it. In many contemporary African polities, dominant ethnic groups enjoy considerable material well-being due to their access to political power, while the non-dominant ones languish at the periphery of the state. If the dominant ethnic groups choose to ignore the concerns of their non-dominant counterparts, the dominant ethnic groups risk suffering the kind of social, political, and economic instability that was experienced after the discredited 2007 and 2017 Kenyan general elections. On the other hand, if non-dominant ethnic groups engage in actions that are destabilising to the state, their dominant counterparts would be inclined to use their access to state resources to suppress, or even further marginalise, their non-dominant counterparts. Consequently, it is necessary that some kind of exchange between the protagonists be undertaken through constitutional provisions that go a considerable way in addressing the concerns of both.

THE NEED TO MITIGATE THE DELETERIOUS EFFECTS OF THE DISCOURSE ON THE NATION-STATE

It has become conventional to refer to post-colonial African polities as "nation-states". These polities boast of national flags, national anthems, national holidays, national assemblies, and national armies, among others. Nevertheless, the concept of a "nation-state" presupposes the existence of a people with a shared culture that seeks to build a polity whose boundaries are coterminus with the homogenous culture of its citizens. Nevertheless, such polities are rare in Africa, where colonial powers arbitrarily lumped up diverse cultural groups into single states, and in fact drew up arbitrary boundaries that left single ethnic groups in two or more states, with deleterious effects on the consequent polities (see Oduor 2018). Thus, one of the main causes of the dysfunctional character of many post-colonial African states is the fact that the masses' loyalties are to their ethnic groups rather than to the state, making them (the masses) easy prey for politicised ethnicity. Yet the masses ought not to be blamed for this, because their incorporation into such states was not voluntary, but rather through colonial coercion.

It is therefore regrettable that politicians in post-colonial African states, along with African and Africanist scholars, have uncritically embraced the concept of "nation-state", thereby perpetuating the colonial agenda of de-ethnicising the African masses in order to form African polities in the image and likeness of Western European ones (see Oduor 2018). Thus, when banning ethnically based associations (such as Gikuyu Embu Meru Association [GEMA] and Luo Union), the late President Daniel arap Moi declared that "These tribal unions distract our attention from national issues. We are, first and foremost, Kenyans. Tribalism is a cancer to the society; so let us do without these tribal organisations" (Moi 1986, 173). Moi is also remembered for repeatedly encouraging his listeners to refrain from revealing their ethnic identities when asked to do so, and instead to simply reply that they were Kenyans. Yet he consistently pursued overtly ethnicised politics, thereby facilitating the crystallisation of ethnic exclusion introduced by his predecessor, Jomo Kenyatta (see Oduor 2011, chapter 3).

Similarly, in his defence of a no-party system of government, Uganda's Yoweri Kaguta Museveni professes a liberal vision of de-ethnicised African states as follows:

> A leader should show the people that those who emphasise ethnicity are messengers of perpetual backwardness. This process of undermining a sectarian mentality of "my tribe, my religion" is linked with the process of modernization and overcoming underdevelopment. When subsistence farming is undermined and the exchange of commodities is introduced, there will be more efficiency and, in time, savings, which will in turn result in investible capital. Eventually, the society will be transformed and modernized. The moment that process takes place, one's tribe or religion cease to be of much consequence. (Museveni 1997, 189)

As Deng (2004, 506) observed, "The process of state formation and nation-building has ... denied Africa's peoples the dignity of building their nations on their own indigenous identities, structures, values, institutions, and practices". Thus Davidson (1992) was justified to refer to the introduction of the state in Africa after the pattern of the modern Western nation-state as a burden and a curse. Consequently, the constitutional recognition of the right to the protection of ethnic identities and interests would mitigate the deleterious impact of the discourse on the nation-state and the attendant pernicious policies that afford some ethnic groups vast economic and political resources while others languish at the periphery of the polity.

In the rest of this chapter, I focus on the Kenyan situation, with the aim of proposing a prototype ethnically based federal model with a communalistic orientation to replace the current avowedly liberal and essentially unitarist constitutional framework.

INTER-ETHNIC RELATIONS IN KENYA: DEMOGRAPHIC AND LEGAL DIMENSIONS

Demographics and Political Opportunities

According to the 1989 Population Census, the largest ethnic groups in Kenya were the Kikuyu (21%), Luhya (14%), Luo (12%), Kalenjin (12%), and Kamba (11%). These groups jointly made up about 70% of the country's population. Other significantly large groups were the Kisii (6%), Meru (5%), and the Mijikenda (5%), that jointly accounted for only 16% of the country's population. Together, the eight groups jointly constituted about 86% of the population. The remaining thirty-four groups were numerically insignificant, jointly making up about 14% of the population and, individually, many were less than 1% of the country's population. These included the Elmolo, Malakote, Ogiek, Sanye, and Waata, among others (Republic of Kenya 1994, Table 6-2).

The government declined to release the 1999 Census figures (Republic of Kenya 2001) disaggregated by ethnicity, purportedly in view of ethnic sensitivities. Yet the 1999 census was more politicized than the preceding ones, so that it would have been difficult to ascertain the accuracy of such data (Kanyinga 2006, 354). The findings of the 2009 Population Census indicated that while the five largest ethnic groups generally maintained their numerical supremacy (except for the Luo who were displaced from the third position by the Kalenjin), ethnic groups such as the Elmolo, Malakote, Ogiek, Sanye and Waata continued to be grossly numerically disadvantaged (Republic of Kenya 2010b).

According to the 2019 Census, Kenya had a population of 47.6 million. The Kikuyu were the largest ethnic group with a population of 8,148,668, followed by the Luhya (6,823,842), Kalenjin (6,358,113), Kamba (5,066,966), and Luo (4,663,910). One of the most noteworthy shifts in the 2019 Census was the Kenyan Somali, with a population of 2,780,502, taking over sixth position from the Kisii with a population of 2,703,235. The Mijikenda, Meru, and Maasai took positions 8, 9, and 10 with populations of 2,488,691,

1,975,869, and 1,189,522 respectively. The ethnic group with the least population was the Dahalo at 575 (Kenya National Bureau of Statistics 2020).

It is crucial to bear in mind that the official number of ethnic groups in Kenya as forty-two is arbitrary, having been arrived at by the British colonisers out of expedience. Thus, several of the communities in the official list are actually clusters of ethnic groups. The sixteen communities known corporately as "Luhya", the nine groups collectively designated "Mijikenda", and the approximately eight jointly referred to as "Kalenjin" are all cases in point (Itebete 1974, 97–101; Atieno-Odhiambo 2002, 231–32; Kipkorir and Welbourn 1973, 1, 70 ff.). As such, going by the peoples of Kenya's own definition of themselves rather than by the colonial definition of them, the ethnic groups in the country are well over seventy and not forty-two.

Furthermore, the whole question of ethnic identity is itself a contested one, because there is no consensus on the indicators to be considered in determining an ethnic group. For example, while language is often seen as an indicator of ethnic identity, there is no agreement among linguists on the difference between languages and dialects (Jenkins 1997; Kellas 1998). Indeed, there is no distinct Luhya, Kalenjin, or Mijikenda language, although the languages spoken by each of these clusters of communities are related. Furthermore, some Kenyan communities that regard themselves as distinct ethnic groups, such as the Ogiek and the Mukogodo, do not currently speak languages of their own (Kamau 2000; Cronk 2004).

Nevertheless, many Kenyans view themselves as belonging to specific ethnic groups, and the country's political life is dominated by cleavage along ethnic lines (that is, politicised ethnicity or ethnicised politics), giving rise to discontent among non-dominant ethnic groups. The larger ethnic groups form alliances which give them the advantage of majority status, as was the case in the alliance between the Kikuyu and the Luo on the eve of political independence in 1963, during the transition elections of 2002 (Ndegwa 1997; Oyugi et al. eds. 2003), and lately under the so-called Building Bridges Initiative following the contested 2017 elections. On the other hand, the very small ethnic groups such as the Elmolo, Malakote, Ogiek, Sanye, and Waata do not have the leverage with which to negotiate to be part of the ethnic cluster enjoying majority status. The Ilchamus of Baringo Central, who have been consistently ignored by the majority Turgen in the constituency, are a case in point (High Court of Kenya 2006).

The nexus between political and economic opportunity in Kenya was highlighted by a 2011 report of the National Cohesion and Integration Commission (NCIC), which indicated that the five most numerous ethnic groups in Kenya (Kikuyu, Kalenjin, Luhya, Kamba, and Luo) occupied nearly 70% of all government jobs. The Kikuyu led the pack with 22.3% of all civil service jobs, followed by the Kalenjin (16.7%), Luhya (11.3%), Kamba (9.7%), and Luo (9.0%). The Kikuyu, Kalenjin, Luhya, Kamba, Luo, Kisii, and Meru had a representation of above 5% in the civil service. All the other communities' representation was below 5%. Two communities alone, the Kikuyu and the Kalenjin, had a combined presence of almost 40% of civil service jobs, and the report inferred that this was due to the fact that each of them had held the presidency for more than twenty years (NCIC 2011). The NCIC published similar findings in its 2012 report (NCIC 2012). Furthermore, a 2018 report by the Kenya Human Rights Commission demonstrates that the allocation of cabinet positions from 1963 to 2018 has been heavily influenced by ethnic loyalty (KHRC 2018).

Consequently, there is an urgent need to address political marginalisation in Kenya with a view to promoting the country's long-term social and political stability. Preaching against "tribalism", as politicians have done since 1963 while vigorously engaging in politicised ethnicity, has clearly not helped. What is desperately needed, I think, is to factor Kenya's ethnic diversity into the country's socio-political engineering, a project to which I seek to contribute through this chapter and several others of my works (e.g. Oduor 2011; 2018; 2019a; 2019b).

Legal Framework and Inter-Ethnic Relations

At the height of the Kenyan post 2007 elections crisis, Kioi Mbugua correctly asserted that it was time to address the major fault line of the Kenyan polity, namely, perceived ethnically based competition for political power. He further observed that constitutional engineering is required to go beyond the winner-takes-all system and eradicate ethnic exclusion and fear of domination and persecution (Mbugua 2008). As a direct result of the mediated resolution of the 2007/2008 post-elections crisis, Kenya undertook some legal reforms to address inter-ethnic tensions, and I outline these below.

Kenya's National Cohesion and Integration Act of 2008 states that "It shall be unlawful for any public officer, while in charge of public resources and without justification, to distribute resources in an ethnically inequitable manner" (Republic of Kenya 2008, Sec.11 (2)). It goes on to require that no single ethnic group occupies more than a third of the positions in a government institution (Republic of Kenya 2008, Sec.7 (2)). Besides, it establishes the National Cohesion and Integration Commission to enforce its provisions (Republic of Kenya 2008, Sec.15). Nevertheless, the tenor of this act is the promotion of a culturally homogenous society rather than the building of a stable pluralist polity. This is evident when we consider the import of the phrase "national integration". However, as indicated in the next section on the history of the struggle for ethnically based federalism in Kenya, integration is a goal which some non-dominant ethnic groups are unwilling to subscribe to, as they are keen to maintain their cultural identities. In other words, such ethnic groups prefer a pluralist rather than an assimilationist legal framework.

The Constitution of Kenya, ratified at the 4 August 2010 Referendum and promulgated on 27 August 2010, acknowledges the country's ethnic diversity. Its preamble includes the declaration that the people of Kenya are "PROUD of our ethnic, cultural and religious diversity, and determined to live in peace and unity as one indivisible sovereign nation". However, this acknowledgement is weakened by the talk of "one indivisible sovereign nation", signifying a homogenizing project in line with the National Cohesion and Integration Act referred to above. Besides, unlike earlier drafts of the Constitution that in their chapters on values and principles explicitly recognised Kenya's ethnic diversity, Article 10 on "National Values and Principles of Governance" is extremely vague in this regard. Indeed, while we might be inclined to interpret the phrase "the marginalised" in Article 10 (2) (b) to include those who have been excluded on ethnic grounds, Article 21 (3) speaks of "members of minority or marginalized communities" and also speaks about ethnicity separately, leading to the inference that the phrase "the marginalised" does not refer to non-dominant ethnic groups.

Furthermore, while Article 11 of the current Kenyan Constitution is dedicated to culture, it seems to disregard the country's cultural diversity, as it refers to Kenyans as a "people" and a "nation" with a single culture. This suggests that the drafters of the constitution had a bias towards assimilationism and against pluralism. The article begins as follows:

> This Constitution recognizes culture as the foundation of the nation and as the cumulative civilization of the Kenyan people and nation. (Republic 2010a, Article 11 [1])

Nevertheless, several provisions in the Constitution acknowledge the collective rights of ethnic groups. Article 21 (3) of the Constitution of Kenya states: "All State organs and all public officers have the duty to address the needs of vulnerable groups within society, including women, older members of society, persons with disabilities, children, youth, members of minority or marginalised communities, and *members of particular ethnic, religious or cultural communities*" (emphasis mine). In addition, the constitution states that "Community land shall vest in and be held by communities identified on the basis of ethnicity, culture or similar community of interest" (Article 63 (1)). The article goes on to stipulate the different conditions under which land could be considered to belong to a community, and acknowledges community forests, grazing areas or shrines, ancestral lands, and lands traditionally occupied by hunter-gatherer communities as falling within this category of land. This is a significant departure from the ethnically blind orientation typical of the Western liberal tradition that greatly informed the independence Kenyan Constitution, where only individuals and corporations were entitled to own land. Similarly, on the issue of special seats in the National Assembly and Senate, the constitution stipulates that they shall be filled on the basis of proportional representation from party lists that reflect "the regional and ethnic diversity of the people of Kenya" (Article 90 (2) (c)).

The Constitution (Republic of Kenya 2010a) also requires parliament to enact legislation to promote the representation in parliament of, among others, "ethnic and other minorities" (Article 100 (d)). It also provides that "The composition of the national executive shall reflect the regional and *ethnic* diversity of the people of Kenya" (Article 130 (2); emphasis mine). In addition, it stipulates that the values and principles of public service include affording adequate and equal opportunities for appointment, training and advancement, at all levels of the public service, for among others, "the members of all ethnic groups" (Article 232 (1) (i) (ii)). Similarly, "The composition of the command of the Defence Forces shall reflect the regional and ethnic diversity of the people of Kenya" (Article 241 (4)). The same requirement applies to the Kenya Police Service (Article 246 (4)), as well as to constitutional commissions and independent offices (Article 250 (4)).

However, in line with the individualist ethnically blind liberal democratic vision, Article 27 (1) of the Constitution of Kenya focuses on the equality of individual persons before the law, with no mention of ethnic groups as legal persons bearing rights. What is more, Article 27 (4) does not speak of "ethnic identity", but rather of "ethnic or social origin", thereby reinforcing the idea that the persons it refers to are individuals rather than members of ethnic groups. It is therefore not surprising that the article on freedom of expression singles out "ethnic incitement" as one of the grounds on which freedom of expression is to be limited (Article 33 (2) (d) (i)). While I agree with the drafters of the Constitution that ethnic incitement ought to be curtailed, singling it out without adequately recognising the right to ethnic identity has the import of criminalising even the most benign ethnically based political mobilisation, thereby unjustifiably limiting the freedoms of association and expression.

Besides, the Constitution of Kenya requires that political parties have a "national character as prescribed by an Act of Parliament" (Article 91 (1) (a)). It goes on to enjoin political parties to "promote and uphold national unity" (Article 91 (1) (c))—a requirement which, in the Kenyan context, is understood to refer to a homogenizing project through the systematic de-emphasizing of ethnic identities. Furthermore, the Constitution states that political parties shall not "be founded on a religious, linguistic, racial, *ethnic*, gender or regional basis or seek to engage in advocacy of hatred on any such basis" (Article 91 (2) (a); emphasis mine). The Political Parties Act had already articulated this approach which criminalises the formation of ethnically based parties, requiring instead that every party be "national in character" (Republic of Kenya 2007, Section 14).

The effect of the provisos on political parties in the Constitution and in the Political Parties Act is to limit the collective right of ethnic groups to pursue their political aspirations through parties of their own. In view of the three grounds for the right to the constitutional recognition and protection of ethnic identities and interests presented in the previous section, and in the light of the constitutional provisions on the collective rights of ethnic groups outlined earlier in this section, it is most regrettable that the Constitution of Kenya and the Political Parties Act proscribe ethnically based political parties.

The pluralist elements in Kenya's National Cohesion and Integration Act (Republic of Kenya 2008) and in the current Constitution of Kenya (Republic of Kenya 2010a) are steps in the right direction, since a policy of officially disregarding ethnicity has for more than five decades failed to stem rampant ethnic discrimination in the country. More than forty years ago, Rawls (1971, 234) asserted that "The public will to consult and to take everyone's beliefs and interests into account lays the foundations for civic friendship and shapes the ethos of political culture". Although Rawls would probably have doubted it, his observation is applicable not only to individual citizens, but also to ethnic groups within the African context. In other words, ethnic groups ought to be treated as interest groups whose views are pivotal to the building of viable democracies in twenty-first century African polities.

THE STRUGGLE FOR ETHNICALLY BASED FEDERALISM IN KENYA: A HISTORICAL SYNOPSIS

The advent of the British invasion and subjugation of the territory now called Kenya commenced with the formal inauguration of the Imperial British East Africa Company rule in 1888, but more officially with the declaration of British East African Protectorate on 1 July 1895 (Kihoro 2005, 8). An 1886 Anglo-German agreement had delineated the sovereignty of the Sultan of Zanzibar from the country's coastline to ten miles into the interior (Brennan 2008, 838), but in 1895 the Sultan of Zanzibar leased the administration of the strip to the British. These events set in motion the process of placing different ethnic communities with their diverse systems of government within one large and new area of central administration (Olumwullah 1990, 88; Jonyo 2002, 90). The territory beyond the Ten-Mile Coastal Strip was declared to be "Kenya Colony" in 1920 (Omolo 2002, 213). Thus, while the Ten-Mile Coastal Strip continued to be referred to as a Protectorate, the rest of the country was henceforth referred to as the Kenya Colony (Brennan 2008, 831). Nevertheless, the British administered the Protectorate and the Colony as a two-in-one unit out of expediency (Hassan 2002). Thus, if you asked my grandmother whether she is Luo or Kenyan, she would be startled by the question, because she knows nothing of a Kenyan identity, but is proud of her Luo identity, which she can trace several generations back.

Kenya's political independence in December 1963 was preceded by three constitutional conferences held in the Lancaster house, London, in 1960, 1962, and 1963 (Ndegwa 1997, 602–4). The Kenya African National Union (KANU), a party mainly of the numerically advantaged Kikuyu and Luo, was in favour of a unitary state. However, the Kenya African Democratic Union (KADU), supported by minority ethnic groups such as the Kalenjin, Maasai, Turkana, Samburu, the Giriama of the Coast, and sections of the Luhya, along with Michael Blundel's European settler-dominated New Kenya Party (NKP) and the Kenya Indian Congress (KIC), favoured a regionalist (*majimbo*)[1] system (Odinga 1967, 226–27). The prospect of Kikuyu-Luo dominance through KANU was real, since the two groups were larger, more politically conscious, and better organized than the KADU groups, and presumably would win overwhelmingly at the polls (Ndegwa 1997, 605). The expectation of a census-type vote was largely fulfilled in the February 1961 elections. Of the thirty-three open seats, KANU won nineteen with 67.4% of the vote, while KADU won eleven seats with a paltry 16.4% of the vote. These proportions roughly approximated the population distribution of the ethnic groups backing each party (Muigai 2004, 210).

Despite the numerical disadvantage of KADU and its European and Indian allies, it managed to put pressure at the Lancaster House conferences that resulted in the independence constitution providing for eight regions (*majimbo*), which were the former more or less ethnically defined colonial administrative units ("provinces"), namely, Nairobi, Coast, Eastern, Central, Rift Valley, Nyanza, Western, and North-Eastern, each with its own legislative and executive bodies (Republic of Kenya 1963, chapter VI). The minority ethnic groups were also assured of representation in the central government through the Senate, whose electoral areas were the even more ethnically homogeneous administrative districts. Moreover, the Regional Boundaries Commission was established to collate the views of all ethnic groups regarding the region to which they wished to belong. However, the Commission did not grant all the petitions it received. For example, it declined the petition of the Sabaot of Mount Elgon to be included in the Rift Valley Region along with their Kalenjin kin (Ndegwa 1997, 602–4).

Following the Lancaster agreement of 1962, elections were held under the new constitution in May 1963. Again, KANU won an overwhelming majority in these "independence elections", with the regional and ethnic spread remaining similar to that of the 1961 elections, each party predominating in the areas largely populated by ethnic groups sympathetic to it (Odinga 1967, 234). When the two parties returned to London in September 1963 to finalize the independence constitution, KANU demanded amendments to the 1962 agreement to reduce regional powers, the special protections for minorities, and the constraints imposed on constitutional change. On the other hand, KADU, having suffered an electoral setback (and the defection of the Luhya and Kamba leaders), insisted on retaining the 1962 agreement as the framework for the final constitution. KADU threatened the integrity of the new state if protections already attained were withdrawn. Consequently, KANU accepted the *majimbo* arrangement as the independence constitution, but a number of changes were made in its favour. One of the most important of these was a concession on constitutional change: Amendment proposals that failed to receive the required majority in the House and Senate would then require a two-thirds majority in a referendum (Odinga 1967, 234). Muigai (2001) identified the two cardinal principles of the independence constitution as parliamentary government and the protection of minorities.

However, KADU could only secure control over two regions, namely, the Rift Valley and the Coast. Furthermore, within the first year of political independence, KANU undermined the regional governments by withholding funds, passing legislation to circumvent regional powers, and forcing major changes to the constitution by threatening to hold a referendum if the Senate—in which KADU could block the proposals—did not accede to the changes. Outnumbered, outmanoeuvred, and with no prospects for enforcing the compromise constitution or, given the reality of census-type voting, for overtaking KANU at the subsequent polls, KADU dissolved and joined KANU to form a centralised single-party state at the beginning of 1964 (Ndegwa 1997, 604; Ajulu 2002, 258–59). This was a major blow to the struggle for ethnic minority rights in Kenya, as it gave the majority ethnic groups an opportunity to entrench their hegemony in the nascent state. They did so by amending the constitution to replace the parliamentary system with a presidential one, and by concentrating power in the presidency.

From the time KADU was dissolved in 1964 to the next period of fundamental political transformation beginning in 1990, agitation for federalism remained muted, as KANU suppressed advocacy for alternatives to the unitary state. Nevertheless, the coming to power of Daniel arap Moi, a former key KADU leader, in 1978, gave the KADU groups an opportunity to influence the direction of Kenyan politics. In effect, while Moi was president on a KANU ticket, he represented the aspirations of the former KADU groups. This might explain Moi's inauguration of the District Focus for Rural Development (Barkan and Chege 1989).

Beginning in 1990, the transition from a single-party dictatorship to a multi-party system of government provided the first significant opportunity since independence to reconsider Kenya's political institutions (Ndegwa 1997, 606–7). Majority ethnic groups continued to advocate for a unitary system, while ethnic minorities continued to advocate for federalism (Oduor 2011, 78 ff.). Nevertheless, in the run-up to the contested 2007 general elections, the Luo broke rank with the Kikuyu to advocate for a new constitution that would provide for a decidedly devolved structure of government to address the rampant marginalisation of the numerous ethnic minorities in the Rift Valley and at the Coast who had thrown their support behind the Luo-led Orange Democratic Movement (IREC 2008, 1).

Furthermore, the controversy over unitarism and devolutionism was predictably impassioned during public debates on the various draft constitutions prepared by the Committee of Experts from the end of 2009, including the Parliamentary Select Committee debates in Naivasha in February 2010. The political elite of the Kalenjin in the Rift Valley and the elites of communities in the Coast and northeastern provinces advocated a highly devolved three-tier structure, comprising national, regional, and county governments. On the other hand, their counterparts from the Kikuyu, Embu, and Meru communities, fearing that strong devolved units could result in their co-ethnics being exposed to evictions from the Rift Valley and other places to which they have migrated from their ancestral lands in the central and upper eastern parts of the country, continued to advocate for an essentially unitary state with weak devolved units. Their fears had been reinforced by the post 2007 general elections crisis, which saw many people from those communities evicted or killed (Kikechi 2010).

It is reported that during the consensus building talks by MPs prior to debate on the draft constitution tabled in Parliament on 2 March 2010, MPs from the largely Kalenjin and Maasai Rift Valley on the one hand, and those from the Kikuyu-populated Central Kenya on the other, had struck a deal that would have seen the two sides supporting each other's proposed amendments in Parliament. However, the central Kenya group beat a hasty retreat upon learning that their Rift Valley colleagues were plotting what they (Central Kenya MPs) perceived to be a *majimbo* system of government (Omanga 2010), and later walked out of Parliament to frustrate the achievement of the 65% threshold for a vote on it (Ndegwa and Mwanzia 2010). Consequently, Parliament adopted the draft constitution without any amendments, and as earlier indicated, it was subsequently ratified in a referendum on 4 August 2010.

Thus, in the end, as indicated in the previous section, the Constitution which Kenyans ratified at the August 2010 referendum, and which was promulgated on 27 August 2010, is essentially unitarist, with a devolved structure that guarantees the dominance of the central government (see Republic of Kenya 2010a, chapter 11).

In 2013, the pastoralist communities of the Rift Valley largely shifted allegiance from the Raila Odinga-led Orange Democratic Movement to the Jubilee Alliance comprised of Uhuru Kenyatta's The National Alliance (TNA) and William Ruto's United Republican Party (URP), and Uhuru Kenyatta was declared winner of the controversial 2013 elections. Following Uhuru Kenyatta's ascent to power, Odinga's ODM repeatedly accused the Uhuru Kenyatta government of seeking to frustrate devolution as Jomo Kenyatta had done at the dawn of independence. Odinga particularly accused Kenyatta of deliberately allocating insufficient funds to the county governments with a view to weakening them—a charge which Kenyatta vehemently denied. In the meantime, Isaac Rutto broke ranks with William Ruto to form Chama cha Mashinani (CCM)—Kiswahili for "The Grassroots Party"—whose mission was to strengthen devolution through adequate funding. Both Raila Odinga's ODM and Isaac Rutto's CCM along with their allies from other parts of the country unsuccessfully worked towards a referendum with the aim of strengthening devolution through adequate funding. Nevertheless, they joined forces to campaign for the 2017 elections on a platform of adequately funded county governments. In the meantime, the Jubilee alliance consolidated itself into a single party—the Jubilee Party (JP). Uhuru Kenyatta was again declared winner of the controversial 2017 elections.

All in all, non-dominant ethnic groups in Kenya continue to feel trapped in a polity which shows little interest in addressing their social, political, and economic marginalization. Consequently, in the next section, I present the outlines of an ethnically based federal system of government for Kenya to replace the essentially unitarist one that has held sway over the country for almost six decades now.

OUTLINES OF AN ETHNICALLY BASED FEDERAL SYSTEM OF GOVERNMENT FOR KENYA

In view of my reflections in the previous three sections, I hold the view that ethnically plural post-colonial African states desperately need models of democracy that recognise and cater for ethnic identities and interests. I opine that a key feature of these models ought to be ethnically based federations that give each ethnic group some autonomy in these hitherto unduly constricting polities. The ethnically based federal units would give ethnic groups some latitude to incorporate their indigenous political thought into the management of public affairs, thereby enabling them to organise the public space around them in a manner that is consistent with their worldviews. Such models would be markedly different from Western liberal democracy, with its ethnically blind vision. While several African states, Kenya included, have adopted devolution and others such as Nigeria have opted for federalism, they have insisted that the devolved or federal units be ethnically pluralistic. This has the undesirable effect of perpetuating the existing gaping inequalities among the ethnic groups, all the preaching against "tribalism" notwithstanding.

In what follows, I propose seven elements for incorporation into an ethnically based federal system of government for Kenya, with a view to illustrating how such a system could adequately address the decades old sense of exclusion among numerous ethnic groups in the country. My secondary goal for this presentation is to motivate political theorists from other ethnically plural African countries to develop ethnically based federal models that respond to the peculiar needs of their respective countries. Nevertheless, as the title of this section indicates, what I present below are only outlines of what an ethnically based federal system of government in the contemporary Kenyan context might look like.

Recognition of Indigenous Systems of Governance in the Central Government and in the Federal Units

A sizeable proportion of Kenyans still cherish their indigenous African systems of governance, as is evident in the influence that ethnic community elders continue to wield, and which they often use to achieve political ends in their locales and even in the country's politics at large. However, the Kenyan state has largely ignored such systems due to its preoccupation with liberal democracy. It is high time we drew from indigenous systems of government in both the central government and the federal units in order to enable the Kenyan masses to feel a sense of ownership of the state.

It is also noteworthy that several Western democracies still cherish institutions that predate liberal democracy, and that are akin to some of the pre-colonial African political institutions (Chweya 2002, 24–25). Examples of these are the monarchies in countries such as Britain and the Netherlands. Monarchs, by definition, are *not* elected after the manner of liberal democracy, but instead inherit their positions. Yet rarely do people question the essentially democratic nature of those Western polities whose heads of state are monarchs. It is therefore strange that the West and Western-oriented African theorists should frown at calls for the incorporation of indigenous African political thought and practice into the architecture of contemporary African democracies. Wamala (2004) contended that in pre-colonial Ganda society under the reign of the Kabaka (monarch), ideas we would today consider crucial for democracy were very much in operation. Consequently, there is absolutely no reason why African states should capitulate to the pressure to adopt political systems that reflect nothing but modern Western models.

A Synthetic Two-Chamber Parliament

In order to further recognise the indigenous political outlook of a sizeable proportion of the Kenyan masses, I propose a two-chamber parliament. To cater for the modern Western outlook taking root in Africa today, members of the Lower House ought to be elected on the typical liberal democratic framework of one-person-one-vote. On the other hand, the upper house ought to be composed of leaders of ethnic groups, with the power to veto all legislation from the lower house on the basis of consensus in the upper house. This would ensure that the perspectives of the ethnic groups are catered for in all legislation.

The Republic of Somaliland, which broke away from the war-torn Somali Republic in May 1991, has a two-chamber ("bicameral") parliament. Its Lower Chamber, called the House of Representatives, is elected through a liberal democracy-type one-person-one-vote election. Its Upper Chamber, called the House of Elders, is indirectly elected by the various clans, and is the revising chamber for legislation, except for financial bills. In Kenya's case, however, it would be expedient to vest the Upper House with powers to veto financial bills because the unfair distribution of resources among the ethnic groups is the main source of inter-ethnic tensions in the country.

Ethnically Based Shared Executive Power

One of the main reasons for political instability in Kenya is that, currently, the head of the executive arm of government is a single individual from one ethnic group, making the rest of the ethnic groups feel that they have lost out. This ought to be replaced by shared executive power, with the office-holders hailing from ethnic groups representing the different modes of life in the country (agriculturalists, pastoralists, and hunter-gatherers). Executive decisions would then be by consensus, failing which there would be a vote. This would lead to greater harmony between the executive and the bicameral legislature, as there would be no outright losers in the race for executive power who would seek to use their representatives in Parliament to frustrate the executive.

In 2009, Thomas Ojanga wrote to the Committee of Experts charged with preparing the final draft of the new Kenyan Constitution recommending the adoption of a system of government specially designed for Kenya's unique circumstances, markedly different from the two main Western liberal democratic Models (parliamentary and Presidential). For Ojanga, a salient feature of this model is the overt recognition of ethnic interests through a council of ethnic elders, with every ethnic group enjoying equal representation in the council, and with the council holding ultimate executive authority (Ojanga 2009). While Ojanga's call for equal representation of all ethnic groups is likely to be contested for violating the majoritarian principle which for many is the hallmark of democracy, the essence of his proposal, that ethnic diversity be adequately reflected in and by the country's governance structure, is admissible as a means to promoting inter-ethnic harmony in the polity.

A No-Party System of Government

As a young man in the 1980s, I yearned for the day when Kenya would restore multi-party politics, convinced that the event would be synonymous with the restoration of democracy. However, more than thirty years after the return of the system, the country is yet to make meaningful democratic gains. Indeed, just as the party leader during the single-party era in Kenya bullied all the party members into doing his bidding, so the multi-party system has simply enabled similar bullying in the numerous parties, so that elected representatives are concerned about towing the party lines to keep their positions rather than about articulating the concerns of those who purportedly elected them. It is therefore high time Kenya designed a no-party system in which the people can meaningfully participate in governance without the impediments that party politics has placed on their way. We must, of course, guard against the kind of counterfeit non-party system that Yoweri Museveni ran in Uganda for almost two decades, and which was really a camouflaged single-party system (see Oduor 2011, 375–84).

Kwasi Wiredu (1996, 82–90) plausibly argued for a consensual, non-party democracy on the ground that it facilitates not only the formal representation of all interest groups in a polity, but also ensures that every shade of opinion is taken seriously (substantive or decisional representation), so that the people are represented not only in council, but also in counsel, thereby promoting political stability. Similarly, Wamala (2004) highlighted three reasons why the party system is actually an obstacle to genuine democratisation:

1. It destroys consensus-building by de-emphasizing the role of the individual in political action and requiring holders of elected positions to be

loyal to the parties on whose tickets they ran for office rather than to the people who they purportedly represent.
2. Parties deploy the Machiavellian approach to gain power and thereby drain political practice of ethical considerations contrary to the traditional African outlook.
3. Even the parties that command the majority and therefore form the government are really ruled by a handful of persons.

Ethnic Equity in Public Appointments

In the name of an ethnically blind public policy, Kenyan citizens who have questioned ethnically-skewed public appointments have often been reminded that all the appointees are Kenyan citizens. The result has often been accumulated resentment which the aggrieved ethnic groups hope to address through elections. When such groups also repeatedly lose elections whose credibility is in doubt due to alleged interference by those in power, they feel further alienated from the state, and easily foment socio-political unrest. As pointed out in the third section of this chapter, the Constitution of Kenya requires ethnic equity in public appointments. However, it does not provide clear guidelines for implementing this proviso, thus giving the President great latitude to make heavily skewed ethnically based appointments. Consequently, there is an urgent need to amend the Constitution to clarify this important proviso and to stipulate effective sanctions for violating it.

The Right to Secession

The United Nations, the African Union, and other bodies of independent states have frequently discouraged secession except after drawn-out civil wars (see Oduor 2011, 292 ff.). It is incomprehensible why this is so, bearing in mind the extensive damage occasioned by civil conflict. I therefore propose a constitutional provision that where ethnic groups are consistently marginalised, and where the legal and political processes consistently fail to address their concerns, they have a right to institute a process leading to secession. The aim of this proposal is to motivate the Kenyan state to refrain from such marginalisation in a bid to sustain its territorial integrity (see Oduor 2019b).

A Liberal Bill of Rights

One of the dangers of recognising ethnic group rights as I have proposed in this chapter is that by virtue of their communalistic outlook, ethnic groups frequently seek to impose their wills on their members. For example, some of them coerce their members to engage in certain cultural practices and would not envisage the possibility of respecting the rights of their members to dissociate themselves from the groups. Thus, to protect individuals against the overbearing demands of their ethnic groups, it would be important to retain the Western style Bill of Rights in Kenya's Constitution, guaranteeing the rights of the individual such as freedom of conscience, movement, association, and expression.

LESSONS FROM BOTSWANA AND ETHIOPIA

Non-governmental organisations (NGOs) have popularized the idea of looking for "best practice"—identifying a country or an institution worth emulating because of its success in a specific venture. Thus, I have been asked if there are any ethnically plural African countries that have successfully deployed ethnically based federalism. In the quest for "best practice", one could also ask if there are any ethnically plural African states that have embraced liberal democracy without inter-ethnic tensions, and if so, why the rest of the African countries could not emulate them instead of resorting to ethnically based federalism. However, in view of the normative rather than descriptive nature of their discipline, political philosophers do not typically feel obligated to offer cases of "best practice". Nevertheless, in this section, I will briefly examine the experiences of Botswana and Ethiopia, the former reputed for embracing liberal democracy within a unitary framework purportedly without the destructive inter-ethnic conflicts characteristic of most ethnically plural African states, the latter unique for its ethnically based federalism.

Botswana

It is often claimed that relative to many other post-colonial African countries, ethnic relations in Botswana have generally been free from tension since the country became politically independent from the British in 1966. Nevertheless, this relative tranquillity is partly due to the British colonial policy of indirect rule there, informed by the fact that the British had no economic interests in the country, their only goal being to maintain access to their territories in the North, especially the two Rhodesias, Thereby reducing their physical presence and the attendant divide-and-rule policy in Botswana (Mulinge 2008, 66–67). The majority Tswana people is comprised of eight groups, namely, the Bangwato, Barolong, Bakwena, Bakgatla, Batlokwa, Balete, Batawana, and Bangwaketse (WorldAtlas.com 2018).

However, things have not been as rosy in Botswana as is often presented, because of tensions between the majority Tswana people on the one hand, and a number of minority ethnic groups on the other. The name of the country is taken from the Tswana and means "the land of the Tswana". This implies that even the non-Tswana must use a Tswana demonym, that is, they have to say they are *Batswana* (plural) or *Motswana* (singular).[2] Thus the non-Tswana peoples can hardly identify with the name of the country that they are meant to call their own. *Similarly, the national anthem, Fatshe leno la rona ("*This Land of Ours"), is in setswana. Furthermore, Seretse Khama, a Tswana Chief, was the first President, and his son, Ian Khama, the fourth. These features, among others, have an alienating effect on the non-Tswana peoples in the country.

In fact, unlike most other African countries, and contrary to the ethnically blind Western liberal democratic vision, Botswana is characterized by constitutionally grounded ethnic differentiation. The country's Constitution delineates the eight Tswana groups earlier listed as "principal tribes". This was carried over from demarcations done between 1899 and 1933 by a Native Reserve Delimitation Commission (Mulinge 2008, 63). The Commission established "native reserves" in the country that consolidated the subordination of non-Tswana peoples (Mulinge 2008, 63–64). The independence constitution retained the boundaries of the native reserves under the new label of "districts". Consequently, chiefs of peoples other than the eight Tswana groups continued to be marginalized: they were regarded as headmen or sub-chiefs without the right to represent their people in the *Ntlo ya Dikgosi* ("House of Chiefs"), that is, the second chamber of the country's legislature (Mulinge 2008, 64). Besides, the state has pursued an aggressive policy of Tswana assimilation through its official language and culture policy. Purportedly in the interest of "nation-building" and "national unity", Setswana and English are the only official languages in the country, with other languages proscribed in official contexts and in schools (Mulinge 2008, 68; Werbner 2002, 676).

The unrest among minority ethnic groups in Botswana has often manifested in their tireless but unsuccessful agitation for the amendment of Sections 77, 78 and 79 of the country's Constitution that delineate the eight Tswana groups as "principal tribes"—provisions that the minority ethnic groups see as constituting the basis for persistent discrimination against them, resulting in the violation of their rights to land and positions in the country's administrative structure (Mulinge 2008, 70–71; Keorapetse 2017; The Zimbabwean Reporter 2018). The experience of the San, often referred to as the "Basarwa", or derogatorily as the "Bushmen", as well as that of the Bakgalagadi, both super-minority ethnic groups that have suffered under state policies that threaten their cultures and livelihoods, graphically highlight the plight of ethnic minorities in Botswana (see Hitchcock 2002, 797–98; Mulinge 2008; Staff Reporter 2011).

In view of the foregoing considerations, it is evident that the relative tranquillity of inter-ethnic relations in Botswana is only that—relative. It was considerably easy for the Tswana-dominated state to muffle the voices of the discontented ethnic minorities for decades, thereby presenting the country as an island of liberal democratic tranquillity in a sea of failing or failed African states. However, the ochestrated "tranquillity" is clearly not sustainable. I therefore take the view that rather than weakening my case for ethnically based federations in ethnically plural post-colonial African states, the experience of Botswana actually strengthens it.

Ethiopia

Ethiopia is unique in that it was not subjected to Western colonialism, except for a brief Italian occupation between 1936 and 1941. According to The *Encyclopedia of the Nations*, the country's principal ethnic groups are the Oromo (40%), Amhara and Tigre (32%), Sidamo (9%), Shankella (6%), Somali (6%), Afar (4%), and Gurage (2%). The remaining 1% comprises of various other ethnic groups. In total, there are more than eighty different ethnic groups within Ethiopia (Advameg, Inc. 2018), and the country has a long history of inter-ethnic conflicts.

In 1989, the Tigrayan People's Liberation Front (TPLF) came together with other ethnically based opposition movements to form the Ethiopian People's Revolutionary Democratic Front (EPRDF), which overthrew Mengistu Haile Mariam's regime in May 1991, adopted ethnic pluralism as an organizing principle, creating ethnic-based federal units with a "right of secession" provision in Article 39 of a constitution that came into force in 1995 (Habtu 2004; Aaron 2005–2006). The regime initially divided the country into fourteen regions in 1992, but later merged five of them to form the multi-ethnic Southern Nations, Nationalities and Peoples' Region.

The change to ethnically based federalism was largely due to the fact that the leader of the Ethiopian People's Revolutionary Democratic Front (EPRDF) ruling coalition in 1991, Meles Zenawi, up to then leader of the Tigrayan People's Liberation Front (TPLF), was determined to bring to an end what he saw as the dominance of the Shewan Amhara ethnic group. The change was not only meant to reduce inter-ethnic conflicts, but also to equalise living standards in different parts of the country, as well as to improve the working of public institutions locally. To reflect the change to ethnically based federalism, the regime renamed the country "Federal Democratic Republic of Ethiopia". It also renamed the country's legislature "Federal Parliamentary

Assembly", with the Upper Chamber called "House of Federation", and the Lower Chamber "House of Peoples' Representatives". According to Habtu (2004), this experiment, in which a state fully acknowledges ethnic pluralism and bases its structures on it, is unique in the African context.[3] In addition to ethnically based federalism, the regime adopted an avowedly Western-style multi-party parliamentary liberal democratic system.

Consequently, Ethiopia is divided into nine ethnically based and politically autonomous regional states (*kililoch*, singular *kilil*). The nine regions are Afar Region, Amhara Region, Benishangul-Gumuz Region, Gambela Region, Harari Region, Oromia Region, Somali Region, Tigray Region, and Southern Nations, Nationalities and Peoples' Region. There are also two multi-ethnic chartered cities (*astedader akababiwoch*, singular *astedader akababi*), namely, Addis Ababa and Dire Dawa. The *kililoch* are subdivided into sixty-eight zones, which are further divided into 550 *woreda* ("districts") and several special *woreda*, and *kebeles* ("neighborhoods"). The federal units have extensive powers to establish their own models of governance as long as they are in line with the Constitution of the federal government. At the apex of each region is a Regional Council whose members are directly elected to represent the districts, with legislative and executive powers to direct the internal affairs of the regions.

However, more than five years after the commencement of the implementation of ethnically based federalism under a multi-party parliamentary system in Ethiopia, the country was still grappling with inter-ethnic strife (Mengisteab 2001). Besides, just over ten years after the inauguration of ethnically based federalism, Keller (2002) and Gudina (2004) observed that rather than empowering citizens at the grassroots, Ethiopia tightly controlled economic development and politics through regional state governments, with very little citizen participation in decision-making. Indeed, the EPDRF regime in Ethiopia earned notoriety for authoritarianism manifested in the violent quelling of peaceful demonstrations, the incarceration of leading opposition figures, and the organizing of elections that tip the scales in its favour. For example, following the May 2005 Ethiopian elections, the regime responded to public protests by unleashing the police on demonstrators in June and November of the same year, leading to the deaths of 193 people, the injury of 763 people, and the detention of more than 30,000 others. In addition, more than 100 opposition leaders, journalists and aid workers were rounded up during the protests and arraigned in courts on charges of treason and attempted genocide. Besides, Wolde-Michael Meshesha, the Ethiopian judge who compiled the report of the atrocities, fled from the country to Europe, claiming to have received anonymous death threats (BBC 2006).

In 2016, Ethiopia again experienced public protests and police violence following the 2015 elections in which the ruling party claimed victory of all parliamentary seats. According to the Ethiopia Human Rights Commission (EHRC), a total of 669 people were killed in the anti-government unrests that hit the Amhara, Oromia, and the Southern Nations and Nationalities and People's (SNNP) regional states in 2016 (Shaban 2017). The state-affiliated FANA Broadcasting Corporate reported that EHRC boss, Dr. Addisu Gebregziabher, said: "deep-rooted problems of good governance, failure to implement the special interest of Oromia in Addis Ababa as per stated [sic] in the constitution and the Addis Ababa master plan were the main causes for unrest in Oromia regional state" (quoted in Shaban 2017).

On February 16, 2018, the Ethiopian government declared a six-month countrywide state of emergency following the resignation of Prime Minister Hailemariam Desalegn who said he wanted to clear the way for reforms. He was the first ruler in contemporary Ethiopia to step down, previous ones having died in office or been overthrown. Abiy Ahmed Ali replaced Desalegn, becoming the country's first leader from the Oromo—the ethnic group at the centre of nearly three years of anti-government protests that left hundreds of people dead. Ali is leader of the Oromo People's Democratic Organisation (OPDO), one of the four ethnic parties comprising the ruling Ethiopian People's Revolutionary Democratic Front (EPRDF) coalition, and was said to have huge support among the Oromo youth, as well as among other ethnic groups (BBC 2018). Ali ended the twenty-year border war with Eritrea, released political prisoners, removed bans on dissident groups and allowed their members to return from exile, declared press freedom, and granted diverse political groups the freedom to mobilize and organize (Mamdani 2019).

What, then, do we make of the civil war that broke out in November 2020 between the Tigray People's Liberation Front (TPLF) and the Abiy Ahmed Ali-led Ethiopian government? Hibist Kassa (2021) cautions against simplistic accounts of the crisis that focus entirely on the internal debate between the TPLF federalists and the Abiy Ahmed Ali led centrists, warning that diverse interests, including the commercial objectives of Ethiopian political elite, as well as those of the United States, the West at large, and Egypt's concerns about the completion of the Grand Ethiopian Renaissance Dam (GERD), among others are also at play. For example, Kassa points out that Ethiopia's forging of alliances with Eritrea and Somalia and its broader goal of stabilising the Horn of Africa "in a manner that has not centred Washington and its 'War on Terror'" is of great concern to the United States. Nevertheless, as I seek to show in the next few paragraphs, the TPLF's insistence on the retention of the 1995 federalist constitution and Abiy Ahmed Ali's endeavour to dilute that federalist model cannot be ignored in any credible account of the conflict.

The government of Ethiopia had been dominated by the Tigray People's Liberation Front (TPLF), which had ruled the country since 1991 when the TPLF joined forces with other armed groups to overthrow the government of Mengistu Haile Mariam (Hoffman 2021). However, on ascending to power in 2018, Prime Minister Abiy Ahmed Ali organized the Prosperity Party out of many ethnic-based parties to challenge the dominance of the TPLF. In response, the TPLF resigned from government, and its leadership retreated to Tigray, a region along the northern border, where it focused on consolidating its authority in the region in order to curtail the influence of the Ethiopian government and military (Hoffman 2021).

In August 2020, the government postponed the general elections purportedly due to the COVID-19 crisis, but the TPLF considered this a betrayal, and conducted its own elections in contravention of the postponement. In addition, the TPLF seized military bases in Tigray, exacerbating tensions between the government and the TPLF. In November 2020, Prime Minister Ali ordered the military to quell the uprising in Tigray, resulting in large-scale conflict (Hoffman 2021). In late June 2021, the TPLF dealt a severe blow to the government by re-capturing Mekelle, the capital of Tigray. Shortly after that, Prime Minister Ali unilaterally declared a ceasefire. Nevertheless, the TPLF did not relent, but instead pushed out Ethiopian forces from the remaining parts of Tigray, and then moved southwards towards the country's capital Addis Ababa (Hoffman 2021). The TPLF also made alliances with other armed opposition groups, resulting in the emergence of the United Front of Ethiopian Federalist and Confederalist Forces in early November 2021, whose professed goal is to preserve the 1995 constitution that recognises federalism and the right to self-determination (Hoffman 2021).

Tragically, Ali's government greatly restricted the amount of aid that could be delivered to Tigray on grounds that such aid would sustain the TPLF. As a result, towards mid November 2021, despite 5.2 million people in Tigray in need of humanitarian aid (over 90% of the population in Tigray) and about 1.7 million displaced, only about 10% of the aid required had been delivered (Hoffman 2021).

According to Bryden and Abdi (2021), the conflict has weakened the country, and confronted all Ethiopians with one inescapable truth—they must acknowledge their diversity or risk disintegration. It is noteworthy that while by 2004 the Ethiopian federation appeared to have undercut the drive for secession by largely doing away with manifest ethnically based oppression, the fact that the ruling elite came predominantly from a small ethnic group raised vigorous protests from other ethnic groups, larger and smaller (Habtu 2004). In addition, the use of what Habtu (2004) called "democratic centralism" undermined effective decentralization and democratization.

Consequently, Habtu (2004) asserted that ethnic pluralism as an organizing principle underpinning the federal government in Ethiopia is a fragile and perilous experiment.

In line with the views of Habtu (2004) above, Mamdani (2019) holds that the clash between ethnic federalism enshrined in Ethiopia's constitution and Prime Minister Abiy Ahmed Ali's liberal reforms threatens to exacerbate competitive ethnic politics and push the country toward inter-ethnic conflict. According to him, ethnic federalism was troubled with internal inconsistencies from the outset because ethnic groups do not live in discrete "homeland" territories, but are also dispersed across the country, giving rise to numerous cases of ethnic minority discontent. He further asserts that ethnic federalism also unleashed a struggle for supremacy among the three dominant ethnic groups, namely, the Tigray, the Amhara, and the Oromo. For Mamdani (2019), Ethiopia can only gain stability in a territorially based federation rather than in an ethnically based one.

However, in response to Mamdani (2019), Serumaga (2019) correctly points out that since Ethiopia was not under Western colonial rule, her ethnically based federal constitution was not inspired by mere sentimental attachment to ethnic identities fuelled by a colonial divide-and-rule policy. Instead, it arose from the need to address the pertinent issue of land, which is itself tied to claims based on cultural loyalties. Serumaga shows that for over a hundred years now, various nationalities (commonly called "ethnicities") in Ethiopia have been fighting against land dispossession occasioned by the empire of Menelik II which Mengistu Hailemariam's Derg regime autocratically perpetuated. Serumaga cogently infers that the real problem in Ethiopia is that Meles Zenawi and Hailemariam Desalegn did not fully implement the ethnically based federal constitution, thereby neglecting to adequately address the long-standing land question.

Consequently, it seems to me that the authoritarian approach of Ethiopia's ruling elite is probably a much greater cause of the fragility and perilousness of the Ethiopian ethnically based federalist experiment than the governance model itself; for as Fanon (1967) correctly observed, violence breeds violence. Besides, Ethiopia's experiment with ethnically based federalism is yet to be allowed to run its course for a considerable period of time—with the resolute facilitation of genuine participation of the citizenry in the ethnically based federal units, and with meaningful input of the representatives of the federal units in the affairs of the federal government.

In view of the foregoing reflections, the Ethiopian experiment cannot be appropriately cited in support of, or in opposition to, ethnically based federalism in multi-ethnic post-colonial African states. Yet the ethnically blind centralist state model, which has been predominant in post-colonial African states, is even more fragile and perilous than the Ethiopian experiment, because, as I pointed out earlier in this chapter, it enables politicians to create cleavage along ethnic lines, all the while insisting that ethnic considerations are irrelevant to the management of public affairs, thereby promoting a dishonest public discourse, and fomenting deep-seated resentment that frequently breaks out into violence, often resulting in the massive loss of life and property.

CONCLUSION

The peoples of Africa continue to experience the dire impact of the Western imperialistic partition of their continent in the late nineteenth century, mainly in the form of dysfunctional multi-ethnic states in which inter-ethnic conflicts often lead to massive loss of life and property. Besides, contemporary geopolitics renders the reversal of that cataclysmic decision virtually impossible. Nevertheless, ethnically based federations can assuage its impact by accommodating the ethnic loyalties of the masses, instead of ignoring or vilifying them as has been regularly done for more than five decades now. Such federations would be of particular benefit to non-dominant ethnic groups, each of which would thereby have some latitude to organise its local public life in a manner consonant with its own worldview. This is why I think an ethnically based federation in Kenya, and in other multi-ethnic states in Africa, could usher in relative stability in these polities.

NOTES

1. *Majimbo* is the Kiswahili word for "regions", but in the Kenyan context it came to refer to a federal form of government.

2. A "demonym" is the way the citizens of a country are referred to, such as "Kenyan" or "Nigerian". In Bantu languages, a demonym is usually formed by prefixing "*m/mu/mo*" (singular) or "*wa/ba*" (plural) to the name of a country. For example, in Kiswahili, the equivalent of "Kenyan" is "*Mkenya*". Thus, a non-Tswana citizen of Botswana has to say that he or she is a "Motswana", which is a blatant misrepresentation. A similar situation pertains to the non-Ganda citizens of Uganda, and to the non-Congo citizens of the two Congos. This highlights the arbitrary nature of the nineteenth-century Western imperialist partition of Africa, and the attendant arbitrary naming of the territories thus created, and that were the basis of post-colonial African states.

3. The case of South Sudan might be cited as somewhat blunting the uniqueness of the Ethiopian experiment. In October 2015, South Sudan's President Salva Kiir issued a decree establishing twenty-eight states largely along ethnic lines in place of

the ten constitutionally established states. In response to objections from a number of opposition parties and civil societies, Kiir sent it to Parliament for approval as a constitutional amendment, and Parliament empowered him to create new states. Nevertheless, I take the view that this experiment is relatively recent, and therefore difficult to assess at this stage.

REFERENCES

Aaron, Tesfaye. 2005–2006. "Identity Politics, Citizenship, and Democratization in Ethiopia". *International Journal of Ethiopian Studies*, Vol. 2 No. 1/2, pp. 55–75. http://www.jstor.org/stable/27828856.

Advameg, Inc. 2018. "Ethiopia". *Encyclopedia of the Nations*. http://www.nationsencyclopedia.com/economies/Africa/Ethiopia.html.

Ajulu, Rok. 2002. "Politicised Ethnicity, Competitive Politics and Conflict in Kenya: A Historical Perspective". *African Studies*, Vol. 61 No. 2, pp. 252–68.

Ake, Claude. 1993. "What is the Problem of Ethnicity in Africa?" *Transformation* 22, 1993. http://digital.lib.msu.edu/projects/africanjournals/pdfs/transformation/tran022/tran022002.pdf.

Atieno-Odhiambo, E.S. 2002. "Hegemonic Enterprises and Instrumentalities of Survival: Ethnicity and Democracy in Kenya". *African Studies*, Vol. 61 No. 2, pp. 223–49.

Barkan, Joel D. and Michael Chege. 1989. "Decentralising the State: District Focus and the Politics of Reallocation in Kenya". *The Journal of Modern African Studies*, Vol. 27 No. 3, 1989, pp. 431–53.

BBC. 2006. "Ethiopian Protesters Massacred". BBC Report, 19 October 2006. http://news.bbc.co.uk/2/hi/africa/6064638.stm.

———. 2018. "Abiy Ahmed becomes Ethiopia's prime minister". BBC Report, 3 April 2018. http://www.bbc.com/news/world-africa-43567007#page.

"Botswana: BDP MPs call for constitutional review". *The Zimbabwean*, 8 May 2018. http://www.thezimbabwean.co/2009/11/botswana-bdp-mps-call-for-constitutional-review.

Brennan, James R. 2008. "Lowering the Sultan's Flag: Sovereignty and Decolonization in Coastal Kenya". *Comparative Studies in Society and History*, Vol. 50 No. 4, pp. 831–61. http://eprints.soas.ac.uk/7484/1/Sultan's_Flag.pdf.

Bryden, Matt and Rashid Abdi. 2021. "Abiy Has Lost His War but Ethiopia Could Reinvent Itself". *The Elephant*, November 29. https://www.theelephant.info/op-eds/2021/11/29/abiy-has-lost-his-war-but-ethiopia-could-reinvent-itself/.

Campbell, John R. 2004. "Ethnic minorities and development: A Prospective Look at the Situation of African Pastoralists and Hunter-Gatherers". *Ethnicities*, Vol. 4 No. 1, pp. 5–26. http://etn.sagepub.com/cgi/content/abstract/4/1/5.

Chweya, Ludeki. 2002. "Western Modernity, African Indigene, and Political Order: Interrogating the Liberal Democratic Orthodoxy". Chweya, Ludeki ed. *Electoral Politics in Kenya*. Nairobi: Claripress, pp. 1–27.

Cronk, Lee. 2004. *From Mukogodo to Maasai: Ethnicity and Cultural Change in Kenya*. Oxford: Westview Press.

Curry, Jr., R. L. and L. L. Wade. 1968. *A Theory of Political Exchange: Economic Reasoning in Political Analysis*. Engelwood Cliffs: Prentice-Hall, Inc.

Davidson, Basil. 1992. *The Black Man's Burden: Africa and the Curse of the Nation-State*. New York: Three Rivers Press.

Deng, Francis M. 2004. "Human Rights in the African Context". Wiredu, Kwasi ed. 2004. *A Companion to African Philosophy*. Malden, MA: Blackwell Publishing Ltd., pp. 499–508.

Gudina, Merera. 2004. "The State, Competing Ethnic Nationalisms and Democratisation in Ethiopia". *African Journal of Political Science*, Vol. 9 No. 1, pp. 27–50. http://www.jstor.org/stable/23493677.

Habtu, Alem. 2004. "Ethnic Pluralism as an Organizing Principle of the Ethiopian Federation". *Dialectical Anthropology*, Vol. 28 No. 2, pp. 91–123. http://www.jstor.org/stable/29790705.

Hameso, Seyoum Y. 2002. "Issues and Dilemmas of Multi-Party Democracy in Africa". *West Africa Review*, Vol. 3 Issue 2. https://www.africaknowledgeproject.org/index.php/war/article/view/326.

Hassan, Ahmed Issack. 2002. "Working Document for the Constitution of Kenya Review Commission on the Kadhi's Courts, Chief Kadhi and Kadhis". KECKRC 10. www.commonlii.org/ke/other/KECKRC/2002/10.html.

Hellsten, Sirkku. 2009. "Afro-Libertarianism and the Social Contract Framework in Post-Colonial Africa: The Case of Post-2007 Elections Kenya". *Thought and Practice: A Journal of the Philosophical Association of Kenya*, New Series, Vol.1 No. 1, June 2009, pp. 127–50. http://ajol.info/index.php/tp/index.

High Court of Kenya. 2006. "The Ilchamus and the Constitution of Kenya", MISC. CIVIL APPLICATION NO.305 OF 2004.

Hitchcock, Robert K. 2002. "'We are the First People': Land, Natural Resources and Identity in the Central Kalahari, Botswana". *Journal of Southern African Studies*, Vol. 28 No. 4, pp. 797–824. http://www.jstor.org/stable/823352.

Hoffman, Peter. 2021. "The Westphalia State System and the Crisis in Ethiopia". *The Elephant*, November 12. https://www.theelephant.info/op-eds/2021/11/12/the-westphalia-state-system-and-the-crisis-in-ethiopia/.

Hunt, Chester L. and Lewis Walker. 1974. *Ethnic Dynamics: Patterns of Intergroup Relations in Various Societies*. Williams, Jr., Robin M. ed. Homewood: The Dorsey Press.

IREC (Independent Review Commission). 2008. "Report on Kenyan 2007 Elections". Nairobi: IREC.

Itebete, P. A. N. 1974. "Language Standardisation in Western Kenya: The Luluyia Experiment". Whiteley, W. H. Ed. 1974. *Language in Kenya*. Nairobi: Oxford University Press, pp. 87–101.

Jenkins, Richard. 1997. *Rethinking Ethnicity: Arguments and Explorations*. London: SAGE Publications.

Johnson, Craig E. 2001. *Meeting the Ethical Chalenges of Leadership: Casting Light or Shadow?* Thousand Oaks: Sage Publications.

Jonyo, Fred. 2002. "Ethnicity in Multi-Party Electoral Politics". Chweya, Ludeki ed. *Electoral Politics in Kenya*. Nairobi: Claripress, pp. 86–107.

Kamau, John. 2000. *The Ogiek: The Ongoing Destruction of a Minority Tribe in Kenya*. Nairobi: Rights News and Features Service. www.Ogiek.org.

Kanyinga, Karuti. 2006. "Governance Institutions and Inequality in Kenya". Society for International Development. *Readings on Inequality in Kenya: Sectoral Dynamics and Perspectives*. Nairobi: Society for International Development, pp. 345–97.

Kassa, Hibist. 2021. "Competing Narratives and the Crisis in Ethiopia". *The Elephant*, September 27. https://www.theelephant.info/features/2021/09/27/competing-narratives-and-the-crisis-in-ethiopia/.

Kellas, James G. 1998. *The Politics of Nationalism and Ethnicity*, Second Edition. London: Macmillan Press Ltd.

Keller, Edmond J. 2002. "Ethnic Federalism, Fiscal Reform, Development and Democracy in Ethiopia". *African Journal of Political Science*, Vol. 7 No. 1, pp. 21–50. http://www.jstor.org/stable/23495556.

Keorapetse, Dithapelo. 2017. "Constitutional review is overdue". Mmegi Blogs, 24 March 2017. http://www.mmegi.bw/index.php?aid=67663&dir=2017/march/24.

Kenya National Bureau of Statistics. 2020. "2019 Kenya Population and Housing Census Volume IV: Distribution of Population by Socio-Economic Characteristics". https://www.kenyagazettepdf.com/tag/2019-kenya-population-and-housing-census-volume-iv-distribution-of-population-by-socio-economic-characteristics/.

KHRC (Kenya Human Rights Commission). 2018. *Ethnicity and Politicization in Kenya*. Nairobi: Kenya Human Rights Commission. https://www.khrc.or.ke/publications/183-ethnicity-and-politicization-in-kenya/file.html.

Kihoro, Wanyiri. 2005. *The Price of Freedom: The Story of Political Resistance in Kenya*. Nairobi: Mvule Africa Publishers.

Kikechi, Biketi. 2010. "Intrigues as Draft Constitution Push Enters Crucial Week". *The Standard on Sunday*, 28 March, 2010. www.eastandard.net.

Kipkorir, B. E. and F. B. Welbourn. 1973. *The Marakwet of Kenya: a Preliminary Study*. Nairobi: East African Literature Bureau.

Kymlicka, Will. 1995. *Multicultural Citizenship: A Liberal Theory of Minority Rights*. Oxford: Clarendon Press.

Lentz, C. 1995. "'Tribalism' and Ethnicity in Africa". *Cahiers des Sciences Humaines*, Vol. 31 No. 2, pp. 303–28.

Lynch, Gabrielle. 2006. "Negotiating Ethnicity: Identity Politics in Contemporary Kenya". *Review of African Political Economy*, Vol. 33 No. 107, pp. 49–65. https://www.jstor.com/stable/4007111.

Mamdani, Mahmood. 2019. "The Trouble With Ethiopia's Ethnic Federalism". *New York Times*, 3 January, 2019. https://www.nytimes.com/2019/01/03/opinion/ethiopia-abiy-ahmed-reforms-ethnic-conflict-ethnic-federalism.html.

Mbaku, John Mukum. 2000. "Minority Rights in Plural Societies". *African Transitions*, June 2000. www.india-seminar.com/2000/490/490%20mbaku.htm.

Mbiti, John S. 1969. *African Religions and Philosophy*. Nairobi: Heineman.

Mbugua, Kioi. 2008. "It's now time to address political/ethnic fault lines". *East African*, 21 January 2008. http://www.theeastafrican.co.ke/news/-/2558/257696 /-/t67dddz/-/index.html.
Mengisteab, Kidane. 2001. "Ethiopia's Ethnic-Based Federalism: 10 Years after". *African Issues*, Vol. 29 No. 1/2: Ethnicity and Recent Democratic Experiments in Africa, pp. 20–25. http://www.jstor.org/stable/1167105.
Miller, David. 2003. *Political Philosophy: A Very Short Introduction*. Oxford: Oxford University Press.
Moi, Daniel T. arap. 1986. *Kenya African Nationalism: Nyayo Philosophy and Principles*. London: Macmillan Publishers Ltd.
Muigai, Githu. 2001. "The Structure and Values of the Independence Constitution". Paper prepared for the Constitution of Kenya Review Commission.
———. 2004. "Jomo Kenyatta and the Rise of the Ethno-Nationalist State in Kenya". Berman, Bruce, Dickson Eyoh and Will Kymlicka eds. *Ethnicity and Democracy in Africa*. Oxford: James Currey, pp. 200–17.
Mulinge, Munyae M. 2008. "Botswana, Africa's Haven of Ethnic Peace and Harmony: Status and Future Prospects". *African Journal of Sociology*, Vol. 4 No. 1. http://journals.uonbi.ac.ke/ajs/article/view/943.
Museveni, Yoweri Kaguta. 1997. *Sowing the Mustard Seed: The Struggle for Freedom and Democracy in Uganda*. London: Macmillan Education Ltd.
Mute, Lawrence M. 2002. "Minority Groups and the Constitutional Review Process". Mute, Lawrence M. and Smokin Wanjala eds. *When the Constitution Begins to Flower: Paradigms for Constitutional Change in Kenya*, Volume 1. Nairobi: Claripress Ltd., pp. 144–84.
Narang, A. S. 2002. "Ethnic Conflicts and Minority Rights". *Economic and Political Weekly*, Vol. 37 No. 27, 6–12 July 2002, pp. 2696–2700. http://www.jstor.org/stable/4412319.
NCIC (National Cohesion and Integration Commission). 2011. *First Ethnic Audit of the Kenya Civil Service*. Nairobi: National Cohesion and Integration Commission.
———. 2012. *Towards national cohesion and unity in Kenya: Ethnic diversity and audit of the civil service*, volume 1. Nairobi: National Cohesion and Integration Commission.
Ndegwa, Alex, and Mutinda Mwanzia. 2010. "Power intrigues that saved the Draft". *The Standard on Saturday*, 3 April 2010. www.eastandard.net.
Ndegwa, S. N. 1997. "Citizenship and Ethnicity: An Examination of Two Transition Moments in Kenyan Politics". *American Political Science Review*, Vol. 91 No. 3, pp. 599–616.
Odinga, Oginga. 1967. *Not Yet Uhuru: An Autobiography*. London: Heinemann.
Oduor, Reginald M. J. 2010. "Research Methodology in Philosophy within an Interdisciplinary and Commercialised African Context: Guarding against Undue Influence from the Social Sciences". *Thought and Practice: A Journal of the Philosophical Association of Kenya (PAK)*, New Series, Vol. 2 No. 1, pp. 87–118. http://ajol.info/index.php/tp/index.

———. 2011. "Ethnic Minorities in Kenya's Emerging Democracy: Philosophical Foundations of their Liberties and Limits". Ph.D. Thesis at the University of Nairobi.

———. 2018. "Nationhood and Statehood: The Impact of a Conflated Discourse on African Polities and their Non-Dominant Ethnic Groups". *Utafiti: Journal of Humanities and Social Sciences*, Vol. 13 No. 2, pp. 45–66. http://journals.udsm.ac.tz/index.php/uj/article/view/2341.

———. 2019a. "Liberal Democracy: An African Critique". *South African Journal of Philosophy*, Vol.38 No.1, pp.108–22. https://doi.org/10.1080/02580136.2019.1583882.

———. 2019b. "The Right to Secession in the Kenyan Context: Philosophical Reflections, with Special Reference to Non-Dominant Ethnic Groups". *Politika*, 5 September 2019. https://www.politika.io/fr/notice/the-right-to-secession-in-the-kenyan-context-philosophical-reflections-with-special.

Ojanga, Thomas O. 2009. "Letter to the Committee of Experts on Constitutional Review".

Okondo, Peter J. H. 1964. "Prospects of Federalism in East Africa". Currie, David P. ed. *Federalism and the New Nations of Africa*. Chicago: The University of Chicago Press, pp. 29–38.

Olumwullah, O. A. L. A. 1990. "Government". Ochieng', William R. Ed. *Themes in Kenyan History*. Nairobi: East African Educational Publishers Ltd.

Omanga, Beauttah. 2010. "How Fears in Uhuru, Ruto Camps Scuttled KIA Talks". *The Standard on Sunday*, 28 March 2010. www.eastandard.net.

Omolo, Ken. 2002. "Political Ethnicity in the Democratisation Process in Kenya". *African Studies*, Vol. 61 No. 2, pp. 209–21. https://www.tandfonline.com/doi/abs/10.1080/0002018022000032938?journalCode=cast20.

Oyugi, W. O., P. Wanyande and C. Odhiambo-Mbai eds. 2003. *The Politics of Transition in Kenya: from KANU to NARC*. Nairobi: Heinrich Boll Foundation.

Preece, Jennifer Jackson. 2001. "Human Rights and Cultural Pluralism: the 'Problem' of Minorities". Draft Prepared for the Cambridge /Dartmouth Conference on the New Human Rights Agenda, Sydney Sussex College, Cambridge, February 18, 2001.

Rawls, John. 1971. *A Theory of Justice*. Oxford: Oxford University Press.

Reilly, Ben and Andrew Reynolds. 1999. *Electoral Systems and Conflict in Divided Societies*. N.P.: National Academies Press. www.nap.edu.

Republic of Kenya. 1963. *Constitution of Kenya*. Nairobi: Government Printer.

———. 1994. *Kenya Population Census, 1989, Vol.1*. Nairobi: Central Bureau of Statistics.

———. 2001. *The 1999 Population and Housing Census*. Nairobi: Central Bureau of Statistics.

———. 2007. *Political Parties Act*, ACT NO. 10 of 2007. http://kenyalaw.org/kl/fileadmin/pdfdownloads/Acts/PoliticalPartiesAct.pdf.

———. 2008. *National Cohesion and Integration Act*, ACT NO. 12 of 2008. http://kenyalaw.org/kl/fileadmin/pdfdownloads/Acts/NationalCohesionandIntegrationAct_No12of2008.pdf.

―――. 2010a. *Constitution of Kenya*. http://kenyalaw.org/kl/index.php?id=398.

―――. 2010b. *The 2009 Kenya Population and Housing Census*. Nairobi: Kenya National Bureau of Statistics.

Sen, Amartya. 2006. *Identity and Violence: The Illusion of Destiny*. New York: W. W. Norton and Co.

Serumaga, Kalundi. 2019. "SPEAK OF ME AS I AM: Ethiopia, Native Identities and the National Question in Africa". *The E Review*, 26 January 2019. https://www.the eastafricanreview.info/op-eds/2019/01/26/speak-of-me-as-i-am.

Shaban, Abdur Rahman Alfa. 2017. "Ethiopia: 2016 Anti-Gov't Protests Claimed over 660 Lives—Report". *Africa News*, 19 April 2017. http://www.africanews .com/2017/04/19/ethiopia-2016-anti-gov-t-protests-claimed-over-660-lives -report//.

Staff Reporter. 2011. "Bushmen boycott Botswana census". *Mail & Guardian*, 27 June 2011. https://mg.co.za/article/2011-06-27-bushmen-boycott-botswana -census.

Sunstein, Cass R. 2001. *Designing Democracy*. New York: Oxford University Press.

Talbott, Strobe. 2000. "Self-determination in an interdependent world". *Foreign Policy*, No. 118, pp. 152–63. https://www.jstor.com/stable/1149676.

Taylor, Charles. 1994. "The Politics of Recognition". Taylor, Charles, K. Anthony Appiah, Jürgen Habermas, Steven C. Rockefeller, Michael Walzer and Susan Wolf. 1994. *Multiculturalism: Examining the Politics of Recognition*. Gutmann, Amy ed. Princeton, NJ: Princeton University Press, pp. 25–73.

United Nations. 1948. *The Universal Declaration of Human Rights*. www.un.org/en /documents/udhr/index.shtml.

―――. 1966a. "International Covenant on Economic, Social and Cultural Rights". www.hrcr.org/docs/Economic&Social/intlconv.html.

―――. 1966b. "International Covenant on Civil and Political Rights". www.hrcr .org/docs/Civil&Political/intlcivpol.html.

Waldron, Jeremy. 1993. *Liberal Rights*. Cambridge: Cambridge University Press.

Walzer, Michael. 1983. *Spheres of Justice: A Defense of Pluralism and Equality*. New York: Basic Books, Inc.

Wamala, Edward. 2004. "Government by Consensus: An Analysis of a Traditional Form of Democracy". Wiredu, Kwasi ed. *A Companion to African Philosophy*. Malden, MA: Blackwell Publishing Ltd., pp. 435–42.

Werbner, Richard. 2002. "Cosmopolitan ethnicity, entrepreneurship and the nation: Minority elites in Botswana". *Journal of Southern African Studies*, Vol. 28 No. 4, pp. 731–53. http://www.jstor.org/stable/823349.

Wiredu, Kwasi. 1996. *Cultural Universals and Particulars: An African Perspective*. Bloomington: Indiana University Press.

WorldAtlas.com. 2018. "The Major Ethnic Groups of Botswana". https://www.world atlas.com/articles/the-major-ethnic-groups-of-botswana.html.

Wrong, Michela. 2009. *It's Our Turn to Eat*. London: Fourth Estate.

Epilogue

Reginald M. J. Oduor

The authors of the chapters in this volume have raised and attempted to answer numerous pertinent questions about future directions of democratization in African states. Nevertheless, upon reflection, it becomes clear that they have focused on two main questions. *First*, there is the question as to whether or not there is a rational basis for the endeavor to replace liberal democracy with indigenous African models of democracy. The four chapters in Section one have largely answered it in the affirmative, while the two in Section 2 have answered it in the negative. *Second*, there is the question of what kinds of alternative models of democracy could more adequately meet the needs of African peoples than does liberal democracy, and the eight chapters in Section 3 have offered diverse answers to it.

It is my earnest hope that this volume will stimulate further scholarship on new paths to democratisation in African states from a wide range of disciplinary perspectives in the humanities and social sciences. This venture is an integral part of the wider decolonising project. Indeed, a governance model does not stand alone—it arises, and is sustained, within a specific economic system, which also determines the legal system, but, perhaps more important, the mode of knowledge production. In the case of contemporary African states, that economic system is, by and large, the capitalist one foisted on them by Western imperialism, and lately reinforced by the rise of neo-liberalism[1] whose tenets were articulated in the so-called Washington Consensus.[2]

Furthermore, as Amin (2014) observes, "Economic 'alienation' is the specific form of capitalism which governs the reproduction of society in its totality and not only the reproduction of its economic system. The law of value governs not only capitalist economic life, but all social life in this society". What Amin, following Karl Marx, describes above is what I call the ecosystem of Western imperialism driven by capitalist ideology, theory, and practice: this is what Immanuel Wallerstein (2011) and Samir Amin (2014) refer to as the modern world system, and many in our day refer to as the capitalist political economy (Manning and Gills eds. 2011). Thus, liberal democracy, having arisen in the context of the eighteenth-century Western industrial revolution, espouses capitalist values, and thereby seeks to commoditise and monetise politics in terms such as demand and supply, and thus the high premium it places on elections and opinion polls.

Besides, going forward, debates on the future of democratisation in Africa will need to pay close attention to the advent of the so-called Fourth Industrial Revolution ("4IR"), characterised by artificial intelligence, robotics and blockchain (Johnson and Markey-Towler 2021; Donovan 2021). This has exposed the inherent weakness of liberal democracy that may result in its replacement by a perverted technocracy in which an elite ownership of large tech companies controls not only the global economy, but also global politics driven by manipulative narratives and the silencing of contrary opinions. 4IR compromises the privacy of citizens through 'big data' that enables large tech companies to create detailed individual profiles of their customers for 'targeted marketing', including the dissemination of manipulative political messaging such as the one for which the infamous Cambridge Analytica stood accused in several elections and referenda around the world.

Indeed, people in Africa are already under the gaze of the technologies of the Fourth Industrial Revolution (4IR): their smartphones, with their "Location" function on, are beaming data about their movements to networks for sale to high-tech transport companies desperate to gather information about traffic flow in cities; unknown to them, phone apps are accessing their microphones and cameras, with the real possibility of their conversations and actions being monitored; their emails and social media posts are being monitored for information about them that is sold to marketers, advertisers, and politicians who use it for targeted advertisements; their faces are increasingly being scanned by cameras connected to face-recognition software ostensibly to enhance security, but with the real possibility of surveillance for purposes unknown to them (Oduor 2021).

In sum, the technologies of the Fourth Industrial Revolution expose humanity to the possibility of an unprecedented tyranny in the fashion of the scenario that George Orwell draws in his dystopian novel, *1984,* where the elite party leadership has a "thought police" which deploys all manner of technology to keep tabs on members of the "outer party", including "telescreens" in homes and in public places that "listen to" and "see" all that the citizens say and do round the clock—reminiscent of the capabilities of the smart phone. One parody of the famous American Civil War–era song, "The

Battle Hymn of the Republic" (commonly known as "Mine Eyes have Seen the Glory" and known by its chorus "Glory, Glory Hallelujah . . .") circulating on WhatsApp before the 2020 U.S. elections, described the current 4IR surveillance capabilities as follows:

> Our right to privacy is gone, devices are the spies.
> For government surveillance those are now the ears and eyes.
> They use the corporate data, no subpoenas, no surprise,
> And still we don't catch on.

Even the line between 'traditional media' and 'social media' is increasingly becoming undiscernible from the point of view of the co-ordinated manipulative political messaging. Besides, the merger of traditional media companies has resulted in a situation in which public debate is subtly manipulated by privileging certain points of view and suppressing others. Elsewhere in the parody quoted in the previous paragraph it states:

> Fifty companies provided all the news in '84,
> Now there's only six, it's forty-four less than it was before.
> A media consensus now exists for every war,
> and the wars go on and on.

Thus, while the present volume focuses on context-relevant African models of democracy for the twenty-first century, its subject cannot be delinked from the politics of knowledge production. Indeed, Western imperialism systematically marginalised, and in some cases obliterated, indigenous African inventions and innovations in areas such as governance, philosophical traditions, medicine, agriculture, environmental conservation, and creative works, terming them as "primitive" or "savage". In his seminal work, *The Invention of Africa*, V. Y. Mudimbe (1988) illustrates that what the West presents as objective knowledge about Africa is a centuries-old discourse of domination that, through the biased works of Western missionaries, anthropologists, and colonial administrators, presents Africa as "primitive" and "savage", and this is, tragically, the basis of scholarship on Africa even in the so-called postcolonial era. Mudimbe goes on to inform us that the terms '*colonialism*' and '*colonization*' basically mean 'organization' or 'arrangement', having been derived from the latin word *colere*, meaning 'to cultivate' or 'to design'. He further notes that Western colonialism organizes and transforms non-European areas into fundamentally European constructs (Mudimbe 1988, 1). He goes on to write:

> It is possible to use three main keys to account for the modulations and methods representative of colonial organization: the procedures of acquiring, distributing, and exploiting lands in colonies; the policies of domesticating natives; and the manner of managing ancient organizations and implementing new modes of production. Thus, three complementary hypotheses and actions emerge: the domination of physical space, the reformation of natives' minds, and the integration of local economic histories into the Western perspective. These complementary projects constitute what might be called the colonizing structure, which completely embraces the physical, human, and spiritual aspects of the colonizing experience. (Mudimbe 1988, 2)

Furthermore, in *Epistemic Injustice: Power and the Ethics of Knowing*, Miranda Fricker (2009) argues that there is a distinctively epistemic type of injustice, in which someone is wronged specifically in his or her capacity as a 'know-er'. She distinguishes two forms of epistemic injustice—testimonial injustice (the injustice that a speaker suffers in receiving deflated credibility from the hearer owing to identity prejudice on the hearer's part), and hermeneutical injustice (suffered by people who participate unequally in the practices through which social meanings are generated). The fact that the West consistently presents liberal democracy as the only viable model of democracy, and thereby ascribes universality to it, is an act of both forms of epistemic injustice identified by Fricker.

Moreover, in the preface to his celebrated work, *Epistemologies of the south: Justice against Epistemicide*, Boaventura de Sousa Santos (2014) indicates that he seeks to defend three important postulates: "First, the understanding of the world by far exceeds the Western understanding of the world. Second, there is no global social justice without global cognitive justice. Third, the emancipatory transformations in the world may follow grammars and scripts other than those developed by Western-centric critical theory, and such diversity should be valorized". As the word "valorized" in the last quotation above indicates, Santos (2014) is clearly drawing from Michel Foucault's corpus on knowledge production. Indeed, in *The Archaeology of Knowledge*, Foucault (2002) argues that systems of thought and knowledge ("epistemes" or "discursive formations") are governed by rules (beyond those of grammar and logic) that operate beneath the consciousness of individual subjects, and that define a system of conceptual possibilities that determines the boundaries of thought and language use in a given domain and period.

Thus, the process of decolonisation must entail the dismantling of economic, legal, political, and knowledge-production structures of Western domination that goes way beyond what has been correctly referred to as the independence of flags and anthems. It is heartening to note that we have already witnessed decolonising efforts through ventures such as Odera Oruka's sage philosophy project (Oruka ed. 1991), the use of indigenous African languages in creative writing and in philosophy (Thiong'o 1986; Wiredu 1996, 81–104; Wiredu 1998; Jeffers ed. 2013), and Wiredu's conceptual decolonisation project (Wiredu 1996, 136–44).

Yet decolonisation always comes at a high cost, not just in terms of casualties on the streets and in the jungles, but also among scholars. Thus several intellectuals who have raised their voices against dictatorship that rides on the back of global capitalism have borne the brunt of state violence: Samir Amin was forced into exile from his native Egypt in 1960 for his Marxist but anti-Stalinist views; Paulo Freire's success in teaching Brazilian peasants how to read landed him in prison and a subsequent long and painful exile; Ngugi wa Thiong'o spent time as a detainee without trial in a Kenyan maximum security prison for organising a peasants' theatre group to perform his anti-capitalist plays, and endured decades of exile; Walter Rodney's exposition of the damage inflicted on Africa by European mercantilism that evolved into capitalism resulted in his imprisonment in his native land of Guyana, and also in his assassination through a car bomb blast in Georgetown, Guyana; Claude Ake was assassinated through a planned plane crush during the autocratic reign of Sani Abacha in Nigeria; Ken Saro-Wiwa was hanged by the Sani Abacha regime in Nigeria, and Wole Soyinka escaped Abacha's murderous hand by a whisker, and later went into decades of exile. The list is much longer than this. Yet the only option to the decolonising project is the perpetuation of colonialism, albeit in its camouflaged form ("neo-colonialism")—a phenomenon so pernicious that it has already reduced African states to the shells of what they were at the dawn of political independence about six decades ago. Let the discourse on authentic decolonisation continue!

NOTES

1. "Neo-liberalism" is widely understood as the late twentieth-century move away from welfare state models towards free market economic policies initially associated with U.K. Prime Minister Margaret Thatcher and U.S. President Ronald Riegan. Neo-liberalism mainly made its debut in African states with the so-called Structural Adjustment Programmes (SAPs) imposed on these states in the early 1990s by the Bretton Woods Institutions (the World Bank and the International Monetary Fund).

2. The Washington Consensus is a set of ten economic policy prescriptions promoted for crisis-ridden economically disadvantaged countries by several institutions based in Washington, D.C., chiefly the World Bank, the International Monetary Fund (IMF), and the United States Department of the Treasury. The prescriptions were grounded on the conviction that "development" strategies should be anchored on

"free markets" that would allegedly promote "economic growth" that would "trickle down" to benefit everyone (see Gore 2000).

REFERENCES

Amin, Samir. 2014. "Understanding the Political Economy of Contemporary Africa". *Africa Development*, 39 (1): 15–36.

Donovan, Paul. 2021. *Profit and Prejudice: The Luddites of the Fourth Industrial Revolution*. New York: Routledge.

Foucault, Michel. 2002 [1969]. *The Archaeology of Knowledge*. Smith, A.M. Sheridan trans. New York: Routledge.

Fricker, Miranda. 2009. *Epistemic Injustice: Power and the Ethics of Knowing*. Oxford: Oxford University Press.

Gore, Charles. 2000. "The Rise and Fall of the Washington Consensus as a Paradigm for Developing Countries". *World Development*, Vol. 28 Issue 5, pp. 789–804. https://www.sciencedirect.com/science/article/pii/S0305750X99001606.

Jeffers, Chike ed. 2013. *Listening to Ourselves: A Multilingual Anthology of African Philosophy*. New York: SUNY Press.

Johnson, Nicholas, and Brendan Markey-Towler. 2021. *Economics of the Fourth Industrial Revolution: Internet, Artificial Intelligence and Blockchain*. New York: Routledge.

Manning, Patrick, and Barry K. Gills. eds. 2011. *Andre Gunder Frank and Global Development: Visions, Remembrances and Explorations*. Oxford: Routledge.

Mudimbe, V. Y. 1988. *The Invention of Africa: Gnosis, Philosophy, and the Order of Knowledge*. Bloomington: Indiana University Press.

Oduor, Reginald M. J. 2021. "The Fourth Industrial Revolution: Inclusiveness, Affordability, Cultural Identity, and Ethical Orientation". Filosofia Theoretica, Vol. 10 No. 3, December, pp. 57–77. DOI: https://dx.doi.org/10.4314/ft.v10i3.5.

Oruka, H. Odera. Ed. 1991. Sage Philosophy: Indigenous Thinkers and Modern Debate on African Philosophy. Nairobi: ACTS Press.

Santos, Boaventura de Sousa. 2014. *Epistemologies of the south: Justice against Epistemicide*. New York: Routledge.

Thiong'o, Ngugi wa. 1986. *Decolonising the Mind: The Politics of Language in African Literature*. Nairobi: Heinemann Kenya.

Wallerstein, Immanuel. 2011. *The Modern World-System IV*. Berkeley: University of California Press.

Wiredu, Kwasi. 1996. *Cultural Universals and Particulars: An African Perspective*. Bloomington: Indiana University Press.

———. 1998. "Toward Decolonizing African Philosophy and Religion". *African Studies Quarterly: The Online Journal for African Studies*, Vol. 1 No. 4. http://web.africa.ufl.edu/asq/v1/4/3.htm.

Index

Achebe, Chinua, 201, 204
Acholi, 213, 215–18, 221–22, 224–25, 227–31
Africa, 32, 137;
  East, 83-84, 89, 203, 221, 230
  North, 202–3
  Partition of, 42, 267
  Southern, 203, 219
  West, 93, 149, 174, 182, 184, 203
African:
  Communalism, 19, 23, 108, 129, 175, 188, 202, 237, 259
  Philosophy, 279
  socialism, 13, 18–20, 24, 185, 218
Afro-Libertarianism, 17, 23, 241
Ajei, Martin Odei, 154, 160
Akan, 6, 137–39, 141–45, 147, 149, 174, 185, 198, 208n1
Ake, Claude, 71, 181, 243, 279
American, 29, 91, 130, 221
Angola, 182, 203
Anthropology, 81;
  Archaeology, 84
  Biology, 81, 86, 94
  Cultural/social, 88
  linguistics, 82-83
Aristotle, 72
Asia, 15–16, 32, 191, 203

Athens, 32, 71, 74, 180–81, 192, 193
authoritarianism, 15-16, 23, 30, 41, 45, 86

Bell, Daniel A., 2
Bemba, Jean-Pierre, 59
Buhari, Mohammadu, 121
Botswana, 203, 237, 260–62, 267n2
Bottom-up, 220
British, 29, 186, 200, 204, 251
Busia, K.A., 181, 187

Cameroon, 2
Capitalism, 13–15, 19, 24, 42, 56, 165–67, 169, 193, 242, 275, 279
Central African Republic, 2
China, 15, 29, 62, 107,
Christianity, 84, 203, 219, 226–27, 229–30
civilisation, 4, 30–31, 38, 42, 149, 153, 166, 214, 249
Cold War, 1, 57, 72, 165, 174, 192, 197
colonialism, 8, 36, 41–46, 81, 88, 90, 125, 153, 161, 173, 176, 183, 196, 200, 203, 206, 214, 216, 219–20, 235, 237, 252, 277–79
communitarianism, 6, 159, 172

community, 159, 160–61, 170–71, 173–74, 186, 192, 196, 198, 202, 205, 226, 249, 251
compatriotism, 171–72, 176n6
Congo, 2, 5, 55, 59, 68–74, 103, 130, 153, 267n2
consensus, 7, 21, 41, 70–71, 160, 173, 180, 184–86, 206, 218
Constitution, 1–2, 21, 59–60, 63, 72–73, 92, 154, 157, 169, 201, 208n2, 220, 235, 237, 240–41, 245, 249–55, 259, 262, 264, 266, 267n3
Cosmopolitanism, 172
cultural identity, 237–38, 240–41, 243, 246, 249, 251
culture, 1–2, 4, 6–7, 28, 37, 47, 50, 81, 92–94, 97, 102–3, 106, 124, 128, 153, 155, 161, 168, 170, 173, 175–76, 179, 184, 188, 191–92, 194–95, 202–4, 206–8, 208n1, 213, 215, 220, 226–27, 238, 241–42, 244, 248–49, 261

Dahl, Robert, 181
de-colonisation, 13, 154, 275, 278–79
democracy, 1, 3, 5, 21, 27–28, 30, 32, 41, 44, 46, 50, 57–58, 70, 72, 74, 81–84, 91–92, 94, 105, 117, 122, 126, 130, 132–33, 137–39, 149, 154–57, 161, 166, 169–70, 179, 181–82, 187, 191, 195, 213–15, 217–19, 251, 257–58;
collegial, 123
communitarian, 153–57, 159–61
consensual, 46, 49–50, 137–38, 180, 184–86, 198, 206, 214, 220
consociational, 129, 133
co-operative collegial, 6, 117, 119, 126–30, 133
constitutional, 138, 235
culture-bound, 191
deliberative, 120
direct, 180
home-grown African models of, 1–2,
indigenous African models of, 5–6, 41, 46–48, 94, 97, 103, 111, 124, 132, 153–55, 162, 165–66, 170–72, 174–75, 185, 188, 236, 256, 275
liberal, 1–2, 6–8, 13–16, 17, 19–20, 24, 41, 45, 47–48, 50, 55, 57, 68, 71–74, 81, 98, 101–5, 108, 110–11, 117–22, 124–26, 129, 132–33, 138, 153–61, 165–71 173–75, 179, 182–84, 191–95, 198–99, 201–2, 204, 206–8, 213, 235–38, 240, 250, 256, 260, 263, 275–76, 278
majoritarian, 16, 137–38, 160, 173, 179, 185–88, 198, 200–1, 217
Marxist, 183
Monolithic, 191, 198, 206–7
multi-party, 1, 6, 48–50, 58, 61, 70–71, 117–22, 124–26, 128, 132–33, 137–40, 147–48, 154, 157–58, 183–84, 187, 216, 235, 241, 258–59, 263
no-party, 133, 180, 185, 198, 258
one-party, 183, 235, 254
participatory, 90, 20
particular, 191–98
social, 157, 183–84
Third World, 192–93
universal, 191–98, 207
Democratic Electoral Filter-ism, 128
democratisation, 1, 28, 41, 56, 58, 97, 239–40, 275–76
deliberation, 179, 186–87
design, 7, 81, 219–20
development, 13–14, 20, 24, 44, 118–19, 166, 194, 243
devolution, 255–56
Dewey, John, 109
dictatorship, 102, 139, 153, 155, 218, 224, 254
Durkheim, Emile, 181

education, 43, 90, 97, 106, 125, 176, 202, 213, 219, 227
elections, 2, 5, 7, 17, 29, 49, 55–60, 61, 64–65, 67–74, 118, 122–23, 129–30, 132–33, 139–40, 146, 149, 154, 157–58, 160, 165, 170, 173, 179, 181–82,

185, 208n1, 216, 218, 231, 235, 244, 248, 252–54, 259, 263–64, 276
electocracy, 56–57, 59, 69, 74
electoral fundamentalism, 73
elite, 27, 35, 74, 120, 129, 265–66, 276
Ethiopia, 230, 237, 260, 262–67
ethnicity, 6–8, 16, 20, 21, 23–24, 29, 60, 121, 124, 128–29, 132, 139, 143, 167–69, 171, 173, 179, 187, 198, 202–4, 235–39, 241, 242–52, 255, 257–62, 266–67
European Union, 16, 60

Fanon, Frantz, 3–4
Fayemi, Ademola Kazeem, 194–95
federalism, 7, 59, 235–37, 249, 251, 254–56, 260, 262–64, 266–67
female, 85–92, 105, 109, 143, 213, 215, 221, 223, 230
feminism, 5, 81–82
followership, 5, 97–100, 102–111;
  classification of, 101, 108
  socialisation of, 104
Foucault, Michel, 278
France, 29, 138, 156, 204
Freud, Sigmund, 107
Fukuyama, Francis, 4, 56, 68, 117, 132, 154, 156–57, 161, 165–68, 172, 195–97

Gandhi, Mahatma, 2, 70
Gender, 97, 102, 109–110, 228
Germany, 60, 156, 204, 222
Gerontocracy, 91, 218–19
Ghana, 2, 139–40, 144, 146–47, 149, 155
globalisation, 13, 19, 24, 236
governance, 44, 46, 58, 63, 70, 72, 81, 109, 117–18, 125, 132–33, 137, 154–56, 159, 162, 165, 170, 175, 182–86, 191, 194, 198, 206–7, 217, 235, 256, 277
government, 49, 58, 69, 73–75, 83, 108, 117, 119, 123–24, 126–27, 130, 132–33, 156, 158, 179–85, 193–95, 201, 213, 215, 246–47, 254–56, 265;
  central, 255–56
  coalition, 184
  county, 169, 173, 255
  federal, 256, 266
  local, 128
  National, 168
  Regional, 29, 263
Greece, 36, 84, 183
groundswell, 7, 213–16, 219–20, 229–31
Gyekye, Kwame, 155, 158–62

Hegel, Georg Wilhelm Friedrich, 165, 167–68
hegemony, 4–5, 13, 42, 46–47, 57, 81, 132
history, 81, 93, 153, 155, 161, 165, 167, 173, 184, 207, 213, 219–20, 224, 231, 237, 249, 251
Hobbes, Thomas, 14, 182, 193
Hountondji, Paulin J., 3–4
Huntington, Samuel, 16, 73, 138, 166, 196

identity, 7, 202, 204–6, 208, 226, 237, 243, 245–47, 250
ideology, 2, 4, 13, 17, 23–24, 125, 154, 161, 165, 167–68, 170, 184, 195, 198
Igbo, 123–24, 133n2, 134n3, 199–201
independence, 1–2, 4, 15, 21, 22, 28–30, 44–46, 65, 72–73, 155, 157, 162, 168, 173, 188, 204, 216, 218, 225, 235, 252–53, 255, 278
India, 15, 29–30, 36, 203
indigeneity, 1, 3–4, 27, 43–44, 166, 170–71, 174–76, 184, 203, 213, 219, 221, 229, 245
inequality, 34, 256
intellectuals, 28, 37–38
Internally displaced people's (IDP) camps, 224–25
International Monetary Fund, 14, 62, 73, 279n2
Islam, 92, 202–3, 227
Italy, 29, 156
Invectives, 142, 147

James, William, 31
justice, 15, 154, 167, 172, 175, 188, 196, 202

Kabila, Joseph, 59, 62, 64–65, 67
Kalenjin, 230, 246, 248
Kant, Immanuel, 14, 17, 198
Kaunda, Kenneth, 20, 24
Kenya, 2, 7, 23, 81, 87–89, 91–92, 120, 122, 153, 169, 227, 230, 235–37, 239, 242, 245–48, 250–52, 255–56, 267
Kenyatta, Jomo, 245, 255
Kenyatta, Uhuru, 255
Kikuyu, 246, 248, 254
Kisii, 246
Kiswahili, 83, 174, 176
Kresse, Kai, 174
Kymlicka, Will, 242

Land, 43, 242
Language, 109, 126, 137–38, 142, 144, 242–43, 247, 261
Latin America, 2, 27, 29
leadership, 5, 35, 97–100, 102–11, 124, 126, 130, 188, 218
legitimacy, 69–70, 173
Lewin, Michael, 166
liberation, 44, 47
liberalism, 156, 159, 161, 167, 170, 182, 193;
 classical, 193
 economic, 4, 15, 19–20, 23, 193
 political, 4, 15, 19–20, 23, 193
 welfare, 193
Lijphart, Arendt, 129, 133
Lincoln, Abraham, 159, 181
Locke, John, 14, 73, 193, 201
Lumumba, Patrice, 59
Lumumba-Kasongo, Tukumbi, 2, 71–72, 156
Luo, 246, 248, 252, 254
Luhya, 246, 248

Maasai, 89–91, 227, 246
Machiavelli, Niccolo, 126
Magufuli, John Pombe, 22
majorities, 6, 48–49, 58, 60, 65, 83, 132, 153, 158, 179, 186, 197–98, 242, 247
male, 86–88, 90–91, 93, 104, 109, 180–81, 216, 218
Mamdani, 266
Marx, Karl, 183, 275
Matolino, Bernard, 153–54, 160
Mazrui, Ali, 18, 155
Mbembe, Achille, 3
Mbiti, John S., 159, 239
media, 140, 149;
 electronic, 90
 mass, 92
 social, 147, 277
 traditional, 147, 277
 Western, 204
men, 109, 111, 143, 228
Menkiti, Ifeanyi, 159
Mignolo, Walter D. 47
Mill, John Stuart, 5, 130, 193
minorities, 6–7, 16, 27, 34–36, 38, 59, 90, 129, 132, 161, 167, 179, 184, 186, 188, 197–98, 235, 243, 249–50, 253–54, 261–62
Moi, Daniel arap, 245, 253
moral authority, 45
Motlanthe, Kgalema, 159
Mozambique, 22, 182
Mudimbe, V.Y., 277
Mugabe, Robert, 157
Muhammed, Murtala, 119
Museveni, Yoweri, 148, 168, 218, 224, 245, 258

Namibia, 203
nation-state, 15, 94, 168–69, 171–72, 174, 237, 244–46
Neo-colonialism, 8, 46–47, 279
Neo-liberalism, 13, 16, 23, 275, 279n1

Nigeria, 2, 6, 119, 121–22, 125, 130–31, 153, 155, 201, 205, 208n2, 256
Nkrumah, Kwame, 1, 15, 20, 24, 46–47, 139, 155, 159
Non-governmental organisations (NGOs), 225, 260
Nyerere, Julius K., 1, 15, 20–21, 24, 124, 129, 155, 159, 185
Nzongola-Ntalaja, 65–67

Obasanjo, Olusegun, 120, 148
Obeng, Samuel, 141, 144
Odinga, Raila, 122
Oduor, Reginald M.J., 47, 101, 125, 153, 156, 162
Offor, Francis, 154
Oloka-Onyango, 58
One-party states, 1, 56, 155, 185
Opposition, 58, 60, 62, 65–68, 123, 133, 138, 147, 235, 263, 265
Oyo Mesi, 199–200, 208n2

Pan-Africanism, 3
parliament, 57, 62–63, 70, 73, 83, 85, 92, 123–24, 130, 139, 168, 201, 216, 243, 254, 257, 262–64
patriarchy, 16, 81, 86
p'Bitek, Okot, 229
Plato, 120–21, 191, 197–98
policy, 149, 182, 184, 240
political parties, 22–23, 48, 58, 61, 65, 70–71, 73, 120, 122, 126, 130, 132, 139, 147, 158, 160, 183–85, 216, 250–51, 276
political philosophy, 18, 126, 236
political science, 18, 126
Popper, Karl, 167
Portugal, 156
post-colonial, 1, 3, 6–7, 14, 120, 126, 153–62, 169, 187–88, 219, 222, 230, 237–38, 245, 266
post-modernism, 82
post-war, 55, 58, 69, 74
poverty, 23, 32, 57, 62

power, 102, 104, 117, 119–21, 123, 125, 130, 132, 137–39, 179, 185–86, 214, 244
Praeg, Leonhard, 175
pre-colonial, 3, 47, 49, 155–57, 159, 161–62, 171, 191, 218, 256

Racism, 43, 90
Ramose, Mogobe Bernard, 47–48
Rawls, John, 251
Recall, power of, 201–2
representation, 49, 57, 70, 83, 124, 130, 132–33, 157, 160, 183, 185–86, 200, 204, 250, 258
revolution, 36–37, 204, 220, 231;
    American, 156, 194
    Fourth Industrial, 276
    Industrial, 14, 276
    English, 156, 194
    French, 36, 156, 165, 194
Rights, 124, 156, 158, 160–61, 167, 169, 174, 182–83, 187–88, 193, 201, 227, 241, 242–43, 259, 261;
    bill of, 73, 169, 240, 259–60
    cultural group, 3, 7–8, 237, 243, 249, 251;
    human, 14, 154, 157, 160, 167, 179, 186, 194–95, 240
Rodney, Walter, 3, 279
Rome, 31, 36, 72, 84–85
Rousseau, Jean-Jacques, 14, 72, 109–11
Russia, 15, 29–30

secession, 259, 265
Seko, Mobutu Sese, 68, 73
Self-determination, 46
Sen, Amartya, 196–97, 243
Senghor, Léopold Sédar, 155, 159
Serumaga, Kalundi, 266
Sithole, Ndambaningi, 185
slavery, 3, 84, 203
Smith, Adam, 14
social contract, 14
socialism, 57

socialisation, 175
the Solomon Islands, 28–29
South Africa, 15, 22, 175, 182, 203
Sovereignty, 45, 71, 167
the Soviet Union, 29, 197
Spain, 29, 31
Structural Adjustment Programmes, 14, 20
subalternity, 3

Tanzania, 21
Taylor, Charles, 238–39
tolerance, 7, 14, 22, 167, 187–88
Toure, Sekou, 1
Toynbee, 30–31, 33–35, 38
traditions, 3, 16, 20, 27–28, 30, 38, 137–38, 144, 149, 153, 155, 159–62, 168, 185, 195, 198, 202–3, 214, 227–31, 236, 277
Trickle-down, 220
Troop formation, 86, 92
Trump, Donald, 140
Tshisekedi, Etienne, 62–64
Tshisekedi, Félix, 66
Tutu, Desmond, 172
Tyranny, 101

Ubuntu, 162, 172, 174–75, 176n7
Uganda, 23, 92, 97, 103, 107–8, 148, 153, 168, 213, 216–18, 222, 225, 229–30, 245, 258, 267n2
United Kingdom, 138, 156
United Nations, 14, 60–62, 240, 259
United States of America, 30, 62, 68, 73, 88–90, 122, 147, 167, 182

values, 4, 6–7, 14, 16–17, 20, 23–24, 27–28, 30, 32, 34, 39, 149, 153, 157, 160–61, 166–67, 169, 171–73, 175–76, 179, 184, 196, 202–5, 236, 250
Verbal:
 Abuse, 144
 aggression, 6, 137–41, 144–45, 147, 149
 conflicts, 146
 discipline, 137–38, 141, 145, 147
violence, 5, 27–28, 35–37, 49, 56, 58, 60, 69–70, 130, 263–64, 267

Walzer, Michael, 157, 160–61, 241
Wamala, Edward, 186, 257–58
Wamba-dia-Wamba, Ernest, 46, 48, 56–57, 155, 195
weddings, 213, 215–16, 219–22, 224–30
Western imperialism, 7, 46–47, 192, 201, 203, 267, 275–76
Wiredu, Kwasi, 48–49, 153, 158–60, 180, 185, 188, 198, 206, 208n1, 258, 279
women, 92–93, 104–5, 109–11, 143, 228
World Bank, 14, 62, 73, 279n2
Wrong, Michella, 236

Yoruba, 84, 196, 205

Zambia, 22
Zimbabwe, 153, 157, 182, 203

About the Contributors

Moses Oludare Aderibigbe earned his B.A. degree at Ogun State University (now Olabisi Onabanjo University), Ago-Iwoye, Nigeria, and his M.A. and Ph.D. from the University of Ibadan, Nigeria. He is the head of Department of General Studies, Federal University of Technology, Akure, Nigeria. He has research interest in social and political philosophy, as well as in ethics. His exposure to a training in the fall of 2016 on research ethics at the National Institute of Environmental Health Sciences (NIH), in the United States, stimulated his current work on research ethics in Nigeria.

Emmanuel Ifeanyi Ani holds a B.A. in philosophy from the University of Ibadan, Nigeria, a B.Phil. in philosophy from the Pontificia Università Urbaniana Roma (Urban Pontifical University, Rome), Italy, and an M.A. and a Ph.D. in philosophy from Nnamdi Azikiwe University, Nigeria. He is senior lecturer in philosophy at the University of Ghana, and the University's external assessor on logic and critical thinking for affiliate institutions. He has been a visiting scholar at the Centre for Deliberative Democracy and Global Governance, University of Canberra, Australia. His research interests are in African philosophy, political philosophy with special focus on consensual democracy and deliberative democracy, as well as philosophy of mind and philosophy of religion.

Christine Buluma holds B.A. and M.A. degrees in philosophy from the University of Nairobi. She is a corporate accounts executive with a rich background in philosophy, political science, and psychology. She has served as a counsellor at Mahero Secondary School and is a member of the National Youth Guidance and Counselling Association University of Nairobi Chapter.

She is currently conducting a research project on "Poverty, Teenage Pregnancy and Patriarchy in South Nyanza".

Munamato Chemhuru holds a B.A. in geography and philosophy, a B.A. special honours in philosophy, and an M.A. in philosophy, all from the University of Zimbabwe. He obtained his Ph.D. in philosophy from the University of Johannesburg. He is associate professor in philosophy at Great Zimbabwe University and a senior research associate in philosophy in the faculty of humanities at the University of Johannesburg (2018–2023). He is also an Alexander von Humboldt Fellow in the department of philosophy and systematic pedagogics at the Katholische Universität Eichstätt-Ingolstadt, KU, Eichstätt, Germany (2020–2022). His research interests are in social and political philosophy. He has just published the book *Environmental Justice in African Philosophy* (Routledge, 2022).

Tayo Raymond Ezekiel Eegunlusi obtained his B.A. degree in philosophy from the University of Ado Ekiti, Nigeria (now Ekiti State University), and his M.A. and Ph.D. in philosophy from the University of Ibadan, Nigeria. He is lecturer in the department of general studies, at the Institute of Technology-Enhanced-Learning and Digital Humanities (INTEDH), Federal University of Technology, Akure, Nigeria. He is a member of the Philosophical Association of Nigeria (PAN), American Philosophical Association (APA), and International Society for Philosophers (ISFP). His research interests are in social and political philosophy, ethics, and the philosophy of the global economic order. He contributes to various community development initiatives by facilitating educative programmes involving non-governmental organisations (NGOs).

Emefiena Ezeani holds a B.Sc. in ICT and development studies from the University of East London, a B.Phil. in philosophy from the Urban University, Rome, a postgraduate certificate in education from the University of London's Institute of Education, an M.A. in education and international development from the University of London (XE "London"), a Ph.D. in social policy and professional studies specialising in political science from the University of Hull, U.K., and a Ph.D. in education specialising in philosophy of education from the University of Port Harcourt, Nigeria. He is senior lecturer in the department of political science, Alex Ekwueme Federal University (A.E-FUNAI), Ebonyi State, Nigeria. He has research interests in politics (specifically party politics, comparative democracy, and cooperative democracy), development, education, culture, religion, and philosophy. An advocate of social justice (XE "Justice") and biodiversity, he also devotes time to promoting endangered languages, especially Igbo, which is his own mother tongue.

Sirkku Hellsten was senior researcher at the Nordic Africa Institute, Uppsala, Sweden, affiliate professor of social and moral philosophy at the University of Helsinki, Finland, and counsellor for governance and human rights, Embassy of Finland, Nairobi, Kenya. She was previously professor of philosophy at the University of Dar es Salaam, Tanzania, and director of the Centre for the Study of Global Ethics, University of Birmingham, U.K. Prior to that, she was a Fulbright Scholar at the Ethics Center at the University of South Florida. She was also the founding editor and later co-editor of the *Journal of Global Ethics*. She published widely on a number of topics, but probably most prominently on the ideological, value, and gender dimensions of the contemporary political crises in Africa.

Dennis Masaka holds a B.A. dual honours in philosophy and religious studies, an M.A. in philosophy, both from the University of Zimbabwe, and a Ph.D. in philosophy from the University of South Africa. He is senior lecturer in philosophy at Great Zimbabwe University, Zimbabwe. He is also research fellow in the Department of Philosophy at the University of the Free State, Bloemfontein, South Africa. His research interests include African philosophy, philosophy of liberation, and epistemic justice.

Thomas Menamparampil, born in Kerala, India, in 1936, is the most senior contributor to this volume. He is retired from his teaching position at Assam University, India. He lives in Guwahati (Asssam, India), and continues to be active in the intellectual world. He studied in Calcutta University and Shillong. His research interests are in history, culture, ethnic diversity, peace, reconciliation, and ethics. He has been in the field of education and social work during the last more than forty years and has been involved in several initiatives for peace. In recent years, he has presented papers in several universities in Asia, Africa and North America on ethical values, healing of historic memories, and inter-ethnic and inter-cultural understanding.

Kisemei Mutisya holds a B.A. in political science from the University of Nairobi, as well as an M.A. in political science and an M.Sc. in public administration from the University of the Western Cape in South Africa. Before joining the University of Nairobi as an adjunct faculty member at the Department of Political Science, he was a programmes officer at the School of Peace Keeping at the African Centre for Constructive Resolution of Disputes (ACCORD) in Durban, and later researcher at the Africa Institute in Pretoria,

South Africa. He has been part-time lecturer at the United States International University—Africa, Catholic University of Eastern Africa, Kenyatta University, and St. Paul's University, Limuru, Kenya. He has research interests in the state and democracy in Africa, ethics, and African philosophy, and ideologies. He is also the managing editor of *The Nile Explorer* magazine.

Robinah Nakabo holds a B.A. in social sciences majoring in gender and development from Makerere University, an M.A. in philosophy from Makerere University, and an M.A. in organizational leadership from the Eastern University, Pennsylvania. She is a research fellow with the school of postgraduate studies and research at Uganda Martyrs University (UMU), central region coordinator of the gender equity in research alliance (GERA) in Uganda, and fellow of the association of research on civil society in Africa (AROCSA). She is also an awardee of the Gerda Henkel Foundation and Makerere University's College of Humanities and Social Sciences doctoral fellowship, where she is undertaking research on "Followership and Women's Empowerment to Sustainable Development: A Case Study of Women in the National Association of Women's Organisations in Uganda". She has gained valuable teaching experience at the department of philosophy at Makerere University. Her research interests are rooted in applied philosophy, specifically philosophy of gender, political philosophy, philosophy of education, and philosophy of economics, as well as in research methodology and theories of knowledge.

David Ngendo-Tshimba holds a B.A. (ethics and development studies) from Uganda Martyrs University, an M.A. (sustainable peace and conflict management) from Uganda Martyrs University, an M.Phil. (social studies) from Makerere University, and a Ph.D. (history and politics) from the interdisciplinary doctoral programme at the Makerere Institute of Social Research (MISR). He is currently chair of the centre for African studies at Uganda Martyrs University under the auspices of its school of postgraduate studies and research. He also teaches both undergraduate and postgraduate courses in the department of Governance, Peace and International Studies in the School of Arts and Social Sciences at the same university. He has benefited from a number of research fellowships, including with the Council for the Development of Social Science Research in Africa (CODESRIA) on a book project on peace and security in Africa's Great Lakes region, with the Refugee Law Project (RLP) in partnership with the Irish Human Rights Centre on a policy research project on 'Human Trafficking, Forced Migration, and Gender Equality in Uganda', and with the Action for Development (ACFODE) on an ethnographic research project about violated bodies in forced displacement contexts in Kyaka II Refugee Settlement, western Uganda. His research interests include (political) violence, (forced) migration, (social) justice, and gender in history, with particular focus on Africa's Great Lakes region.

Reginald M. J. Oduor holds a B.Ed. (Arts) and an M.A. in philosophy both from Kenyatta University, and a Ph.D. in political philosophy from the University of Nairobi. He is the first person with total visual disability to be appointed to a substantive teaching position in a public university in Kenya. He is senior lecturer in philosophy at the University of Nairobi. He is the lead editor of *Odera Oruka in the Twenty-First Century* (RVP, 2018). He also played a pivotal role in establishing the New Series of *Thought and Practice: A Journal of the Philosophical Association of Kenya*, an open access, online publication, in which he served as founding editor-in-chief from 2009 to 2015. He was African Studies Association (ASA) Presidential Fellow in 2016. In addition, he has given guest lectures in South Africa, Germany, Austria, and the United States. His research interests include political philosophy, African philosophy, research methodology in philosophy, ethics, disability rights, and philosophy of religion. He is also co-founder of the Society of Professionals with Visual Disabilities (SOPVID).

Donna Pido is an American anthropologist with five decades of professional experience in jewellery and product design. She holds a B.A. in anthropology from Indiana University, an M.Phil. in education, and a Ph.D. in anthropology, both from Columbia University. She is senior lecturer in design at The Technical University of Kenya, and research affiliate in the department of archaeology in the National Museums of Kenya, Nairobi. She is the former chair of the College of Arms in the Office of the Attorney General in Nairobi. Dr. Pido has written extensively on Maasai art among other topics related to aesthetic production in Kenya. She is an active member of the Kenya Quilt Guild and the Kenya Embroiderers Guild. She has assembled and deposited several collections of Kenyan material culture in American and European museums.

J. P. Odoch Pido holds B.A., M.A., and Ph.D. degrees in design, all from the University of Nairobi where he also taught until 2012, and a postgraduate certificate in industrial design from Eindhoven, The Netherlands. He is currently director of the School of Creative Arts and Technologies at the Technical University of Kenya in Nairobi. He has taught over one thousand Kenyan designers over the last fifty years. His professional work has focused on exhibition, product, and graphic design. He is also a noted voice in the elucidation and analysis of East African cultures. Many of his writings are critical looks at his own Acholi culture in the face of war and upheaval.

Joseph Situma holds B.A., M.A., and Ph.D. in philosophy, all from the University of Nairobi. He is senior lecturer in philosophy at the University of Nairobi, Kenya. His research interests include ethics, politics, and aesthetics. Apart from his philosophical publications, he is the author of several novels, among them *Mpuonzi's Dream*, *The Mysterious Killer* (2000), *Seizing the Night* (2006), and *The Gift of the Night* (2010).

www.ingramcontent.com/pod-product-compliance
Lightning Source LLC
Chambersburg PA
CBHW020110010526
44115CB00008B/775